ENGLISH CRITICAL ESSAYS

(SIXTEENTH, SEVENTEENTH AND EIGHTEENTH CENTURIES)

SELECTED AND EDITED
BY
EDMUND D. JONES

D1639620

LONDON
OXFORD UNIVERSITY PRESS

The present selection of English Critical Essays (Sixteenth, Seventeenth, and Eighteenth Centuries) was first published in The World's Classics *in* 1922, *and reprinted in* 1924, 1930, 1933, 1936, 1940, 1941, 1943. *Reset in* 1947 *and reprinted in* 1952, 1956, 1959, 1961, 1963, 1965, *and* 1968.

PRINTED IN GREAT BRITAIN

PREFACE

IT is hoped that the present selection of critical essays will be found comprehensive enough to enable the reader to follow the main movements and counter-movements of English critical thought from the Renaissance to the Revival of Romanticism. Except in the few cases indicated, the texts have been given in full. But in order to avoid placing unnecessary difficulties in the way of readers unfamiliar with early English spelling and punctuation, the practice of modern editors of Shakespeare has been followed: the spelling has been modernized throughout, and the punctuation brought into closer conformity with modern usage.

E. D. J.

CONTENTS

SIR PHILIP SIDNEY

AN APOLOGY FOR POETRY

[1595]

WHEN the right virtuous Edward Wotton and I
were at the Emperor's Court together, we gave
ourselves to learn horsemanship of John Pietro Pugliano, one that with great commendation had the place
of an esquire in his stable. And he, according to the
fertileness of the Italian wit, did not only afford us the
demonstration of his practice, but sought to enrich
our minds with the contemplations therein which he
thought most precious. But with none I remember
mine ears were at any time more loaden, than when
(either angered with slow payment, or moved with
our learner-like admiration) he exercised his speech in
the praise of his faculty. He said, soldiers were the
noblest estate of mankind, and horsemen the noblest
of soldiers. He said they were the masters of war and
ornaments of peace; speedy goers and strong abiders;
triumphers both in camps and courts. Nay, to so un-
believed a point he proceeded, as that no earthly thing
bred such wonder to a prince as to be a good horseman. Skill of government was but a *pedanteria* in comparison. Then would he add certain praises, by telling
what a peerless beast a horse was, the only serviceable
courtier without flattery, the beast of most beauty,
faithfulness, courage, and such more, that, if I had not
been a piece of a logician before I came to him, I think
he would have persuaded me to have wished myself
a horse. But thus much at least with his no few
words he drove into me, that self-love is better than any
gilding to make that seem gorgeous wherein ourselves
are parties.

Wherein, if Pugliano's strong affection and weak
arguments will not satisfy you, I will give you a nearer

example of myself, who (I know not by what mis-chance) in these my not old years and idlest times having slipped into the title of a poet, am provoked to say something unto you in the defence of that my un-elected vocation, which if I handle with more good will than good reasons, bear with me, since the scholar is to be pardoned that followeth the steps of his master. And yet I must say that, as I have just cause to make a pitiful defence of poor Poetry, which from almost the highest estimation of learning is fallen to be the laugh-ing-stock of children, so have I need to bring some more available proofs, since the former is by no man barred of his deserved credit, the silly latter hath had even the names of philosophers used to the defacing of it, with great danger of civil war among the Muses.

And first, truly, to all them that professing learning inveigh against Poetry may justly be objected, that they go very near to ungratefulness, to seek to deface that which, in the noblest nations and languages that are known, hath been the first light-giver to ignorance, and first nurse, whose milk by little and little enabled them to feed afterwards of tougher knowledges. And will they now play the hedgehog that, being received into the den, drove out his host, or rather the vipers, that with their birth kill their parents? Let learned Greece in any of her manifold sciences be able to show me one book before Musaeus, Homer, and Hesiod, all three nothing else but poets. Nay, let any history be brought that can say any writers were there before them, if they were not men of the same skill, as Or-pheus, Linus, and some other are named, who, having been the first of that country that made pens deliverers of their knowledge to their posterity, may justly chal-lenge to be called their fathers in learning, for not only in time they had this priority (although in itself anti-quity be venerable) but went before them, as causes to draw with their charming sweetness the wild untamed wits to an admiration of knowledge, so, as Amphion was said to move stones with his poetry to build

Thebes, and Orpheus to be listened to by beasts—indeed stony and beastly people. So among the Romans were Livius Andronicus, and Ennius. So in the Italian language the first that made it aspire to be a treasure-house of Science were the poets Dante, Boccaccio, and Petrarch. So in our English were Gower and Chaucer, after whom, encouraged and delighted with their excellent fore-going, others have followed, to beautify our mother tongue, as well in the same kind as in other arts.

This did so notably show itself, that the philosophers of Greece durst not a long time appear to the world but under the masks of poets. So Thales, Empedocles, and Parmenides sang their natural philosophy in verses; so did Pythagoras and Phocylides their moral counsels; so did Tyrtaeus in war matters, and Solon in matters of policy: or rather, they, being poets, did exercise their delightful vein in those points of highest knowledge, which before them lay hid to the world. For that wise Solon was directly a poet it is manifest, having written in verse the notable fable of the Atlantic Island, which was continued by Plato. And truly, even Plato, whosoever well considereth shall find that in the body of his work, though the inside and strength were Philosophy, the skin as it were and beauty depended most of Poetry: for all standeth upon dialogues, wherein he feigneth many honest burgesses of Athens to speak of such matters, that, if they had been set on the rack, they would never have confessed them, besides his poetical describing the circumstances of their meetings, as the well ordering of a banquet, the delicacy of a walk, with interlacing mere tales, as Gyges' Ring, and others, which who knoweth not to be flowers of poetry did never walk into Apollo's garden.

And even historiographers (although their lips sound of things done, and verity be written in their foreheads) have been glad to borrow both fashion and perchance weight of poets. So Herodotus entitled his history by the name of the nine Muses; and both he and all the rest that followed him either stole or usurped of Poetry their passionate describing of passions, the many particularities of battles, which no man could affirm, or, if that be denied me, long orations put in the mouths of great kings and captains, which it is certain they never pronounced. So that, truly, neither philosopher nor historiographer could at the first have entered into the gates of popular judgements, if they had not taken a great passport of Poetry, which in all nations at this day, where learning flourisheth not, is plain to be seen, in all which they have some feeling of Poetry.

In Turkey, besides their law-giving divines, they have no other writers but poets. In our neighbour country Ireland, where truly learning goeth very bare, yet are their poets held in a devout reverence. Even among the most barbarous and simple Indians where no writing is, yet have they their poets, who make and sing songs, which they call *Areytos*, both of their ancestors' deeds and praises of their gods—a sufficient probability that, if ever learning come among them, it must be by having their hard dull wits softened and sharpened with the sweet delights of Poetry. For until they find a pleasure in the exercises of the mind, great promises of much knowledge will little persuade them that know not the fruits of knowledge. In Wales, the true remnant of the ancient Britons, as there are good authorities to show the long time they had poets, which they called bards, so through all the conquests of Romans, Saxons, Danes, and Normans, some of whom did seek to ruin all memory of learning from among them, yet do their poets, even to this day, last; so as it is not more notable in soon beginning than in long continuing. But since the authors of most of our sciences were the Romans, and before them the Greeks, let us a little stand upon their authorities, but even so far as to see what names they have given unto this now scorned skill.

Among the Romans a poet was called *Vates*, which is as much as a diviner, foreseer, or prophet, as by his conjoined words *vaticinium* and *vaticinari* is manifest: so heavenly a title did that excellent people bestow upon this heart-ravishing knowledge. And so far were they carried into the admiration thereof, that they thought in the chanceable hitting upon any such verses great foretokens of their following fortunes were placed. Whereupon grew the word of *Sortes Virgilianae*, when, by sudden opening Virgil's book, they lighted upon any verse of his making: whereof the histories of the emperors' lives are full, as of Albinus, the governor of our island, who in his childhood met with this verse,

> *Arma amens capio nec sat rationis in armis;*

and in his age performed it: which, although it were a very vain and godless superstition, as also it was to think that spirits were commanded by such verses—whereupon this word charms, derived of *carmina*, cometh—so yet serveth it to show the great reverence those wits were held in. And altogether not without ground, since both the Oracles of Delphos and Sibylla's prophecies were wholly delivered in verses. For that same exquisite observing of number and measure in words, and that high flying liberty of conceit proper to the poet, did seem to have some divine force in it.

And may not I presume a little further, to show the reasonableness of this word *Vates*, and say that the holy David's Psalms are a divine poem? If I do, I shall not do it without the testimony of great learned men, both ancient and modern. But even the name Psalms will speak for me, which, being interpreted, is nothing but Songs; then that it is fully written in metre, as all learned Hebricians agree, although the rules be not yet fully found; lastly and principally, his handling his prophecy, which is merely poetical. For what else is the awaking his musical instruments, the often and free changing of persons, his notable *prosopopeias*, when he maketh you, as it were, see God coming in His majesty, his telling of the beasts' joyfulness, and hills' leaping, but a heavenly poesy, wherein almost he showeth himself a passionate lover of that unspeakable and everlasting beauty to be seen by the eyes of the mind, only cleared by faith? But truly now having named him, I fear me I seem to profane that holy name, applying it to Poetry, which is among us thrown down to so ridiculous an estimation. But they that with quiet judgements will look a little deeper into it, shall find the end and working of it such, as, being rightly applied, deserveth not to be scourged out of the Church of God.

But now, let us see how the Greeks named it, and how they deemed of it. The Greeks called him 'a poet', which name hath, as the most excellent, gone through other languages. It cometh of this word *Poiein*, which is 'to make': wherein, I know not whether by luck or wisdom, we Englishmen have met with the Greeks in calling him 'a maker': which name, how high and incomparable a title it is, I had rather were known by marking the scope of other sciences than by my partial allegation.

There is no art delivered to mankind that hath not the works of Nature for his principal object, without which they could not consist, and on which they so depend, as they become actors and players, as it were, of what Nature will have set forth. So doth the astronomer look upon the stars, and, by that he seeth, setteth down what order Nature hath taken therein. So do the geometrician and arithmetician in their diverse sorts of quantities. So doth the musician in times tell you which by nature agree, which not. The natural philosopher thereon hath his name, and the moral philosopher standeth upon the natural virtues, vices, and passions of man; and 'follow Nature' (saith he) 'therein, and thou shalt not err'. The lawyer saith what men have determined; the historian what men have done. The grammarian speaketh only of the rules of speech; and the rhetorician and logician, considering what in Nature will soonest prove and persuade, thereon give artificial rules, which still are compassed within the circle of a question according to the proposed matter. The physician weigheth the nature of a man's body, and the nature of things helpful or hurtful unto it. And the metaphysic, though it be in the second and abstract notions, and therefore be counted supernatural, yet doth he indeed build upon the depth of Nature. Only the poet, disdaining to be tied to any such subjection, lifted up with the vigour of his own invention, doth grow in effect another nature, in making things either better than Nature bringeth forth, or, quite anew, forms such as never were in Nature, as the Heroes, Demigods, Cyclops, Chimeras, Furies, and such like: so as he goeth hand in hand with Nature, not enclosed within the narrow warrant of her gifts, but freely ranging only within the zodiac of his own wit.

Nature never set forth the earth in so rich tapestry as divers poets have done—neither with pleasant rivers, fruitful trees, sweet-smelling flowers, nor whatsoever else may make the too much loved earth more lovely. Her world is brazen, the poets only deliver a golden. But let those things alone, and go to man—for whom as the other things are, so it seemeth in him her uttermost cunning is employed—and know whether she have brought forth so true a lover as Theagenes, so constant a friend as Pylades, so valiant a man as Orlando, so right a prince as Xenophon's Cyrus, so excellent a man every way as Virgil's Aeneas. Neither let this be jestingly conceived, because the works of the one be essential, the other in imitation or fiction; for any understanding knoweth the skill of the artificer standeth in that idea or foreconceit of the work, and not in the work itself. And that the poet hath that idea is manifest, by delivering them forth in such excellency as he hath imagined them. Which delivering forth also is not wholly imaginative, as we are wont to say by them that build castles in the air: but so far substantially it worketh, not only to make a Cyrus, which had been but a particular excellency, as Nature might have done, but to bestow a Cyrus upon the world, to make many Cyruses, if they will learn aright why and how that maker made him.

Neither let it be deemed too saucy a comparison to balance the highest point of man's wit with the efficacy of Nature; but rather give right honour to the heavenly Maker of that maker, who, having made man to His own likeness, set him beyond and over all the works of that second nature: which in nothing he showeth so much as in Poetry, when with the force of a divine breath He bringeth things forth far surpassing her doings, with no small argument to the incredulous of that first accursed fall of Adam, since our erected wit maketh us know what perfection is, and yet our infected will keepeth us from reaching unto it. But these arguments will by few be understood, and by fewer granted. Thus much (I hope) will be given me, that the Greeks with some probability of reason gave him the name above all names of learning. Now let us go to a more ordinary opening of him, that the truth may be more palpable: and so I hope, though we get not so unmatched a praise as the etymology of his names will grant, yet his very description, which no man will deny, shall not justly be barred from a principal commendation.

Poesy therefore is an art of imitation, for so Aristotle termeth it in his word *Mimesis*, that is to say, a representing, counterfeiting, or figuring forth—to speak metaphorically, a speaking picture; with this end, to teach and delight. Of this have been three several kinds.

The chief, both in antiquity and excellency, were they that did imitate the inconceivable excellencies of God. Such were David in his Psalms; Solomon in his Song of Songs, in his Ecclesiastes, and Proverbs; Moses and Deborah in their Hymns; and the writer of

Job, which, beside other, the learned Emanuel Tremellius and Franciscus Junius do entitle the poetical part of the Scripture. Against these none will speak that hath the Holy Ghost in due holy reverence. In this kind, though in a full wrong divinity, were Orpheus, Amphion, Homer in his Hymns, and many other, both Greeks and Romans, and this poesy must be used by whosoever will follow St. James's counsel in singing psalms when they are merry, and I know is used with the fruit of comfort by some, when, in sorrowful pangs of their death-bringing sins, they find the consolation of the never-leaving goodness.

The second kind is of them that deal with matters philosophical: either moral, as Tyrtaeus, Phocylides, and Cato; or natural, as Lucretius and Virgil's Georgics; or astronomical, as Manilius and Pontanus; or historical, as Lucan; which who mislike, the fault is in their judgements quite out of taste, and not in the sweet food of sweetly uttered knowledge.

But because this second sort is wrapped within the fold of the proposed subject, and takes not the course of his own invention, whether they properly be poets or no let grammarians dispute; and go to the third, indeed right poets, of whom chiefly this question ariseth, betwixt whom and these second is such a kind of difference as betwixt the meaner sort of painters, who counterfeit only such faces as are set before them, and the more excellent, who, having no law but wit, bestow that in colours upon you which is fittest for the eye to see, as the constant though lamenting look of Lucretia, when she punished in herself another's fault (wherein he painteth not Lucretia whom he never saw, but painteth the outward beauty of such a virtue). For these third be they which most properly do imitate to teach and delight, and to imitate borrow nothing of what is, hath been, or shall be; but range, only reined with learned discretion, into the divine consideration of what may be, and should be. These be they that, as the first and most noble sort may justly be termed *Vates*, so these are waited on in the excellentest languages and best understandings, with the fore-described name of Poets; for these indeed do merely make to imitate, and imitate both to delight and teach, and delight to move men to take that goodness in hand, which without delight they would fly as from a stranger, and teach, to make them know that goodness whereunto they are moved: which being the noblest scope to which ever any learning was directed, yet want there not idle tongues to bark at them.

These be subdivided into sundry more special denominations. The most notable be the Heroic, Lyric, Tragic, Comic, Satiric, Iambic, Elegiac, Pastoral, and certain others, some of these being termed according to the matter they deal with, some by the sorts of verses they liked best to write in; for indeed the greatest part of poets have apparelled their poetical inventions in that numbrous kind of writing which is called verse—indeed but apparelled, verse being but an ornament and no cause to Poetry, since there have been many most excellent poets that never versified, and now swarm many versifiers that need never answer to the name of poets. For Xenophon, who did imitate so excellently as to give us *effigiem iusti imperii*, 'the portraiture of a just Empire,' under name of Cyrus (as Cicero saith of him), made therein an absolute heroical poem. So did Heliodorus in his sugared invention of that picture of love in Theagenes and Chariclea; and yet both these writ in prose: which I speak to show that it is not rhyming and versing that maketh a poet —no more than a long gown maketh an advocate, who though he pleaded in armour should be an advocate and no soldier. But it is that feigning notable images of virtues, vices, or what else, with that delightful teaching, which must be the right describing note to know a poet by, although indeed the Senate of Poets hath chosen verse as their fittest raiment, meaning, as in matter they passed all in all, so in manner to go beyond them—not speaking (table talk fashion or

like men in a dream) words as they chanceably fall
from the mouth, but peizing each syllable of each
word by just proportion according to the dignity of
the subject.

Now therefore it shall not be amiss first to weigh
this latter sort of Poetry by his works, and then by his
parts, and, if in neither of these anatomies he be con-
demnable, I hope we shall obtain a more favourable
sentence. This purifying of wit, this enriching of
memory, enabling of judgement, and enlarging of
conceit, which commonly we call learning, under
what name soever it come forth, or to what immediate
end soever it be directed, the final end is to lead and
draw us to as high a perfection as our degenerate
souls, made worse by their clayey lodgings, can be
capable of. This, according to the inclination of the
man, bred many formed impressions. For some that
thought this felicity principally to be gotten by knowledge and no knowledge to be so high and heavenly
as acquaintance with the stars, gave themselves to
Astronomy; others, persuading themselves to be demigods if they knew the causes of things, became natural
and supernatural philosophers; some an admirable
delight drew to Music; and some the certainty of
demonstration to the Mathematics. But all, one and
other, having this scope—to know, and by knowledge
to lift up the mind from the dungeon of the body to
the enjoying his own divine essence. But when by the
balance of experience it was found that the astronomer
looking to the stars might fall into a ditch, that the inquiring philosopher might be blind in himself, and the
mathematician might draw forth a straight line with
a crooked heart, then, lo, did proof, the overruler of
opinions, make manifest that all these are but serving
sciences, which, as they have each a private end in
themselves, so yet are they all directed to the highest end of the mistress-knowledge, by the Greeks
called *Architectonike*, which stands (as I think) in the
knowledge of a man's self, in the ethic and politic

consideration, with the end of well doing and not of well knowing only:—even as the saddler's next end is to make a good saddle, but his farther end to serve a nobler faculty, which is horsemanship; so the horseman's to soldiery, and the soldier not only to have the skill, but to perform the practice of a soldier. So that, the ending end of all earthly learning being virtuous action, those skills, that most serve to bring forth that, have a most just title to be princes over all the rest. Wherein we can show the poet's nobleness, by setting him before his other competitors, among whom as principal challengers step forth the moral philosophers, whom, me thinketh, I see coming towards me with a sullen gravity, as though they could not abide vice by daylight, rudely clothed for to witness outwardly their contempt of outward things, with books in their hands against glory, whereto they set their names, sophistically speaking against subtlety, and angry with any man in whom they see the foul fault of anger. These men casting largesse as they go of definitions, divisions, and distinctions, with a scornful interrogative do soberly ask whether it be possible to find any path so ready to lead a man to virtue as that which teacheth what virtue is—and teacheth it not only by delivering forth his very being, his causes, and effects, but also by making known his enemy, Vice (which must be destroyed), and his cumbersome servant, Passion (which must be mastered), by showing the generalities that containeth it, and the specialities that are derived from it; lastly, by plain setting down, how it extendeth itself out of the limits of a man's own little world to the government of families, and maintaining of public societies.

The historian scarcely giveth leisure to the moralist to say so much, but that he, laden with old mouse-eaten records, authorizing himself (for the most part) upon other histories, whose greatest authorities are built upon the notable foundation of hearsay; having much ado to accord differing writers and to pick truth out of partiality; better acquainted with a thousand years ago than with the present age, and yet better knowing how this world goeth than how his own wit runneth; curious for antiquities and inquisitive of novelties; a wonder to young folks and a tyrant in table talk, denieth, in a great chafe, that any man for teaching of virtue, and virtuous actions, is comparable to him. 'I am *Lux vitae, Temporum magistra, Vita memoriae, Nuncia vetustatis,*' &c. The philosopher (saith he) 'teacheth a disputative virtue, but I do an active. His virtue is excellent in the dangerless Academy of Plato, but mine showeth forth her honourable face in the battles of Marathon, Pharsalia, Poitiers, and Agincourt. He teacheth virtue by certain abstract considerations, but I only bid you follow the footing of them that have gone before you. Old-aged experience goeth beyond the fine-witted philosopher, but I give the experience of many ages. Lastly, if he make the song-book, I put the learner's hand to the lute; and if he be the guide, I am the light.'

Then would he allege you innumerable examples, conferring story by story, how much the wisest senators and princes have been directed by the credit of history, as Brutus, Alphonsus of Aragon, and who not, if need be? At length the long line of their disputation maketh a point in this, that the one giveth the precept, and the other the example.

Now, whom shall we find (since the question standeth for the highest form in the School of Learning) to be Moderator? Truly, as me seemeth, the poet; and if not a Moderator, even the man that ought to carry the title from them both, and much more from all other serving sciences. Therefore compare we the poet with the historian, and with the moral philosopher; and, if he go beyond them both, no other human skill can match him. For as for the Divine, with all reverence it is ever to be excepted, not only for having his scope as far beyond any of these as eternity exceedeth a moment, but even for passing each of these in themselves. And for the lawyer, though Jus be the daughter of Justice, and Justice the chief of virtues, yet because he seeketh to make men good rather *formidine poenae* than *virtutis amore*, or, to say righter, doth not endeavour to make men good, but that their evil hurt not others, having no care, so he be a good citizen, how bad a man he be: therefore, as our wickedness maketh him necessary, and necessity maketh him honourable, so is he not in the deepest truth to stand in rank with these who all endeavour to take naughtiness away, and plant goodness even in the secretest cabinet of our souls. And these four are all that any way deal in that consideration of men's manners, which being the supreme knowledge, they that best breed it deserve the best commendation.

The philosopher therefore and the historian are they which would win the goal, the one by precept, the other by example. But both, not having both, do both halt. For the philosopher, setting down with thorny argument the bare rule, is so hard of utterance, and so misty to be conceived, that one that hath no other guide but him shall wade in him till he be old before he shall find sufficient cause to be honest. For his knowledge standeth so upon the abstract and general, that happy is that man who may understand him, and more happy that can apply what he doth understand. On the other side, the historian, wanting the precept, is so tied, not to what should be but to what is, to the particular truth of things and not to the general reason of things, that his example draweth no necessary consequence, and therefore a less fruitful doctrine.

Now doth the peerless poet perform both: for whatsoever the philosopher saith should be done, he giveth a perfect picture of it in some one by whom he presupposeth it was done; so as he coupleth the general notion with the particular example. A perfect picture I say, for he yieldeth to the powers of the mind an image of that whereof the philosopher bestoweth but a wordish description: which doth neither strike, pierce, nor possess the sight of the soul so much as that other doth.

For as in outward things, to a man that had never seen an elephant or a rhinoceros, who should tell him most exquisitely all their shapes, colour, bigness, and particular marks, or of a gorgeous palace the architecture, with declaring the full beauties might well make the hearer able to repeat, as it were by rote, all he had heard, yet should never satisfy his inward conceits with being witness to itself of a true lively knowledge: but the same man, as soon as he might see those beasts well painted, or the house well in model, should straightways grow, without need of any description, to a judicial comprehending of them: so no doubt the philosopher with his learned definition—be it of virtue, vices, matters of public policy or private government—replenisheth the memory with many infallible grounds of wisdom, which, notwithstanding, lie dark before the imaginative and judging power, if they be not illuminated or figured forth by the speaking picture of Poesy.

Tully taketh much pains, and many times not without poetical helps, to make us know the force love of our country hath in us. Let us but hear old Anchises speaking in the midst of Troy's flames, or see Ulysses in the fullness of all Calypso's delights bewail his absence from barren and beggarly Ithaca. Anger, the Stoics say, was a short madness: let but Sophocles bring you Ajax on a stage, killing and whipping sheep and oxen, thinking them the army of Greeks, with their chieftains Agamemnon and Menelaus, and tell me if you have not a more familiar insight into anger than finding in the Schoolmen his genus and difference. See whether wisdom and temperance in Ulysses and Diomedes, valour in Achilles, friendship in Nisus and Euryalus, even to an ignorant man carry not an apparent shining, and, contrarily, the remorse of conscience in Oedipus, the soon repenting pride of

Agamemnon, the self-devouring cruelty in his father Atreus, the violence of ambition in the two Theban brothers, the sour-sweetness of revenge in Medea, and, to fall lower, the Terentian Gnatho and our Chaucer's Pandar so expressed that we now use their names to signify their trades; and finally, all virtues, vices, and passions so in their own natural seats laid to the view, that we seem not to hear of them, but clearly to see through them. But even in the most excellent determination of goodness, what philosopher's counsel can so readily direct a prince, as the feigned Cyrus in Xenophon; or a virtuous man in all fortunes, as Aeneas in Virgil; or a whole Commonwealth, as the way of Sir Thomas More's *Utopia*? I say the way, because where Sir Thomas More erred, it was the fault of the man and not of the poet, for that way of patterning a Commonwealth was most absolute, though he perchance hath not so absolutely performed it. For the question is, whether the feigned image of Poesy or the regular instruction of Philosophy hath the more force in teaching: wherein if the philosophers have more rightly showed themselves philosophers than the poets have attained to the high top of their profession, as in truth,

> *Mediocribus esse poetis,*
> *Non Dii, non homines, non concessere Columnae;*

it is, I say again, not the fault of the art, but that by few men that art can be accomplished. Certainly, even our Saviour Christ could as well have given the moral commonplaces of uncharitableness and humbleness as the divine narration of Dives and Lazarus; or of disobedience and mercy, as that heavenly discourse of the lost child and the gracious father; but that His through-searching wisdom knew the estate of Dives burning in hell, and of Lazarus being in Abraham's bosom, would more constantly (as it were) inhabit both the memory and judgement. Truly, for myself, meseems I see before my eyes the lost child's disdainful prodigality, turned to envy a swine's dinner: which by the learned Divines are thought not historical acts, but instructing parables. For conclusion, I say the Philosopher teacheth, but he teacheth obscurely, so as the learned only can understand him; that is to say, he teacheth them that are already taught. But the poet is the food for the tenderest stomachs, the poet is indeed the right popular philosopher, whereof Aesop's tales give good proof: whose pretty allegories, stealing under the formal tales of beasts, make many, more beastly than beasts, begin to hear the sound of virtue from these dumb speakers.

But now may it be alleged that, if this imagining of matters be so fit for the imagination, then must the historian needs surpass, who bringeth you images of true matters, such as indeed were done, and not such as fantastically or falsely may be suggested to have been done. Truly, Aristotle himself, in his discourse of Poesy, plainly determineth this question, saying that Poetry is *Philosophoteron* and *Spoudaioteron*, that is to say, it is more philosophical and more studiously serious than history. His reason is, because Poesy dealeth with *Katholou*, that is to say, with the universal consideration, and the history with *Kathekaston*, the particular: 'now', saith he, 'the universal weighs what is fit to be said or done, either in likelihood or necessity (which the Poesy considereth in his imposed names), and the particular only marks whether Alcibiades did, or suffered, this or that.' Thus far Aristotle: which reason of his (as all his) is most full of reason. For indeed, if the question were whether it were better to have a particular act truly or falsely set down, there is no doubt which is to be chosen, no more than whether you had rather have Vespasian's picture right as he was, or at the painter's pleasure nothing resembling. But if the question be for your own use and learning, whether it be better to have it set down as it should be, or as it was, then certainly is more doctrinable the feigned Cyrus in Xenophon than the true Cyrus in Justin, and the feigned Aeneas in Virgil than

the right Aeneas in Dares Phrygius: as to a lady that
desired to fashion her countenance to the best grace,
a painter should more benefit her to portrait a most
sweet face, writing Canidia upon it, than to paint
Canidia as she was, who, Horace sweareth, was foul
and ill favoured.

If the poet do his part aright, he will show you in
Tantalus, Atreus, and such like, nothing that is not to
be shunned; in Cyrus, Aeneas, Ulysses, each thing to
be followed; where the historian, bound to tell things
as things were, cannot be liberal (without he will be
poetical) of a perfect pattern, but, as in Alexander or
Scipio himself, show doings, some to be liked, some to
be misliked. And then how will you discern what to
follow but by your own discretion, which you had
without reading Quintus Curtius? And whereas a
man may say, though in universal consideration of
doctrine the poet prevaileth, yet that the history, in
his saying such a thing was done, doth warrant a man
more in that he shall follow; the answer is manifest:
that if he stand upon that *was*—as if he should argue,
because it rained yesterday, therefore it should rain
to-day—then indeed it hath some advantage to a
gross conceit; but if he know an example only informs
a conjectured likelihood, and so go by reason, the
poet doth so far exceed him, as he is to frame his
example to that which is most reasonable, be it in
warlike, politic, or private matters; where the historian
in his bare *was* hath many times that which we call
fortune to overrule the best wisdom. Many times he
must tell events whereof he can yield no cause: or, if
he do, it must be poetical.

For that a feigned example hath as much force to
teach as a true example (for as for to move, it is clear,
since the feigned may be tuned to the highest key of
passion), let us take one example wherein a poet and
a historian do concur. Herodotus and Justin do both
testify that Zopyrus, King Darius's faithful servant,
seeing his master long resisted by the rebellious Baby-

lonians, feigned himself in extreme disgrace of his
king: for verifying of which, he caused his own nose
and ears to be cut off, and so flying to the Babylonians,
was received, and for his known valour so far credited,
that he did find means to deliver them over to Darius.
Much like matter doth Livy record of Tarquinius and
his son. Xenophon excellently feigneth such another
stratagem performed by Abradates in Cyrus's behalf.
Now would I fain know, if occasion be presented unto
you to serve your prince by such an honest dissimula-
tion, why you do not as well learn it of Xenophon's
fiction as of the other's verity—and truly so much the
better, as you shall save your nose by the bargain; for
Abradates did not counterfeit so far. So then the best
of the historian is subject to the poet; for whatsoever
action, or faction, whatsoever counsel, policy, or war
stratagem the historian is bound to recite, that may
the poet (if he list) with his imitation make his own,
beautifying it both for further teaching, and more delighting, as it pleaseth him, having all, from Dante's
heaven to his hell, under the authority of his pen.
Which if I be asked what poets have done so, as I
might well name some, yet say I, and say again, I
speak of the art, and not of the artificer.

Now, to that which commonly is attributed to the
praise of histories, in respect of the notable learning is
gotten by marking the success, as though therein a
man should see virtue exalted and vice punished—
truly that commendation is peculiar to Poetry, and
far off from History. For indeed Poetry ever setteth
virtue so out in her best colours, making Fortune her
well-waiting handmaid, that one must needs be
enamoured of her. Well may you see Ulysses in a
storm, and in other hard plights; but they are but
exercises of patience and magnanimity, to make them
shine the more in the near-following prosperity. And
of the contrary part, if evil men come to the stage,
they ever go out (as the tragedy writer answered to
one that misliked the show of such persons) so

manacled as they little animate folks to follow them.
But the historian, being captived to the truth of a
foolish world, is many times a terror from well doing,
and an encouragement to unbridled wickedness.

For see we not valiant Miltiades rot in his fetters:
the just Phocion and the accomplished Socrates put
to death like traitors; the cruel Severus live pros-
perously; the excellent Severus miserably murdered;
Sylla and Marius dying in their beds; Pompey and
Cicero slain then when they would have thought exile
a happiness? See we not virtuous Cato driven to kill
himself, and rebel Caesar so advanced that his name
yet, after 1,600 years, lasteth in the highest honour?
And mark but even Caesar's own words of the fore-
named Sylla (who in that only did honestly, to put
down his dishonest tyranny), *Literas nescivit*, as if want
of learning caused him to do well. He meant it not
by Poetry, which, not content with earthly plagues,
deviseth new punishments in hell for tyrants, nor yet
by Philosophy, which teacheth *Occidendos esse*; but no
doubt by skill in History, for that indeed can afford
your Cypselus, Periander, Phalaris, Dionysius, and
I know not how many more of the same kennel, that
speed well enough in their abominable injustice or
usurpation. I conclude, therefore, that he excelleth
History, not only in furnishing the mind with knowledge, but in setting it forward to that which deserveth
to be called and accounted good: which setting forward, and moving to well doing, indeed setteth the
laurel crown upon the poet as victorious, not only of
the historian, but over the philosopher, howsoever in
teaching it may be questionable.

For suppose it be granted (that which I suppose
with great reason may be denied) that the philosopher, in respect of his methodical proceeding, doth
teach more perfectly than the poet, yet do I think
that no man is so much *Philophilosophos* as to compare
the philosopher, in moving, with the poet.

And that moving is of a higher degree than teaching, it may by this appear, that it is wellnigh the cause and the effect of teaching. For who will be taught, if he be not moved with desire to be taught, and what so much good doth that teaching bring forth (I speak still of moral doctrine) as that it moveth one to do that which it doth teach? For, as Aristotle saith, it is not *Gnosis* but *Praxis* must be the fruit. And how *Praxis* cannot be, without being moved to practise, it is no hard matter to consider.

The philosopher showeth you the way, he informeth you of the particularities, as well of the tediousness of the way, as of the pleasant lodging you shall have when your journey is ended, as of the many by-turnings that may divert you from your way. But this is to no man but to him that will read him, and read him with attentive studious painfulness; which constant desire whosoever hath in him, hath already passed half the hardness of the way, and therefore is beholding to the philosopher but for the other half. Nay truly, learned men have learnedly thought that where once reason hath so much overmastered passion as that the mind hath a free desire to do well, the inward light each mind hath in itself is as good as a philosopher's book; seeing in nature we know it is well to do well, and what is well and what is evil, although not in the words of art which philosophers bestow upon us. For out of natural conceit the philosophers drew it; but to be moved to do that which we know, or to be moved with desire to know, *Hoc opus, hic labor est.*

Now therein of all sciences (I speak still of human, and according to the humane conceits) is our poet the monarch. For he doth not only show the way, but giveth so sweet a prospect into the way, as will entice any man to enter into it. Nay, he doth, as if your journey should lie through a fair vineyard, at the first give you a cluster of grapes, that, full of that taste, you may long to pass further. He beginneth not with obscure definitions, which must blur the margent with interpretations, and load the memory with doubtfulness; but he cometh to you with words set in delightful proportion, either accompanied with, or prepared for, the well enchanting skill of music; and with a tale forsooth he cometh unto you, with a tale which holdeth children from play, and old men from the chimney corner. And, pretending no more, doth intend the winning of the mind from wickedness to virtue: even as the child is often brought to take most wholesome things by hiding them in such other as have a pleasant taste: which, if one should begin to tell them the nature of aloes or rhubarb they should receive, would sooner take their physic at their ears than at their mouth. So is it in men (most of which are childish in the best things, till they be cradled in their graves): glad they will be to hear the tales of Hercules, Achilles, Cyrus, and Aeneas; and, hearing them, must needs hear the right description of wisdom, valour, and justice; which, if they had been barely, that is to say philosophically, set out, they would swear they be brought to school again.

That imitation whereof Poetry is, hath the most conveniency to Nature of all other, insomuch that, as Aristotle saith, those things which in themselves are horrible, as cruel battles, unnatural monsters, are made in poetical imitation delightful. Truly, I have known men, that even with reading *Amadis de Gaule* (which God knoweth wanteth much of a perfect poesy) have found their hearts moved to the exercise of courtesy, liberality, and especially courage. Who readeth Aeneas carrying old Anchises on his back, that wisheth not it were his fortune to perform so excellent an act? Whom do not the words of Turnus move, the tale of Turnus having planted his image in the imagination?—

> *Fugientem haec terra videbit?*
> *Usque adeone mori miserum est?*

Where the philosophers, as they scorn to delight, so must they be content little to move, saving wrangling whether Virtue be the chief or the only good, whether the contemplative or the active life do excel: which Plato and Boethius well knew, and therefore made Mistress Philosophy very often borrow the masking raiment of Poesy. For even those hard-hearted evil men who think virtue a school name, and know no other good but *indulgere genio*, and therefore despise the austere admonitions of the philosopher, and feel not the inward reason they stand upon, yet will be content to be delighted—which is all the good fellow poet seemeth to promise—and so steal to see the form of goodness, which seen they cannot but love ere themselves be aware, as if they took a medicine of cherries.

Infinite proofs of the strange effects of this poetical invention might be alleged; only two shall serve, which are so often remembered as I think all men know them; the one of Menenius Agrippa, who, when the whole people of Rome had resolutely divided themselves from the Senate, with apparent show of utter ruin, though he were (for that time) an excellent orator, came not among them upon trust of figurative speeches or cunning insinuations, and much less with farfetched maxims of Philosophy, which (especially if they were Platonic) they must have learned geometry before they could well have conceived; but forsooth he behaves himself like a homely and familiar poet. He telleth them a tale, that there was a time when all the parts of the body made a mutinous conspiracy against the belly, which they thought devoured the fruits of each other's labour: they concluded they would let so unprofitable a spender starve. In the end, to be short (for the tale is notorious, and as notorious that it was a tale), with punishing the belly they plagued themselves. This applied by him wrought such effect in the people, as I never read that ever words brought forth but then so sudden and so good an alteration; for upon reasonable conditions a perfect reconcilement ensued. The other is of

Nathan the Prophet, who, when the holy David had so far forsaken God as to confirm adultery with murder, when he was to do the tenderest office of a friend, in laying his own shame before his eyes, sent by God to call again so chosen a servant, how doth he it but by telling of a man whose beloved lamb was ungratefully taken from his bosom?—the application most divinely true, but the discourse itself feigned. Which made David (I speak of the second and instrumental cause) as in a glass to see his own filthiness, as that heavenly Psalm of Mercy well testifieth.

By these, therefore, examples and reasons, I think it may be manifest that the Poet, with that same hand of delight, doth draw the mind more effectually than any other art doth: and so a conclusion not unfitly ensueth, that, as Virtue is the most excellent resting place for all worldly learning to make his end of, so Poetry, being the most familiar to teach it, and most princely to move towards it, in the most excellent work is the most excellent workman. But I am content not only to decipher him by his works (although works in commendation or dispraise must ever hold an high authority), but more narrowly will examine his parts: so that, as in a man, though all together may carry a presence full of majesty and beauty, perchance in some one defectious piece we may find a blemish. Now in his parts, kinds, or species (as you list to term them), it is to be noted that some poesies have coupled together two or three kinds, as tragical and comical, whereupon is risen the tragi-comical. Some, in the like manner, have mingled prose and verse, as Sannazzaro and Boethius. Some have mingled matters heroical and pastoral. But that cometh all to one in this question, for, if severed they be good, the conjunction cannot be hurtful. Therefore, perchance forgetting some, and leaving some as needless to be remembered, it shall not be amiss in a word to cite the special kinds, to see what faults may be found in the right use of them.

Is it then the Pastoral Poem which is misliked? For perchance where the hedge is lowest they will soonest leap over. Is the poor pipe disdained, which sometime out of Melibaeus' mouth can show the misery of people under hard lords or ravening soldiers, and again, by Tityrus, what blessedness is derived to them that lie lowest from the goodness of them that sit highest? sometimes, under the pretty tales of wolves and sheep, can include the whole considerations of wrongdoing and patience; sometimes show that contention for trifles can get but a trifling victory; where perchance a man may see that even Alexander and Darius, when they strave who should be cock of this world's dunghill, the benefit they got was that the afterlivers may say,

> *Haec memini et victum frustra contendere Thirsin:*
> *Ex illo Coridon, Coridon est tempore nobis.*

Or is it the lamenting Elegiac, which in a kind heart would move rather pity than blame, who bewails with the great philosopher Heraclitus the weakness of mankind and the wretchedness of the world; who surely is to be praised, either for compassionate accompanying just causes of lamentation, or for rightly pointing out how weak be the passions of woefulness? Is it the bitter but wholesome Iambic, which rubs the galled mind, in making shame the trumpet of villainy with bold and open crying out against naughtiness? Or the Satiric, who

> *Omne vafer vitium ridenti tangit amico;*

who sportingly never leaveth until he make a man laugh at folly, and, at length ashamed, to laugh at himself, which he cannot avoid, without avoiding the folly; who, while

> *circum praecordia ludit,*

giveth us to feel how many headaches a passionate life bringeth us to; how, when all is done,

> *Est Ulubris animus si nos non deficit aequus?*

No, perchance it is the Comic, whom naughty play-makers and stage-keepers have justly made odious. To the argument of abuse I will answer after. Only thus much now is to be said, that the Comedy is an imitation of the common errors of our life, which he representeth in the most ridiculous and scornful sort that may be, so as it is impossible that any beholder can be content to be such a one.

Now, as in Geometry the oblique must be known as well as the right, and in Arithmetic the odd as well as the even, so in the actions of our life who seeth not the filthiness of evil wanteth a great foil to perceive the beauty of virtue. This doth the Comedy handle so in our private and domestical matters, as with hearing it we get as it were an experience, what is to be looked for of a niggardly Demea, of a crafty Davus, of a flattering Gnatho, of a vainglorious Thraso; and not only to know what effects are to be expected, but to know who be such, by the signifying badge given them by the comedian. And little reason hath any man to say that men learn evil by seeing it so set out; since, as I said before, there is no man living but, by the force truth hath in nature, no sooner seeth these men play their parts, but wisheth them in *pistrinum;* although perchance the sack of his own faults lie so behind his back that he seeth not himself dance the same measure; whereto yet nothing can more open his eyes than to find his own actions contemptibly set forth.

So that the right use of Comedy will (I think) by nobody be blamed, and much less of the high and excellent Tragedy, that openeth the greatest wounds, and showeth forth the ulcers that are covered with tissue; that maketh kings fear to be tyrants, and tyrants manifest their tyrannical humours; that, with stirring the affects of admiration and commiseration, teacheth the uncertainty of this world, and upon how weak foundations gilden roofs are builded; that maketh us know,

Qui sceptra saevus duro imperio regit,
Timet timentes, metus in auctorem redit.

But how much it can move, Plutarch yieldeth a notable testimony of the abominable tyrant Alexander Phereaus, from whose eyes a tragedy, well made and represented, drew abundance of tears, who, without all pity, had murdered infinite numbers, and some of his own blood, so as he, that was not ashamed to make matters for tragedies, yet could not resist the sweet violence of a tragedy. And if it wrought no further good in him, it was that he, in despite of himself, withdrew himself from hearkening to that which might mollify his hardened heart.

But it is not the Tragedy they do mislike; for it were too absurd to cast out so excellent a representation of whatsoever is most worthy to be learned. Is it the Lyric that most displeaseth, who with his tuned lyre, and well-accorded voice, giveth praise, the reward of virtue, to virtuous acts, who gives moral precepts, and natural problems, who sometimes raiseth up his voice to the height of the heavens, in singing the lauds of the immortal God? Certainly, I must confess my own barbarousness, I never heard the old song of Percy and Douglas that I found not my heart moved more than with a trumpet; and yet is it sung but by some blind crowder, with no rougher voice than rude style; which, being so evil apparelled in the dust and cobwebs of that uncivil age, what would it work, trimmed in the gorgeous eloquence of Pindar? In Hungary I have seen it the manner at all feasts, and other such meetings, to have songs of their ancestors' valour; which that right soldierlike nation think the chiefest kindlers of brave courage. The incomparable Lacedemonians did not only carry that kind of music ever with them to the field, but even at home, as such songs were made, so were they all content to be the singers of them, when the lusty men were to tell what they did, the old men what they had done, and the young men what they would do. And where a man may say that Pindar many times praiseth highly victories of small moment, matters rather of sport than virtue; as it may be answered, it was the fault of the poet, and not of the poetry, so indeed the chief fault was in the time and custom of the Greeks, who set those toys at so high a price that Philip of Macedon reckoned a horserace won at Olympus among his three fearful felicities. But as the inimitable Pindar often did, so is that kind most capable and most fit to awake the thoughts from the sleep of idleness, to embrace honourable enterprises.

There rests the Heroical, whose very name (I think) should daunt all backbiters; for by what conceit can a tongue be directed to speak evil of that which draweth with it no less champions than Achilles, Cyrus, Aeneas, Turnus, Tydeus, and Rinaldo? who doth not only teach and move to a truth, but teacheth and moveth to the most high and excellent truth; who maketh magnanimity and justice shine throughout all misty fearfulness and foggy desires; who, if the saying of Plato and Tully be true, that who could see Virtue would be wonderfully ravished with the love of her beauty—this man sets her out to make her more lovely in her holiday apparel, to the eye of any that will deign not to disdain until they understand. But if anything be already said in the defence of sweet Poetry, all concurreth to the maintaining the Heroical, which is not only a kind, but the best and most accomplished kind of Poetry. For as the image of each action stirreth and instructeth the mind, so the lofty image of such worthies most inflameth the mind with desire to be worthy, and informs with counsel how to be worthy. Only let Aeneas be worn in the tablet of your memory, how he governeth himself in the ruin of his country, in the preserving his old father, and carrying away his religious ceremonies, in obeying the god's commandment to leave Dido, though not only all passionate kindness, but even the human consideration of virtuous gratefulness, would have craved other of him; how in storms, how in sports, how in war, how in peace, how a fugitive, how victorious, how besieged, how besieging, how to strangers, how to allies, how to enemies, how to his own; lastly, how in his inward self, and how in his outward government, and I think, in a mind not prejudiced with a prejudicating humour, he will be found in excellency fruitful, yea, even as Horace saith,

Melius Chrysippo et Crantore.

But truly I imagine it falleth out with these poet-whippers, as with some good women, who often are sick, but in faith they cannot tell where. So the name of Poetry is odious to them, but neither his cause nor effects, neither the sum that contains him nor the particularities descending from him, give any fast handle to their carping dispraise.

Since then Poetry is of all human learning the most ancient and of most fatherly antiquity, as from whence other learnings have taken their beginnings; since it is so universal that no learned nation doth despise it, nor no barbarous nation is without it; since both Roman and Greek gave divine names unto it, the one of 'prophesying', the other of 'making', and that indeed that name of 'making' is fit for him, considering that whereas other Arts retain themselves within their subject, and receive, as it were, their being from it, the poet only bringeth his own stuff, and doth not learn a conceit out of a matter, but maketh matter for a conceit; since neither his description nor his end containeth any evil, the thing described cannot be evil; since his effects be so good as to teach goodness and to delight the learners; since therein (namely in moral doctrine, the chief of all knowledges) he doth not only far pass the historian, but, for instructing, is wellnigh comparable to the philosopher, and, for moving, leaves him behind him; since the Holy Scripture (wherein there is no uncleanness) hath whole parts in it poetical, and that even our Saviour Christ vouchsafed to use the flowers of it; since all his kinds are not only in their united forms but in their severed dissections fully commendable; I think (and think I think rightly) the laurel crown appointed for triumphing captains doth worthily (of all other learnings) honour the poet's triumph. But because we have ears as well as tongues, and that the lightest reasons that may be will seem to weigh greatly, if nothing be put in the counterbalance, let us hear, and, as well as we can, ponder, what objections may be made against this art, which may be worthy either of yielding or answering.

First, truly I note not only in these *Mysomousoi*, poet-haters, but in all that kind of people who seek a praise by dispraising others, that they do prodigally spend a great many wandering words in quips and scoffs, carping and taunting at each thing, which, by stirring the spleen, may stay the brain from a thorough beholding the worthiness of the subject. Those kind of objections, as they are full of very idle easiness, since there is nothing of so sacred a majesty but that an itching tongue may rub itself upon it, so deserve they no other answer, but, instead of laughing at the jest, to laugh at the jester. We know a playing wit can praise the discretion of an ass, the comfortableness of being in debt, and the jolly commodity of being sick of the plague. So of the contrary side, if we will turn Ovid's verse,

Ut lateat virtus proximitate mali,

that 'good lie hid in nearness of the evil', Agrippa will be as merry in showing the vanity of Science as Erasmus was in commending of folly. Neither shall any man or matter escape some touch of these smiling railers. But for Erasmus and Agrippa, they had another foundation than the superficial part would promise. Marry, these other pleasant faultfinders, who will correct the verb before they understand the noun, and confute others' knowledge before they confirm their own, I would have them only remember that scoffing cometh not of wisdom; so as the best title in true English they get with their merriments is to be called good fools, for so have our grave forefathers ever termed that humorous kind of jesters.

But that which giveth greatest scope to their scorning humours is rhyming and versing. It is already said (and, as I think, truly said) it is not rhyming and versing that maketh Poesy. One may be a poet without versing, and a versifier without poetry. But yet presuppose it were inseparable (as indeed it seemeth Scaliger judgeth) truly it were an inseparable commendation. For if *Oratio* next to *Ratio*, Speech next to Reason, be the greatest gift bestowed upon mortality, that cannot be praiseless which doth most polish that blessing of speech; which considers each word, not only (as a man may say) by his forcible quality, but by his best measured quantity, carrying even in themselves a harmony (without, perchance, number, measure, order, proportion be in our time grown odious). But lay aside the just praise it hath, by being the only fit speech for Music (Music, I say, the most divine striker of the senses), thus much is undoubtedly true, that if reading be foolish without remembering, memory being the only treasurer of knowledge, those words which are fittest for memory are likewise most convenient for knowledge.

Now, that verse far exceedeth prose in the knitting up of the memory, the reason is manifest,—the words (besides their delight, which hath a great affinity to memory) being so set as one word cannot be lost but the whole work fails; which accuseth itself, calleth the remembrance back to itself, and so most strongly confirmeth it. Besides, one word so, as it were, begetting another, as, be it in rhyme or measured verse, by the former a man shall have a near guess to the follower: lastly, even they that have taught the art of memory have showed nothing so apt for it as a certain room divided into many places well and thoroughly known. Now, that hath the verse in effect perfectly, every word having his natural seat, which seat must needs

make the words remembered. But what needeth more
in a thing so known to all men? Who is it that ever
was a scholar that doth not carry away some verses of
Virgil, Horace, or Cato, which in his youth he learned,
and even to his old age serve him for hourly lessons?
But the fitness it hath for memory is notably proved by
all delivery of Arts: wherein for the most part, from
Grammar to Logic, Mathematic, Physic, and the rest,
the rules chiefly necessary to be borne away are com-
piled in verses. So that, verse being in itself sweet and
orderly, and being best for memory, the only handle
of knowledge, it must be in jest that any man can
speak against it.

Now then go we to the most important imputations
laid to the poor poets. For aught I can yet learn, they
are these. First, that there being many other more
fruitful knowledges, a man might better spend his
time in them than in this. Secondly, that it is the
mother of lies. Thirdly, that it is the nurse of abuse,
infecting us with many pestilent desires, with a siren's
sweetness drawing the mind to the serpent's tale of
sinful fancy,—and herein, especially, comedies give
the largest field to ear (as Chaucer saith),—how both
in other nations and in ours, before poets did soften
us, we were full of courage, given to martial exercises,
the pillars of manlike liberty, and not lulled asleep in
shady idleness with poets' pastimes. And lastly, and
chiefly, they cry out with an open mouth, as if they
outshot Robin Hood, that Plato banished them out of
his Commonwealth. Truly, this is much, if there be
much truth in it. First, to the first, that a man might
better spend his time is a reason indeed: but it doth
(as they say) but *petere principium*: for if it be, as I
affirm, that no learning is so good as that which
teacheth and moveth to virtue, and that none can
both teach and move thereto so much as Poetry, then
is the conclusion manifest that ink and paper cannot
be to a more profitable purpose employed. And
certainly, though a man should grant their first

assumption, it should follow (methinks) very unwillingly, that good is not good because better is better. But I still and utterly deny that there is sprung out of earth a more fruitful knowledge. To the second therefore, that they should be the principal liars, I answer paradoxically, but truly, I think truly, that of all writers under the sun the poet is the least liar, and, though he would, as a poet can scarcely be a liar. The astronomer, with his cousin the geometrician, can hardly escape, when they take upon them to measure the height of the stars. How often, think you, do the physicians lie, when they aver things good for sicknesses, which afterwards send Charon a great number of souls drowned in a potion before they come to his ferry? And no less of the rest, which take upon them to affirm. Now, for the poet, he nothing affirms, and therefore never lieth. For, as I take it, to lie is to affirm that to be true which is false; so as the other artists, and especially the historian, affirming many things, can, in the cloudy knowledge of mankind, hardly escape from many lies. But the poet (as I said before) never affirmeth. The poet never maketh any circles about your imagination, to conjure you to believe for true what he writes. He citeth not authorities of other histories, but even for his entry calleth the sweet Muses to inspire into him a good invention; in truth, not labouring to tell you what is, or is not, but what should or should not be. And therefore, though he recount things not true, yet because he telleth them not for true, he lieth not,—without we will say that Nathan lied in his speech, before alleged, to David; which as a wicked man durst scarce say, so think I none so simple would say that Aesop lied in the tales of his beasts: for who thinks that Aesop writ it for actually true were well worthy to have his name chronicled among the beasts he writeth of. What child is there that, coming to a play, and seeing *Thebes* written in great letters upon an old door, doth believe that it is Thebes? If then a man can arrive, at that child's age, to know that the poets' persons and doings are but pictures what should be, and not stories what have been, they will never give the lie to things not affirmatively but allegorically and figuratively written. And therefore, as in History, looking for truth, they go away full fraught with falsehood, so in Poesy, looking for fiction, they shall use the narration but as an imaginative ground-plot of a profitable invention.

But hereto is replied, that the poets give names to men they write of, which argueth a conceit of an actual truth, and so, not being true, proves a falsehood. And doth the lawyer lie then, when under the names of 'John a Stile' and 'John a Noakes' he puts his case? But that is easily answered. Their naming of men is but to make their picture the more lively, and not to build any history; painting men, they cannot leave men nameless. We see we cannot play at chess but that we must give names to our chessmen; and yet, methinks, he were a very partial champion of truth that would say we lied for giving a piece of wood the reverend title of a bishop. The poet nameth Cyrus or Aeneas no other way than to show what men of their fames, fortunes, and estates should do.

Their third is, how much it abuseth men's wit, training it to wanton sinfulness and lustful love: for indeed that is the principal, if not the only, abuse I can hear alleged. They say the Comedies rather teach than reprehend amorous conceits. They say the Lyric is larded with passionate sonnets, the Elegiac weeps the want of his mistress, and that even to the Heroical Cupid hath ambitiously climbed. Alas, Love, I would thou couldst as well defend thyself as thou canst offend others. I would those on whom thou dost attend could either put thee away, or yield good reason why they keep thee. But grant love of beauty to be a beastly fault (although it be very hard, since only man, and no beast, hath that gift to discern beauty); grant that lovely name of Love to deserve all hateful reproaches (although even some of my masters the philosophers spent a good deal of their lamp-oil in setting forth the excellency of it); grant, I say, whatsoever they will have granted; that not only love, but lust, but vanity, but (if they list) scurrility, possesseth many leaves of the poets' books: yet think I, when this is granted, they will find their sentence may with good manners put the last words foremost, and not say that Poetry abuseth man's wit, but that man's wit abuseth Poetry.

For I will not deny but that man's wit may make Poesy, which should be *Eikastike*, which some learned have defined, 'figuring forth good things', to be *Phantastike*, which doth, contrariwise, infect the fancy with unworthy objects, as the painter, that should give to the eye either some excellent perspective, or some fine picture, fit for building or fortification, or containing in it some notable example, as Abraham sacrificing his son Isaac, Judith killing Holofernes, David fighting with Goliath, may leave those, and please an ill-pleased eye with wanton shows of better hidden matters. But what, shall the abuse of a thing make the right use odious? Nay truly, though I yield that Poesy may not only be abused, but that being abused, by the reason of his sweet charming force, it can do more hurt than any other army of words, yet shall it be so far from concluding that the abuse should give reproach to the abused, that contrariwise it is a good reason, that whatsoever, being abused, doth most harm, being rightly used (and upon the right use each thing conceiveth his title), doth most good.

Do we not see the skill of Physic (the best rampire to our often-assaulted bodies), being abused, teach poison, the most violent destroyer? Doth not knowledge of Law, whose end is to even and right all things, being abused, grow the crooked fosterer of horrible injuries? Doth not (to go to the highest) God's word abused breed heresy, and His Name abused become blasphemy? Truly, a needle cannot do much hurt, and as truly (with leave of ladies be it spoken) it

cannot do much good. With a sword thou mayest kill
thy father, and with a sword thou mayest defend thy
prince and country. So that, as in their calling poets
the fathers of lies they say nothing, so in this their
argument of abuse they prove the commendation.

They allege herewith, that before poets began to be
in price our nation hath set their heart's delight upon
action, and not upon imagination, rather doing things
worthy to be written, than writing things fit to be
done. What that before-time was, I think scarcely
Sphinx can tell, since no memory is so ancient that
hath the precedence of Poetry. And certain it is that,
in our plainest homeliness, yet never was the Albion
nation without Poetry. Marry, this argument, though
it be levelled against Poetry, yet is it indeed a chain-
shot against all learning, or bookishness, as they commonly term it. Of such mind were certain Goths, of
whom it is written that, having in the spoil of a famous
city taken a fair library, one hangman, belike, fit to
execute the fruits of their wits, who had murdered
a great number of bodies, would have set fire on it.
'No,' said another very gravely, 'take heed what you
do, for while they are busy about these toys, we shall
with more leisure conquer their countries.'

This indeed is the ordinary doctrine of ignorance,
and many words sometimes I have heard spent in it:
but because this reason is generally against all learning, as well as Poetry, or rather, all learning but
Poetry; because it were too large a digression to
handle, or at least too superfluous (since it is manifest
that all government of action is to be gotten by knowledge, and knowledge best by gathering many knowledges, which is reading), I only, with Horace, to him
that is of that opinion,

Iubeo stultum esse libenter;

for as for Poetry itself, it is the freest from this objection. For Poetry is the companion of the camps.

I dare undertake, Orlando Furioso, or honest King

Arthur, will never displease a soldier: but the quiddity of *Ens* and *Prima materia* will hardly agree with a corslet. And therefore, as I said in the beginning, even Turks and Tartars are delighted with poets. Homer, a Greek, flourished before Greece flourished. And if to a slight conjecture a conjecture may be opposed, truly it may seem, that, as by him their learned men took almost their first light of knowledge, so their active men received their first motions of courage. Only Alexander's example may serve, who by Plutarch is accounted of such virtue, that Fortune was not his guide but his footstool; whose acts speak for him, though Plutarch did not,—indeed the Phoenix of warlike princes. This Alexander left his schoolmaster, living Aristotle, behind him, but took dead Homer with him. He put the philosopher Callisthenes to death for his seeming philosophical, indeed mutinous, stubbornness, but the chief thing he ever was heard to wish for was that Homer had been alive. He well found he received more bravery of mind by the pattern of Achilles than by hearing the definition of fortitude: and therefore, if Cato misliked Fulvius for carrying Ennius with him to the field, it may be answered that, if Cato misliked it, the noble Fulvius liked it, or else he had not done it: for it was not the excellent Cato Uticensis (whose authority I would much more have reverenced), but it was the former, in truth a bitter punisher of faults, but else a man that had never well sacrificed to the Graces. He misliked and cried out upon all Greek learning, and yet, being 80 years old, began to learn it, belike fearing that Pluto understood not Latin. Indeed, the Roman laws allowed no person to be carried to the wars but he that was in the soldier's roll, and therefore, though Cato misliked his unmustered person, he misliked not his work. And if he had, Scipio Nasica, judged by common consent the best Roman, loved him. Both the other Scipio brothers, who had by their virtues no less surnames than of Asia and Afric, so loved him that they caused his body to be buried in their sepulchre. So as Cato's authority being but against his person, and that answered with so far greater than himself, is herein of no validity.

But now indeed my burden is great; now Plato's name is laid upon me, whom, I must confess, of all philosophers I have ever esteemed most worthy of reverence, and with great reason, since of all philosophers he is the most poetical. Yet if he will defile the fountain out of which his flowing streams have proceeded, let us boldly examine with what reasons he did it. First truly, a man might maliciously object that Plato, being a philosopher, was a natural enemy of poets. For indeed, after the philosophers had picked out of the sweet mysteries of Poetry the right discerning true points of knowledge, they forthwith, putting it in method, and making a school art of that which the poets did only teach by a divine delightfulness, beginning to spurn at their guides, like ungrateful prentices, were not content to set up shops for themselves, but sought by all means to discredit their masters; which by the force of delight being barred them, the less they could overthrow them, the more they hated them. For indeed, they found for Homer seven cities strove who should have him for their citizen; where many cities banished philosophers as not fit members to live among them. For only repeating certain of Euripides' verses, many Athenians had their lives saved of the Syracusians, when the Athenians themselves thought many philosophers unworthy to live. Certain poets, as Simonides and Pindarus, had so prevailed with Hiero the First, that of a tyrant they made him a just king; where Plato could do so little with Dionysius, that he himself of a philosopher was made a slave. But who should do thus, I confess, should requite the objections made against poets with like cavillation against philosophers; as likewise one should do that should bid one read Phaedrus or Symposium in Plato, or the discourse of love in Plutarch, and see whether any poet do authorize abominable filthiness, as they do. Again, a man might ask out of what Commonwealth Plato did banish them. In sooth, thence where he himself alloweth community of women. So as belike this banishment grew not for effeminate wantonness, since little should poetical sonnets be hurtful when a man might have what woman he listed. But I honour philosophical instructions, and bless the wits which bred them: so as they be not abused, which is likewise stretched to Poetry.

St. Paul himself, who yet, for the credit of poets, allegeth twice two poets, and one of them by the name of a prophet, setteth a watchword upon Philosophy,— indeed upon the abuse. So doth Plato upon the abuse, not upon Poetry. Plato found fault that the poets of his time filled the world with wrong opinions of the gods, making light tales of that unspotted essence, and therefore would not have the youth depraved with such opinions. Herein may much be said; let this suffice: the poets did not induce such opinions, but did imitate those opinions already induced. For all the Greek stories can well testify that the very religion of that time stood upon many and many-fashioned gods, not taught so by the poets, but followed according to their nature of imitation. Who list may read in Plutarch the discourses of Isis and Osiris, of the cause why oracles ceased, of the divine providence, and see whether the theology of that nation stood not upon such dreams which the poets indeed superstitiously observed, and truly (since they had not the light of Christ) did much better in it than the philosophers, who, shaking off superstition, brought in atheism. Plato therefore (whose authority I had much rather justly construe than unjustly resist) meant not in general of poets, in those words of which Julius Scaliger saith, *Qua authoritate barbari quidam atque hispidi abuti velint ad poetas e republica exigendos*; but only meant to drive out those wrong opinions of the Deity (where-of now, without further law, Christianity hath taken

away all the hurtful belief), perchance (as he thought)
nourished by the then esteemed poets. And a man
need go no further than to Plato himself to know his
meaning: who, in his Dialogue called *Ion*, giveth high
and rightly divine commendation to Poetry. So as
Plato, banishing the abuse, not the thing, not banishing it, but giving due honour unto it, shall be our
patron and not our adversary. For indeed I had much
rather (since truly I may do it) show their mistaking
of Plato (under whose lion's skin they would make an
ass-like braying against Poesy) than go about to overthrow his authority; whom, the wiser a man is, the
more just cause he shall find to have in admiration;
especially since he attributeth unto Poesy more than
myself do, namely, to be a very inspiring of a divine
force, far above man's wit, as in the afore-named
Dialogue is apparent.

Of the other side, who would show the honours
have been by the best sort of judgements granted
them, a whole sea of examples would present themselves: Alexanders, Caesars, Scipios, all favourers of
poets; Laelius, called the Roman Socrates, himself a
poet, so as part of *Heautontimorumenos* in Terence was
supposed to be made by him, and even the Greek
Socrates, whom Apollo confirmed to be the only wise
man, is said to have spent part of his old time in putting Aesop's fables into verses. And therefore, full
evil should it become his scholar Plato to put such
words in his master's mouth against poets. But what
need more? Aristotle writes the Art of Poesy: and
why, if it should not be written? Plutarch teacheth
the use to be gathered of them, and how, if they should
not be read? And who reads Plutarch's either history or philosophy, shall find he trimmeth both their
garments with guards of Poesy. But I list not to defend Poesy with the help of her underling Historio-
graphy. Let it suffice that it is a fit soil for praise to
dwell upon; and what dispraise may set upon it, is
either easily overcome, or transformed into just com-

mendation. So that, since the excellencies of it may
be so easily and so justly confirmed, and the low-
creeping objections so soon trodden down; it not
being an art of lies, but oft true doctrine; not of effemi-
nateness, but of notable stirring of courage; not of
abusing man's wit, but of strengthening man's wit;
not banished, but honoured by Plato; let us rather
plant more laurels for to engarland our poets' heads
(which honour of being laureate, as besides them only
triumphant captains wear, is a sufficient authority to
show the price they ought to be had in) than suffer the
ill-favouring breath of such wrong-speakers once to
blow upon the clear springs of Poesy.

But since I have run so long a career in this matter,
methinks, before I give my pen a full stop, it shall be
but a little more lost time to inquire why England
(the mother of excellent minds) should be grown so
hard a stepmother to poets, who certainly in wit ought
to pass all other, since all only proceedeth from their
wit, being indeed makers of themselves, not takers of
others. How can I but exclaim,

Musa, mihi causas memora, quo numine laeso!

Sweet Poesy, that hath anciently had kings, emperors,
senators, great captains, such as, besides a thousand
others, David, Adrian, Sophocles, Germanicus, not
only to favour poets, but to be poets; and of our nearer
times can present for her patrons a Robert, king of
Sicily, the great King Francis of France, King James
of Scotland; such cardinals as Bembus and Bibbiena:
such famous preachers and teachers as Beza and
Melancthon; so learned philosophers as Fracastorius
and Scaliger; so great orators as Pontanus and Mure-
tus; so piercing wits as George Buchanan; so grave
counsellors as, besides many, but before all, that
Hospital of France, than whom (I think) that realm
never brought forth a more accomplished judgement,
more firmly builded upon virtue—I say these, with
numbers of others, not only to read others' poesies, but

to poetize for others' reading—that Poesy, thus embraced in all other places, should only find in our
time a hard welcome in England, I think the very
earth lamenteth it, and therefore decketh our soil
with fewer laurels than it was accustomed. For heretofore poets have in England also flourished, and,
which is to be noted, even in those times when the
trumpet of Mars did sound loudest. And now that an
overfaint quietness should seem to strew the house for
poets, they are almost in as good reputation as the
mountebanks at Venice. Truly even that, as of the
one side it giveth great praise to Poesy, which like
Venus (but to better purpose) hath rather be troubled
in the net with Mars than enjoy the homely quiet of
Vulcan; so serves it for a piece of a reason why they
are less grateful to idle England, which now can
scarce endure the pain of a pen. Upon this necessarily
followeth, that base men with servile wits undertake
it, who think it enough if they can be rewarded of the
printer. And so as Epaminondas is said, with the
honour of his virtue, to have made an office, by his
exercising it, which before was contemptible, to become highly respected, so these, no more but setting
their names to it, by their own disgracefulness disgrace the most graceful Poesy. For now, as if all the
Muses were got with child, to bring forth bastard
poets, without any commission they do post over the
banks of Helicon, till they make the readers more
weary than posthorses, while, in the meantime, they,

Queis meliore luto finxit praecordia Titan,

are better content to suppress the outflowing of their
wit, than, by publishing them, to be accounted
knights of the same order. But I that, before ever I
durst aspire unto the dignity, am admitted into the
company of the paper-blurrers, do find the very true
cause of our wanting estimation is want of desert,
taking upon us to be poets in despite of Pallas. Now,
wherein we want desert were a thankworthy labour to

express: but if I knew, I should have mended myself. But I, as I never desired the title, so have I neglected the means to come by it. Only, overmastered by some thoughts, I yielded an inky tribute unto them. Marry, they that delight in Poesy itself should seek to know what they do, and how they do, and, especially, look themselves in an unflattering glass of reason, if they be inclinable unto it. For Poesy must not be drawn by the ears; it must be gently led, or rather it must lead; which was partly the cause that made the ancient-learned affirm it was a divine gift, and no human skill; since all other knowledges lie ready for any that hath strength of wit; a poet no industry can make, if his own genius be not carried unto it; and therefore is it an old proverb, *Orator fit, Poeta nascitur.* Yet confess I always that as the fertilest ground must be manured, so must the highest-flying wit have a Daedalus to guide him. That Daedalus, they say, both in this and in other, hath three wings to bear itself up into the air of due commendation: that is, Art, Imitation, and Exercise. But these, neither artificial rules nor imitative patterns, we much cumber ourselves withal. Exercise indeed we do, but that very fore-backwardly: for where we should exercise to know, we exercise as having known: and so is our brain delivered of much matter which never was begotten by knowledge. For, there being two principal parts—matter to be expressed by words and words to express the matter—in neither we use Art or Imitation rightly. Our matter is *Quodlibet* indeed, though wrongly performing Ovid's verse,

Quicquid conabar dicere, versus erat:

never marshalling it into an assured rank, that almost the readers cannot tell where to find themselves.

Chaucer, undoubtedly, did excellently in his *Troilus and Cressida*; of whom, truly, I know not whether to marvel more, either that he in that misty time could see so clearly, or that we in this clear age walk so stumblingly after him. Yet had he great wants, fit to be forgiven in so reverent antiquity. I account the *Mirrour of Magistrates* meetly furnished of beautiful parts, and in the Earl of Surrey's *Lyrics* many things tasting of a noble birth, and worthy of a noble mind. The *Shepheard's Calendar* hath much poetry in his Eclogues, indeed worthy the reading, if I be not deceived. That same framing of his style to an old rustic language I dare not allow, since neither Theocritus in Greek, Virgil in Latin, nor Sannazaro in Italian did affect it. Besides these, do I not remember to have seen but few (to speak boldly) printed, that have poetical sinews in them: for proof whereof, let but most of the verses be put in prose, and then ask the meaning; and it will be found that one verse did but beget another, without ordering at the first what should be at the last; which becomes a confused mass of words, with a tingling sound of rhyme, barely accompanied with reason.

Our Tragedies and Comedies (not without cause cried out against), observing rules neither of honest civility nor of skilful Poetry, excepting *Gorboduc* (again, I say, of those that I have seen), which notwithstanding, as it is full of stately speeches and well-sounding phrases, climbing to the height of Seneca's style, and as full of notable morality, which it doth most delightfully teach, and so obtain the very end of Poesy, yet in truth it is very defectious in the circumstances, which grieveth me, because it might not remain as an exact model of all Tragedies. For it is faulty both in place and time, the two necessary companions of all corporal actions. For where the stage should always represent but one place, and the uttermost time presupposed in it should be, both by Aristotle's precept and common reason, but one day, there is both many days, and many places, inartificially imagined. But if it be so in *Gorboduc*, how much more in all the rest, where you shall have Asia of the one side, and Afric of the other, and so many other under-kingdoms, that the player, when he cometh in, must ever begin with telling where he is, or else the tale will not be conceived? Now ye shall have three ladies walk to gather flowers and then we must believe the stage to be a garden. By and by we hear news of shipwreck in the same place, and then we are to blame if we accept it not for a rock. Upon the back of that comes out a hideous monster, with fire and smoke, and then the miserable beholders are bound to take it for a cave. While in the meantime two armies fly in, represented with four swords and bucklers, and then what hard heart will not receive it for a pitched field? Now, of time they are much more liberal, for ordinary it is that two young princes fall in love. After many traverses, she is got with child, delivered of a fair boy; he is lost, groweth a man, falls in love, and is ready to get another child; and all this in two hours' space: which, how absurd it is in sense, even sense may imagine, and Art hath taught, and all ancient examples justified, and, at this day, the ordinary players in Italy will not err in. Yet will some bring in an example of Eunuchus in Terence, that containeth matter of two days, yet far short of twenty years. True it is, and so was it to be played in two days, and so fitted to the time it set forth. And though Plautus hath in one place done amiss, let us hit with him, and not miss with him. But they will say, How then shall we set forth a story, which containeth both many places and many times? And do they not know that a Tragedy is tied to the laws of Poesy, and not of History; not bound to follow the story, but, having liberty, either to feign a quite new matter, or to frame the history to the most tragical conveniency? Again, many things may be told which cannot be showed, if they know the difference betwixt reporting and representing. As, for example, I may speak (though I am here) of Peru, and in speech digress from that to the description of Calicut; but in action I cannot represent it without Pacolet's horse.

And so was the manner the ancients took, by some Nuncius to recount things done in former time or other place. Lastly, if they will represent an history, they must not (as Horace saith) begin *ab ovo*, but they must come to the principal point of that one action which they will represent. By example this will be best expressed. I have a story of young Polydorus, delivered for safety's sake, with great riches, by his father Priam to Polymnestor, king of Thrace, in the Trojan war time. He, after some years, hearing the overthrow of Priam, for to make the treasure his own, murdereth the child. The body of the child is taken up by Hecuba. She, the same day, findeth a slight to be revenged most cruelly of the tyrant. Where now would one of our tragedy writers begin, but with the delivery of the child? Then should he sail over into Thrace, and so spend I know not how many years, and travel numbers of places. But where doth Euripides? Even with the finding of the body, leaving the rest to be told by the spirit of Polydorus. This need no further to be enlarged; the dullest wit may conceive it.

But besides these gross absurdities, how all their plays be neither right tragedies, nor right comedies, mingling kings and clowns, not because the matter so carrieth it, but thrust in clowns by head and shoulders, to play a part in majestical matters, with neither decency nor discretion, so as neither the admiration and commiseration, nor the right sportfulness, is by their mongrel tragi-comedy obtained. I know Apuleius did somewhat so, but that is a thing recounted with space of time, not represented in one moment: and I know the ancients have one or two examples of tragi-comedies, as Plautus hath *Amphitrio*. But, if we mark them well, we shall find, that they never, or very daintily, match hornpipes and funerals. So falleth it out that, having indeed no right comedy, in that comical part of our tragedy we have nothing but scurrility, unworthy of any chaste ears, or some extreme show of doltishness, indeed fit to lift up a loud laughter, and nothing else: where the whole tract of a comedy should be full of delight, as the tragedy should be still maintained in a well-raised admiration. But our comedians think there is no delight without laughter; which is very wrong, for though laughter may come with delight, yet cometh it not of delight, as though delight should be the cause of laughter; but well may one thing breed both together. Nay, rather in themselves they have, as it were, a kind of contrariety: for delight we scarcely do but in things that have a conveniency to ourselves or to the general nature: laughter almost ever cometh of things most disproportioned to ourselves and nature. Delight hath a joy in it, either permanent or present. Laughter hath only a scornful tickling. For example, we are ravished with delight to see a fair woman, and yet are far from being moved to laughter. We laugh at deformed creatures, wherein certainly we cannot delight. We delight in good chances, we laugh at mischances; we delight to hear the happiness of our friends, or country, at which he were worthy to be laughed at that would laugh. We shall, contrarily, laugh sometimes to find a matter quite mistaken and go down the hill against the bias, in the mouth of some such men, as for the respect of them one shall be heartily sorry, yet he cannot choose but laugh; and so is rather pained than delighted with laughter. Yet deny I not but that they may go well together. For as in Alexander's picture well set out we delight without laughter, and in twenty mad antics we laugh without delight, so in Hercules, painted with his great beard and furious countenance, in woman's attire, spinning at Omphale's commandment, it breedeth both delight and laughter. For the representing of so strange a power in love procureth delight: and the scornfulness of the action stirreth laughter. But I speak to this purpose, that all the end of the comical part be not upon such scornful matters as stirreth laughter only, but, mixed with it, that delightful teaching which is the end of Poesy. And the great fault even in that point of laughter, and forbidden plainly by Aristotle, is that they stir laughter in sinful things, which are rather execrable than ridiculous; or in miserable, which are rather to be pitied than scorned. For what is it to make folks gape at a wretched beggar, or a beggarly clown; or, against law of hospitality, to jest at strangers, because they speak not English so well as we do? What do we learn, since it is certain

> *Nil habet infelix paupertas durius in se,*
> *Quam quod ridiculos homines facit?*

But rather a busy loving courtier, a heartless threatening Thraso, a self-wise-seeming schoolmaster, an awry-transformed traveller—these if we saw walk in stage names, which we play naturally, therein were delightful laughter, and teaching delightfulness: as in the other, the tragedies of Buchanan do justly bring forth a divine admiration. But I have lavished out too many words of this play matter. I do it because, as they are excelling parts of Poesy, so is there none so much used in England, and none can be more pitifully abused; which, like an unmannerly daughter showing a bad education, causeth her mother Poesy's honesty to be called in question.

Other sorts of Poetry almost have we none, but that lyrical kind of songs and sonnets: which, Lord, if He gave us so good minds, how well it might be employed, and with how heavenly fruit, both private and public, in singing the praises of the immortal beauty, the immortal goodness of that God who giveth us hands to write and wits to conceive; of which we might well want words, but never matter; of which we could turn our eyes to nothing, but we should ever have new budding occasions. But truly many of such writings as come under the banner of unresistible love, if I were a mistress, would never

persuade me they were in love; so coldly they apply
fiery speeches, as men that had rather read lovers'
writings, and so caught up certain swelling phrases
(which hang together like a man which once told me
the wind was at north-west, and by south, because he
would be sure to name winds enough), than that in
truth they feel those passions, which easily (as I think)
may be betrayed by that same forcibleness or *Energia*
(as the Greeks call it) of the writer. But let this be a
sufficient though short note, that we miss the right
use of the material point of Poesy.

Now, for the outside of it, which is words, or (as
I may term it) Diction, it is even well worse. So is
that honey-flowing matron Eloquence apparelled, or
rather disguised, in a courtesan-like painted affectation: one time with so far-fetched words, they may
seem monsters, but must seem strangers, to any poor
Englishman; another time, with coursing of a letter,
as if they were bound to follow the method of a
dictionary; another time, with figures and flowers,
extremely winter-starved. But I would this fault were
only peculiar to versifiers, and had not as large possession among prose-printers, and (which is to be mar-
velled) among many scholars, and (which is to be
pitied) among some preachers. Truly I could wish,
if at least I might be so bold to wish in a thing beyond
the reach of my capacity, the diligent imitators of
Tully and Demosthenes (most worthy to be imitated)
did not so much keep Nizolian paper-books of their
figures and phrases, as by attentive translation (as it
were) devour them whole, and make them wholly
theirs. For now they cast sugar and spice upon every
dish that is served to the table, like those Indians, not
content to wear earrings at the fit and natural place of
the ears, but they will thrust jewels through their nose
and lips, because they will be sure to be fine. Tully,
when he was to drive out Catiline, as it were with a
thunderbolt of eloquence, often used that figure of repetition, *Vivit. Vivit? Imo in Senatum venit*, &c. Indeed,

inflamed with a well-grounded rage, he would have his words (as it were) double out of his mouth, and so do that artificially which we see men do in choler naturally. And we, having noted the grace of those words, hale them in sometime to a familiar epistle, when it were too much choler to be choleric.

Now for similitudes in certain printed discourses, I think all Herberists, all stories of beasts, fowls, and fishes are rifled up, that they come in multitudes to wait upon any of our conceits; which certainly is as absurd a surfeit to the ears as is possible: for the force of a similitude not being to prove anything to a contrary disputer, but only to explain to a willing hearer; when that is done, the rest is a most tedious prattling, rather over-swaying the memory from the purpose whereto they were applied, than any whit informing the judgement, already either satisfied, or by similitudes not to be satisfied. For my part, I do not doubt, when Antonius and Crassus, the great forefathers of Cicero in eloquence, the one (as Cicero testifieth of them) pretended not to know art, the other not to set by it, because with a plain sensibleness they might win credit of popular ears; which credit is the nearest step to persuasion; which persuasion is the chief mark of Oratory—I do not doubt (I say) that but they used these knacks very sparingly; which, who doth generally use, any man may see doth dance to his own music; and so be noted by the audience more careful to speak curiously than to speak truly.

Undoubtedly (at least to my opinion undoubtedly) I have found in divers small-learned courtiers a more sound style than in some professors of learning: of which I can guess no other cause, but that the courtier, following that which by practice he findeth fittest to nature, therein (though he know it not) doth according to Art, though not by Art: where the other, using Art to show Art, and not to hide Art (as in these cases he should do), flieth from nature, and indeed abuseth Art.

But what? Methinks I deserve to be pounded for straying from Poetry to Oratory: but both have such an affinity in this wordish consideration, that I think this digression will make my meaning receive the fuller understanding—which is not to take upon me to teach poets how they should do, but only, finding myself sick among the rest, to show some one or two spots of the common infection grown among the most part of writers: that, acknowledging ourselves somewhat awry, we may bend to the right use both of matter and manner; whereto our language giveth us great occasion, being indeed capable of any excellent exercising of it. I know some will say it is a mingled language. And why not so much the better, taking the best of both the other? Another will say it wanteth grammar. Nay truly, it hath that praise, that it wanteth not grammar: for grammar it might have, but it needs it not; being so easy of itself, and so void of those cumbersome differences of cases, genders, moods, and tenses, which I think was a piece of the Tower of Babylon's curse, that a man should be put to school to learn his mother-tongue. But for the uttering sweetly and properly the conceits of the mind, which is the end of speech, that hath it equally with any other tongue in the world: and is particularly happy in compositions of two or three words together, near the Greek, far beyond the Latin: which is one of the greatest beauties can be in a language.

Now, of versifying there are two sorts, the one ancient, the other modern: the ancient marked the quantity of each syllable, and according to that framed his verse; the modern observing only number (with some regard of the accent), the chief life of it standeth in that like sounding of the words, which we call rhyme. Whether of these be the most excellent, would bear many speeches. The ancient (no doubt) more fit for music, both words and tune observing quantity, and more fit lively to express divers passions, by the low and lofty sound of the well-weighed syllable.

The latter likewise, with his rhyme, striketh a certain music to the ear: and, in fine, since it doth delight, though by another way, it obtains the same purpose: there being in either sweetness, and wanting in neither majesty. Truly the English, before any other vulgar language I know, is fit for both sorts: for, for the ancient, the Italian is so full of vowels that it must ever be cumbered with elisions; the Dutch so, of the other side, with consonants, that they cannot yield the sweet sliding fit for a verse; the French, in his whole language, hath not one word that hath his accent in the last syllable saving two, called *Antepenultima*; and little more hath the Spanish: and, therefore, very gracelessly may they use dactyls. The English is subject to none of these defects.

Now, for the rhyme, though we do not observe quantity, yet we observe the accent very precisely: which other languages either cannot do, or will not do so absolutely. That *caesura*, or breathing place in the midst of the verse, neither Italian nor Spanish have, the French, and we, never almost fail of. Lastly, even the very rhyme itself the Italian cannot put in the last syllable, by the French named the 'masculine rhyme', but still in the next to the last, which the French call the 'female', or the next before that, which the Italians term *sdrucciola*. The example of the former is *buono : suono*, of the *sdrucciola*, *femina : semina*. The French, of the other side, hath both the male, as *bon : son*, and the female, as *plaise : taise*, but the *sdrucciola* he hath not: where the English hath all three, as *due : true*, *father : rather*, *motion : potion*, with much more which might be said, but that I find already the triflingness of this discourse is much too much enlarged.

So that since the ever-praiseworthy Poesy is full of virtue-breeding delightfulness, and void of no gift that ought to be in the noble name of learning; since the blames laid against it are either false or feeble; since the cause why it is not esteemed in England is the fault of poet-apes, not poets; since, lastly, our tongue is most fit to honour Poesy, and to be honoured by Poesy; I conjure you all that have had the evil luck to read this ink-wasting toy of mine, even in the name of the Nine Muses, no more to scorn the sacred mysteries of Poesy, no more to laugh at the name of 'poets', as though they were next inheritors to fools, no more to jest at the reverent title of a 'rhymer'; but to believe, with Aristotle, that they were the ancient treasurers of the Grecians' Divinity; to believe, with Bembus, that they were first bringers-in of all civility; to believe, with Scaliger, that no philosopher's precepts can sooner make you an honest man than the reading of Virgil; to believe, with Clauserus, the translator of Cornutus, that it pleased the heavenly Deity, by Hesiod and Homer, under the veil of fables, to give us all knowledge, Logic, Rhetoric, Philosophy, natural and moral, and *Quid non?*; to believe, with me, that there are many mysteries contained in Poetry, which of purpose were written darkly, lest by profane wits it should be abused; to believe, with Landino, that they are so beloved of the gods that whatsoever they write proceeds of a divine fury; lastly, to believe themselves, when they tell you they will make you immortal by their verses.

Thus doing, your name shall flourish in the printers' shops; thus doing, you shall be of kin to many a poetical preface; thus doing, you shall be most fair, most rich, most wise, most all; you shall dwell upon superlatives. Thus doing, though you be *libertino patre natus*, you shall suddenly grow *Herculea proles*,

Si quid mea carmina possunt.

Thus doing, your soul shall be placed with Dante's Beatrix, or Virgil's Anchises. But if (fie of such a but) you be born so near the dull-making cataract of Nilus that you cannot hear the planet-like music of Poetry, if you have so earth-creeping a mind that it cannot lift itself up to look to the sky of Poetry, or rather, by a certain rustical disdain, will become such a Mome as to be a Momus of Poetry; then, though I will not wish unto you the ass's ears of Midas, nor to be driven by a poet's verses (as Bubonax was) to hang himself, nor to be rhymed to death, as is said to be done in Ireland; yet thus much curse I must send you, in the behalf of all poets, that while you live, you live in love, and never get favour for lacking skill of a Sonnet, and, when you die, your memory die from the earth for want of an Epitaph.

THOMAS CAMPION

From OBSERVATIONS IN THE ART OF ENGLISH POESY

[1602]

THE FIRST CHAPTER, INTREATING OF NUMBERS IN GENERAL

THERE is no writing too brief that, without obscurity, comprehends the intent of the writer. These my late observations in English Poesy I have thus briefly gathered, that they might prove the less troublesome in perusing, and the more apt to be retained in memory. And I will first generally handle the nature of Numbers. Number is *discreta quantitas*: so that when we speak simply of number, we intend only the dissevered quantity; but when we speak of a poem written in number, we consider not only the distinct number of the syllables, but also their value, which is contained in the length or shortness of their sound. As in Music we do not say a strain of so many notes, but so many semibreves (though sometimes there are no more notes than semibreves), so in a verse the numeration of the syllables is not so much to be observed as their weight and due proportion. In joining of words to harmony there is nothing more offensive to the ear than to place a long syllable with a short note, or a short syllable with a long note, though in the last the vowel often bears it out. The world is made by symmetry and proportion, and is in that respect compared to Music, and Music to Poetry: for Terence saith, speaking of poets, *artem qui tractant musicam*, confounding Music and Poesy together. What music can there be where there is no proportion observed? Learning first flourished in Greece; from whence it was derived unto the Romans, both diligent observers of the number and quantity of syllables, not in their verses only but likewise in their prose. Learning, after the declining of the Roman Empire and the pollution of their language through the conquest of the Barbarians, lay most pitifully deformed till the time of Erasmus, Reuchlin, Sir Thomas More, and other learned men of that age, who brought the Latin tongue again to light, redeeming it with much labour out of the hands of the illiterate monks and friars: as a scoffing book, entitled *Epistolae obscurorum virorum,* may sufficiently testify. In those lack-learning times, and in barbarized Italy, began that vulgar and easy kind of Poesy which is now in use throughout most parts of Christendom, which we abusively call Rhyme and Metre, of *Rithmus* and *Metrum,* of which I will now discourse.

THE SECOND CHAPTER, DECLARING THE INAPTNESS OF RHYME IN POESY

I am not ignorant that whosoever shall by way of reprehension examine the imperfections of Rhyme must encounter with many glorious enemies, and those very expert and ready at their weapon, that can if need be extempore (as they say) rhyme a man to death. Besides, there is grown a kind of prescription in the use of Rhyme, to forestall the right of true numbers, as also the consent of many nations, against all which it may seem a thing almost impossible and vain to contend. All this and more cannot yet deter me from a lawful defence of perfection, or make me any whit the sooner adhere to that which is lame and unbeseeming. For custom I allege that ill uses are to be abolished, and that things naturally imperfect cannot be perfected by use. Old customs, if they be better, why should they not be recalled, as the yet flourishing custom of numerous poesy used among the Romans and Grecians? But the unaptness of our tongues and the difficulty of imitation disheartens us: again, the facility and popularity of Rhyme creates as many poets as a hot summer flies.

But let me now examine the nature of that which we call Rhyme. By Rhyme is understood that which ends in the like sound, so that verses in such manner composed yield but a continual repetition of that rhetorical figure which we term *similiter desinentia*, and that, being but *figura verbi*, ought (as Tully and all other rhetoricians have judicially observed) sparingly to be used, lest it should offend the ear with tedious affectation. Such was that absurd following of the letter amongst our English so much of late affected, but now hissed out of Paul's Churchyard: which foolish figurative repetition crept also into the Latin tongue, as it is manifest in the book of P's called *praelia porcorum*, and another pamphlet all of F's which I have seen imprinted. But I will leave these follies to their own ruin, and return to the matter intended. The ear is a rational sense and a chief judge of proportion; but in our kind of rhyming what proportion is there kept where there remains such a confused inequality of syllables? Iambic and trochaic feet, which are opposed by nature, are by all rhymers confounded; nay, oftentimes they place instead of an iambic the foot *Pyrrhichius*, consisting of two short syllables, curtailing their verse, which they supply in reading with a ridiculous and unapt drawing of their speech. As for example:

> Was it my destiny, or dismal chance?

In this verse the two last syllables of the word 'destiny', being both short, and standing for a whole foot in the verse, cause the line to fall out shorter than it ought by nature. The like impure errors have in time of rudeness been used in the Latin tongue, as the *Carmina proverbialia* can witness, and many other such reverend baubles. But the noble Grecians and Romans, whose skilful monuments outlive barbarism, tied themselves to the strict observation of poetical numbers, so abandoning the childish titillation of rhyming that it was imputed a great error to Ovid for setting forth this one rhyming verse,

Quot caelum stellas tot habet tua Roma puellas.

For the establishing of this argument, what better confirmation can be had than that of Sir Thomas More in his book of Epigrams, where he makes two sundry epitaphs upon the death of a singing man at Westminster, the one in learned numbers and disliked, the other in rude rhyme and highly extolled: so that he concludes, *tales lactucas talia labra petunt,* like lips like lettuce.

But there is yet another fault in Rhyme altogether intolerable, which is, that it enforceth a man oftentimes to abjure his matter and extend a short conceit beyond all bounds of art; for in quatorzains, methinks, the poet handles his subject as tyrannically as Procrustes the thief his prisoners, whom, when he had taken, he used to cast upon a bed which if they were too short to fill, he would stretch them longer, if too long, he would cut them shorter. Bring before me now any the most self-loved rhymer, and let me see if without blushing he be able to read his lame halting rhymes. Is there not a curse of nature laid upon such rude Poesy, when the writer is himself ashamed of it, and the hearers in contempt call it rhyming and ballading? What divine in his sermon, or grave counsellor in his oration, will allege the testimony of a rhyme? But the divinity of the Romans and Grecians was all written in verse; and Aristotle, Galen, and the books of all the excellent philosophers are full of the testimonies of the old poets. By them was laid the foundation of all human wisdom, and from them the knowledge of all antiquity is derived. I will propound but one question, and so conclude this point. If the Italians, Frenchmen, and Spaniards, that with commendation have written in rhyme, were demanded whether they had rather the books they have published (if their tongue would bear it) should remain as they are in rhyme or be translated into the ancient numbers of the Greeks and Romans, would they not answer, Into numbers? What honour were it then for our English language to be the first that after so many years of barbarism could second the perfection of the industrious Greeks and Romans? Which how it may be effected I will now proceed to demonstrate.

THE THIRD CHAPTER: OF OUR ENGLISH NUMBERS IN GENERAL

There are but three feet which generally distinguish the Greek and Latin verses, the Dactyl, consisting of one long syllable and two short, as *vĭvĕrĕ*; the Trochee, of one long and one short, as *vītă*; and the Iambic, of one short and one long, as *ămŏr*. The Spondee of two long, the Tribrach of three short, the Anapaestic of two short and a long, are but as servants to the first. Divers other feet I know are by the Grammarians cited, but to little purpose. The Heroical Verse that is distinguished by the dactyl hath been oftentimes attempted in our English tongue, but with passing pitiful success; and no wonder, seeing it is an attempt altogether against the nature of our language. For both the concourse of our monosyllables make our verses unapt to slide, and also, if we examine our polysyllables, we shall find few of them, by reason of their heaviness, willing to serve in place of a dactyl. Thence it is that the writers of English heroics do so often repeat *Amyntas, Olympus, Avernus, Erinnis*, and suchlike borrowed words, to supply the defect of our hardly entreated dactyl. I could in this place set down many ridiculous kinds of dactyls which they use, but that it is not my purpose here to incite men to laughter. If we therefore reject the dactyl as unfit for our use (which of necessity we are enforced to do), there remain only the iambic foot, of which the iambic verse is framed, and the trochee, from which the trochaic numbers have their original. Let us now then examine the property of these two feet, and try if they consent with the nature of our English syllables. And first for the iambics, they fall out so naturally in our tongue, that, if we examine our own writers, we shall find they unawares hit oftentimes upon the true iambic numbers, but always aim at them as far as their ear without the guidance of art can attain unto, as it shall hereafter more evidently appear. The trochaic foot, which is but an iambic turned over and over, must of force in like manner accord in proportion with our British syllables, and so produce an English trochaical verse. Then having these two principal kinds of verses, we may easily out of them derive other forms, as the Latins and Greeks before us have done.

SAMUEL DANIEL

A DEFENCE OF RHYME

[? 1603]

TO WILLIAM HERBERT, EARL OF PEMBROKE

THE general custom and use of Rhyme in this kingdom, noble lord, having been so long (as if from a grant of Nature) held unquestionable, made me to imagine that it lay altogether out of the way of contradiction, and was become so natural, as we should never have had a thought to cast it off into reproach, or be made to think that it ill became our language. But now I see, when there is opposition made to all things in the world by words, we must now at length likewise fall to contend for words themselves, and make a question whether they be right or not. For we are told how that our measures go wrong, all rhyming is gross, vulgar, barbarous; which if it be so, we have lost much labour to no purpose; and, for mine own particular, I cannot but blame the fortune of the times and mine own genius, that cast me upon so wrong a course, drawn with the current of custom and an unexamined example. Having been first encouraged or framed thereunto by your most worthy and honourable mother, and receiving the first notion for the formal ordering of those compositions at Wilton—which I must ever acknowledge to have been my best school, and thereof always am to hold a feeling and grateful memory—, afterward drawn farther on by the well liking and approbation of my worthy lord, the fosterer of me and my Muse; I adventured to bestow all my whole powers therein, perceiving it agreed so well, both with the complexion of the times and mine own constitution, as I found not wherein I might better employ me. But yet now, upon the great discovery of these new measures, threatening to overthrow the whole state of Rhyme in this kingdom, I must either stand out to defend, or else be forced to forsake myself and give over all. And though irresolution and a self-distrust be the most apparent faults of my nature, and that the least check of reprehension, if it savour of reason, will as easily shake my resolution as any man's living; yet in this case I know not how I am grown more resolved, and, before I sink, willing to examine what those powers of judgement are that must bear me down and beat me off from the station of my profession, which by the law of nature I am set to defend. And the rather for that this detractor (whose commendable rhymes, albeit now himself an enemy to Rhyme, have given heretofore to the world the best notice of his worth) is a man of fair parts and good reputation; and therefore the reproach forcibly cast from such a hand may throw down more at once than the labours of many shall in long time build up again, specially upon the slippery foundation of opinion, and the world's inconstancy, which knows not well what it would have, and

> *Discit enim citius meminitque libentius illud*
> *Quod quis deridet, quam quod probat et veneratur.*

And he who is thus become our unkind adversary must pardon us if we be as jealous of our fame and reputation as he is desirous of credit by his new-old art, and must consider that we cannot, in a thing that concerns us so near, but have a feeling of the wrong done, wherein every rhymer in this universal island, as well as myself, stands interested. So that if his charity had equally drawn with his learning, he would have forborne to procure the envy of so powerful a number upon him, from whom he cannot but expect the return of a like measure of blame, and only have made way to his own grace by the proof of his ability, without the disparaging of us, who would have been glad to have stood quietly by him, and perhaps commended his adventure; seeing that ever-more of one science another be may born, and that these sallies made out of the quarter of our set knowledges are the gallant proffers only of attemptive spirits, and commendable, though they work no other effect than make a bravado: and I know it were *Indecens et morosum nimis alienae industriae modum ponere*.

We could well have allowed of his numbers, had he not disgraced our Rhyme, which both custom and nature doth most powerfully defend: custom that is before all law, nature that is above all art. Every language hath her proper number or measure fitted to use and delight, which custom, entertaining by the allowance of the ear, doth endenize and make natural. All verse is but a frame of words confined within certain measure, differing from the ordinary speech, and introduced the better to express men's conceits, both for delight and memory. Which frame of words consisting of *rhythmus* or *metrum*, number or measure, are disposed into divers fashions, according to the humour of the composer and the set of the time. And these *rhythmi*, as Aristotle saith, are familiar amongst all nations, and *e naturali et sponte fusa compositione*: and they fall as naturally already in our language as ever art can make them, being such as the ear of itself doth marshal in their proper rooms; and they of themselves will not willingly be put out of their rank, and that in such a verse as best comports with the nature of our language. And for our Rhyme (which is an excellency added to this work of measure, and a harmony far happier than any proportion antiquity could ever shew us) doth add more grace, and hath more of delight than ever bare numbers, howsoever they can be forced to run in our slow language, can possibly yield. Which, whether it be derived of *rhythmus* or of romance, which were songs the Bards and Druids about rhymes used, and thereof were called *Remensi*, as some Italians hold, or how-soever, it is likewise number and harmony of words,

consisting of an agreeing sound in the last syllables
of several verses, giving both to the ear an echo of a
delightful report, and to the memory a deeper impression of what is delivered therein. For as Greek
and Latin verse consists of the number and quantity
of syllables, so doth the English verse of measure and
accent. And though it doth not strictly observe long
and short syllables, yet it most religiously respects the
accent; and as the short and the long make number,
so the acute and grave accent yield harmony. And
harmony is likewise number; so that the English verse
then hath number, measure, and harmony in the best
proportion of music. Which, being more certain and
more resounding, works that effect of motion with as
happy success as either the Greek or Latin. And so
natural a melody is it, and so universal, as it seems to
be generally born with all the nations of the world as
an hereditary eloquence proper to all mankind. The
universality argues the general power of it: for if
the barbarian use it, then it shews that it sways the
affection of the barbarian; if civil nations practise it,
it proves that it works upon the hearts of civil nations;
if all, then that it hath a power in nature on all.
Georgeviez, *De Turcarum Moribus*, hath an example of
the Turkish rhymes just of the measure of our verse
of eleven syllables, in feminine rhyme; never begotten,
I am persuaded, by any example in Europe, but born
no doubt in Scythia, and brought over Caucasus and
Mount Taurus. The Sclavonian and Arabian tongues
acquaint a great part of Asia and Africa with it; the
Moscovite, Polack, Hungarian, German, Italian,
French, and Spaniard use no other harmony of words.
The Irish, Briton, Scot, Dane, Saxon, English, and all
the inhabiters of this island either have hither brought
or here found the same in use. And such a force hath
it in nature, or so made by nature, as the Latin
numbers, notwithstanding their excellence, seemed
not sufficient to satisfy the ear of the world thereunto
accustomed, without this harmonical cadence: which

made the most learned of all nations labour with exceeding travail to bring those numbers likewise unto it; which many did with that happiness as neither their purity of tongue nor their material contemplations are thereby any way disgraced, but rather deserve to be reverenced of all grateful posterity, with the due regard of their worth. And for *Schola Salerna*, and those *Carmina proverbialia*, who finds not therein more precepts for use, concerning diet, health, and conversation, than Cato, Theognis, or all the Greeks and Latins can show us in that kind of teaching? and that in so few words, both for delight to the ear and the hold of memory, as they are to be embraced of all modest readers that study to know and not to deprave.

Methinks it is a strange imperfection that men should thus overrun the estimation of good things with so violent a censure, as though it must please none else because it likes not them: whereas *Oportet arbitratores esse non contradictores eos qui verum indicaturi sunt*, saith Aristotle, though he could not observe it himself. And mild charity tells us:

> ——*Non ego paucis*
> *Offendar maculis quas aut incuria fudit*
> *Aut humana parum cavit natura.*

For all men have their errors, and we must take the best of their powers, and leave the rest as not appertaining unto us.

'Ill customs are to be left.' I grant it; but I see not how that can be taken for an ill custom which nature hath thus ratified, all nations received, time so long confirmed, the effects such as it performs those offices of motion for which it is employed; delighting the ear, stirring the heart, and satisfying the judgement in such sort as I doubt whether ever single numbers will do in our climate, if they show no more work of wonder than yet we see. And if ever they prove to become anything, it must be by the approbation of many ages that must give them their strength for any operation, as before the world will feel where the pulse, life, and energy lies; which now we are sure where to have in our rhymes, whose known frame hath those due stays for the mind, those encounters of touch, as makes the motion certain, though the variety be infinite.

Nor will the general sort for whom we write (the wise being above books) taste these laboured measures but as an orderly prose when we have all done. For this kind acquaintance and continual familiarity ever had betwixt our ear and this cadence is grown to so intimate a friendship, as it will now hardly ever be brought to miss it. For be the verse never so good, never so full, it seems not to satisfy nor breed that delight, as when it is met and combined with a like sounding accent: which seems as the jointure without which it hangs loose, and cannot subsist, but runs wildly on, like a tedious fancy without a close. Suffer then the world to enjoy that which it knows, and what it likes: seeing that whatsoever force of words doth move, delight, and sway the affections of men, in what Scythian sort soever it be disposed or uttered, that is true number, measure, eloquence, and the perfection of speech: which I said hath as many shapes as there be tongues or nations in the world, nor can with all the tyrannical rules of idle rhetoric be governed otherwise than custom and present observation will allow. And being now the trim and fashion of the times, to suit a man otherwise cannot but give a touch of singularity; for when he hath all done, he hath but found other clothes to the same body, and peradventure not so fitting as the former. But could our adversary hereby set up the music of our times to a higher note of judgement and discretion, or could these new laws of words better our imperfections, it were a happy attempt; but when hereby we shall but as it were change prison, and put off these fetters to receive others, what have we gained? As good still to use rhyme and a little reason as neither rhyme nor reason; for, no doubt, as idle wits will write in that kind, as do now in this,—imitation will after, though it break her neck. *Scribimus indocti doctique poemata passim.* And this multitude of idle writers can be no disgrace to the good; for the same fortune in one proportion or other is proper in a like season to all states in their turn; and the same unmeasurable confluence of scribblers happened when measures were most in use among the Romans, as we find by this reprehension:

> *Mutavit mentem populus levis, et calet uno*
> *Scribendi studio; pueri[que] patresque severi*
> *Fronde comas vincti cenant et carmina dictant.*

So that their plenty seems to have bred the same waste and contempt as ours doth now, though it had not power to disvalue what was worthy of posterity, nor keep back the reputation of excellences destined to continue for many ages. For seeing it is matter that satisfies the judicial, appear it in what habit it will, all these pretended proportions of words, howsoever placed, can be but words, and peradventure serve but to embroil our understanding; whilst seeking to please our ear, we enthral our judgement; to delight an exterior sense, we smooth up a weak confused sense, affecting sound to be unsound, and all to seem *Servum pecus*, only to imitate Greeks and Latins, whose felicity in this kind might be something to themselves, to whom their own *idioma* was natural; but to us it can yield no other commodity than a sound. We admire them not for their smooth-gliding words, nor their measures, but for their inventions; which treasure if it were to be found in Welsh and Irish, we should hold those languages in the same estimation; and they may thank their sword that made their tongues so famous and universal as they are. For to say truth, their verse is many times but a confused deliverer of their excellent conceits, whose scattered limbs we are fain to look out and join together, to discern the image of what they represent unto us. And even the Latins, who profess not to be so licentious as the Greeks, show us many times examples, but of strange cruelty in torturing and dismembering of words in the midst, or disjoining such as naturally should be married and march together, by setting them as far asunder as they can possibly stand: that sometimes, unless the kind reader out of his own good nature will stay them up by their measure, they will fall down into flat prose, and sometimes are no other indeed in their natural sound: and then again, when you find them disobedient to their own laws, you must hold it to be *licentia poetica*, and so dispensable. The striving to show their change-able measures in the variety of their odes have been very painful no doubt unto them, and forced them thus to disturb the quiet stream of their words which by a natural succession otherwise desire to follow in their due course.

But such affliction doth laboursome curiosity still lay upon our best delights (which ever must be made strange and variable), as if Art were ordained to afflict Nature, and that we could not go but in fetters. Every science, every profession, must be so wrapped up in unnecessary intrications, as if it were not to fashion but to confound the understanding: which makes me much to distrust man, and fear that our presumption goes beyond our ability, and our curiosity is more than our judgement; labouring ever to seem to be more than we are, or laying greater burdens upon our minds than they are well able to bear, because we would not appear like other men.

And indeed I have wished that there were not that multiplicity of rhymes as is used by many in sonnets, which yet we see in some so happily to succeed, and hath been so far from hindering their inventions, as it hath begot conceit beyond expectation, and com-parable to the best inventions of the world: for sure in an eminent spirit, whom Nature hath fitted for that mystery, Rhyme is no impediment to his conceit, but rather gives him wings to mount, and carries him, not out of his course, but as it were beyond his power to a far happier flight. All excellences being sold us at the hard price of labour, it follows, where we bestow most thereof we buy the best success: and Rhyme, being far more laborious than loose measures (whatsoever is objected), must needs, meeting with wit and industry, breed greater and worthier effects in our language. So that, if our labours have wrought out a manumission from bondage, and that we go at liberty, notwithstanding these ties, we are no longer the slaves of Rhyme, but we make it a most excellent instrument to serve us. Nor is this certain limit observed in sonnets any tyrannical bounding of the conceit, but rather reducing it in *girum* and a just form, neither too long for the shortest project, nor too short for the longest, being but only employed for a present passion. For the body of our imagination being as an unformed chaos without fashion, without day, if by the divine power of the spirit it be wrought into an orb of order and form, is it not more pleasing to Nature, that desires a certainty and comports not with that which is infinite, to have these closes, rather than not to know where to end, or how far to go, especially seeing our passions are often without measure? And we find the best of the Latins many times either not concluding or else otherwise in the end than they began. Besides, is it not most delightful to see much excellently ordered in a small room, or little gallantly disposed and made to fill up a space of like capacity, in such sort that the one would not appear so beautiful in a larger circuit, nor the other do well in a less?— which often we find to be so, according to the powers of nature in the workman. And these limited proportions and rests of stanzas, consisting of six, seven, or eight lines, are of that happiness both for the disposition of the matter, the apt planting the sentence where it may best stand to hit, the certain close of delight with the full body of a just period well carried, is such as neither the Greeks or Latins ever attained unto. For their boundless running-on often so confounds the reader, that, having once lost himself, must either give off unsatisfied, or uncertainly cast back to retrieve the escaped sense, and to find way again into this matter.

Methinks we should not so soon yield our consents captive to the authority of antiquity, unless we saw more reason; all our understandings are not to be built by the square of Greece and Italy. We are the children of nature as well as they; we are not so placed out of the way of judgement, but that the same sun of discretion shineth upon us; we have our portion of the same virtues as well as of the same vices: *Et Catilinam quocunque in populo videas, quocunque sub axe.* Time and the turn of things bring about these faculties according to the present estimation: and *Res temporibus non tempora rebus servire oportet.* So that we must never rebel against use: *Quem penes arbitrium est et vis et norma loquendi.* It is not the observing of trochaics nor their iambics that will make our writings aught the wiser. All their Poesy, all their Philosophy is nothing, unless we bring the discerning light of conceit with us to apply it to use. It is not books, but only that great book of the world and the all-overspreading grace of heaven that makes men truly judicial. Nor can it be but a touch of arrogant ignorance to hold this or that nation barbarous, these or those times gross, considering how this manifold creature man, wheresoever he stand in the world, hath always some disposition of worth, entertains the order of society, affects that which is most in use, and is eminent in some one thing or other that fits his humour and the times. The Grecians held all other nations barbarous but themselves; yet Pyrrhus, when he saw the well-ordered marching of the Romans, which made them see their presumptuous error, could say it was no barbarous manner of proceeding. The Goths, Vandals, and

Lombards, whose coming down like an inundation overwhelmed, as they say, all the glory of learning in Europe, have yet left us still their laws and customs as the originals of most of the provincial constitutions of Christendom, which well considered with their other courses of government may serve to clear them from this imputation of ignorance. And though the vanquished never yet spake well of the conqueror, yet even through the unsound coverings of malediction appear those monuments of truth as argue well their worth and proves them not without judgement, though without Greek and Latin.

Will not experience confute us, if we should say the state of China, which never heard of Anapaestics, Trochees, and Tribrachs, were gross, barbarous, and uncivil? And is it not a most apparent ignorance, both of the succession of learning in Europe and the general course of things, to say 'that all lay pitifully deformed in those lack-learning times from the declining of the Roman Empire till the light of the Latin tongue was revived by Reuchlin, Erasmus, and More'?—when for three hundred years before them, about the coming down of Tamerlane into Europe, Francis Petrarch (who then no doubt likewise found whom to imitate) showed all the best notions of learning, in that degree of excellency both in Latin, prose and verse, and in the vulgar Italian, as all the wits of posterity have not yet much overmatched him in all kinds to this day: his great volumes in moral philosophy show his infinite reading and most happy power of disposition; his twelve Eclogues, his *Africa*, containing nine books of the last Punic war, with his three books of Epistles in Latin verse show all the transformations of wit and invention that a spirit naturally born to the inheritance of poetry and judicial knowledge could express: all which notwithstanding wrought him not that glory and fame with his own nation as did his poems in Italian, which they esteem above all whatsoever wit could have invented

in any other form than wherein it is; which questionless they will not change with the best measures
Greeks or Latins can show them, howsoever our
adversary imagines. Nor could this very same innovation in verse, begun amongst them by C. Tolomei, but
die in the attempt; and was buried as soon as it came
born, neglected as a prodigious and unnatural issue
amongst them. Nor could it never induce Tasso, the
wonder of Italy, to write that admirable poem of
Jerusalem, comparable to the best of the ancients, in
any other form than the accustomed verse. And with
Petrarch lived his scholar Boccaccio, and near about
the same time Johannis Ravenensis; and from these,
tanquam ex equo Troiano, seems to have issued all those
famous Italian writers, Leonardus Aretinus, Lauren-
tius Valla, Poggius, Biondus, and many others. Then
Emanuel Chrysolaras, a Constantinopolitan gentleman, renowned for his learning and virtue, being
employed by John Paleologus, Emperor of the East,
to implore the aid of Christian princes for the suc-
couring of perishing Greece, and understanding in the
meantime how Bajazet was taken prisoner by Tamerlane, and his country freed from danger, stayed still
at Venice, and there taught the Greek tongue, dis-
continued before in these parts the space of seven
hundred years. Him followed Bessarion, George
Trapezuntius, Theodorus Gaza, and others, transporting Philosophy, beaten by the Turk out of Greece,
into Christendom. Hereupon came that mighty confluence of Learning in these parts, which, returning
as it were *per postliminium*, and here meeting then
with the new invented stamp of Printing, spread
itself indeed in a more universal sort than the world
ever heretofore had it; when Pomponius Laetus,
Aeneas Sylvius, Angelus Politianus, Hermolaus Bar-
barus, Johannes Picus de Mirandula (the miracle and
phoenix of the world) adorned Italy, and wakened
other nations likewise with this desire of glory, long
before it brought forth Reuchlin, Erasmus, and More

—worthy men, I confess, and the last a great ornament to this land, and a rhymer.

And yet long before all these, and likewise with these, was not our nation behind in her portion of spirit and worthiness, but concurrent with the best of all this lettered world; witness venerable Bede, that flourished above a thousand years since; Aldelmus Durotelmus, that lived in the year 739, of whom we find this commendation registered: *Omnium Poetarum sui temporis facile primus, tantae eloquentiae, maiestatis, et eruditionis homo fuit, ut nunquam satis admirari possim unde illi in tam barbara ac rudi aetate facundia accreverit, usque adeo omnibus numeris tersa, elegans, et rotunda, versus edidit cum antiquitate de palma contendentes.* Witness Josephus Devonius, who wrote *de bello Troiano* in so excellent a manner, and so near resembling antiquity, as printing his work beyond the seas they have ascribed it to Cornelius Nepos, one of the ancients. What should I name Walterus Mape, Gulielmus Nigellus, Gervasius Tilburiensis, Bracton, Bacon, Occam, and an infinite catalogue of excellent men, most of them living about four hundred years since, and have left behind them monuments of most profound judgement and learning in all sciences! So that it is but the clouds gathered about our own judgement that makes us think all other ages wrapped up in mists, and the great distance betwixt us that causes us to imagine men so far off to be so little in respect of ourselves.

We must not look upon the immense course of times past as men overlook spacious and wide countries from off high mountains, and are never the near to judge of the true nature of the soil or the particular site and face of those territories they see. Nor must we think, viewing the superficial figure of a region in a map, that we know straight the fashion and place as it is. Or reading an history (which is but a map of men, and doth no otherwise acquaint us with the true substance of circumstances than a superficial card doth the seaman with a coast never seen, which always

proves other to the eye than the imagination forecast
it), that presently we know all the world, and can
distinctly judge of times, men, and manners, just as
they were: when the best measure of man is to be
taken by his own foot bearing ever the nearest proportion to himself, and is never so far different and
unequal in his powers, that he hath all in perfection
at one time, and nothing at another. The distribution
of gifts are universal, and all seasons have them in some
sort. We must not think but that there were Scipios,
Caesars, Catos, and Pompeys born elsewhere than at
Rome; the rest of the world hath ever had them in
the same degree of nature, though not of state. And
it is our weakness that makes us mistake or miscon-
ceive in these delineations of men the true figure of
their worth. And our passion and belief is so apt to
lead us beyond truth, that unless we try them by the
just compass of humanity, and as they were men, we
shall cast their figures in the air, when we should
make their models upon earth. It is not the con-
texture of words, but the effects of action, that gives
glory to the times: we find they had *mercurium in
pectore*, though not *in lingua*; and in all ages, though
they were not Ciceronians, they knew the art of
men, which only is *Ars Artium*, the great gift of heaven,
and the chief grace and glory on earth; they had the
learning of government, and ordering their state;
eloquence enough to show their judgements. And it
seems the best times followed Lycurgus's counsel;
*Literas ad usum saltem discebant, reliqua omnis disciplina
erat ut pulchre pararent ut labores preferrent, &c.* Had not
unlearned Rome laid the better foundation, and built
the stronger frame of an admirable state, eloquent
Rome had confounded it utterly, which we saw ran
the way of all confusion, the plain course of dissolu-
tion, in her greatest skill: and though she had not
power to undo herself, yet wrought she so that she
cast herself quite away from the glory of a commonwealth, and fell upon the form of state she ever most

feared and abhorred of all other: and then scarce was
there seen any shadow of policy under her first
emperors, but the most horrible and gross confusion
that could be conceived; notwithstanding, it still
endured, preserving not only a monarchy, locked up
in her own limits, but therewithal held under her
obedience so many nations so far distant, so ill affected,
so disorderly commanded and unjustly conquered, as
it is not to be attributed to any other fate but to the
first frame of that commonwealth; which was so
strongly jointed, and with such infinite combinations
interlinked as one nail or other ever held up the
majesty thereof. There is but one learning, which
omnes gentes habent scriptum in cordibus suis, one and the
self-same spirit that worketh in all. We have but one
body of justice, one body of wisdom throughout the
whole world; which is but apparelled according to
the fashion of every nation.

Eloquence and gay words are not of the substance
of wit; it is but the garnish of a nice time, the ornaments that do but deck the house of a state, and
imitatur publicos mores. Hunger is as well satisfied with
meat served in pewter as silver. Discretion is the best
measure, the rightest foot in what habit soever it run.
Erasmus, Reuchlin, and More brought no more wisdom into the world with all their new revived words
than we find was before; it bred not a profounder
divine than St. Thomas, a greater lawyer than Bar-
tolus, a more acute logician than Scotus; nor are the
effects of all this great mass of eloquence so admirable
or of that consequence, but that *impexa illa antiquitas*
can yet compare with them.

Let us go no further but look upon the wonderful
architecture of this state of England, and see whether
they were deformed times that could give it such a
form: where there is no one the least pillar of majesty
but was set with most profound judgement, and borne
up with the just convenience of prince and people;
no court of justice but laid by the rule and square of

Nature, and the best of the best commonwealths that ever were in the world; so strong and substantial as it hath stood against all the storms of factions, both of belief and ambition, which so powerfully beat upon it, and all the tempestuous alterations of humorous times whatsoever; being continually in all ages furnished with spirits fit to maintain the majesty of her own greatness, and to match in an equal concurrency all other kingdoms round about her with whom it had to encounter.

But this innovation, like a viper, must ever make way into the world's opinion, through the bowels of her own breeding, and is always borne with reproach in her mouth; the disgracing others is the best grace it can put on to win reputation of wit; and yet it is never so wise as it would seem, nor doth the world ever get so much by it as it imagineth; which being so often deceived, and seeing it never performs so much as it promises, methinks men should never give more credit unto it. For, let us change never so often, we cannot change man; our imperfections must still run on with us. And therefore the wiser nations have taught men always to use *moribus legibusque praesentibus etiamsi deteriores sint.* The Lacedaemonians, when a musician, thinking to win himself credit by his new invention and be before his fellows, had added one string more to his crowd, brake his fiddle and banished him the city, holding the innovator, though in the least things, dangerous to a public society. It is but a fantastic giddiness to forsake the way of other men, especially where it lies tolerable: *Ubi nunc est respublica, ibi simus potius quam dum illam veterem sequimur simus in nulla.*

But shall we not tend to perfection? Yes; and that ever best by going on in the course we are in, where we have advantage, being so far onward, of him that is but now setting forth. For we shall never proceed, if we be ever beginning; nor arrive at any certain port, sailing with all winds that blow—*non convalescit*

planta quae saepius transfertur—and therefore let us hold
on in the course we have undertaken, and not still
be wandering. Perfection is not the portion of man;
and if it were, why may we not as well get to it this
way as another, and suspect those great undertakers,
lest they have conspired with envy to betray our proceedings, and put us by the honour of our attempts,
with casting us back upon another course, of purpose
to overthrow the whole action of glory when we lay
the fairest for it, and were so near our hopes? I think
God that I am none of these great scholars, if thus
their high knowledges do but give them more eyes to
look out into uncertainty and confusion, accounting
myself rather beholding to my ignorance that hath
set me in so low an under-room of conceit with other
men, and hath given me as much distrust as it hath
done hope, daring not adventure to go alone, but
plodding on the plain tract I find beaten by custom
and the time, contenting me with what I see in use.

And surely methinks these great wits should rather
seek to adorn than to disgrace the present; bring something to it, without taking from it what it hath. But
it is ever the misfortune of Learning to be wounded
by her own hand. *Stimulos dat emula virtus*, and where
there is not ability to match what is, malice will find
out engines, either to disgrace or ruin it, with a per-
verse encounter of some new impression; and, which
is the greatest misery, it must ever proceed from the
powers of the best reputation, as if the greatest spirits
were ordained to endanger the world, as the gross are
to dishonour it, and that we were to expect *ab optimic
periculum, a pessimis dedecus publicum.* Emulation, the
strongest pulse that beats in high minds, is oftentimes
a wind, but of the worst effect; for whilst the soul
comes disappointed of the object it wrought on, it
presently forges another, and even cozens itself, and
crosses all the world, rather than it will stay to be
under her desires, falling out with all it hath, to
flatter and make fair that which it would have.

So that it is the ill success of our longings that with Xerxes makes us to whip the sea, and send a cartel of defiance to Mount Athos: and the fault laid upon others' weakness is but a presumptuous opinion of our own strength, who must not seem to be mastered. But had our adversary taught us by his own proceedings this way of perfection, and therein framed us a poem of that excellence as should have put down all, and been the masterpiece of these times, we should all have admired him. But to deprave the present form of writing, and to bring us nothing but a few loose and uncharitable epigrams—and yet would make us believe those numbers were come to raise the glory of our language—giveth us cause to suspect the performance, and to examine whether this new art *constat sibi*, or *aliquid sit dictum quod non sit dictum prius*.

First, we must here imitate the Greeks and Latins, and yet we are here showed to disobey them, even in their own numbers and quantities; taught to produce what they make short, and make short what they produce; make believe to be showed measures in that form we have not seen, and no such matter; told that here is the perfect art of versifying, which in conclusion is yet confessed to be unperfect—as if our adversary, to be opposite to us, were become unfaithful to himself, and seeking to lead us out of the way of reputation, hath adventured to intricate and confound him in his own courses, running upon most uneven grounds, with imperfect rules, weak proofs, and unlawful laws. Whereunto the world, I am persuaded, is not so unreasonable as to subscribe, considering the unjust authority of the lawgiver: for who hath constituted him to be the Rhadamanthus, thus to torture syllables and adjudge them their perpetual doom, setting his *Theta* or mark of condemnation upon them, to endure the appointed sentence of his cruelty, as he shall dispose? As though there were that disobedience in our words, as they would not be ruled or stand in order without so many intricate laws;

which would argue a great perverseness amongst them, according to that *in pessima republica plurimae leges*, or that they were so far gone from the quiet freedom of nature that they must thus be brought back again by force. And now in what case were this poor state of words, if in like sort another tyrant the next year should arise and abrogate these laws and ordain others clean contrary according to his humour, and say that they were only right, the others unjust? What disturbance were there here, to whom should we obey? Were it not far better to hold us fast to our old custom than to stand thus distracted with uncertain laws, wherein Right shall have as many faces as it pleases passion to make it, that wheresoever men's affections stand, it shall still look that way? What trifles doth our unconstant curiosity call up to contend for? what colours are there laid upon indifferent things to make them seem other than they are, as if it were but only to entertain contestation amongst men, who, standing according to the prospective of their own humour, seem to see the self-same things to appear otherwise to them than either they do to other, or are indeed in themselves, being but all one in nature? For what ado have we here? what strange precepts of art about the framing of an iambic verse in our language? which, when all is done, reaches not by a foot, but falleth out to be the plain ancient verse, consisting of ten syllables or five feet, which hath ever been used amongst us time out of mind, and, for all this cunning and counterfeit name, can or will [not] be any other in nature than it hath been ever heretofore: and this new *dimeter* is but the half of this verse divided in two, and no other than the *caesura* or breathing-place in the midst thereof, and therefore it had been as good to have put two lines in one, but only to make them seem diverse. Nay, it had been much better for the true English reading and pronouncing thereof, without violating the accent, which now our adversary hath herein most unkindly done: for, being as we are to sound it, according to our English march, we must make a rest, and raise the last syllable, which falls out very unnatural in *desolate, funeral, Elizabeth, prodigal*, and in all the rest, saving the monosyllables. Then follows the English trochaic, which is said to be a simple verse, and so indeed it is, being without rhyme: having here no other grace than that in sound it runs like the known measure of our former ancient verse, ending (as we term it according to the French) in a feminine foot, saving that it is shorter by one syllable at the beginning, which is not much missed, by reason it falls full at the last. Next comes the elegiac, being the fourth kind, and that likewise is no other than our old accustomed measure of five feet: if there be any difference, it must be made in the reading, and therein we must stand bound to stay where often we would not, and sometimes either break the accent or the due course of the word. And now for the other four kinds of numbers, which are to be employed for odes, they are either of the same measure, or such as have ever been familiarly used among us.

So that of all these eight several kinds of new promised numbers, you see what we have—only what was our own before, and the same but apparelled in foreign titles; which had they come in their kind and natural attire of rhyme, we should never have suspected that they had affected to be other, or sought to degenerate into strange manners which now we see was the cause why they were turned out of their proper habit, and brought in as aliens, only to induce men to admire them as far-comers. But see the power of Nature; it is not all the artificial coverings of wit that can hide their native and original condition, which breaks out through the strongest bands of affectation, and will be itself, do singularity what it can. And as for those imagined quantities of syllables, which have been ever held free and indifferent in our language, who can enforce us to take knowledge of them, being *in nullius verba iurati*, and owing fealty to no foreign

invention? especially in such a case where there is
no necessity in Nature, or that it imports either the
matter or form, whether it be so or otherwise. But
every versifier that well observes his work finds in our
language, without all these unnecessary precepts,
what numbers best fit the nature of her idiom, and
the proper places destined to such accents as she will
not let into any other rooms than in those for which
they were born. As for example, you cannot make
this fall into the right sound of a verse—

> None thinks reward rend'red worthy his worth,

unless you thus misplace the accent upon 'rend'rèd'
and 'worthỳ', contrary to the nature of these words:
which showeth that two feminine numbers (or trochees, if so you will call them) will not succeed in the
third and fourth place of the verse. And so likewise
in this case,

> Though death doth consume, yet virtue preserves,

it will not be a verse, though it hath the just syllables,
without the same number in the second, and the
altering of the fourth place in this sort,

> Though death doth ruin, virtue yet preserves.

Again, who knows not that we cannot kindly answer
a feminine number with a masculine rhyme, or (if you
will so term it) a trochee with a spondee, as *weakness*
with *confess*, *nature* and *endure*, only for that thereby we
shall wrong the accent, the chief lord and grave
governor of numbers? Also you cannot in a verse of
four feet place a trochee in the first, without the like
offence, as, *Yearly out of his wat'ry Cell*; for so you shall
sound it Yearlỳ, which is unnatural. And other such
like observations usually occur, which Nature and a
judicial ear of themselves teach us readily to avoid.

But now for whom hath our adversary taken all
this pains? For the learned, or for the ignorant, or
for himself, to show his own skill? If for the learned,
it was to no purpose, for every grammarian in this

land hath learned his *Prosodia*, and already knows all this art of numbers: if for the ignorant, it was vain, for if they become versifiers, we are like to have lean numbers instead of fat rhyme; and if Tully would have his orator skilled in all the knowledges appertaining to God and man, what should they have who would be a degree above orators? Why then it was to show his own skill, and what himself had observed; so he might well have done without doing wrong to the fame of the living, and wrong to England, in seeking to lay reproach upon her native ornaments, and to turn the fair stream and full course of her accents into the shallow current of a less uncertainty, clean out of the way of her known delight. And I had thought it could never have proceeded from the pen of a scholar (who sees no profession free from the impure mouth of the scorner) to say the reproach of others' idle tongues is the curse of Nature upon us, when it is rather her curse upon him, that knows not how to use his tongue. What, doth he think himself is now gotten so far out of the way of contempt, that his numbers are gone beyond the reach of obloquy, and that, how frivolous or idle soever they shall run, they shall be protected from disgrace? as though that light rhymes and light numbers did not weigh all alike in the grave opinion of the wise. And that is not rhyme but our idle arguments that hath brought down to so base a reckoning the price and estimation of writing in this kind; when the few good things of this age, by coming together in one throng and press with the many bad, are not discerned from them, but overlooked with them, and all taken to be alike. But when after-times shall make a quest of enquiry, to examine the best of this age, peradventure there will be found in the now contemned records of Rhyme matter not unfitting the gravest divine and severest lawyer in this kingdom. But these things must have the date of antiquity to make them reverend and authentical. For ever in the collation of writers men rather weigh their age than their merit, and *legunt priscos cum reverentia, quando coaetaneos non possunt sine invidia.* And let no writer in rhyme be any way discouraged in his endeavour by this brave alarum, but rather animated to bring up all the best of their powers, and charge with all the strength of nature and industry upon contempt, that the show of their real forces may turn back insolency into her own hold. For be sure that innovation never works any overthrow, but upon the advantage of a careless idleness. And let this make us look the better to our feet, the better to our matter, better to our manners. Let the adversary that thought to hurt us bring more profit and honour by being against us than if he had stood still on our side. For that (next to the awe of heaven) the best rein, the strongest hand to make men keep their way, is that which their enemy bears upon them: and let this be the benefit we make by being oppugned, and the means to redeem back the good opinion vanity and idleness have suffered to be won from us; which nothing but substance and matter can effect. For *scribendi recte sapere est et principium et fons.*

When we hear music, we must be in our ear in the outer-room of sense, but when we entertain judgement, we retire into the cabinet and innermost withdrawing chamber of the soul. And it is but as music for the ear *verba sequi fidibus modulanda Latinis*; but it is a work of power for the soul *numerosque modusque ediscere vitae.* The most judicial and worthy spirits of this land are not so delicate, or will owe so much to their ear, as to rest upon the outside of words, and be entertained with sound; seeing that both number, measure, and rhyme is but as the ground or seat, whereupon is raised the work that commends it, and which may be easily at the first found out by any shallow conceit: as we see some fantastic to begin a fashion, which afterward gravity itself is fain to put on, because it will not be out of the wear of other men, and *recti apud nos locum tenet error ubi publicus factus est.* And power and strength that can plant itself anywhere, having built within this compass, and reared it of so high a respect, we now embrace it as the fittest dwelling for our invention, and have thereon bestowed all the substance of our understanding to furnish it as it is. And therefore here I stand forth, only to make good the place we have thus taken up, and to defend the sacred monuments erected therein, which contain the honour of the dead, the fame of the living, the glory of peace, and the best power of our speech; and wherein so many honourable spirits have sacrificed to memory their dearest passions, showing by what divine influence they have been moved, and under what stars they lived.

But yet, notwithstanding all this which I have here delivered in the defence of rhyme, I am not so far in love with mine own mystery, or will seem so froward, as to be against the reformation and the better settling these measures of ours. Wherein there be many things I could wish were more certain and better ordered, though myself dare not take upon me to be a teacher therein, having so much need to learn of others. And I must confess that to mine own ear those continual cadences of couplets used in long and continued poems are very tiresome and unpleasing, by reason that still, methinks, they run on with a sound of one nature, and a kind of certainty which stuffs the delight rather than entertains it. But yet, notwithstanding, I must not out of mine own daintiness condemn this kind of writing, which peradventure to another may seem most delightful; and many worthy compositions we see to have passed with commendation in that kind. Besides, methinks, sometimes to beguile the ear with a running out, and passing over the rhyme, as no bound to stay us in the line where the violence of the matter will break through, is rather graceful than otherwise.

Wherein I find my Homer-Lucan, as if he gloried to seem to have no bounds, albeit he were confined within his measures, to be in my conceit most happy. For so thereby they who care not for verse or rhyme may pass it over with taking notice thereof, and please themselves with a well-measured prose. And I must confess my adversary hath wrought this much upon me, that I think a tragedy would indeed best comport with a blank verse, and dispense with rhyme, saving in the chorus, or where a sentence shall require a couplet. And to avoid this over-glutting the ear with that always certain and full encounter of rhyme, I have assayed in some of my Epistles to alter the usual place of meeting, and to set it further off by one verse, to try how I could disuse mine own ear and to ease it of this continual burden which indeed seems to surcharge it a little too much: but as yet I cannot come to please myself therein, this alternate or cross rhyme holding still the best place in my affection.

Besides, to me this change of number in a poem of one nature fits not so well as to mix uncertainly feminine rhymes with masculine, which ever since I was warned of that deformity by my kind friend and countryman Master Hugh Samford, I have always so avoided it, as there are not above two couplets in that kind in all my poem of the Civil Wars: and I would willingly if I could have altered it in all the rest, holding feminine rhymes to be fittest for ditties, and either to be set for certain, or else by themselves. But in these things, I say, I dare not take upon me to teach that they ought to be so, in respect myself holds them to be so, or that I think it right: for indeed there is no right in these things that are continually in a wandering motion, carried with the violence of uncertain likings, being but only the time that gives them their power. For if this right or truth should be no other thing than that we make it, we shall shape it into a thousand figures,

seeing this excellent painter, Man, can so well lay
the colours which himself grinds in his own affections,
as that he will make them serve for any shadow and
any counterfeit. But the greatest hinderer to our
proceedings and the reformation of our errors is this
self-love, whereunto we versifiers are ever noted to
be specially subject; a disease of all other the most
dangerous and incurable, being once seated in the
spirits, for which there is no cure but only by a
spiritual remedy. *Multos puto ad sapientiam potuisse
pervenire, nisi putassent se pervenisse*: and this opinion
of our sufficiency makes so great a crack in our judgement, as it will hardly ever hold anything of worth.
Caecus amor sui; and though it would seem to see all
without it, yet certainly it discerns but little within.
For there is not the simplest writer that will ever tell
himself he doth ill, but, as if he were the parasite
only to sooth his own doings, persuades him that his
lines cannot but please others which so much delight
himself: *Suffenus est quisque sibi*

> *—neque idem unquam*
> *Aeque est beatus, ac poema cum scribit.*
> *Tam gaudet in se tamque se ipse miratur.*

And the more to show that he is so, we shall see him
evermore in all places, and to all persons repeating
his own compositions; and

> *Quem vero arripuit, tenet, occiditque legendo.*

Next to this deformity stands our affectation, wherein we always betray ourselves to be both unkind and
unnatural to our own native language, in disguising
or forging strange or unusual words, as if it were to
make our verse seem another kind of speech out of
the course of our usual practice, displacing our words,
or inventing new, only upon a singularity, when our
own accustomed phrase, set in the due place, would
express us more familiarly and to better delight than
all this idle affectation of antiquity or novelty can
ever do. And I cannot but wonder at the strange

presumption of some men, that dare so audaciously adventure to introduce any whatsoever foreign words, be they never so strange, and of themselves, as it were, without a parliament, without any consent or allowance, establish them as free denizens in our language. But this is but a character of that perpetual revolution which we see to be in all things that never remain the same: and we must herein be content to submit ourselves to the law of time, which in few years will make all that for which we now contend nothing.

FRANCIS BACON

THE NATURE OF POETRY

[From *The Advancement of Learning*, Book II, 1605]

THE parts of human learning have reference to the three parts of man's understanding, which is the seat of learning: History to his memory, Poesy to his imagination, and Philosophy to his reason. Divine learning receiveth the same distribution, for the spirit of man is the same, though the revelation of oracle and sense be diverse; so as Theology consisteth also of History of the Church, of Parables, which is Divine Poesy, and of holy Doctrine or Precept. For as for that part which seemeth supernumerary, which is Prophecy, it is but Divine History, which hath that prerogative over human as the narration may be before the fact as well as after.

History is natural, civil, ecclesiastical, and literary, whereof the three first I allow as extant, the fourth I note as deficient. For no man hath propounded to himself the general state of learning to be described and represented from age to age, as many have done the works of Nature and the State civil and ecclesiastical, without which the History of the world seemeth to me to be as the statua of Polyphemus with his eye out, that part being wanting which doth most show the spirit and life of the person. And yet I am not ignorant that in divers particular sciences, as of the Jurisconsults, the Mathematicians, the Rhetoricians, the Philosophers, there are set down some small memorials of the schools, authors, and books; and so likewise some barren relations touching the invention of arts or usages. But a just story of learning, containing the antiquities and originals of knowledges and their sects, their inventions, their traditions, their diverse administrations and managings, their flourish-ings, their oppositions, decays, depressions, oblivions, removes, with the causes and occasions of them, and all other events concerning learning throughout the ages of the world, I may truly affirm to be wanting. The use and end of which work I do not so much design for curiosity or satisfaction of those that are the lovers of learning, but chiefly for a more serious and grave purpose, which is this in few words, that it will make learned men wise in the use and administration of learning. For it is not Saint Augustine's nor Saint Ambrose's works that will make so wise a divine as Ecclesiastical History thoroughly read and observed, and the same reason is of Learning.

.   .   .   .

Poesy is a part of Learning in measure of words for the most part restrained, but in all other points extremely licensed, and doth truly refer to the imagination, which, being not tied to the laws of matter, may at pleasure join that which Nature hath severed, and sever that which Nature hath joined, and so make unlawful matches and divorces of things: *Pictoribus atque Poetis, &c.* It is taken in two senses in respect of words or matter. In the first sense it is but a *character* of style, and belongeth to arts of speech, and is not pertinent for the present. In the later it is, as hath been said, one of the principal portions of learning, and is nothing else but FEIGNED HISTORY, which may be styled as well in prose as in verse.

The use of this FEIGNED HISTORY hath been to give some shadow of satisfaction to the mind of man in those points wherein the nature of things doth deny it, the world being in proportion inferior to the soul; by reason whereof there is agreeable to the spirit of man a more ample greatness, a more exact goodness, and a more absolute variety than can be found in the nature of things. Therefore, because the acts or events of true History have not that magnitude which satisfieth the mind of man, Poesy feigneth acts and events greater and more heroical; because true History propoundeth the successes and issues of actions not so agreeable to the merits of virtue and vice, therefore Poesy feigns them more just in retribution and more according to revealed Providence; because true History representeth actions and events more ordinary and less interchanged, therefore Poesy endueth them with more rareness and more unexpected and alternative variations: so as it appeareth that Poesy serveth and conferreth to magnanimity, morality, and to delectation. And therefore it was ever thought to have some participation of divineness, because it doth raise and erect the mind, by submitting the shows of things to the desires of the mind, whereas reason doth buckle and bow the mind unto the nature of things. And we see that by these insinuations and congruities with man's nature and pleasure, joined also with the agreement and consort it hath with music, it hath had access and estimation in rude times and barbarous regions, where other learning stood excluded.

The division of Poesy which is aptest in the propriety thereof (besides those divisions which are common unto it with History, as feigned chronicles, feigned lives, and the appendices of History, as feigned epistles, feigned orations, and the rest) is into Poesy Narrative, Representative, and Allusive. The Narrative is a mere imitation of History with the excesses before remembered, choosing for subject commonly wars and love, rarely state, and sometimes pleasure or mirth. Representative is as a visible History, and is an image of actions as if they were present, as History is of actions in nature as they are, that is past; Allusive, or Parabolical, is a narration applied only to express some special purpose or conceit: which later kind of parabolical wisdom was much more in use in the ancient times, as by the Fables of Aesop, and the brief sentences of the Seven, and the use of hieroglyphics may appear. And the cause was for that it was then of necessity to express any point of reason which was more sharp or subtle than the vulgar in that manner, because men in those times wanted both variety of examples and subtlety of conceit: and as hieroglyphics were before letters, so parables were before arguments: and nevertheless now and at all times they do retain much life and vigour, because reason cannot be sensible, nor examples so fit.

But there remaineth yet another use of Poesy parabolical opposite to that which we last mentioned; for that tendeth to demonstrate and illustrate that which is taught or delivered, and this other to retire and obscure it: that is, when the secrets and mysteries of Religion, Policy, or Philosophy, are involved in fables or parables. Of this in divine Poesy we see the use is authorized. In heathen Poesy we see the exposition of fables doth fall out sometimes with great felicity, as in the fable that the Giants being overthrown in their war against the Gods, the Earth their mother in revenge thereof brought forth Fame:

> *Illam terra Parens ira irritata Deorum,*
> *Extremam, ut perhibent, Coeo Enceladoque Sororem*
> *Progenuit:*

expounded, that when princes and monarchs have suppressed actual and open rebels, then the malignity of people, which is the mother of Rebellion, doth bring forth libels and slanders, and taxations of the states, which is of the same kind with rebellion, but more feminine: so in the fable that the rest of the gods having conspired to bind Jupiter, Pallas called Briareus with his hundred hands to his aid, expounded, that monarchies need not fear any curbing of their absoluteness by mighty subjects, as long as by wisdom they keep the hearts of the people, who will be sure to come in on their side: so in the fable that Achilles was brought up under Chiron the Centaur, who was part a man and part a beast, expounded ingenuously but corruptly by Machiavell, that it belongeth to the education and discipline of princes to know as well how to play the part of the lion in violence and the fox in guile, as of the man in virtue and justice. Nevertheless, in many the like encounters, I do rather think that the fable was first and the exposition devised than that the moral was first and thereupon the fable framed. For I find it was an ancient vanity in Chrysippus that troubled himself with great contention to fasten the assertions of the Stoics upon the fictions of the ancient poets: but yet that all the fables and fictions of the poets were but pleasure and not figure, I interpose no opinion. Surely of those poets which are now extant, even Homer himself (notwithstanding he was made a kind of Scripture by the later schools of the Grecians), yet I should without any difficulty pronounce that his fables had no such inwardness in his own meaning: but what they might have, upon a more original tradition, is not easy to affirm, for he was not the inventor of many of them. In this third part of Learning which is Poesy, I can report no deficiency. For being as a plant that cometh of the lust of the earth, without a formal seed, it hath sprung up and spread abroad, more than any other kind: but to ascribe unto it that which is due for the expressing of affections, passions, corruptions, and customs, we are beholden to Poets more than to the Philosophers' works, and for wit and eloquence not much less than to Orators' harangues.

BEN JONSON

Extracts from *TIMBER, OR DISCOVERIES*

(1620-35)

i. *De Shakespeare nostrat*

I REMEMBER the players have often mentioned it as an honour to Shakespeare, that in his writing, whatsoever he penned, he never blotted out a line. My answer hath been, 'Would he had blotted a thousand,' which they thought a malevolent speech. I had not told posterity this but for their ignorance who chose that circumstance to commend their friend by wherein he most faulted; and to justify mine own candour, for I loved the man, and do honour his memory on this side idolatry as much as any. He was, indeed, honest, and of an open and free nature; had an excellent fantasy, brave notions, and gentle expressions, wherein he flowed with that facility that sometimes it was necessary he should be stopped. '*Sufflaminandus erat*,' as Augustus said of Haterius. His wit was in his own power; would the rule of it had been so, too! Many times he fell into those things, could not escape laughter, as when he said in the person of Caesar, one speaking to him, 'Caesar, thou dost me wrong.' He replied, 'Caesar did never wrong but with just cause;' and such like, which were ridiculous. But he redeemed his vices with his virtues. There was ever more in him to be praised than to be pardoned.

ii. *Ingeniorum Discrimina*

It cannot but come to pass that these men who commonly seek to do more than enough may sometimes happen on something that is good and great; but very seldom: and when it comes, it doth not recompense the rest of their ill. For their jests and their sentences, which they only and ambitiously seek for, stick out and are more eminent, because all is sordid and vile about them; as lights are more discerned in a thick darkness than a faint shadow. Now because they speak all they can, however unfitly, they are thought to have the greater copy. Where the learned use ever election and a mean they look back to what they intended at first, and make all an even and proportioned body. The true artificer will not run away from Nature, as he were afraid of her, or depart from life and the likeness of Truth, but speak to the capacity of his hearers. And though his language differ from the vulgar somewhat, it shall not fly from all humanity, with the Tamerlanes and Tamer-Chams of the late age, which had nothing in them but the scenical strutting and furious vociferation to warrant them to the ignorant gapers. He knows it is his only art so to carry it, as none but artificers perceive it. In the meantime perhaps he is called barren, dull, lean, a poor writer, or by what contumelious words can come in their cheeks, by these men who, without labour, judgement, knowledge, or almost sense, are received or preferred before him. He gratulates them and their fortune. Another age or juster men will acknowledge the virtues of his studies, his wisdom in dividing, his subtilty in arguing, with what strength he doth inspire his readers, with what sweetness he strokes them; in inveighing, what sharpness; in jest, what urbanity he uses; how he doth reign in men's affections; how invade and break in upon them, and makes their minds like the thing he writes. Then in his elocution, to behold what word is proper, which hath ornament, which height, what is beautifully translated, where figures are fit, which gentle, which strong to show the composition manly: and how he hath avoided faint, obscure, obscene, sordid, humble, improper, or effeminate phrase, which is not only praised of the most, but commended, which is worse, especially for that it is naught.

iii. *Scriptorum Catalogus*

Cicero is said to be the only wit that the people of Rome had equalled to their Empire. *Ingenium par imperio.* We have had many, and in their several ages (to take in but the former *seculum*) Sir Thomas More, the elder Wyatt, Henry Earl of Surrey, Chaloner, Smith, Elyot, B. Gardiner, were for their times admirable; and the more because they began eloquence with us. Sir Nicholas Bacon was singular and almost alone in the beginning of Queen Elizabeth's times. Sir Philip Sidney and Mr. Hooker, in different matter, grew great masters of wit and language, and in whom all vigour of invention and strength of judgement met. The Earl of Essex, noble and high, and Sir Walter Raleigh, not to be contemned either for judgement or style; Sir Henry Savile, grave and truly lettered; Sir Edwin Sandes, excellent in both; Lord Egerton, the Chancellor, a grave and great orator, and best when he was provoked. But his learned and able, though unfortunate, successor is he who hath filled up all numbers, and performed that in our tongue which may be compared or preferred either to insolent Greece or haughty Rome. In short, within his view and about his times were all the wits born that could honour a language or help study. Now things daily fall; wits grow downward and eloquence grows backward: so that he may be named and stand as the mark and ἀκμή of our language.

I have ever observed it to have been the office of a wise patriot, among the greatest affairs of the state, to take care of the commonwealth of learning. For schools, they are the seminaries of state; and nothing is worthier the study of a statesman than that part of the republic which we call the advancement of letters. Witness the care of Julius Caesar, who in the heat of the civil war writ his books of Analogy, and

dedicated them to Tully. This made the late Lord
St. Albans entitle his work *Novum Organum*: which,
though by the most of superficial men, who cannot
get beyond the title of Nominals, it is not penetrated
nor understood, it really openeth all defects of Learning whatsoever, and is a book

Qui longum noto scriptori porriget aevum.

iv. *Praecipiendi Modi*

I take this labour in teaching others, that they
should not be always to be taught, and I would bring
my precepts into practice. For rules are ever of less
force and value than experiments: yet with this purpose, rather to show the right way to those that
come after, than to detect any that have slipped
before by error; and I hope it will be more profitable: for men do more willingly listen, and with more
favour, to precept than reprehension. Among diverse
opinions of an art, and most of them contrary in
themselves, it is hard to make election; and therefore,
though a man cannot invent new things after so many,
he may do a welcome work yet to help posterity to
judge rightly of the old. But arts and precepts avail
nothing, except Nature be beneficial and aiding. And
therefore these things are no more written to a dull
disposition than rules of husbandry to a barren soil.
No precepts will profit a fool, no more than beauty
will the blind, or music the deaf. As we should take
care that our style in writing be neither dry nor
empty, we should look again it be not winding, or
wanton with far-fetched descriptions: either is a vice.
But that is worse which proceeds out of want than
that which riots out of plenty. The remedy of fruit-
fulness is easy, but no labour will help the contrary.
I will like and praise some things in a young writer
which yet, if he continue in, I cannot but justly hate
him for the same. There is a time to be given all
things for maturity, and that even your country

husbandman can teach, who to a young plant will
not put the pruning knife, because it seems to fear
the iron, as not able to admit the scar. No more
would I tell a green writer all his faults, lest I should
make him grieve and faint, and at last despair. For
nothing doth more hurt than to make him so afraid
of all things as he can endeavour nothing. Therefore
youth ought to be instructed betimes, and in the best
things; for we hold those longest we take soonest: as
the first scent of a vessel lasts, and that tinct the wool
first receives. Therefore a master should temper his
own powers, and descend to the other's infirmity. If
you pour a glut of water upon a bottle, it receives
little of it; but with a funnel, and by degrees, you
shall fill many of them, and spill little of your own;
to their capacity they will all receive and be full. And
as it is fit to read the best authors to youth first, so let
them be of the openest and clearest: as Livy before
Sallust, Sidney before Donne; and beware of letting
them taste Gower or Chaucer at first, lest falling too
much in love with antiquity, and not apprehending
the weight, they grow rough and barren in language
only. When their judgements are firm and out of
danger, let them read both the old and the new;
but no less take heed that their new flowers and
sweetness do not as much corrupt as the others' dry-
ness and squalor, if they choose not carefully. Spenser,
in affecting the ancients, writ no language: yet I
would have him read for his matter, but as Virgil
read Ennius. The reading of Homer and Virgil is
counselled by Quintilian as the best way of informing
youth and confirming man. For, besides that the
mind is raised with the height and sublimity of such
a verse, it takes spirit from the greatness of the matter,
and is tincted with the best things. Tragic and Lyric
Poetry is good too; and Comic with the best, if the
manners of the reader be once in safety. In the Greek
poets, as also in Plautus, we shall see the economy
and disposition of poems better observed than in

Terence and the later, who thought the sole grace
and virtue of their fable the sticking in of sentences,
as ours do the forcing in of jests.

TO THE MEMORY OF MY BELOVED

MASTER WILLIAM SHAKESPEARE

AND WHAT HE HATH LEFT US

[1623]

To draw no envy, Shakespeare, on thy name,
Am I thus ample to thy book and fame;
While I confess thy writings to be such,
As neither man, nor Muse, can praise too much.
'Tis true, and all men's suffrage. But these ways
Were not the paths I meant unto thy praise;
For silliest ignorance on these may light,
Which, when it sounds at best, but echoes right;
Or blind affection, which doth ne'er advance
The truth, but gropes, and urgeth all by chance;
Or crafty malice might pretend this praise,
And think to ruin, where it seem'd to raise.
These are, as some infámous bawd, or whore,
Should praise a matron; what could hurt her more?
But thou art proof against them, and, indeed,
Above the ill fortune of them, or the need.
I therefore will begin. Soul of the age!
The applause! delight! the wonder of our stage!
My Shakespeare, rise! I will not lodge thee by
Chaucer, or Spenser, or bid Beaumont lie
A little further to make thee a room:
Thou art a monument without a tomb,
And art alive still, while thy book doth live,
And we have wits to read, and praise to give.
That I not mix thee so, my brain excuses,
I mean with great, but disproportion'd Muses:
For if I thought my judgement were of years,
I should commit thee surely with thy peers,

And tell how far thou didst our Lyly outshine,
Or sporting Kyd, or Marlowe's mighty line.
And though thou hadst small Latin and less Greek,
From thence to honour thee, I will not seek
For names: but call forth thund'ring Aeschylus,
Euripides, and Sophocles to us,
Pacuvius, Accius, him of Cordova dead,
To life again, to hear thy buskin tread,
And shake a stage: or when thy socks were on,
Leave thee alone for the comparison
Of all, that insolent Greece, or haughty Rome
Sent forth, or since did from their ashes come.
Triumph, my Britain, thou hast one to show,
To whom all scenes of Europe homage owe.
He was not of an age, but for all time!
And all the Muses still were in their prime,
When like Apollo, he came forth to warm
Our ears, or like a Mercury to charm!
Nature herself was proud of his designs,
And joy'd to wear the dressing of his lines!
Which were so richly spun; and woven so fit,
As, since, she will vouchsafe no other wit.
The merry Greek, tart Aristophanes,
Neat Terence, witty Plautus, now not please;
But antiquated and deserted lie,
As they were not of nature's family.
Yet must I not give nature all; thy art,
My gentle Shakespeare, must enjoy a part.
For though the poet's matter nature be,
His art doth give the fashion: and, that he
Who casts to write a living line, must sweat,
(Such as thine are) and strike the second heat
Upon the Muses' anvil; turn the same,
And himself with it, that he thinks to frame;
Or for the laurel, he may gain a scorn;
For a good poet's made, as well as born.
And such wert thou! Look how the father's face
Lives in his issue, even so the race
Of Shakespeare's mind and manners brightly shines

In his well turned and true filed lines:
In each of which he seems to shake a lance,
As brandish'd at the eyes of ignorance.
Sweet Swan of Avon! what a sight it were
To see thee in our waters yet appear,
And make those flights upon the banks of Thames,
That so did take Eliza, and our James!
But stay! I see thee in the hemisphere
Advanced, and made a constellation there!
Shine forth, thou Star of poets, and with rage,
Or influence, chide, or cheer the drooping stage,
Which, since thy flight from hence, hath mourn'd
    like night,
And despairs day, but for thy volume's light.

JOHN MILTON

PREFACE TO *SAMSON AGONISTES*

[1671]

Of that sort of Dramatic Poem which is called
Tragedy

TRAGEDY, as it was anciently composed, hath
been ever held the gravest, moralest, and most
profitable of all other poems; therefore said by Aristotle to be of power, by raising pity and fear, or terror,
to purge the mind of those and such like passions,
that is, to temper and reduce them to just measure
with a kind of delight, stirred up by reading or seeing
those passions well imitated. Nor is Nature wanting
in her own effects to make good his assertion; for so,
in Physic, things of melancholic hue and quality are
used against melancholy, sour against sour, salt to
remove salt humours. Hence philosophers and other
gravest writers, as Cicero, Plutarch, and others, frequently cite out of Tragic poets, both to adorn and
illustrate their discourse. The Apostle Paul himself
thought it not unworthy to insert a verse of Euripides
into the text of Holy Scripture, *1 Cor. xv. 33*; and
Paraeus, commenting on the *Revelation*, divides the
whole book, as a tragedy, into acts, distinguished each
by a Chorus of heavenly harpings and song between.
Heretofore men in highest dignity have laboured not
a little to be thought able to compose a tragedy. Of
that honour Dionysius the elder was no less ambitious
than before of his attaining to the tyranny. Augustus
Caesar also had begun his *Ajax*, but, unable to please
his own judgement with what he had begun, left it
unfinished. Seneca the Philosopher is by some thought
the author of those tragedies (at least the best of them)
that go under that name. Gregory Nazianzen, a

Father of the Church, thought it not unbeseeming the
sanctity of his person to write a tragedy, which he
entitled *Christ Suffering*. This is mentioned to vindicate Tragedy from the small esteem, or rather
infamy, which in the account of many it undergoes at
this day, with other common interludes; happening
through the poets' error of intermixing comic stuff
with tragic sadness and gravity, or introducing trivial and vulgar persons: which by all judicious hath
been counted absurd, and brought in without discretion, corruptly to gratify the people. And though
ancient Tragedy use no Prologue, yet using sometimes,
in case of self defence or explanation, that which
Martial calls an Epistle, in behalf of this tragedy,
coming forth after the ancient manner, much different
from what among us passes for best, thus much
beforehand may be epistled: that Chorus is here
introduced after the Greek manner, not ancient only
but modern, and still in use among the Italians.
In the modelling therefore of this poem, with good
reason, the ancients and Italians are rather followed,
as of much more authority and fame. The measure
of verse used in the Chorus is of all sorts, called by
the Greeks Monostrophic, or rather Apolelymenon,
without regard had to strophe, antistrophe, or epode;
which were a kind of stanzas framed only for the
music, then used with the Chorus that sung, not
essential to the poem, and therefore not material;
or being divided into stanzas or pauses, they may be
called Alloeostropha. Division into Act and Scene,
referring chiefly to the stage (to which this work
never was intended), is here omitted.

It suffices if the whole drama be found not produced beyond the fifth act; of the style and uniformity,
and that commonly called the plot, whether intricate or explicit—which is nothing indeed but such
economy or disposition of the fable as may stand best
with verisimilitude and decorum—they only will best
judge who are not unacquainted with Aeschylus,

Sophocles, and Euripides, the three tragic poets unequalled yet by any, and the best rule to all who endeavour to write Tragedy. The circumscription of time wherein the whole Drama begins and ends, is, according to ancient rule and best example, within the space of twenty-four hours.

JOHN DRYDEN

AN ESSAY OF DRAMATIC POESY

[1668]

IT was that memorable day, in the first summer of the late war, when our navy engaged the Dutch —a day wherein the two most mighty and best appointed fleets which any age had ever seen, disputed the command of the greater half of the globe, the commerce of nations, and the riches of the universe. While these vast floating bodies, on either side, moved against each other in parallel lines, and our countrymen, under the happy conduct of his royal highness, went breaking, by little and little, into the line of the enemies; the noise of the cannon from both navies reached our ears about the city, so that all men being alarmed with it, and in a dreadful suspense of the event, which they knew was then deciding, every one went following the sound as his fancy led him; and leaving the town almost empty, some took towards the park, some cross the river, others down it; all seeking the noise in the depth of silence.

Among the rest, it was the fortune of Eugenius, Crites, Lisideius, and Neander, to be in company together; three of them persons whom their wit and quality have made known to all the town; and whom I have chose to hide under these borrowed names, that they may not suffer by so ill a relation as I am going to make of their discourse.

2. Taking then a barge, which a servant of Lisideius had provided for them, they made haste to shoot the bridge, and left behind them that great fall of waters which hindered them from hearing what they desired: after which, having disengaged themselves from many vessels which rode at anchor in

the Thames, and almost blocked up the passage towards Greenwich, they ordered the watermen to let fall their oars more gently; and then, every one favouring his own curiosity with a strict silence, it was not long ere they perceived the air to break about them like the noise of distant thunder, or of swallows in a chimney—those little undulations of sound, though almost vanishing before they reached them, yet still seeming to retain somewhat of their first horror, which they had betwixt the fleets. After they had attentively listened till such time as the sound by little and little went from them, Eugenius, lifting up his head, and taking notice of it, was the first who congratulated to the rest that happy omen of our nation's victory: adding, that we had but this to desire in confirmation of it, that we might hear no more of that noise, which was now leaving the English coast. When the rest had concurred in the same opinion, Crites, a person of a sharp judgement, and somewhat too delicate a taste in wit (which the world have mistaken in him for ill-nature), said, smiling to us, that if the concernment of this battle had not been so exceeding great, he could scarce have wished the victory at the price he knew he must pay for it, in being subject to the reading and hearing of so many ill verses as he was sure would be made on that subject. Adding, that no argument could escape some of those eternal rhymers, who watch a battle with more diligence than the ravens and birds of prey; and the worst of them surest to be first in upon the quarry: while the better able, either out of modesty writ not at all, or set that due value upon their poems, as to let them be often desired and long expected. 'There are some of those impertinent people of whom you speak,' answered Lisideius, 'who to my knowledge are already so provided, either way, that they can produce not only a panegyric upon the victory, but, if need be, a funeral elegy on the duke; wherein, after they have crowned his valour with

many laurels, they will at last deplore the odds under
which he fell, concluding that his courage deserved
a better destiny.' All the company smiled at the
conceit of Lisideius; but Crites, more eager than
before, began to make particular exceptions against
some writers, and said, the public magistrate ought to
send betimes to forbid them; and that it concerned
the peace and quiet of all honest people, that ill
poets should be as well silenced as seditious preachers.
'In my opinion,' replied Eugenius, 'you pursue your
point too far; for as to my own particular, I am so
great a lover of poesy, that I could wish them all
rewarded, who attempt but to do well; at least, I
would not have them worse used than one of their
brethren was by Sylla the Dictator:—*Quem in concione
vidimus* (says Tully) *cum ei libellum malus poeta de populo
subjecisset, quod epigramma in eum fecisset tantummodo
alternis versibus longiusculis, statim ex iis rebus quas tunc
vendebat jubere ei praemium tribui, sub ea conditione ne quid
postea scriberet.*' 'I could wish with all my heart,'
replied Crites, 'that many whom we know were as
bountifully thanked upon the same condition,—that
they would never trouble us again. For amongst
others, I have a mortal apprehension of two poets,
whom this victory, with the help of both their wings,
will never be able to escape.' ' 'Tis easy to guess
whom you intend,' said Lisideius; 'and without naming them, I ask you, if one of them does not perpetually pay us with clenches upon words, and a certain
clownish kind of raillery? if now and then he does not
offer at a catachresis or Clevelandism, wresting and
torturing a word into another meaning: in fine, if he
be not one of those whom the French would call *un
mauvais bouffon*; one who is so much a well-willer to
the satire, that he intends at least to spare no man;
and though he cannot strike a blow to hurt any,
yet he ought to be punished for the malice of the
action, as our witches are justly hanged, because they
think themselves to be such; and suffer deservedly for

believing they did mischief, because they meant it.'
'You have described him,' said Crites, 'so exactly, that
I am afraid to come after you with my other extremity
of poetry. He is one of those who, having had some
advantage of education and converse, knows better
than the other what a poet should be, but puts it
into practice more unluckily than any man; his style
and matter are everywhere alike: he is the most calm,
peaceable writer you ever read: he never disquiets
your passions with the least concernment, but still
leaves you in as even a temper as he found you;
he is a very leveller in poetry: he creeps along with
ten little words in every line, and helps out his numbers with *For to*, and *Unto*, and all the pretty expletives
he can find, till he drags them to the end of another
line; while the sense is left tired half way behind it:
he doubly starves all his verses, first for want of
thought, and then of expression; his poetry neither
has wit in it, nor seems to have it; like him in Martial:

Pauper videri Cinna vult, et est pauper.

'He affects plainness, to cover his want of imagination: when he writes the serious way, the highest
flight of his fancy is some miserable antithesis, or
seeming contradiction; and in the comic he is still
reaching at some thin conceit, the ghost of a jest, and
that too flies before him, never to be caught; these
swallows which we see before us on the Thames are
the just resemblance of his wit: you may observe how
near the water they stoop, how many proffers they
make to dip, and yet how seldom they touch it; and
when they do, it is but the surface: they skim over it
but to catch a gnat, and then mount into the air
and leave it.'

3. 'Well, gentlemen,' said Eugenius, 'you may
speak your pleasure of these authors; but though I
and some few more about the town may give you a
peaceable hearing, yet assure yourselves, there are
multitudes who would think you malicious and them

injured: especially him whom you first described; he is the very Withers of the city: they have bought more editions of his works than would serve to lay under all their pies at the lord mayor's Christmas. When his famous poem first came out in the year 1660, I have seen them reading it in the midst of 'Change time; nay, so vehement they were at it, that they lost their bargain by the candles' ends; but what will you say, if he has been received amongst great persons? I can assure you he is, this day, the envy of one who is lord in the art of quibbling; and who does not take it well, that any man should intrude so far into his province.' 'All I would wish,' replied Crites, 'is, that they who love his writings, may still admire him, and his fellow poet: *Qui Bavium non odit*, &c., is curse sufficient.' 'And farther,' added Lisideius, 'I believe there is no man who writes well, but would think he had hard measure, if their admirers should praise anything of his: *Nam quos contemnimus, eorum quoque laudes contemnimus.*' 'There are so few who write well in this age,' said Crites, 'that methinks any praises should be welcome; they neither rise to the dignity of the last age, nor to any of the ancients: and we may cry out of the writers of this time, with more reason than Petronius of his, *Pace vestrâ liceat dixisse, primi omnium eloquentiam perdidistis:* you have debauched the true old poetry so far, that Nature, which is the soul of it, is not in any of your writings.'

4. 'If your quarrel,' said Eugenius, 'to those who now write, be grounded only on your reverence to antiquity, there is no man more ready to adore those great Greeks and Romans than I am: but on the other side, I cannot think so contemptibly of the age in which I live, or so dishonourably of my own country, as not to judge we equal the ancients in most kinds of poesy, and in some surpass them; neither know I any reason why I may not be as zealous for the reputation of our age, as we find the ancients themselves were in reference to those

who lived before them. For you hear your Horace
saying,

> *Indignor quidquam reprehendi, non quia crassè*
> *Compositum, illepidève putetur, sed quia nuper.*

And after:

> *Si meliora dies, ut vina, poemata reddit,*
> *Scire velim, pretium chartis quotus arroget annus?*

'But I see I am engaging in a wide dispute, where
the arguments are not like to reach close on either
side; for poesy is of so large an extent, and so many
both of the ancients and moderns have done well in
all kinds of it, that in citing one against the other, we
shall take up more time this evening than each man's
occasions will allow him: therefore I would ask Crites
to what part of poesy he would confine his arguments,
and whether he would defend the general cause of
the ancients against the moderns, or oppose any age
of the moderns against this of ours?'

5. Crites, a little while considering upon this demand, told Eugenius, that if he pleased, he would
limit their dispute to Dramatic Poesy; in which he
thought it not difficult to prove, either that the ancients were superior to the moderns, or the last age
to this of ours.

Eugenius was somewhat surprised, when he heard
Crites make choice of that subject. 'For aught I
see,' said he, 'I have undertaken a harder province
than I imagined; for though I never judged the plays
of the Greek or Roman poets comparable to ours,
yet, on the other side, those we now see acted come
short of many which were written in the last age:
but my comfort is, if we are overcome, it will be only
by our own countrymen: and if we yield to them in
this one part of poesy, we more surpass them in all
the other: for in the epic or lyric way, it will be
hard for them to show us one such amongst them,
as we have many now living, or who lately were:
they can produce nothing so courtly writ, or which

expresses so much the conversation of a gentleman, as Sir John Suckling; nothing so even, sweet, and flowing, as Mr. Waller; nothing so majestic, so correct, as Sir John Denham; nothing so elevated, so copious, and full of spirit, as Mr. Cowley. As for the Italian, French, and Spanish plays, I can make it evident that those who now write surpass them; and that the drama is wholly ours.'

All of them were thus far of Eugenius his opinion, that the sweetness of English verse was never understood or practised by our fathers; even Crites himself did not much oppose it: and every one was willing to acknowledge how much our poesy is improved by the happiness of some writers yet living; who first taught us to mould our thoughts into easy and significant words,—to retrench the superfluities of expression,—and to make our rhyme so properly a part of the verse, that it should never mislead the sense, but itself be led and governed by it.

6. Eugenius was going to continue this discourse, when Lisideius told him that it was necessary, before they proceeded further, to take a standing measure of their controversy; for how was it possible to be decided who writ the best plays, before we know what a play should be? But, this once agreed on by both parties, each might have recourse to it, either to prove his own advantages, or to discover the failings of his adversary.

He had no sooner said this, but all desired the favour of him to give the definition of a play; and they were the more importunate, because neither Aristotle, nor Horace, nor any other who had writ of that subject, had ever done it.

Lisideius, after some modest denials, at last confessed he had a rude notion of it; indeed, rather a description than a definition; but which served to guide him in his private thoughts, when he was to make a judgement of what others writ: that he conceived a play ought to be, *A just and lively image of*

*human nature, representing its passions and humours, and
the changes of fortune to which it is subject, for the delight
and instruction of mankind.*

This definition, though Crites raised a logical
objection against it—that it was only *a genere et fine*,
and so not altogether perfect—was yet well received
by the rest: and after they had given order to the
watermen to turn their barge, and row softly, that
they might take the cool of the evening in their return,
Crites, being desired by the company to begin, spoke
on behalf of the ancients, in this manner:

'If confidence presage a victory, Eugenius, in his
own opinion, has already triumphed over the ancients:
nothing seems more easy to him, than to overcome
those whom it is our greatest praise to have imitated
well; for we do not only build upon their foundations,
but by their models. Dramatic Poesy had time
enough, reckoning from Thespis (who first invented
it) to Aristophanes, to be born, to grow up, and to
flourish in maturity. It has been observed of arts and
sciences, that in one and the same century they have
arrived to great perfection; and no wonder, since
every age has a kind of universal genius, which in-
clines those that live in it to some particular studies:
the work then, being pushed on by many hands, must
of necessity go forward.

'Is it not evident, in these last hundred years, when
the study of philosophy has been the business of all
the virtuosi in Christendom, that almost a new nature
has been revealed to us? that more errors of the
School have been detected, more useful experiments
in philosophy have been made, more noble secrets
in optics, medicine, anatomy, astronomy discovered,
than in all those credulous and doting ages from
Aristotle to us?—so true it is, that nothing spreads
more fast than science, when rightly and generally
cultivated.

'Add to this, the more than common emulation
that was in those times of writing well; which though

it be found in all ages and all persons that pretend to
the same reputation, yet poesy, being then in more
esteem than now it is, had greater honours decreed
to the professors of it, and consequently the rivalship
was more high between them; they had judges
ordained to decide their merit, and prizes to reward
it; and historians have been diligent to record of
Aeschylus, Euripides, Sophocles, Lycophron, and the
rest of them, both who they were that vanquished in
these wars of the theatre, and how often they were
crowned: while the Asian kings and Grecian commonwealths scarce afforded them a nobler subject than
the unmanly luxuries of a debauched court, or giddy
intrigues of a factious city: *Alit aemulatio ingenia*
(says Paterculus), *et nunc invidia, nunc admiratio incita-
tionem accendit:* 'emulation is the spur of wit; and
sometimes envy, sometimes admiration, quickens our
endeavours.'

'But now, since the rewards of honour are taken
away, that virtuous emulation is turned into direct
malice; yet so slothful, that it contents itself to condemn and cry down others, without attempting to do
better: it is a reputation too unprofitable, to take the
necessary pains for it; yet, wishing they had it, that
desire is incitement enough to hinder others from it.
And this, in short, Eugenius, is the reason why you
have now so few good poets, and so many severe
judges. Certainly, to imitate the ancients well, much
labour and long study is required; which pains, I
have already shown, our poets would want encouragement to take, if yet they had ability to go through the
work. Those ancients have been faithful imitators
and wise observers of that nature which is so torn and
ill represented in our plays; they have handed down
to us a perfect resemblance of her; which we, like
ill copiers, neglecting to look on, have rendered
monstrous, and disfigured. But, that you may know
how much you are indebted to those your masters,
and be ashamed to have so ill requited them, I must

remember you, that all the rules by which we practise the drama at this day, (either such as relate to the justness and symmetry of the plot, or the episodical ornaments, such as descriptions, narrations, and other beauties, which are not essential to the play), were delivered to us from the observations which Aristotle made of those poets who either lived before him, or were his contemporaries: we have added nothing of our own, except we have the confidence to say our wit is better; of which, none boast in this our age, but such as understand not theirs. Of that book which Aristotle has left us, περὶ τῆς Ποιητικῆς, Horace his *Art of Poetry* is an excellent comment, and, I believe, restores to us that second book of his concerning Comedy, which is wanting in him.

'Out of these two have been extracted the famous rules, which the French call *Des Trois Unités*, or, The Three Unities, which ought to be observed in every regular play; namely, of time, place, and action.

'The unity of time they comprehend in twenty-four hours, the compass of a natural day, or as near as it can be contrived; and the reason of it is obvious to every one,—that the time of the feigned action, or fable of the play, should be proportioned as near as can be to the duration of that time in which it is represented: since therefore, all plays are acted on the theatre in the space of time much within the compass of twenty-four hours, that play is to be thought the nearest imitation of nature, whose plot or action is confined within that time; and, by the same rule which concludes this general proportion of time, it follows, that all the parts of it are (as near as may be) to be equally subdivided; namely, that one act take not up the supposed time of half a day, which is out of proportion to the rest; since the other four are then to be straightened within the compass of the remaining half: for it is unnatural that one act, which being spoke or written is not longer than the rest, should be supposed longer by the audience; it is therefore the poet's duty, to take care that no act should be imagined to exceed the time in which it is represented on the stage; and that the intervals and inequalities of time be supposed to fall out between the acts.

'This rule of time, how well it has been observed by the ancients, most of their plays will witness; you see them in their tragedies (wherein to follow this rule, is certainly most difficult), from the very beginning of their plays, falling close into that part of the story which they intend for the action or principal object of it, leaving the former part to be delivered by narration: so that they set the audience, as it were, at the post where the race is to be concluded; and, saving them the tedious expectation of seeing the poet set out and ride the beginning of the course, they suffer you not to behold him, till he is in sight of the goal and, just upon you.

For the second unity, which is that of place, the ancients meant by it, that the scene ought to be continued through the play, in the same place where it was laid in the beginning: for, the stage on which it is represented being but one and the same place, it is unnatural to conceive it many,—and those far distant from one another. I will not deny but, by the variation of painted scenes, the fancy, which in these cases will contribute to its own deceit, may sometimes imagine it several places, with some appearance of probability; yet it still carries the greater likelihood of truth, if those places be supposed so near each other, as in the same town or city, which may all be comprehended under the larger denomination of one place; for a greater distance will bear no proportion to the shortness of time which is allotted, in the acting, to pass from one of them to another; for the observation of this, next to the ancients, the French are to be most commended. They tie themselves so strictly to the unity of place, that you never see in any of their plays, a scene changed in the middle of an act: if the act begins in a garden, a street, or chamber, 'tis ended in the same place; and that you may know it to be the same, the stage is so supplied with persons, that it is never empty all the time: he who enters second has business with him who was on before; and before the second quits the stage, a third appears who has business with him. This Corneille calls *la liaison des scènes*, the continuity or joining of the scenes; and 'tis a good mark of a well-contrived play, when all the persons are known to each other, and every one of them has some affairs with all the rest.

'As for the third unity, which is that of action, the ancients meant no other by it than what the logicians do by their *finis*, the end or scope of any action—that which is the first in intention, and last in execution: now the poet is to aim at one great and complete action, to the carrying on of which all things in his play, even the very obstacles, are to be subservient; and the reason of this is as evident as any of the former. For two actions, equally laboured and driven on by the writer, would destroy the unity of the poem; it would be no longer one play, but two: not but that there may be many actions in a play, as Ben Jonson has observed in his *Discoveries*; but they must be all subservient to the great one (which our language happily expresses in the name of *under-plots*): such as in Terence's *Eunuch* is the difference and recon- cilement of Thais and Phaedria, which is not the chief business of the play, but promotes the marriage of Chaerea and Chremes's sister, principally intended by the poet. There ought to be but one action, says Corneille, that is, one complete action, which leaves the mind of the audience in a full repose; but this cannot be brought to pass but by many other im- perfect actions, which conduce to it, and hold the audience in a delightful suspense of what will be.

'If by these rules (to omit many other drawn from the precepts and practice of the ancients) we should judge our modern plays, 'tis probable that few of them would endure the trial: that which should be the business of a day, takes up in some of them an age; instead of one action, they are the epitomes of a man's life; and for one spot of ground, which the stage should represent, we are sometimes in more countries than the map can show us.

'But if we allow the ancients to have contrived well, we must acknowledge them to have written better. Questionless we are deprived of a great stock of wit in the loss of Menander among the Greek poets, and of Caecilius, Afranius, and Varius, among the Romans; we may guess at Menander's excellency by the plays of Terence, who translated some of his; and yet wanted so much of him, that he was called by C. Caesar the half-Menander; and may judge of Varius, by the testimonies of Horace, Martial, and Velleius Paterculus. 'Tis probable that these, could they be recovered, would decide the controversy; but so long as Aristophanes and Plautus are extant, while the tragedies of Euripides, Sophocles, and Seneca, are in our hands, I can never see one of those plays which are now written, but it increases my admiration of the ancients. And yet I must acknowledge further, that to admire them as we ought, we should understand them better than we do. Doubtless many things appear flat to us, the wit of which depended on some custom or story which never came to our knowledge; or perhaps on some criticism in their language, which being so long dead, and only remaining in their books, 'tis not possible they should make us understand perfectly. To read Macrobius, explaining the propriety and elegancy of many words in Virgil, which I had before passed over without consideration as common things, is enough to assure me that I ought to think the same of Terence; and that in the purity of his style (which Tully so much valued that he ever carried his works about him) there is yet left in him great room for admiration, if I knew but where to place it. In the meantime I must desire you to take notice, that the greatest man of the last age, Ben Jonson, was willing to give place to them in all things: he was not only a professed imitator of Horace, but a learned plagiary of all the others; you track him everywhere in their snow: if Horace, Lucan, Petronius Arbiter, Seneca, and Juvenal, had their own from him, there are few serious thoughts which are new in him: you will pardon me, therefore, if I presume he loved their fashion, when he wore their clothes. But since I have otherwise a great veneration for him, and you, Eugenius, prefer him above all other poets, I will use no further argument to you than his example: I will produce before you Father Ben, dressed in all the ornaments and colours of the ancients; you will need no other guide to our party, if you follow him; and whether you consider the bad plays of our age, or regard the good plays of the last, both the best and worst of the modern poets will equally instruct you to admire the ancients.'

Crites had no sooner left speaking, but Eugenius, who had waited with some impatience for it, thus began:

'I have observed in your speech, that the former part of it is convincing as to what the moderns have profited by the rules of the ancients; but in the latter you are careful to conceal how much they have excelled them; we own all the helps we have from them, and want neither veneration nor gratitude, while we acknowledge that, to overcome them, we must make use of the advantages we have received from them: but to these assistances we have joined our own industry; for, had we sat down with a dull imitation of them, we might then have lost somewhat of the old perfection, but never acquired any that was new. We draw not therefore after their lines, but those of nature; and having the life before us, besides the experience of all they knew, it is no wonder if we hit

some airs and features which they have missed. I deny
not what you urge of arts and sciences, that they
have flourished in some ages more than others; but
your instance in philosophy makes for me: for if
natural causes be more known now than in the time
of Aristotle, because more studied, it follows that
poesy and other arts may, with the same pains, arrive
still nearer to perfection; and, that granted, it will
rest for you to prove that they wrought more perfect
images of human life than we; which seeing in your
discourse you have avoided to make good, it shall now
be my task to show you some part of their defects,
and some few excellencies of the moderns. And I
think there is none among us can imagine I do it
enviously, or with purpose to detract from them; for
what interest of fame or profit can the living lose by
the reputation of the dead? On the other side, it is
a great truth which Velleius Paterculus affirms:
*Audita visis libentius laudamus; et praesentia invidia,
praeterita admiratione prosequimur; et his nos obrui, illis
instrui credimus:* that praise or censure is certainly the
most sincere, which unbribed posterity shall give us.

'Be pleased then in the first place to take notice,
that the Greek poesy, which Crites has affirmed to
have arrived to perfection in the reign of the old
comedy, was so far from it, that the distinction of it
into acts was not known to them; or if it were, it is yet
so darkly delivered to us that we cannot make it out.

'All we know of it is, from the singing of their
Chorus; and that too is so uncertain, that in some of
their plays we have reason to conjecture they sung
more than five times. Aristotle indeed divides the
integral parts of a play into four. First, the *Protasis*,
or entrance, which gives light only to the characters
of the persons, and proceeds very little into any part of
the action. Secondly, the *Epitasis*, or working up of the
plot; where the play grows warmer, the design or
action of it is drawing on, and you see something
promising that it will come to pass. Thirdly, the

Catastasis, called by the Romans, *Status*, the height and full growth of the play: we may call it properly the counterturn, which destroys that expectation, embroils the action in new difficulties, and leaves you far distant from that hope in which it found you; as you may have observed in a violent stream resisted by a narrow passage,—it runs round to an eddy, and carries back the waters with more swiftness than it brought them on. Lastly, the *Catastrophe*, which the Grecians called λύσις, the French *le dénouement*, and we the discovery, or unravelling of the plot: there you see all things settling again upon their first foundations; and, the obstacles which hindered the design or action of the play once removed, it ends with that resemblance of truth and nature, that the audience are satisfied with the conduct of it. Thus this great man delivered to us the image of a play; and I must confess it is so lively, that from thence much light has been derived to the forming it more perfectly into acts and scenes: but what poet first limited to five the number of the acts, I know not; only we see it so firmly established in the time of Horace, that he gives it for a rule in comedy, *Neu brevior quinto, neu sit productior actu*. So that you see the Grecians cannot be said to have consummated this art; writing rather by entrances, than by acts, and having rather a general indigested notion of a play, than knowing how and where to bestow the particular graces of it.

'But since the Spaniards at this day allow but three acts, which they call *Jornadas*, to a play, and the Italians in many of theirs follow them, when I condemn the ancients, I declare it is not altogether because they have not five acts to every play, but because they have not confined themselves to one certain number: it is building a house without a model; and when they succeeded in such undertakings, they ought to have sacrificed to Fortune, not to the Muses.

'Next, for the plot, which Aristotle called τὸ μυθὸς, and often τῶν πραγμάτων σύνθεσις, and from him the Romans *Fabula*; it has already been judiciously observed by a late writer, that in their tragedies it was only some tale derived from Thebes or Troy, or at least something that happened in those two ages; which was worn so threadbare by the pens of all the epic poets, and even by tradition itself of the talkative Greeklings (as Ben Jonson calls them), that before it came upon the stage, it was already known to all the audience: and the people, so soon as ever they heard the name of Oedipus, knew as well as the poet, that he had killed his father by a mistake, and committed incest with his mother, before the play; that they were now to hear of a great plague, an oracle, and the ghost of Laius: so that they sat with a yawning kind of expectation, till he was to come with his eyes pulled out, and speak a hundred or more verses in a tragic tone, in complaint of his misfortunes. But one Oedipus, Hercules, or Medea, had been tolerable: poor people, they escaped not so good cheap; they had still the *chapon bouillé* set before them, till their appetites were cloyed with the same dish, and, the novelty being gone, the pleasure vanished; so that one main end of Dramatic Poesy in its definition, which was to cause delight, was of consequence destroyed.

'In their comedies, the Romans generally borrowed their plots from the Greek poets; and theirs was commonly a little girl stolen or wandered from her parents, brought back unknown to the city, there [falling into the hands of] some young fellow, who, by the help of his servant, cheats his father; and when her time comes, to cry, *Juno Lucina, fer opem*, one or other sees a little box or cabinet which was carried away with her, and so discovers her to her friends, if some god do not prevent it, by coming down in a machine, and taking the thanks of it to himself.

'By the plot you may guess much of the characters of the persons. An old father, who would willingly, before he dies, see his son well married; his debauched son, kind in his nature to his mistress, but miserably in want of money; a servant or slave, who has so much wit to strike in with him, and help to dupe his father; a braggadocio captain, a parasite, and a lady of pleasure.

'As for the poor honest maid, on whom the story is built, and who ought to be one of the principal actors in the play, she is commonly a mute in it: she has the breeding of the old Elizabeth way, which was for maids to be seen and not to be heard; and it is enough you know she is willing to be married when the fifth act requires it.

'These are plots built after the Italian mode of houses,—you see through them all at once: the characters are indeed the imitation of nature, but so narrow, as if they had imitated only an eye or an hand, and did not dare to venture on the lines of a face, or the proportion of a body.

'But in how straight a compass soever they have bounded their plots and characters, we will pass it by, if they have regularly pursued them, and perfectly observed those three unities of time, place, and action; the knowledge of which you say is derived to us from them. But in the first place give me leave to tell you, that the unity of place, however it might be practised by them, was never any of their rules: we neither find it in Aristotle, Horace, or any who have written of it, till in our age the French poets first made it a precept of the stage. The unity of time, even Terence himself, who was the best and most regular of them, has neglected: his *Heautontimorumenos*, or Self-Punisher, takes up visibly two days, says Scaliger; the two first acts concluding the first day, the three last the day ensuing; and Euripides, in tying himself to one day, has committed an absurdity never to be forgiven him; for in one of his tragedies he has made Theseus go from Athens to Thebes, which was about forty English miles, under the walls of it to give battle, and appear victorious in the next act; and yet, from the time of his departure to the return of the Nuntius, who gives the relation of his victory, Aethra and the chorus have but thirty-six verses; which is not for every mile a verse.

'The like error is as evident in Terence his *Eunuch*, when Laches, the old man, enters by mistake into the house of Thais; where, betwixt his exit and the entrance of Pythias, who comes to give ample relation of the disorders he has raised within, Parmeno, who was left upon the stage, has not above five lines to speak. *C'est bien employer un temps si court*, says the French poet, who furnished me with one of the observations: and almost all their tragedies will afford us examples of the like nature.

'It is true they have kept the continuity, or, as you called it, *liaison des scènes*, somewhat better: two do not perpetually come in together, talk, and go out together; and other two succeed them, and do the same throughout the act, which the English call by the name of single scenes; but the reason is, because they have seldom above two or three scenes, properly so called, in every act; for it is to be accounted a new scene, not only every time the stage is empty; but every person who enters, though to others, makes it so; because he introduces a new business. Now the plots of their plays being narrow, and the persons few, one of their acts was written in a less compass than one of our well-wrought scenes; and yet they are often deficient even in this. To go no further than Terence; you find in the *Eunuch*, Antipho entering single in the midst of the third act, after Chremes and Pythias were gone off; in the same play you have likewise Dorias beginning the fourth act alone; and after she had made a relation of what was done at the Soldier's entertainment (which by the way was very inartificial, because she was presumed to speak directly to the audience, and to acquaint them with what was necessary to be known, but yet should have been so contrived by the poet as to have been told by persons of the drama to one another, and so by them to have come to the knowledge of the people), she quits the stage, and Phaedria enters next, alone likewise: he also gives you an account of himself, and of his returning from the country, in monologue; to which unnatural way of narration Terence is subject in all his plays. In his *Adelphi*, or brothers, Syrus and Demea enter after the scene was broken by the departure of Sostrata, Geta, and Canthara; and indeed you can scarce look into any of his comedies, where you will not presently discover the same interruption.

'But as they have failed both in laying of their plots, and in the management, swerving from the rules of their own art by misrepresenting nature to us, in which they have ill satisfied one intention of a play, which was delight; so in the instructive part they have erred worse: instead of punishing vice and rewarding virtue, they have often shown a prosperous wickedness, and an unhappy piety: they have set before us a bloody image of revenge in Medea, and given her dragons to convey her safe from punishment; a Priam and Astyanax murdered, and Cassandra ravished, and the lust and murder ending in the victory of him who acted them: in short, there is no indecorum in any of our modern plays, which if I would excuse, I could not shadow with some authority from the ancients.

'And one further note of them let me leave you: tragedies and comedies were not writ then as they are now, promiscuously, by the same person; but he who found his genius bending to the one, never attempted the other way. This is so plain, that I need not instance to you, that Aristophanes, Plautus, Terence, never any of them writ a tragedy; Aeschylus, Euripides, Sophocles, and Seneca, never meddled with comedy: the sock and buskin were not worn by the same poet. Having then so much care to excel in one kind, very little is to be pardoned them, if they miscarried in it; and this would lead me to the consideration of their wit, had not Crites given me sufficient warning not to be too bold in my judgement of it; because, the languages being dead, and many of the customs and little accidents on which it depended lost to us, we are not competent judges of it. But though I grant that here and there we may miss the application of a proverb or a custom, yet a thing well said will be wit in all languages; and though it may lose something in the translation, yet to him who reads it in the original, 'tis still the same: he has an idea of its excellency, though it cannot pass from his mind into any other expression or words than those in which he finds it. When Phaedria, in the *Eunuch*, had a command from his mistress to be absent two days, and, encouraging himself to go through with it, said, *Tandem ego non illa caream, si sit opus, vel totum triduum?* Parmeno, to mock the softness of his master, lifting up his hands and eyes, cries out, as it were in admiration, *Hui! universum triduum!* the elegancy of which *universum*, though it cannot be rendered in our language, yet leaves an impression on our souls: but this happens seldom in him; in Plautus oftener, who is infinitely too bold in his metaphors and coining words, out of which many times his wit is nothing; which questionless was one reason why Horace falls upon him so severely in those verses:

> *Sed proavi nostri Plautinos et numeros et*
> *Laudavere sales, nimium patienter utrumque,*
> *Ne dicam stolidè.*

For Horace himself was cautious to obtrude a new word on his readers, and makes custom and common use the best measure of receiving it into our writings:

> *Multa renascentur quae nunc [iam] cecidere, cadentque*
> *Quae nunc sunt in honore vocabula, si volet usus,*
> *Quem penes arbitrium est, et ius, et norma loquendi.*

'The not observing this rule is that which the world has blamed in our satirist, Cleveland: to express a thing hard and unnaturally, is his new way of elocution. 'Tis true, no poet but may sometimes use a catachresis: Virgil does it:—

> *Mistaque ridenti colocasia fundet acantho—*

in his eclogue of Pollio; and in his seventh Aeneid,

> —— *mirantur et undae,*
> *Miratur nemus insuetum fulgentia longe*
> *Scuta virum fluvio pictasque innare carinas.*

And Ovid once so modestly that he asks leave to do it:

> —— *quem, si verbo audacia detur,*
> *Haud metuam summi dixisse Palatia caeli,*

calling the court of Jupiter by the name of Augustus his palace; though in another place he is more bold, where he says, *et longas visent Capitolia pompas.* But to do this always, and never be able to write a line without it, though it may be admired by some few pedants, will not pass upon those who know that wit is best conveyed to us in the most easy language; and is most to be admired when a great thought comes dressed in words so commonly received that it is understood by the meanest apprehensions, as the best meat is the most easily digested: but we cannot read a verse of Cleveland's without making a face at it, as if every word were a pill to swallow: he gives us many times a hard nut to break our teeth, without a kernel for our pains. So that there is this difference betwixt his satires and Doctor Donne's; that the one gives us deep thoughts in common language, though rough cadence; the other gives us common thoughts in abstruse words: 'tis true, in some places his wit is independent of his words, as in that of the *Rebel Scot*:

Had Cain been Scot, God would have chang'd his doom;
Not forc'd him wander, but confin'd him home.

'*Si sic omnia dixisset!* This is wit in all languages:

it is like mercury, never to be lost or killed:—and so that other—

> For beauty, like white powder, makes no noise,
> And yet the silent hypocrite destroys.

You see, the last line is highly metaphorical, but it is so soft and gentle, that it does not shock us as we read it.

'But to return from whence I have digressed, to the consideration of the ancients' writing, and their wit (of which by this time you will grant us in some measure to be fit judges). Though I see many excellent thoughts in Seneca, yet he of them who had a genius most proper for the stage, was Ovid; he had a way of writing so fit to stir up a pleasing admiration and concernment, which are the objects of a tragedy, and to show the various movements of a soul combating betwixt two different passions, that, had he lived in our age, or in his own could have writ with our advantages, no man but must have yielded to him; and therefore I am confident the *Medea* is none of his: for, though I esteem it for the gravity and sententiousness of it, which he himself concludes to be suitable to a tragedy,—*Omne genus scripti gravitate tragoedia vincit*,—yet it moves not my soul enough to judge that he, who in the epic way wrote things so near the drama as the story of Myrrha, of Caunus and Biblis, and the rest, should stir up no more concernment where he most endeavoured it. The masterpiece of Seneca I hold to be that scene in the *Troades*, where Ulysses is seeking for Astyanax to kill him: there you see the tenderness of a mother so represented in Andromache that it raises compassion to a high degree in the reader, and bears the nearest resemblance of anything in the tragedies of the ancients to the excellent scenes of passion in Shakespeare, or in Fletcher: for love scenes, you will find few among them; their tragic poets dealt not with that soft passion, but with lust, cruelty, revenge, ambition, and those bloody actions they produced; which were more capable of raising horror than compassion in an audience: leaving love untouched, whose gentleness would have tempered them; which is the most frequent of all the passions, and which, being the private concernment of every person, is soothed by viewing its own image in a public entertainment.

'Among their comedies, we find a scene or two of tenderness, and that where you would least expect it, in Plautus; but to speak generally, their lovers say little, when they see each other, but *anima mea, vita mea*; Ζωὴ καὶ ψυχῇ, as the women in Juvenal's time used to cry out in the fury of their kindness. Any sudden gust of passion (as an ecstasy of love in an unexpected meeting) cannot better be expressed than in a word and a sigh, breaking one another. Nature is dumb on such occasions; and to make her speak, would be to represent her unlike herself. But there are a thousand other concernments of lovers, as jealousies, complaints, contrivances, and the like, where not to open their minds at large to each other were to be wanting to their own love, and to the expectation of the audience; who watch the movements of their minds, as much as the changes of their fortunes. For the imaging of the first is properly the work of a poet; the latter he borrows from the historian.'

Eugenius was proceeding in that part of his discourse, when Crites interrupted him. 'I see,' said he, 'Eugenius and I are never like to have this question decided betwixt us; for he maintains the moderns have acquired a new perfection in writing; I can only grant they have altered the mode of it. Homer described his heroes men of great appetites, lovers of beef broiled upon the coals, and good fellows; contrary to the practice of the French Romances, whose heroes neither eat, nor drink, nor sleep, for love. Virgil makes Aeneas a bold avower of his own virtues:

Sum pius Aeneas, fama super aethera notus;

which, in the civility of our poets, is the character of a fanfaron or Hector: for with us the knight takes occasion to walk out, or sleep, to avoid the vanity of telling his own story, which the trusty squire is ever to perform for him. So in their love scenes, of which Eugenius spoke last, the ancients were more hearty, we more talkative: they writ love as it was then the mode to make it; and I will grant thus much to Eugenius, that perhaps one of their poets, had he lived in our age, *si foret hoc nostrum fato delapsus in aevum* (as Horace says of Lucilius), he had altered many things; not that they were not natural before, but that he might accommodate himself to the age in which he lived. Yet in the mean time we are not to conclude anything rashly against those great men, but preserve to them the dignity of masters, and give that honour to their memories, *quos Libitina sacravit*, part of which we expect may be paid to us in future times.'

This moderation of Crites, as it was pleasing to all the company, so it put an end to that dispute; which Eugenius, who seemed to have the better of the argument, would urge no farther; but Lisideius, after he had acknowledged himself of Eugenius his opinion concerning the ancients, yet told him, he had forborne, till his discourse were ended, to ask him why he preferred the English plays above those of other nations? and whether we ought not to submit our stage to the exactness of our next neighbours?

'Though,' said Eugenius, 'I am at all times ready to defend the honour of my country against the French, and to maintain we are as well able to vanquish them with our pens, as our ancestors have been with their swords; yet, if you please,' added he, looking upon Neander, 'I will commit this cause to my friend's management; his opinion of our plays is the same with mine: and besides, there is no reason that Crites and I, who have now left the stage, should reenter so suddenly upon it; which is against the laws of comedy.'

'If the question had been stated,' replied Lisideius, 'who had writ best, the French or English, forty years ago, I should have been of your opinion, and adjudged the honour to our own nation; but since that time,' (said he, turning towards Neander), 'we have been so long together bad Englishmen, that we had not leisure to be good poets. Beaumont, Fletcher, and Ionson (who were only capable of bringing us to that degree of perfection which we have), were just then leaving the world; as if in an age of so much horror, wit, and those milder studies of humanity, had no further business among us. But the Muses, who ever follow peace, went to plant in another country: it was then, that the great Cardinal of Richelieu began to take them into his protection; and that, by his encouragement, Corneille, and some other Frenchmen, reformed their theatre (which before was as much below ours, as it now surpasses it and the rest of Europe). But because Crites in his discourse for the ancients has prevented me, by observing many rules of the stage which the moderns have borrowed from them, I shall only, in short, demand of you, whether you are not convinced that of all nations the French have best observed them? In the unity of time you find them so scrupulous, that it yet remains a dispute among their poets, whether the artificial day of twelve hours, more or less, be not meant by Aristotle, rather than the natural one of twenty-four; and consequently, whether all plays ought not to be reduced into that compass. This I can testify, that in all their dramas writ within these last twenty years and upwards, I have not observed any that have extended the time to thirty hours: in the unity of place they are full as scrupulous; for many of their critics limit it to that very spot of ground where the play is supposed to begin; none of them exceed the compass of the same town or city. The unity of action in all plays is yet more conspicuous; for they do not burden them with underplots, as the English do: which is the reason

why many scenes of our tragi-comedies carry on a
design that is nothing of kin to the main plot; and that
we see two distinct webs in a play, like those in ill-
wrought stuffs; and two actions, that is, two plays,
carried on together, to the confounding of the audience; who, before they are warm in their concernments for one part, are diverted to another; and by
that means espouse the interest of neither. From
hence likewise it arises, that the one half of our actors
are not known to the other. They keep their distances,
as if they were Montagues and Capulets, and seldom
begin an acquaintance till the last scene of the fifth
act, when they are all to meet upon the stage. There
is no theatre in the world has anything so absurd as the
English tragi-comedy; 'tis a drama of our own invention, and the fashion of it is enough to proclaim it so;
here a course of mirth, there another of sadness and
passion, and a third of honour and a duel: thus, in
two hours and a half, we run through all the fits of
Bedlam. The French affords you as much variety on
the same day, but they do it not so unseasonably, or
mal à propos, as we: our poets present you the play and
the farce together; and our stages still retain somewhat of the original civility of the Red Bull:

    Atque ursum et pugiles media inter carmina poscunt.

The end of tragedies or serious plays, says Aristotle,
is to beget admiration, compassion or concernment;
but are not mirth and compassion things incompatible? and is it not evident that the poet must of
necessity destroy the former by intermingling of the
latter? that is, he must ruin the sole end and object
of his tragedy to introduce somewhat that is forced
into it, and is not of the body of it. Would you not
think that physician mad, who, having prescribed a
purge, should immediately order you to take restrin-
gents?

   'But to leave our plays, and return to theirs. I have
noted one great advantage they have had in the

plotting of their tragedies; that is, they are always grounded upon some known history: according to that of Horace, *Ex noto fictum carmen sequar*; and in that they have so imitated the ancients that they have surpassed them. For the ancients, as was observed before, took for the foundation of their plays some poetical fiction, such as under that consideration could move but little concernment in the audience, because they already knew the event of it. But the French goes farther:

> *Atque ita mentitur, sic veris falsa remiscet,*
> *Primo ne medium, medio ne discrepet imum.*

He so interweaves truth with probable fiction that he puts a pleasing fallacy upon us; mends the intrigues of fate, and dispenses with the severity of history, to reward that virtue which has been rendered to us there unfortunate. Sometimes the story has left the success so doubtful, that the writer is free, by the privilege of a poet, to take that which of two or more relations will best suit with his design: as for example, in the death of Cyrus, whom Justin and some others report to have perished in the Scythian war, but Xenophon affirms to have died in his bed of extreme old age. Nay more, when the event is past dispute, even then we are willing to be deceived, and the poet, if he contrives it with appearance of truth, has all the audience of his party; at least during the time his play is acting: so naturally we are kind to virtue, when our own interest is not in question, that we take it up as the general concernment of mankind. On the other side, if you consider the historical plays of Shakespeare, they are rather so many chronicles of kings, or the business many times of thirty or forty years, cramped into a representation of two hours and a half; which is not to imitate or paint nature, but rather to draw her in miniature, to take her in little; to look upon her through the wrong end of a perspective, and receive her images not only much less, but infinitely more imperfect than the life: this, instead of making a play delightful, renders it ridiculous:—

> *Quodcunque ostendis mihi sic, incredulus odi.*

For the spirit of man cannot be satisfied but with truth, or at least verisimility; and a poem is to contain, if not τὰ ἔτυμα, yet ἐτύμοισιν ὁμοῖα, as one of the Greek poets has expressed it.

'Another thing in which the French differ from us and from the Spaniards is, that they do not embarrass or cumber themselves with too much plot; they only represent so much of a story as will constitute one whole and great action sufficient for a play; we, who undertake more, do but multiply adventures; which, not being produced from one another, as effects from causes, but barely following, constitute many actions in the drama, and consequently make it many plays.

'But by pursuing closely one argument, which is not cloyed with many turns, the French have gained more liberty for verse, in which they write; they have leisure to dwell on a subject which deserves it; and to represent the passions (which we have acknowledged to be the poet's work), without being hurried from one thing to another, as we are in the plays of Calderon, which we have seen lately upon our theatres, under the name of Spanish plots. I have taken notice but of one tragedy of ours, whose plot has that uniformity and unity of design in it which I have commended in the French; and that is *Rollo*, or rather, under the name of Rollo, the Story of Bassianus and Geta in Herodian: there indeed the plot is neither large nor intricate, but just enough to fill the minds of the audience, not to cloy them. Besides, you see it founded upon the truth of history,—only the time of the action is not reduceable to the strictness of the rules; and you see in some places a little farce mingled, which is below the dignity of the other parts; and in this all our poets are extremely peccant: even Ben Jonson himself, in *Sejanus* and *Catiline*, has given us this oleo of a play, this unnatural mixture of comedy and tragedy; which to me sounds just as ridiculously as the history of David with the merry humours of Golia's. In *Sejanus* you may take notice of the scene betwixt Livia and the physician, which is a pleasant satire upon the artificial helps of beauty: in *Catiline* you may see the parliament of women; the little envies of them to one another; and all that passes betwixt Curio and Fulvia: scenes admirable in their kind, but of an ill mingle with the rest.

'But I return again to the French writers, who, as I have said, do not burden themselves too much with plot, which has been reproached to them by an ingenious person of our nation as a fault; for, he says, they commonly make but one person considerable in a play; they dwell on him and his concernments, while the rest of the persons are only subservient to set him off. If he intends this by it—that there is one person in the play who is of greater dignity than the rest, he must tax, not only theirs, but those of the ancients, and (which he would be loth to do) the best of ours; for it is impossible but that one person must be more conspicuous in it than any other, and consequently the greatest share in the action must devolve on him. We see it so in the management of all affairs; even in the most equal aristocracy the balance cannot be so justly poised, but some one will be superior to the rest, either in parts, fortune, interest, or the consideration of some glorious exploit; which will reduce the greatest part of business into his hands.

'But, if he would have us to imagine that in exalting one character the rest of them are neglected, and that all of them have not some share or other in the action of the play, I desire him to produce any of Corneille's tragedies, wherein every person, like so many servants in a well-governed family, has not some employment, and who is not necessary to the carrying on of the plot, or at least to your understanding it.

'There are indeed some protatic persons in the

ancients, whom they make use of in their plays, either
to hear or give the relation: but the French avoid this
with great address, making their narrations only to
or by such, who are some way interested in the main
design. And now I am speaking of relations, I cannot
take a fitter opportunity to add this in favour of the
French, that they often use them with better judgement and more *à propos* than the English do. Not that
I commend narrations in general—but there are two
sorts of them. One, of those things which are antecedent to the play, and are related to make the conduct of it more clear to us. But 'tis a fault to choose
such subjects for the stage as will force us on that rock,
because we see they are seldom listened to by the
audience, and that is many times the ruin of the play;
for, being once let pass without attention, the audience
can never recover themselves to understand the plot:
and indeed it is somewhat unreasonable that they
should be put to so much trouble, as that, to comprehend what passes in their sight, they must have recourse to what was done, perhaps, ten or twenty years
ago.

'But there is another sort of relations, that is, of
things happening in the action of the play, and supposed to be done behind the scenes; and this is many
times both convenient and beautiful; for by it the
French avoid the tumult to which we are subject in
England by representing duels, battles, and the like;
which renders our stage too like the theatres where
they fight prizes. For what is more ridiculous than to
represent an army with a drum and five men behind
it; all which the hero of the other side is to drive in
before him; or to see a duel fought, and one slain with
two or three thrusts of the foils, which we know are so
blunted, that we might give a man an hour to kill
another in good earnest with them.

'I have observed that in all our tragedies the audience cannot forbear laughing when the actors are to
die; it is the most comic part of the whole play. All

passions may be lively represented on the stage, if to the well-writing of them the actor supplies a good commanded voice, and limbs that move easily, and without stiffness; but there are many *actions* which can never be imitated to a just height: dying especially is a thing which none but a Roman gladiator could naturally perform on the stage, when he did not imitate or represent, but do it; and therefore it is better to omit the representation of it.

'The words of a good writer, which describe it lively, will make a deeper impression of belief in us than all the actor can insinuate into us, when he seems to fall dead before us; as a poet in the description of a beautiful garden, or a meadow, will please our imagination more than the place itself can please our sight. When we see death represented, we are convinced it is but fiction; but when we hear it related, our eyes, the strongest witnesses, are wanting, which might have undeceived us; and we are all willing to favour the sleight, when the poet does not too grossly impose on us. They therefore who imagine these relations would make no concernment in the audience, are deceived, by confounding them with the other, which are of things antecedent to the play: those are made often in cold blood, as I may say, to the audience; but these are warmed with our concernments, which were before awakened in the play. What the philosophers say of motion, that, when it is once begun, it continues of itself, and will do so to eternity, without some stop put to it, is clearly true on this occasion: the soul, being already moved with the characters and fortunes of those imaginary persons, continues going of its own accord; and we are no more weary to hear what becomes of them when they are not on the stage than we are to listen to the news of an absent mistress. But it is objected, that if one part of the play may be related, then why not all? I answer, some parts of the action are more fit to be represented, some to be related. Corneille says judiciously, that the poet is not

obliged to expose to view all particular actions which
conduce to the principal: he ought to select such of
them to be seen, which will appear with the greatest
beauty, either by the magnificence of the show, or the
vehemence of passions which they produce, or some
other charm which they have in them; and let the
rest arrive to the audience by narration. 'Tis a great
mistake in us to believe the French present no part of
the action on the stage; every alteration or crossing
of a design, every new-sprung passion and turn of it,
is a part of the action, and much the noblest, except
we conceive nothing to be action till the players come
to blows; as if the painting of the hero's mind were
not more properly the poet's work than the strength
of his body. Nor does this anything contradict the
opinion of Horace, where he tells us,

> *Segnius irritant animos demissa per aurem,*
> *Quam quae sunt oculis subiecta fidelibus.*

For he says immediately after,

> —————— *Non tamen intus*
> *Digna geri promes in scenam; multaq; tolles*
> *Ex oculis, quae mox narret facundia praesens.*

Among which 'many' he recounts some:

> *Nec pueros coram populo Medea trucidet,*
> *Aut in avem Progne mutetur, Cadmus in anguem; &c.*

That is, those actions which by reason of their cruelty
will cause aversion in us, or by reason of their impossi-
bility, unbelief, ought either wholly to be avoided by
a poet, or only delivered by narration. To which we
may have leave to add, such as, to avoid tumult (as
was before hinted), or to reduce the plot into a more
reasonable compass of time, or for defect of beauty in
them, are rather to be related than presented to the
eye. Examples of all these kinds are frequent, not only
among all the ancients, but in the best received of our
English poets. We find Ben Jonson using them in his
Magnetic Lady, where one comes out from dinner, and

relates the quarrels and disorders of it, to save the undecent appearance of them on the stage, and to abbreviate the story; and this in express imitation of Terence, who had done the same before him in his *Eunuch*, where Pythias makes the like relation of what had happened within at the soldier's entertainment. The relations likewise of Sejanus's death, and the prodigies before it, are remarkable; the one of which was hid from sight, to avoid the horror and tumult of the representation; the other, to shun the introducing of things impossible to be believed. In that excellent play, *The King and no King*, Fletcher goes yet farther; for the whole unravelling of the plot is done by narration in the fifth act, after the manner of the ancients; and it moves great concernment in the audience, though it be only a relation of what was done many years before the play. I could multiply other instances, but these are sufficient to prove that there is no error in choosing a subject which requires this sort of narrations; in the ill management of them, there may.

'But I find I have been too long in this discourse, since the French have many other excellencies not common to us; as that you never see any of their plays end with a conversion, or simple change of will, which is the ordinary way which our poets use to end theirs. It shows little art in the conclusion of a dramatic poem, when they who have hindered the felicity during the four acts, desist from it in the fifth, without some powerful cause to take them off their design; and though I deny not but such reasons may be found, yet it is a path that is cautiously to be trod, and the poet is to be sure he convinces the audience that the motive is strong enough. As, for example, the conversion of the Usurer in *The Scornful Lady*, seems to me a little forced; for, being an Usurer, which implies a lover of money to the highest degree of covetousness—and such the poet has represented him—the account he gives for the sudden change is, that he has been duped by the wild young fellow; which in reason might render him more wary another time, and make him punish himself with harder fare and coarser clothes, to get up again what he had lost: but that he should look on it as a judgement, and so repent, we may expect to hear in a sermon, but I should never endure it in a play.

'I pass by this; neither will I insist on the care they take, that no person after his first entrance shall ever appear, but the business which brings him upon the stage shall be evident; which rule, if observed, must needs render all the events in the play more natural; for there you see the probability of every accident, in the cause that produced it; and that which appears chance in the play, will seem so reasonable to you, that you will there find it almost necessary: so that in the exit of the actor you have a clear account of his purpose and design in the next entrance (though, if the scene be well wrought, the event will commonly deceive you); for there is nothing so absurd, says Corneille, as for an actor to leave the stage, only because he has no more to say.

'I should now speak of the beauty of their rhyme, and the just reason I have to prefer that way of writing in tragedies before ours in blank verse; but because it is partly received by us, and therefore not altogether peculiar to them, I will say no more of it in relation to their plays. For our own, I doubt not but it will exceedingly beautify them; and I can see but one reason why it should not generally obtain, that is, because our poets write so ill in it. This indeed may prove a more prevailing argument than all others which are used to destroy it, and therefore I am only troubled when great and judicious poets, and those who are acknowledged such, have written or spoke against it: as for others, they are to be answered by that one sentence of an ancient author: *Sed ut primo ad consequendos eos quos priores ducimus, accendimur, ita ubi aut praeteriri, aut aequari eos posse desperavimus, studium cum spe senescit: quod, scilicet, assequi non potest, sequi*

*desinit; . . . praeteritoque eo in quo eminere non possumus,
aliquid in quo nitamur, conquirimus.'*

Lisideius concluded in this manner; and Neander,
after a little pause, thus answered him:

'I shall grant Lisideius, without much dispute, a
great part of what he has urged against us; for I
acknowledge that the French contrive their plots
more regularly, and observe the laws of comedy, and
decorum of the stage (to speak generally), with more
exactness than the English. Farther, I deny not but
he has taxed us justly in some irregularities of ours,
which he has mentioned; yet, after all, I am of opinion
that neither our faults nor their virtues are considerable enough to place them above us.

'For the lively imitation of nature being in the
definition of a play, those which best fulfil that law
ought to be esteemed superior to the others. 'Tis
true, those beauties of the French poesy are such as
will raise perfection higher where it is, but are not
sufficient to give it where it is not: they are indeed the
beauties of a statue, but not of a man, because not
animated with the soul of poesy, which is imitation of
humour and passions: and this Lisideius himself, or
any other, however biassed to their party, cannot but
acknowledge, if he will either compare the humours
of our comedies, or the characters of our serious plays,
with theirs. He who will look upon theirs which have
been written till these last ten years, or thereabouts,
will find it a hard matter to pick out two or three
passable humours amongst them. Corneille himself,
their arch-poet, what has he produced except *The
Liar*? and you know how it was cried up in France;
but when it came upon the English stage, though well
translated, and that part of Dorant acted to so much
advantage as I am confident it never received in its
own country, the most favourable to it would not
put it in competition with many of Fletcher's or Ben
Jonson's. In the rest of Corneille's comedies you have
little humour; he tells you himself his way is, first to

show two lovers in good intelligence with each other; in the working up of the play to embroil them by some mistake, and in the latter end to clear it, and reconcile them.

'But of late years Molière, the younger Corneille, Quinault, and some others, have been imitating afar off the quick turns and graces of the English stage. They have mixed their serious plays with mirth, like our tragi-comedies, since the death of Cardinal Richelieu; which Lisideius and many others not observing, have commended that in them for a virtue which they themselves no longer practise. Most of their new plays are, like some of ours, derived from the Spanish novels. There is scarce one of them without a veil, and a trusty Diego, who drolls much after the rate of *The Adventures*. But their humours, if I may grace them with that name, are so thin-sown, that never above one of them comes up in any play. I dare take upon me to find more variety of them in some one play of Ben Jonson's, than in all theirs together; as he who has seen *The Alchemist*, *The Silent Woman*, or *Bartholomew Fair*, cannot but acknowledge with me.

'I grant the French have performed what was possible on the ground-work of the Spanish plays; what was pleasant before, they have made regular: but there is not above one good play to be writ on all those plots; they are too much alike to please often; which we need not the experience of our own stage to justify. As for their new way of mingling mirth with serious plot, I do not, with Lisideius, condemn the thing, though I cannot approve their manner of doing it. He tells us, we cannot so speedily recollect ourselves after a scene of great passion and concernment, as to pass to another of mirth and humour, and to enjoy it with any relish: but why should he imagine the soul of man more heavy than his senses? Does not the eye pass from an unpleasant object to a pleasant in a much shorter time than is required to this? and does not the unpleasantness of the first commend the beauty of the latter? The old rule of logic might have convinced him that contraries, when placed near, set off each other. A continued gravity keeps the spirit too much bent; we must refresh it sometimes, as we bait in a journey that we may go on with greater ease. A scene of mirth, mixed with tragedy, has the same effect upon us which our music has between the acts; which we find a relief to us from the best plots and language of the stage, if the discourses have been long. I must therefore have stronger arguments, ere I am convinced that compassion and mirth in the same subject destroy each other; and in the meantime cannot but conclude, to the honour of our nation, that we have invented, increased, and perfected a more pleasant way of writing for the stage than was ever known to the ancients or moderns of any nation, which is tragi-comedy.

'And this leads me to wonder why Lisideius and many others should cry up the barrenness of the French plots above the variety and copiousness of the English. Their plots are single; they carry on one design, which is pushed forward by all the actors, every scene in the play contributing and moving towards it. Our plays, besides the main design, have under-plots or by-concernments, of less considerable persons and intrigues, which are carried on with the motion of the main plot: as they say the orb of the fixed stars and those of the planets, though they have motions of their own, are whirled about by the motion of the *primum mobile*, in which they are contained. That similitude expresses much of the English stage; for if contrary motions may be found in nature to agree, if a planet can go east and west at the same time—one way by virtue of his own motion, the other by the force of the first mover—it will not be difficult to imagine how the under-plot, which is only different, not contrary to the great design, may naturally be conducted along with it.

'Eugenius has already shown us, from the confession of the French poets, that the unity of action is sufficiently preserved, if all the imperfect actions of the play are conducing to the main design; but when those petty intrigues of a play are so ill ordered, that they have no coherence with the other, I must grant that Lisideius has reason to tax that want of due connexion; for co-ordination in a play is as dangerous and unnatural as in a state. In the meantime he must acknowledge our variety, if well ordered, will afford a greater pleasure to the audience.

'As for his other argument, that by pursuing one single theme they gain an advantage to express and work up the passions, I wish any example he could bring from them would make it good; for I confess their verses are to me the coldest I have ever read. Neither, indeed, is it possible for them, in the way they take, so to express passion as that the effects of it should appear in the concernment of an audience, their speeches being so many declamations which tire us with the length; so that instead of persuading us to grieve for their imaginary heroes, we are concerned for our own trouble, as we are in tedious visits of bad company; we are in pain till they are gone. When the French stage came to be reformed by Cardinal Richelieu, those long harangues were introduced to comply with the gravity of a churchman. Look upon the *Cinna* and the *Pompey*; they are not so properly to be called plays, as long discourses of reason of state; and *Polyeucte* in matters of religion is as solemn as the long stops upon our organs. Since that time it is grown into a custom and their actors speak by the hour-glass, like our parsons; nay, they account it the grace of their parts, and think themselves disparaged by the poet, if they may not twice or thrice in a play entertain the audience with a speech of an hundred lines. I deny not but this may suit well enough with the French; for as we, who are a more sullen people, come to be diverted at our plays, so they, who are of an airy and gay temper, come thither to make themselves more serious: and this I conceive to be one reason why comedies are more pleasing to us, and tragedies to them. But to speak generally: it cannot be denied that short speeches and replies are more apt to move the passions and beget concernment in us, than the other; for it is unnatural for any one in a gust of passion to speak long together, or for another in the same condition to suffer him, without interruption. Grief and passion are like floods raised in little brooks by a sudden rain; they are quickly up; and if the concernment be poured unexpectedly in upon us, it overflows us: but a long sober shower gives them leisure to run out as they came in, without troubling the ordinary current. As for comedy, repartee is one of its chiefest graces; the greatest pleasure of the audience is a chase of wit, kept up on both sides, and swiftly managed. And this our forefathers, if not we, have had in Fletcher's plays, to a much higher degree of perfection than the French poets can reasonably hope to reach.

'There is another part of Lisideius his discourse, in which he has rather excused our neighbours, than commended them; that is, for aiming only to make one person considerable in their plays. 'Tis very true what he has urged, that one character in all plays, even without the poet's care, will have advantage of all the others; and that the design of the whole drama will chiefly depend on it. But this hinders not that there may be more shining characters in the play; many persons of a second magnitude, nay, some so very near, so almost equal to the first, that greatness may be opposed to greatness, and all the persons be made considerable, not only by their quality, but their action. 'Tis evident that the more the persons are, the greater will be the variety of the plot. If then the parts are managed so regularly, that the beauty of the whole be kept entire, and that the variety become not a perplexed and confused mass of accidents,

you will find it infinitely pleasing to be led in a laby-
rinth of design, where you see some of your way before
you, yet discern not the end till you arrive at it. And
that all this is practicable, I can produce for examples
many of our English plays: as *The Maid's Tragedy,
The Alchemist, The Silent Woman*: I was going to have
named *The Fox*, but the unity of design seems not
exactly observed in it; for there appear two actions
in the play; the first naturally ending with the fourth
act; the second forced from it in the fifth: which yet is
the less to be condemned in him, because the disguise
of Volpone, though it suited not with his character
as a crafty or covetous person, agreed well enough
with that of a voluptuary; and by it the poet gained
the end at which he aimed, the punishment of vice
and the reward of virtue, both which that disguise
produced. So that to judge equally of it, it was an
excellent fifth act, but not so naturally proceeding from
the former.

'But to leave this, and pass to the latter part of
Lisideius his discourse, which concerns relations: I
must acknowledge with him, that the French have
reason to hide that part of the action which would
occasion too much tumult on the stage, and to choose
rather to have it made known by narration to the
audience. Farther, I think it very convenient, for
the reasons he has given, that all incredible actions
were removed; but, whether custom has so insinuated
itself into our countrymen, or nature has so formed
them to fierceness, I know not; but they will scarcely
suffer combats and other objects of horror to be taken
from them. And indeed, the indecency of tumults is
all which can be objected against fighting; for why
may not our imagination as well suffer itself to be
deluded with the probability of it, as with any other
thing in the play? For my part, I can with as great
ease persuade myself that the blows are given in good
earnest, as I can, that they who strike them are kings
or princes, or those persons whom they represent. For

objects of incredibility—I would be satisfied from Lisideius, whether we have any so removed from all appearance of truth, as are those of Corneille's *Andromède*; a play which has been frequented the most of any he has written. If the Perseus, or the son of an heathen god, the Pegasus, and the Monster, were not capable to choke a strong belief, let him blame any representation of ours hereafter. Those indeed were objects of delight; yet the reason is the same as to the probability: for he makes it not a ballet or masque, but a play, which is to resemble truth. But for death, that it ought not to be represented, I have, besides the arguments alleged by Lisideius, the authority of Ben Jonson, who has forborne it in his tragedies; for both the death of Sejanus and Catiline are related: though in the latter I cannot but observe one irregularity of that great poet; he has removed the scene in the same act from Rome to Catiline's army, and from thence again to Rome; and besides, has allowed a very inconsiderable time after Catiline's speech for the striking of the battle, and the return of Petreius who is to relate the event of it to the senate: which I should not animadvert on him, who was otherwise a painful observer of τὸ πρέπον, or the *decorum* of the stage, if he had not used extreme severity in his judgement on the incomparable Shakespeare for the same fault. To conclude on this subject of relations; if we are to be blamed for showing too much of the action, the French are as faulty for discovering too little of it: a mean betwixt both should be observed by every judicious writer, so as the audience may neither be left unsatisfied by not seeing what is beautiful, or shocked by beholding what is either incredible or undecent.

'I hope I have already proved in this discourse that though we are not altogether so punctual as the French in observing the laws of comedy, yet our errors are so few and little, and those things wherein we excel them so considerable, that we ought of right to be preferred before them. But what will Lisideius say, if they themselves acknowledge they are too strictly bounded by those laws, for breaking which he has blamed the English? I will allege Corneille's words as I find them in the end of his discourse of the three Unities: *Il est facile aux speculatifs d'être sévères &c.* " 'Tis easy for speculative persons to judge severely; but if they would produce to public view ten or twelve pieces of this nature, they would perhaps give more latitude to the rules than I have done, when, by experience, they have known how much we are limited and constrained by them, and how many beauties of the stage they banished from it." To illustrate a little what he has said: By their servile observations of the unities of time and place, and integrity of scenes, they have brought on themselves that dearth of plot, and narrowness of imagination, which may be observed in all their plays. How many beautiful accidents might naturally happen in two or three days, which cannot arrive with any probability in the compass of twenty-four hours? There is time to be allowed also for maturity of design, which, amongst great and prudent persons, such as are often represented in tragedy, cannot, with any likelihood of truth, be brought to pass at so short a warning. Farther; by tying themselves strictly to the unity of place and unbroken scenes, they are forced many times to omit some beauties which cannot be shown where the act began; but might, if the scene were interrupted and the stage cleared for the persons to enter in another place; and therefore the French poets are often forced upon absurdities; for if the act begins in a chamber, all the persons in the play must have some business or other to come hither, or else they are not to be shown that act; and sometimes their characters are very unfitting to appear there: as, suppose it were the king's bed-chamber; yet the meanest man in the tragedy must come and dispatch his business there, rather than in the lobby or courtyard (which is fitter for him), for fear the stage should be cleared, and the scenes broken. Many times they fall by it in a greater inconvenience; for they keep their scenes unbroken, and yet change the place; as in one of their newest plays, where the act begins in the street. There a gentleman is to meet his friend; he sees him with his man, coming out from his father's house; they talk together, and the first goes out: the second, who is a lover, has made an appointment with his mistress; she appears at the window, and then we are to imagine the scene lies under it. This gentleman is called away, and leaves his servant with his mistress; presently her father is heard from within; the young lady is afraid the serving-man should be discovered, and thrusts him into a place of safety, which is supposed to be her closet. After this, the father enters to the daughter, and now the scene is in a house; for he is seeking from one room to another for this poor Philipin, or French Diego, who is heard from within, drolling and breaking many a miserable conceit on the subject of his sad condition. In this ridiculous manner the play goes forward, the stage being never empty all the while: so that the street, the window, the houses, and the closet, are made to walk about, and the persons to stand still. Now what, I beseech you, is more easy than to write a regular French play, or more difficult than to write an irregular English one, like those of Fletcher, or of Shakespeare?

'If they content themselves, as Corneille did, with some flat design, which, like an ill riddle, is found out ere it be half proposed, such plots we can make every way regular, as easily as they; but whenever they endeavour to rise to any quick turns and counter-turns of plot, as some of them have attempted, since Corneille's plays have been less in vogue, you see they write as irregularly as we, though they cover it more speciously. Hence the reason is perspicuous why no French plays, when translated, have or ever can succeed on the English stage. For, if you consider the plots, our own are fuller of variety; if the writing, ours are more quick and fuller of spirit; and therefore 'tis a strange mistake in those who decry the way of writing plays in verse, as if the English therein imitated the French. We have borrowed nothing from them; our plots are weaved in English looms: we endeavour therein to follow the variety and greatness of characters which are derived to us from Shakespeare and Fletcher; the copiousness and well-knitting of the intrigues we have from Jonson; and for the verse itself we have English precedents of elder date than any of Corneille's plays. Not to name our old comedies before Shakespeare, which were all writ in verse of six feet, or Alexandrines, such as the French now use, I can show in Shakespeare many scenes of rhyme together, and the like in Ben Jonson's tragedies; in *Catiline* and *Sejanus* sometimes thirty or forty lines—I mean besides the Chorus, or the monologues; which, by the way, showed Ben no enemy to this way of writing, especially if you read his *Sad Shepherd*, which goes sometimes on rhyme, sometimes on blank verse, like an horse who eases himself on trot and amble. You find him likewise commending Fletcher's pastoral of *The Faithful Shepherdess*, which is for the most part rhyme, though not refined to that purity to which it hath since been brought. And these examples are enough to clear us from a servile imitation of the French.

'But to return whence I have digressed: I dare boldly affirm these two things of the English drama: First, that we have many plays of ours as regular as any of theirs, and which, besides, have more variety of plot and characters; and secondly, that in most of the irregular plays of Shakespeare or Fletcher (for Ben Jonson's are for the most part regular), there is a more masculine fancy and greater spirit in the writing than there is in any of the French. I could produce, even in Shakespeare's and Fletchers' works, some plays which are almost exactly formed; as *The Merry Wives of Windsor*, and *The Scornful Lady*: but because (generally speaking) Shakespeare, who writ first, did not perfectly observe the laws of comedy, and Fletcher, who came nearer to perfection, yet through carelessness made many faults; I will take the pattern of a perfect play from Ben Jonson, who was a careful and learned observer of the dramatic laws, and from all his comedies I shall select *The Silent Woman*; of which I will make a short examen, according to those rules which the French observe.'

As Neander was beginning to examine *The Silent Woman*, Eugenius, earnestly regarding him, 'I beseech you, Neander,' said he, 'gratify the company, and me in particular, so far as, before you speak of the play, to give us a character of the author; and tell us frankly your opinion, whether you do not think all writers, both French and English, ought to give place to him.'

'I fear,' replied Neander, 'that in obeying your commands I shall draw some envy on myself. Besides, in performing them, it will be first necessary to speak somewhat of Shakespeare and Fletcher, his rivals in poesy; and one of them, in my opinion, at least his equal, perhaps his superior.

'To begin, then, with Shakespeare. He was the man who of all modern, and perhaps ancient poets, had the largest and most comprehensive soul. All the images of nature were still present to him, and he drew them, not laboriously, but luckily; when he describes anything, you more than see it, you feel it too. Those who accuse him to have wanted learning, give him the greater commendation: he was naturally learned; he needed not the spectacles of books to read nature; he looked inwards, and found her there. I cannot say he is everywhere alike; were he so, I should do him injury to compare him with the greatest of mankind. He is many times flat, insipid; his comic wit degenerating into clenches, his serious swelling into bombast. But he is always great, when some great occasion is presented to him; no man can say he ever had a fit subject for his wit, and did not then raise himself as high above the rest of poets.

Quantum lenta solent inter viburna cupressi.

The consideration of this made Mr. Hales of Eaton say, that there was no subject of which any poet ever wrote but he would produce it much better done in Shakespeare; and however others are now generally preferred before him, yet the age wherein he lived, which had contemporaries with him Fletcher and Jonson, never equalled them to him in their esteem: and in the last king's court, when Ben's reputation was at highest, Sir John Suckling, and with him the greater part of the courtiers, set our Shakespeare far above him.

'Beaumont and Fletcher, of whom I am next to speak, had, with the advantage of Shakespeare's wit, which was their precedent, great natural gifts, improved by study: Beaumont especially being so accurate a judge of plays that Ben Jonson, while he lived, submitted all his writings to his censure, and, 'tis thought, used his judgement in correcting, if not contriving, all his plots. What value he had for him, appears by the verses he writ to him; and therefore I need speak no farther of it. The first play that brought Fletcher and him in esteem was their *Philaster*: for before that, they had written two or three very unsuccessfully, as the like is reported of Ben Jonson, before he wrote *Every Man in his Humour*. Their plots were generally more regular than Shakespeare's, especially those which were made before Beaumont's death; and they understood and imitated the conversation of gentlemen much better; whose wild debaucheries, and quickness of wit in repartees, no poet before them could paint as they have done. Humour which Ben Jonson derived from particular persons they made it not their business to describe: they represented all the passions very lively, but above all, love. I am apt to believe the English language in them arrived to its highest perfection; what words have since been taken in, are rather superfluous than ornamental. Their plays are now the most pleasant and frequent entertainments of the stage; two of theirs being acted through the year for one of Shakespeare's or Jonson's: the reason is, because there is a certain gaiety in their comedies and pathos in their more serious plays, which suits generally with all men's humours. Shakespeare's language is likewise a little obsolete, and Ben Jonson's wit comes short of theirs.

'As for Jonson, to whose character I am now arrived, if we look upon him while he was himself (for his last plays were but his dotages), I think him the most learned and judicious writer which any theatre ever had. He was a most severe judge of himself, as well as others. One cannot say he wanted wit, but rather that he was frugal of it. In his works you find little to retrench or alter. Wit, and language, and humour also in some measure, we had before him; but something of art was wanting to the drama, till he came. He managed his strength to more advantage than any who preceded him. You seldom find him making love in any of his scenes, or endeavouring to move the passions; his genius was too sullen and saturnine to do it gracefully, especially when he knew he came after those who had performed both to such a height. Humour was his proper sphere; and in that he was delighted most to represent mechanic people. He was deeply conversant in the ancients, both Greek and Latin, and he borrowed boldly from them: there is scarce a poet or historian among the Roman authors of those times whom he has not translated in *Sejanus* and *Catiline*. But he has done his robberies so openly, that one may see he fears not to be taxed by any law. He invades authors like a monarch; and what would be theft in other poets is only victory in him. With the spoils of these writers he so represents old Rome to us, in its rites, ceremonies, and customs, that if one of their poets had written either of his tragedies, we had seen less of it than in him. If there was any fault in his language, 'twas that he weaved it too closely and laboriously, in his comedies especially: perhaps too, he did a little too much Romanize our tongue, leaving the words which he translated almost as much Latin as he found them: wherein, though he learnedly followed their language, he did not enough comply with the idiom of ours. If I would compare him with Shakespeare, I must acknowledge him the more correct poet, but Shakespeare the greater wit. Shakespeare was the Homer, or father of our dramatic poets; Jonson was the Virgil, the pattern of elaborate writing; I admire him, but I love Shakespeare. To conclude of him; as he has given us the most correct plays, so in the precepts which he has laid down in his *Discoveries*, we have as many and profitable rules for perfecting the stage, as any wherewith the French can furnish us.

'Having thus spoken of the author, I proceed to the examination of his comedy, *The Silent Woman*.

EXAMEN OF 'THE SILENT WOMAN'.

'To begin first with the length of the action; it is so far from exceeding the compass of a natural day, that it takes not up an artificial one. 'Tis all included in the limits of three hours and a half, which is no more than is required for the presentment on the stage: a beauty perhaps not much observed; if it had, we should not have looked on the Spanish translation of *Five Hours* with so much wonder. The scene of it is laid in London; the latitude of place is almost as little as you can imagine; for it lies all within the compass of two houses, and after the first act, in one. The continuity of scenes is observed more than in any of our plays, except his own *Fox* and *Alchemist*. They are not broken above twice or thrice at most in the whole comedy; and in the two best of Corneille's plays, the *Cid* and *Cinna*, they are interrupted once. The action of the play is entirely one; the end or aim of which is the settling Morose's estate on Dauphine. The intrigue of it is the greatest and most noble of any pure unmixed comedy in any language; you see in it many persons of various characters and humours, and all delightful: as first, Morose, or an old man, to whom all noise but his own talking is offensive. Some who would be thought critics, say this humour of his is forced: but to remove that objection, we may consider him first to be naturally of a delicate hearing, as many are, to whom all sharp sounds are unpleasant; and secondly, we may attribute much of it to the peevishness of his age, or the wayward authority of an old man in his own house, where he may make himself obeyed; and to this the poet seems to allude in his name Morose. Besides this, I am assured from divers persons, that Ben Jonson was actually acquainted with such a man, one altogether as ridiculous as he is here represented. Others say, it is not enough to find one man of such a humour; it must be common to more, and the more common the more natural. To prove this, they instance in the best of comical characters, Falstaff. There are many men resembling him; old, fat, merry, cowardly, drunken, amorous, vain, and lying. But to convince these people, I need but tell them, that humour is the ridiculous extravagance of conversation, wherein one man differs from all others. If then it be common, or communicated to many, how differs it from other men's? or what indeed causes it to be ridiculous so much as the singularity of it? As for Falstaff, he is not properly one humour, but a miscellany of humours or images, drawn from so many several men: that wherein he is singular is his wit, or those things he says *praeter expectatum*, unexpected by the audience; his quick evasions, when you imagine him surprised, which, as they are extremely diverting of themselves, so receive a great addition from his person; for the

very sight of such an unwieldy old debauched fellow
is a comedy alone. And here, having a place so proper
for it, I cannot but enlarge somewhat upon this subject of humour into which I am fallen. The ancients
had little of it in their comedies; for the τὸ γελοῖον of
the old comedy, of which Aristophanes was chief, was
not so much to imitate a man, as to make the people
laugh at some odd conceit, which had commonly
somewhat of unnatural or obscene in it. Thus, when
you see Socrates brought upon the stage, you are not
to imagine him made ridiculous by the imitation of
his actions, but rather by making him perform something very unlike himself; something so childish and
absurd as by comparing it with the gravity of the
true Socrates makes a ridiculous object for the spectators. In their new comedy which succeeded, the poets
sought indeed to express the ἦθος, as in their tragedies
the πάθος of mankind. But this ἦθος contained only
the general characters of men and manners; as old
men, lovers, serving-men, courtesans, parasites, and
such other persons as we see in their comedies; all
which they made alike; that is, one old man or father,
one lover, one courtesan, so like another, as if the first
of them had begot the rest of every sort: *Ex homine
hunc natum dicas*. The same custom they observed likewise in their tragedies. As for the French, though they
have the word *humeur* among them, yet they have
small use of it in their comedies or farces; they being
but ill imitations of the *ridiculum*, or that which stirred
up laughter in the old comedy. But among the English
'tis otherwise: where by humour is meant some ex-
travagant habit, passion, or affection, particular (as
I said before) to some one person, by the oddness of
which he is immediately distinguished from the rest
of men; which being lively and naturally represented,
most frequently begets that malicious pleasure in the
audience which is testified by laughter; as all things
which are deviations from customs are ever the aptest
to produce it: though by the way this laughter is only

accidental, as the person represented is fantastic or bizarre; but pleasure is essential to it, as the imitation of what is natural. The description of these humours, drawn from the knowledge and observation of particular persons, was the peculiar genius and talent of Ben Jonson; to whose play I now return.

'Besides Morose, there are at least nine or ten different characters and humours in *The Silent Woman*; all which persons have several concernments of their own, yet are all used by the poet to the conducting of the main design to perfection. I shall not waste time in commending the writing of this play; but I will give you my opinion, that there is more wit and acuteness of fancy in it than in any of Ben Jonson's. Besides that he has here described the conversation of gentlemen in the persons of True-Wit and his friends, with more gaiety, air, and freedom, than in the rest of his comedies. For the contrivance of the plot, 'tis extreme elaborate, and yet withal easy; for the λύσις, or untying of it, 'tis so admirable, that when it is done, no one of the audience would think the poet could have missed it; and yet it was concealed so much before the last scene that any other way would sooner have entered into your thoughts. But I dare not take upon me to commend the fabric of it, because it is altogether so full of art, that I must unravel every scene in it to commend it as I ought. And this excellent contrivance is still the more to be admired, because 'tis comedy, where the persons are only of common rank, and their business private, not elevated by passions or high concernments, as in serious plays. Here every one is a proper judge of all he sees, nothing is represented but that with which he daily converses: so that by consequence all faults lie open to discovery, and few are pardonable. 'Tis this which Horace has judiciously observed:

> Creditur, ex medio quia res arcessit, habere
> Sudoris minimum; sed habet Comedia tanto
> Plus oneris, quanto veniae minus.

But our poet who was not ignorant of these difficulties, has made use of all advantages; as he who designs a large leap takes his rise from the highest ground. One of these advantages is that which Corneille has laid down as the greatest which can arrive to any poem, and which he himself could never compass above thrice in all his plays; viz. the making choice of some signal and long-expected day, whereon the action of the play is to depend. This day was that designed by Dauphine for the settling of his uncle's estate upon him; which to compass, he contrives to marry him. That the marriage had been plotted by him long beforehand is made evident by what he tells True-Wit in the second act, that in one moment he had destroyed what he had been raising many months.

'There is another artifice of the poet, which I cannot here omit, because by the frequent practice of it in his comedies he has left it to us almost as a rule; that is, when he has any character or humour wherein he would show a *coup de maître*, or his highest skill, he recommends it to your observation by a pleasant description of it before the person first appears. Thus, in *Bartholomew Fair* he gives you the picture of Numps and Cokes, and in this those of Daw, Lafoole, Morose, and the Collegiate Ladies; all which you hear described before you see them. So that before they come upon the stage, you have a longing expectation of them, which prepares you to receive them favourably; and when they are there, even from their first appearance you are so far acquainted with them, that nothing of their humour is lost to you.

'I will observe yet one thing further of this admirable plot; the business of it rises in every act. The second is greater than the first; the third than the second; and so forward to the fifth. There too you see, till the very last scene, new difficulties arising to obstruct the action of the play; and when the audience is brought into despair that the business can naturally be effected, then, and not before, the discovery is made. But that the poet might entertain you with more variety all this while, he reserves some new characters to show you, which he opens not till the second and third act; in the second Morose, Daw, the Barber, and Otter; in the third the Collegiate Ladies: all which he moves afterwards in by-walks, or under-plots, as diversions to the main design, lest it should grow tedious, though they are still naturally joined with it, and somewhere or other subservient to it. Thus, like a skilful chess-player, by little and little he draws out his men, and makes his pawns of use to his greater persons.

'If this comedy and some others of his were trans-lated into French prose (which would now be no wonder to them, since Molière has lately given them plays out of verse, which have not displeased them), I believe the controversy would soon be decided betwixt the two nations, even making them the judges. But we need not call our heroes to our aid. Be it spoken to the honour of the English, our nation can never want in any age such who are able to dispute the empire of wit with any people in the universe. And though the fury of a civil war, and power for twenty years together abandoned to a barbarous race of men, enemies of all good learning, had buried the muses under the ruins of monarchy; yet, with the restoration of our happiness, we see revived poesy lifting up its head, and already shaking off the rubbish which lay so heavy on it. We have seen since his majesty's return many dramatic poems which yield not to those of any foreign nation, and which deserve all laurels but the English. I will set aside flattery and envy: it cannot be denied but we have had some little blemish either in the plot or writing of all those plays which have been made within these seven years; (and perhaps there is no nation in the world so quick to discern them, or so difficult to pardon them, as ours): yet if we can persuade ourselves to use the candour of that poet, who, though the most severe of

critics, has left us this caution by which to moderate
our censures—

> ——*ubi plura nitent in carmine, non ego paucis*
> *Offendar maculis;*—

if, in consideration of their many and great beauties
we can wink at some slight and little imperfections,
if we, I say, can be thus equal to ourselves, I ask no
favour from the French. And if I do not venture upon
any particular judgement of our late plays, 'tis out of
the consideration which an ancient writer gives me:
vivorum, ut magna admiratio, ita censura difficilis: "betwixt
the extremes of admiration and malice, 'tis hard to
judge uprightly of the living." Only I think it may
be permitted me to say, that as it is no lessening to us
to yield to some plays, and those not many, of our own
nation in the last age, so it can be no addition to pronounce of our present poets that they have far surpassed all the ancients, and the modern writers of
other countries.'

    This was the substance of what was then spoke on
that occasion; and Lisideius, I think, was going to
reply, when he was prevented thus by Crites: 'I am
confident,' said he, 'that the most material things that
can be said have been already urged on either side;
if they have not, I must beg of Lisideius that he will
defer his answer till another time: for I confess I have
a joint quarrel to you both, because you have concluded, without any reason given for it, that rhyme is
proper for the stage. I will not dispute how ancient
it hath been among us to write this way; perhaps our
ancestors knew no better till Shakespeare's time. I
will grant it was not altogether left by him, and that
Fletcher and Ben Jonson used it frequently in their
Pastorals, and sometimes in other plays. Farther—I
will not argue whether we received it originally from
our own countrymen, or from the French; for that is
an inquiry of as little benefit, as theirs who, in the
midst of the late plague, were not so solicitous to

provide against it, as to know whether we had it from the malignity of our own air, or by transportation from Holland. I have therefore only to affirm that it is not allowable in serious plays; for comedies, I find you already concluding with me. To prove this, I might satisfy myself to tell you how much in vain it is for you to strive against the stream of the people's inclination; the greatest part of which are prepossessed so much with those excellent plays of Shakespeare, Fletcher, and Ben Jonson, which have been written out of rhyme, that except you could bring them such as were written better in it, and those too by persons of equal reputation with them, it will be impossible for you to gain your cause with them, who will still be judges. This it is to which, in fine, all your reasons must submit. The unanimous consent of an audience is so powerful, that even Julius Caesar (as Macrobius reports of him), when he was perpetual dictator, was not able to balance it on the other side; but when Laberius, a Roman knight, at his request contended in the *Mime* with another poet, he was forced to cry out, *Etiam favente me victus es, Laberi*. But I will not on this occasion take the advantage of the greater number, but only urge such reasons against rhyme, as I find in the writings of those who have argued for the other way. First then, I am of opinion, that rhyme is unnatural in a play, because dialogue there is presented as the effect of sudden thought: for a play is the imitation of nature; and since no man without premeditation speaks in rhyme, neither ought he to do it on the stage. This hinders not but the fancy may be there elevated to a higher pitch of thought than it is in ordinary discourse; for there is a probability that men of excellent and quick parts may speak noble things *extempore*: but those thoughts are never fettered with the numbers or sound of verse without study, and therefore it cannot be but unnatural to present the most free way of speaking in that which is the most constrained. For this reason, says Aristotle, 'tis best to write tragedy in that kind of verse which is the least such, or which is nearest prose: and this amongst the ancients was the Iambic, and with us is blank verse, or the measure of verse kept exactly without rhyme. These numbers therefore are fittest for a play; the others for a paper of verses, or a poem; blank verse being as much below them, as rhyme is improper for the drama. And if it be objected that neither are blank verses made *extempore*, yet, as nearest nature, they are still to be preferred. But there are two particular exceptions, which many besides myself have had to verse; by which it will appear yet more plainly how improper it is in plays. And the first of them is grounded on that very reason for which some have commended rhyme; they say the quickness of repartees in argumentative scenes receives an ornament from verse. Now what is more unreasonable than to imagine that a man should not only light upon the wit, but the rhyme too, upon the sudden? This nicking of him who spoke before both in sound and measure, is so great a happiness that you must at least suppose the persons of your play to be born poets: *Arcades omnes, et cantare pares, et respondere parati*: they must have arrived at the degree of *quicquid conabar dicere*; to make verses almost whether they will or no. If they are anything below this, it will look rather like the design of two, than the answer of one: it will appear that your actors hold intelligence together; that they perform their tricks like fortune-tellers, by confederacy. The hand of art will be too visible in it, against that maxim of all professions—*Ars est celare artem*; that it is the greatest perfection of art to keep itself undiscovered. Nor will it serve you to object, that however you manage it, 'tis still known to be a play; and, consequently, the dialogue of two persons understood to be the labour of one poet. For a play is still an imitation of nature; we know we are to be deceived, and we desire to be so; but no man ever was deceived but with a probability of truth; for who will suffer a gross lie to be fastened on him? Thus we sufficiently understand, that the scenes which represent cities and countries to us are not really such, but only painted on boards and canvas; but shall that excuse the ill painture or designment of them? Nay, rather ought they not to be laboured with so much the more diligence and exactness, to help the imagination? since the mind of man does naturally tend to truth; and therefore the nearer any thing comes to the imitation of it, the more it pleases.

'Thus, you see, your rhyme is uncapable of expressing the greatest thoughts naturally, and the lowest it cannot with any grace: for what is more unbefitting the majesty of verse than to call a servant, or bid a door be shut, in rhyme? and yet you are often forced on this miserable necessity. But verse, you say, circumscribes a quick and luxuriant fancy, which would extend itself too far on every subject, did not the labour which is required to well-turned and polished rhyme set bounds to it. Yet this argument, if granted, would only prove that we may write better in verse, but not more naturally. Neither is it able to evince that; for he who wants judgement to confine his fancy in blank verse, may want it as much in rhyme: and he who has it will avoid errors in both kinds. Latin verse was as great a confinement to the imagination of those poets, as rhyme to ours; and yet you find Ovid saying too much on every subject. *Nescivit* (says Seneca) *quod bene cessit relinquere*: of which he gives you one famous instance in his description of the deluge:

> *Omnia pontus erat, deerant quoque litora ponto.*
> Now all was sea, nor had that sea a shore.

Thus Ovid's fancy was not limited by verse, and Virgil needed not verse to have bounded his.

'In our own language we see Ben Jonson confining himself to what ought to be said, even in the liberty of blank verse; and yet Corneille, the most judicious of the French poets, is still varying the same sense a hundred ways, and dwelling eternally on the same subject, though confined by rhyme. Some other exceptions I have to verse; but since these I have named are for the most part already public, I conceive it reasonable they should first be answered.'

'It concerns me less than any,' said Neander (seeing he had ended), 'to reply to this discourse; because when I should have proved that verse may be natural in plays, yet I should always be ready to confess, that those which I have written in this kind come short of that perfection which is required. Yet since you are pleased I should undertake this province, I will do it, though with all imaginable respect and deference, both to that person from whom you have borrowed your strongest arguments and to whose judgement, when I have said all, I finally submit. But before I proceed to answer your objections, I must first remember you, that I exclude all comedy from my defence; and next that I deny not but blank verse may be also used; and content myself only to assert, that in serious plays where the subject and characters are great, and the plot unmixed with mirth, which might allay or divert these concernments which are produced, rhyme is there as natural and more effectual than blank verse.

'And now having laid down this as a foundation— to begin with Crites—I must crave leave to tell him, that some of his arguments against rhyme reach no farther than, from the faults or defects of ill rhyme, to conclude against the use of it in general. May not I conclude against blank verse by the same reason? If the words of some poets who write in it are either ill chosen, or ill placed, which makes not only rhyme, but all kinds of verse in any language unnatural, shall I, for their vicious affectation, condemn those excellent lines of Fletcher which are written in that kind? Is there anything in rhyme more constrained than this line in blank verse?—*I heaven invoke, and strong resistance make*; where you see both the clauses are placed unnaturally, that is, contrary to the common way of speaking, and that without the excuse of a rhyme to cause it: yet you would think me very ridiculous, if I should accuse the stubbornness of blank verse for this, and not rather the stiffness of the poet. Therefore, Crites, you must either prove that words, though well chosen, and duly placed, yet render not rhyme natural in itself: or that, however natural and easy the rhyme may be, yet it is not proper for a play. If you insist on the former part, I would ask you, what other conditions are required to make rhyme natural in itself, besides an election of apt words, and a right disposition of them? For the due choice of your words expresses your sense naturally, and the due placing them adapts the rhyme to it. If you object that one verse may be made for the sake of another, though both the words and rhyme be apt, I answer, it cannot possibly so fall out; for either there is a dependance of sense betwixt the first line and the second, or there is none: if there be that connexion, then in the natural position of the words the latter line must of necessity flow from the former; if there be no dependance, yet still the due ordering of words makes the last line as natural in itself as the other: so that the necessity of a rhyme never forces any but bad or lazy writers to say what they would not otherwise. 'Tis true, there is both care and art required to write in verse. A good poet never establishes the first line, till he has sought out such a rhyme as may fit the sense, already prepared to heighten the second: many times the close of the sense falls into the middle of the next verse, or farther off, and he may often prevail himself of the same advantages in English which Virgil had in Latin —he may break off in the hemistich, and begin another line. Indeed, the not observing these two last things makes plays which are written in verse so tedious: for though, most commonly, the sense is to be confined to the couplet, yet nothing that does *perpetuo tenore fluere*, "run in the same channel", can please always. 'Tis like the murmuring of a stream, which not varying in the fall, causes at first attention, at last drowsiness. Variety of cadences is the best rule; the greatest help to the actors, and refreshment to the audience.

'If then verse may be made natural in itself, how becomes it unnatural in a play? You say the stage is the representation of nature, and no man in ordinary conversation speaks in rhyme. But you foresaw when you said this, that it might be answered—neither does any man speak in blank verse, or in measure without rhyme. Therefore you concluded, that which is nearest nature is still to be preferred. But you took no notice that rhyme might be made as natural as blank verse, by the well placing of the words, &c. All the difference between them, when they are both correct, is, the sound in one, which the other wants; and if so, the sweetness of it, and all the advantage resulting from it, which are handled in the Preface to *The Rival Ladies*, will yet stand good. As for that place of Aristotle, where he says, plays should be written in that kind of verse which is nearest prose, it makes little for you; blank verse being properly but measured prose. Now measure alone, in any modern language, does not constitute verse; those of the ancients in Greek and Latin consisted in quantity of words, and a determinate number of feet. But when, by the inundation of the Goths and Vandals into Italy, new languages were introduced, and barbarously mingled with the Latin, of which the Italian, Spanish, French, and ours (made out of them and the Teutonic) are dialects, a new way of poesy was practised; new, I say, in those countries, for in all probability it was that of the conquerors in their own nations: at least we are able to prove that the eastern people have used it from all antiquity. This new way consisted in measure or number of feet, and rhyme; the sweetness of rhyme, and observation of accent, supplying the place of quantity in words, which could neither exactly be observed by those barbarians, who knew not the rules of it, neither was it suitable to their tongues, as it had been to the Greek and Latin. No man is tied in modern poesy to observe any farther rule in the feet of his verse, but that they be dissyllables; whether Spondee, Trochee, or Iambic, it matters not; only he is obliged to rhyme: neither do the Spanish, French, Italian, or Germans acknowledge at all, or very rarely, any such kind of poesy as blank verse amongst them. Therefore, at most 'tis but a poetic prose, a *sermo pedestris*; and as such, most fit for comedies, where I acknowledge rhyme to be improper. Farther; as to that quotation of Aristotle, our couplet verses may be rendered as near prose as blank verse itself, by using those advantages I lately named—as breaks in an hemistich, or running the sense into another line—thereby making art and order appear as loose and free as nature: or, not tying ourselves to couplets strictly, we may use the benefit of the Pindaric way practised in *The Siege of Rhodes*; where the numbers vary, and the rhyme is disposed carelessly and far from often chiming. Neither is that other advantage of the ancients to be despised, of changing the kind of verse when they please, with the change of the scene, or some new entrance; for they confine not themselves always to iambics, but extend their liberty to all lyric numbers, and sometimes even to hexameter. But I need not go so far to prove that rhyme, as it succeeds to all other offices of Greek and Latin verse, so especially to this of plays, since the custom of nations at this day confirms it; the French, Italian, and Spanish tragedies are generally writ in it; and sure the universal consent of the most civilized parts of the world ought in this, as it doth in other customs, to include the rest.

'But perhaps you may tell me, I have proposed such a way to make rhyme natural, and consequently proper to plays, as is unpracticable; and that I shall scarce find six or eight lines together in any play, where the words are so placed and chosen as is required to make it natural. I answer, no poet need constrain himself at all times to it. It is enough he makes it his general rule; for I deny not but sometimes there may be a greatness in placing the words otherwise; and sometimes they may sound better; sometimes also the variety itself is excuse enough. But if, for the most part, the words be placed as they are in the negligence of prose, it is sufficient to denominate the way practicable; for we esteem that to be such, which in the trial oftener succeeds than misses. And thus far you may find the practice made good in many plays: where you do not, remember still that if you cannot find six natural rhymes together, it will be as hard for you to produce as many lines in blank verse, even among the greatest of our poets, against which I cannot make some reasonable exception.

'And this, Sir, calls to my remembrance the beginning of your discourse, where you told us we should never find the audience favourable to this kind of writing, till we could produce as good plays in rhyme, as Ben Jonson, Fletcher, and Shakespeare had written out of it. But it is to raise envy to the living, to compare them with the dead. They are honoured, and almost adored by us, as they deserve; neither do I know any so presumptuous of themselves as to contend with them. Yet give me leave to say thus much, without injury to their ashes; that not only we shall never equal them, but they could never equal themselves, were they to rise and write again. We acknowledge them our fathers in wit; but they have ruined their estates themselves, before they came to their children's hands. There is scarce a humour, a character, or any kind of plot, which they have not used. All comes sullied or wasted to us: and were they to entertain this age, they could not now make so plenteous treatments out of such decayed fortunes. This therefore will be a good argument to us, either not to write at all, or to attempt some other way. There is no bays to be expected in their walks: *tentanda via est, quà me quoque possum tollere humo.*

This way of writing in verse they have only left free to us; our age is arrived to a perfection in it, which they never knew; and which (if we may guess by what of theirs we have seen in verse, as *The Faithful Shepherdess*, and *Sad Shepherd*) 'tis probable they never could have reached. For the genius of every age is different; and though ours excel in this, I deny not but to imitate nature in that perfection which they did in prose, is a greater commendation than to write in verse exactly. As for what you have added—that the people are not generally inclined to like this way —if it were true, it would be no wonder that betwixt the shaking off an old habit, and the introducing of a new, there should be difficulty. Do we not see them stick to Hopkins' and Sternhold's psalms, and forsake those of David, I mean Sandys his translation of them? If by the people you understand the multitude, the οἱ πολλοί, 'tis no matter what they think; they are sometimes in the right, sometimes in the wrong: their judgement is a mere lottery. *Est ubi plebs rectè putat, est ubi peccat.* Horace says it of the vulgar judging poesy. But if you mean the mixed audience of the populace and the noblesse, I dare confidently affirm that a great part of the latter sort are already favourable to verse; and that no serious plays written since the king's return have been more kindly received by them than *The Siege of Rhodes*, the *Mustapha*, *The Indian Queen*, and *Indian Emperor*.

'But I come now to the inference of your first argument. You said that the dialogue of plays is presented as the effect of sudden thought, but no man speaks suddenly, or *extempore*, in rhyme; and you inferred from thence, that rhyme, which you acknowledge to be proper to epic poesy, cannot equally be proper to dramatic, unless we could suppose all men born so much more than poets, that verses should be made in them, not by them.

'It has been formerly urged by you, and confessed by me, that since no man spoke any kind of verse *extempore*, that which was nearest nature was to be preferred. I answer you, therefore, by distinguishing betwixt what is nearest to the nature of comedy, which is the imitation of common persons and ordinary speaking, and what is nearest the nature of a serious play: this last is indeed the representation of nature, but 'tis nature wrought up to a higher pitch. The plot, the characters, the wit, the passions, the descriptions, are all exalted above the level of common converse, as high as the imagination of the poet can carry them, with proportion to verisimility. Tragedy, we know, is wont to image to us the minds and fortunes of noble persons, and to portray these exactly; heroic rhyme is nearest nature, as being the noblest kind of modern verse.

> *Indignatur enim privatis et prope socco*
> *Dignis carminibus narrari coena Thyestae*—

says Horace: and in another place,

> *Effutire leves indigna tragoedia versus*—.

Blank verse is acknowledged to be too low for a poem, nay more, for a paper of verses; but if too low for an ordinary sonnet, how much more for tragedy, which is by Aristotle in the dispute betwixt the epic poesy and the dramatic, for many reasons he there alleges, ranked above it?

'But setting this defence aside, your argument is almost as strong against the use of rhyme in poems as in plays; for the epic way is everywhere interlaced in dialogue, or discursive scenes; and therefore you must either grant rhyme to be improper there, which is contrary to your assertion, or admit it into plays by the same title which you have given it to poems. For though tragedy be justly preferred above the other, yet there is a great affinity between them, as may easily be discovered in that definition of a play which Lisideius gave us. The *genus* of them is the same—a just and lively image of human nature, in its actions, passions, and traverses of fortune: so is the end—namely, for the delight and benefit of mankind. The characters and persons are still the same, viz. the greatest of both sorts; only the manner of acquainting us with those actions, passions, and fortunes is different. Tragedy performs it *viva voce*, or by action, in dialogue; wherein it excels the epic poem, which does it chiefly by narration, and therefore is not so lively an image of human nature. However, the agreement between them is such that if rhyme be proper for one, it must be for the other. Verse, 'tis true, is not the effect of sudden thought; but this hinders not that sudden thought may be represented in verse, since those thoughts are such as must be higher than nature can raise them without premeditation, especially to a continuance of them, even out of verse; and consequently you cannot imagine them to have been sudden either in the poet or in the actors. A play, as I have said, to be like nature, is to be set above it; as statues which are placed on high are made greater than the life, that they may descend to the sight in their just proportion.

'Perhaps I have insisted too long on this objection; but the clearing of it will make my stay shorter on the rest. You tell us, Crites, that rhyme appears most unnatural in repartees, or short replies: when he who answers (it being presumed he knew not what the other would say, yet) makes up that part of the verse which was left incomplete, and supplies both the sound and measure of it. This, you say, looks rather like the confederacy of two, than the answer of one.

'This, I confess, is an objection which is in every man's mouth, who loves not rhyme: but suppose, I beseech you, the repartee were made only in blank verse, might not part of the same argument be turned against you? for the measure is as often supplied there, as it is in rhyme; the latter half of the hemistich as commonly made up, or a second line subjoined as a reply to the former; which any one leaf in Jonson's plays will sufficiently clear to you. You will often find in the Greek tragedians, and in Seneca, that when a scene grows up into the warmth of repartees, which is the close fighting of it, the latter part of the trimeter is supplied by him who answers; and yet it was never observed as a fault in them by any of the ancient or modern critics. The case is the same in our verse, as it was in theirs; rhyme to us being in lieu of quantity to them. But if no latitude is to be allowed a poet, you take from him not only his licence of *quidlibet audendi*, but you tie him up in a straighter compass than you would a philosopher. This is indeed *Musas colere severiores*. You would have him follow nature, but he must follow her on foot: you have dismounted him from his Pegasus. But you tell us, this supplying the last half of a verse, or adjoining a whole second to the former, looks more like the design of two, than the answer of one. Suppose we acknowledge it: how comes this confederacy to be more displeasing to you than in a dance which is well contrived? You see there the united design of many persons to make up one figure: after they have separated themselves in many petty divisions, they rejoin one by one into a gross: the confederacy is plain amongst them, for chance could never produce anything so beautiful; and yet there is nothing in it, that shocks your sight. I acknowledge the hand of art appears in repartee, as of necessity it must in all kind of verse. But there is also the quick and poignant brevity of it (which is an high imitation of nature in those sudden gusts of passion) to mingle with it; and this, joined with the cadency and sweetness of the rhyme, leaves nothing in the soul of the hearer to desire. 'Tis an art which appears; but it appears only like the shadowings of painture, which being to cause the rounding of it cannot be absent; but while that is considered, they are lost: so while we attend to the other beauties of

the matter, the care and labour of the rhyme is carried
from us, or at least drowned in its own sweetness, as
bees are sometimes buried in their honey. When a
poet has found the repartee, the last perfection he can
add to it is to put it into verse. However good the
thought may be, however apt the words in which
'tis couched, yet he finds himself at a little unrest
while rhyme is wanting: he cannot leave it till that
comes naturally, and then is at ease, and sits down
contented.

'From replies, which are the most elevated thoughts
of verse, you pass to those which are most mean, and
which are common with the lowest of household conversation. In these, you say, the majesty of verse
suffers. You instance in the calling of a servant, or
commanding a door to be shut, in rhyme. This,
Crites, is a good observation of yours, but no argument: for it proves no more but that such thoughts
should be waived, as often as may be, by the address
of the poet. But suppose they are necessary in the
places where he uses them, yet there is no need to put
them into rhyme. He may place them in the beginning of a verse, and break it off, as unfit, when so
debased, for any other use; or granting the worst—
that they require more room than the hemistich will
allow, yet still there is a choice to be made of the best
words, and least vulgar (provided they be apt), to
express such thoughts. Many have blamed rhyme in
general for this fault, when the poet with a little care
might have redressed it. But they do it with no more
justice than if English poesy should be made ridiculous
for the sake of the Water-poet's rhymes. Our language
is noble, full, and significant; and I know not why he
who is master of it may not clothe ordinary things in
it as decently as the Latin, if he use the same diligence
in his choice of words: *delectus verborum origo est eloquentiae.* It was the saying of Julius Caesar, one so
curious in his, that none of them can be changed but
for a worse. One would think *unlock the door* was a

thing as vulgar as could be spoken; and yet Seneca could make it sound high and lofty in his Latin:

> *Reserate clusos regii postes laris.*
> Set wide the palace gates.

'But I turn from this exception, both because it happens not above twice or thrice in any play that those vulgar thoughts are used; and then too, (were there no other apology to be made, yet) the necessity of them, which is alike in all kind of writing, may excuse them. For if they are little and mean in rhyme, they are of consequence such in blank verse. Besides that the great eagerness and precipitation with which they are spoken makes us rather mind the substance than the dress; that for which they are spoken, rather than what is spoke. For they are always the effect of some hasty concernment, and something of consequence depends on them.

'Thus, Crites, I have endeavoured to answer your objections; it remains only that I should vindicate an argument for verse, which you have gone about to overthrow. It had formerly been said, that the easiness of blank verse renders the poet too luxuriant, but that the labour of rhyme bounds and circumscribes an over-fruitful fancy; the sense there being commonly confined to the couplet, and the words so ordered that the rhyme naturally follows them, not they the rhyme. To this you answered, that it was no argument to the question in hand; for the dispute was not which way a man may write best, but which is most proper for the subject on which he writes.

'First, give me leave, Sir, to remember you, that the argument against which you raised this objection was only secondary: it was built on this hypothesis—that to write in verse was proper for serious plays. Which supposition being granted (as it was briefly made out in that discourse by showing how verse might be made natural), it asserted, that this way of writing was an help to the poet's judgement, by putting bounds to a wild overflowing fancy. I think, therefore, it will not be hard for me to make good what it was to prove on that supposition. But you add, that were this let pass, yet he who wants judgement in the liberty of his fancy, may as well show the defect of it when he is confined to verse; for he who has judgement will avoid errors, and he who has it not will commit them in all kinds of writing.

'This argument, as you have taken it from a most acute person, so I confess it carries much weight in it: but by using the word "judgement" here indefinitely, you seem to have put a fallacy upon us. I grant, he who has judgement, that is, so profound, so strong, or rather so infallible a judgement that he needs no helps to keep it always poised and upright, will commit no faults either in rhyme or out of it. And on the other extreme, he who has a judgement so weak and crazed that no helps can correct or amend it, shall write scurvily out of rhyme, and worse in it. But the first of these judgements is no where to be found, and the latter is not fit to write at all. To speak therefore of judgement as it is in the best poets; they who have the greatest proportion of it, want other helps than from it, within. As for example you would be loath to say, that he who is endued with a sound judgement has no need of history, geography, or moral philosophy, to write correctly. Judgement is indeed the master-workman in a play; but he requires many subordinate hands, many tools to his assistance. And verse I affirm to be one of these; 'tis a rule and line by which he keeps his building compact and even, which otherwise lawless imagination would raise either irregularly or loosely; at least, if the poet commits errors with this help, he would make greater and more without it: 'tis, in short, a slow and painful, but the surest kind of working. Ovid, whom you accuse for luxuriancy in verse, had perhaps been farther guilty of it, had he writ in prose. And for your instance of Ben Jonson, who, you say, wrote exactly without the help of rhyme; you are to remember, 'tis only an aid to a luxuriant fancy, which his was not: as he did not want imagination, so none ever said he had much to spare. Neither was verse then refined so much, to be an help to that age, as it is to ours. Thus then the second thoughts being usually the best, as receiving the maturest digestion from judgement, and the last and most mature product of those thoughts being artful and laboured verse, it may well be inferred, that verse is a great help to a luxuriant fancy; and this is what that argument which you opposed was to evince.'

Neander was pursuing this discourse so eagerly, that Eugenius had called to him twice or thrice, ere he took notice that the barge stood still, and that they were at the foot of Somerset Stairs, where they had appointed it to land. The company were all sorry to separate so soon, though a great part of the evening was already spent; and stood awhile looking back on the water, upon which the moonbeams played, and made it appear like floating quicksilver: at last they went up through a crowd of French people, who were merrily dancing in the open air, and nothing concerned for the noise of guns which had alarmed the town that afternoon. Walking thence together to the Piazze, they parted there; Eugenius and Lisideius to some pleasant appointment they had made, and Crites and Neander to their several lodgings.

PREFACE TO THE FABLES

[1700]

'Tis with a poet, as with a man who designs to build, and is very exact, as he supposes, in casting up the cost beforehand; but, generally speaking, he is mistaken in his account, and reckons short of the expense he first intended. He alters his mind as the work proceeds, and will have this or that convenience more, of which he had not thought when he began. So has it happened to me; I have built a house, where I intended but a lodge; yet with better success than a certain nobleman, who, beginning with a dog-kennel, never lived to finish the palace he had contrived.

From translating the First of Homer's *Iliads* (which I intended as an essay to the whole work), I proceeded to the translation of the Twelfth Book of Ovid's *Metamorphoses*, because it contains, among other things, the causes, the beginning, and ending, of the Trojan war. Here I ought in reason to have stopped; but the speeches of Ajax and Ulysses lying next in my way I could not balk 'em. When I had compassed them, I was so taken with the former part of the Fifteenth Book (which is the masterpiece of the whole *Metamorphoses*), that I enjoined myself the pleasing task of rendering it into English. And now I found, by the number of my verses, that they began to swell into a little volume; which gave me an occasion of looking backward on some beauties of my author, in his former books: there occurred to me the *Hunting of the Boar*, *Cinyras and Myrrha*, the good-natured story of *Baucis and Philemon*, with the rest, which I hope I have translated closely enough, and given them the same turn of verse which they had in the original; and this, I may say, without vanity, is not the talent of every poet. He who has arrived the nearest to it is the ingenious and learned Sandys, the best versifier of the former age; if I may properly call it by that name, which was the former part of this concluding century. For Spenser and Fairfax both flourished in the reign of Queen Elizabeth; great masters in our language, and who saw much farther into the beauties of our numbers than those who immediately followed them. Milton was the poetical son of Spenser, and Mr. Waller of Fairfax; for we have our lineal descents and clans as well as other families. Spenser more than once insinuates, that the soul of Chaucer was transfused into his body; and that he was begotten by him two hundred years after his decease. Milton has acknowledged to me, that Spenser was his original; and many besides myself have heard our famous Waller own, that he derived the harmony of his numbers from *Godfrey of Bulloigne*, which was turned into English by Mr. Fairfax.

But to return: having done with Ovid for this time, it came into my mind, that our old English poet, Chaucer, in many things resembled him, and that with no disadvantage on the side of the modern author, as I shall endeavour to prove when I compare them; and as I am, and always have been, studious to promote the honour of my native country, so I soon resolved to put their merits to the trial, by turning some of the *Canterbury Tales* into our language, as it is now refined; for by this means, both the poets being set in the same light and dressed in the same English habit, story to be compared with story, a certain judgement may be made betwixt them by the reader, without obtruding my opinion on him. Or, if I seem partial to my countryman and predecessor in the laurel, the friends of antiquity are not few; and, besides many of the learned, Ovid has almost all the beaux and the whole fair sex, his declared patrons. Perhaps I have assumed somewhat more to myself than they allow me, because I have adventured to sum up the evidence; but the readers are the jury, and their privilege remains entire, to decide according to the merits of the cause; or, if they please, to bring it to another hearing before some other court. In the meantime, to follow the thread of my discourse (as thoughts, according to Mr. Hobbes, have always some connexion), so from Chaucer I was led to think on Boccace, who was not only his contemporary, but also pursued the same studies; wrote novels in prose, and many works in verse; particularly is said to have invented the octave rhyme, or stanza of eight lines, which ever since has been maintained by the practice of all Italian writers who are, or at least assume the title of, heroic poets. He and Chaucer, among other things, had this in common, that they refined their mother-tongues; but with this difference, that Dante had begun to file their language, at least in verse, before the time of Boccace, who likewise received no little help from his master Petrarch; but the reformation of their prose was wholly owing to Boccace himself, who is yet the standard of purity in the Italian tongue, though many of his phrases are become obsolete, as in process of time it must needs happen. Chaucer (as you have formerly been told by our learned Mr. Rymer) first adorned and amplified our barren tongue from the Provençal, which was then the most polished of all the modern languages; but this subject has been copiously treated by that great critic, who deserves no little commendation from us his countrymen. For these reasons of time, and resemblance of genius, in Chaucer and Boccace, I resolved to join them in my present work; to which I have added some original papers of my own, which whether they are equal or inferior to my other poems, an author is the most improper judge; and therefore I leave them wholly to the mercy of the reader. I will hope the best, that they will not be condemned; but if they should, I have the excuse of an old gentleman, who, mounting on horseback before some ladies, when I was present, got up somewhat heavily, but desired of the fair spectators, that they would count fourscore and eight before they judged him. By the mercy of God, I am already come within twenty years of his number; a cripple in my limbs, but what decays are in my mind, the reader must determine. I think myself as vigorous as ever in the faculties of my soul, excepting only my memory, which is not impaired to any great degree; and if I lose not more of it, I have no great reason to complain. What judgement I had, increases rather than diminishes; and thoughts, such as they are, come crowding in so fast upon me, that my only difficulty is to choose or to reject, to run them into verse, or to give them the other harmony of prose: I have so long studied and practised both, that they are grown into a habit, and become familiar to me. In short, though I may lawfully plead some part of the old gentleman's excuse, yet I will reserve it till I think I have greater need, and ask no grains of allowance for the faults of this my present work, but those which are given of course to human frailty. I will not trouble my reader with the shortness of time in which I wrote it, or the several intervals of sickness. They who think too well of their own performances, are apt to boast in their prefaces how little time their works have cost them, and what other business of more importance interfered; but the reader will be as apt to ask the question, why they allowed not a longer time to make their works more perfect? and why they had so despicable an opinion of their judges as to thrust their indigested stuff upon them, as if they deserved no better?

With this account of my present undertaking, I conclude the first part of this discourse: in the second part, as at a second sitting, though I alter not the draught, I must touch the same features over again, and change the dead-colouring of the whole. In general I will only say, that I have written nothing which savours of immorality or profaneness; at least, I am not conscious to myself of any such intention. If there happen to be found an irreverent expression, or a thought too wanton, they are crept into my verses through my inadvertency: if the searchers find any in the cargo, let them be staved or forfeited, like counterbanded goods; at least, let their authors be answerable for them, as being but imported merchandise, and not of my own manufacture. On the other side, I have endeavoured to choose such fables, both ancient and modern, as contain in each of them some instructive moral; which I could prove by induction, but the way is tedious, and they leap foremost into sight, without the reader's trouble of looking after them. I wish I could affirm, with a safe conscience, that I had taken the same care in all my former writings; for it must be owned, that supposing verses are never so beautiful or pleasing, yet, if they contain anything which shocks religion or good manners, they are at best what Horace says of good numbers without good sense, *Versus inopes rerum, nugaeque canorae.* Thus far, I hope, I am right in court, without renouncing to my other right of self-defence, where I have been wrongfully accused, and my sense wire-drawn into blasphemy or bawdry, as it has often been by a religious lawyer, in a late pleading against the stage; in which he mixes truth with falsehood, and has not forgotten the old rule of calumniating strongly, that something may remain.

I resume the thrid of my discourse with the first of my translations, which was the first *Iliad* of Homer. If it shall please God to give me longer life, and moderate health, my intentions are to translate the whole *Ilias*; provided still that I meet with those encouragements from the public, which may enable me to proceed in my undertaking with some cheerfulness. And this I dare assure the world beforehand, that I have found, by trial, Homer a more pleasing task than Virgil, though I say not the translation will be less laborious; for the Grecian is more according to my genius than the Latin poet. In the works of the two authors we may read their manners, and natural inclinations, which are wholly different. Virgil was of a quiet, sedate temper; Homer was violent, impetuous, and full of fire. The chief talent of Virgil was propriety of thoughts, and ornament of words: Homer was rapid in his thoughts, and took all the liberties, both of numbers and of expressions, which his language, and the age in which he lived, allowed him. Homer's invention was more copious, Virgil's more confined; so that if Homer had not led the way, it was not in Virgil to have begun heroic poetry; for nothing can be more evident, than that the Roman poem is but the second part of the *Ilias*; a continuation of the same story, and the persons already formed. The manners of Aeneas are those of Hector, super-added to those which Homer gave him. The adventures of Ulysses in the *Odysseis* are imitated in the first six books of Virgil's *Aeneis*; and though the accidents are not the same (which would have argued him of a servile copying, and total barrenness of invention), yet the seas were the same in which both the heroes wandered; and Dido cannot be denied to be the poetical daughter of Calypso. The six latter books of Virgil's poem are the four-and-twenty *Iliads* contracted; a quarrel occasioned by a lady, a single combat, battles fought, and a town besieged. I say not this in derogation to Virgil, neither do I contradict anything which I have formerly said in his just praise; for his episodes are almost wholly of his own invention, and the form which he has given to the telling makes the tale his own, even though the original story had been the same. But this proves, however, that Homer taught Virgil to design; and if invention be the first virtue of an epic poet, then the Latin poem can only be allowed the second place. Mr. Hobbes, in the preface to his own bald translation of the *Ilias* (studying poetry as he did mathematics, when it was too late), Mr. Hobbes, I say, begins the praise of Homer where he should have ended it. He tells us, that the first beauty of an epic poem consists in diction; that is, in the choice of words, and harmony of numbers. Now the words are the colouring of the work, which, in the order of nature, is last to be considered. The design, the disposition, the manners, and the thoughts, are all before it: where any of those are wanting or imperfect, so much wants or is imperfect in the imitation of human life, which is in the very definition of a poem. Words, indeed, like glaring colours, are the first beauties that arise and strike the sight; but, if the draught be false or lame, the figures ill disposed, the manners obscure or inconsistent, or the thoughts un-

natural, then the finest colours are but daubing, and
the piece is a beautiful monster at the best. Neither
Virgil nor Homer were deficient in any of the former
beauties; but in this last, which is expression, the
Roman poet is at least equal to the Grecian, as I have
said elsewhere: supplying the poverty of his language
by his musical ear, and by his diligence.

But to return: our two great poets being so different
in their tempers, one choleric and sanguine, the other
phlegmatic and melancholic; that which makes them
excel in their several ways is, that each of them has
followed his own natural inclination, as well in forming the design, as in the execution of it. The very
heroes show their authors: Achilles is hot, impatient,
revengeful:

> *Impiger, iracundus, inexorabilis, acer, &c.,*

Aeneas patient, considerate, careful of his people, and
merciful to his enemies; ever submissive to the will of
heaven:

> *. . . quo fata trahunt retrahuntque, sequamur.*

I could please myself with enlarging on this subject,
but am forced to defer it to a fitter time. From all I
have said, I will only draw this inference, that the
action of Homer, being more full of vigour than that
of Virgil, according to the temper of the writer, is of
consequence more pleasing to the reader. One warms
you by degrees; the other sets you on fire all at once,
and never intermits his heat. 'Tis the same difference
which Longinus makes betwixt the effects of eloquence
in Demosthenes and Tully; one persuades, the other
commands. You never cool while you read Homer,
even not in the Second Book (a graceful flattery to
his countrymen); but he hastens from the ships, and
concludes not that book till he has made you an
amends by the violent playing of a new machine.
From thence he hurries on his action with variety of
events, and ends it in less compass than two months.
This vehemence of his, I confess, is more suitable to

my temper; and, therefore, I have translated his First Book with greater pleasure than any part of Virgil; but it was not a pleasure without pains. The continual agitations of the spirits must needs be a weakening of any constitution, especially in age; and many pauses are required for refreshment betwixt the heats; the *Iliad* of itself being a third part longer than all Virgil's works together.

This is what I thought needful in this place to say of Homer. I proceed to Ovid and Chaucer; considering the former only in relation to the latter. With Ovid ended the golden age of the Roman tongue; from Chaucer the purity of the English tongue began. The manners of the poets were not unlike. Both of them were well-bred, well-natured, amorous, and libertine, at least in their writings; it may be, also in their lives. Their studies were the same, philosophy and philology. Both of them were knowing in astronomy; of which Ovid's books of the *Roman Feasts*, and Chaucer's *Treatise of the Astrolabe*, are sufficient witnesses. But Chaucer was likewise an astrologer, as were Virgil, Horace, Persius, and Manilius. Both writ with wonderful facility and clearness; neither were great inventors: for Ovid only copied the Grecian fables, and most of Chaucer's stories were taken from his Italian contemporaries, or their predecessors. Boccace his *Decameron* was first published, and from thence our Englishman has borrowed many of his *Canterbury Tales*: yet that of *Palamon and Arcite* was written, in all probability, by some Italian wit, in a former age, as I shall prove hereafter. The tale of *Grizild* was the invention of Petrarch; by him sent to Boccace, from whom it came to Chaucer. *Troilus and Cressida* was also written by a Lombard author, but much amplified by our English translator, as well as beautified; the genius of our countrymen, in general, being rather to improve an invention than to invent themselves, as is evident not only in our poetry, but in many of our manufactures. I find I have anticipated already, and taken up from Boccace before I come to him but there is so much less behind; and I am of the temper of most kings, who love to be in debt, are all for present money, no matter how they pay it afterwards: besides, the nature of a preface is rambling, never wholly out of the way, nor in it. This I have learned from the practice of honest Montaigne, and return at my pleasure to Ovid and Chaucer, of whom I have little more to say.

Both of them built on the inventions of other men; yet, since Chaucer had something of his own, as *The Wife of Bath's Tale*, *The Cock and the Fox*, which I have translated, and some others, I may justly give our countryman the precedence in that part; since I can remember nothing of Ovid which was wholly his. Both of them understood the manners; under which name I comprehend the passions, and, in a larger sense, the descriptions of persons, and their very habits. For an example, I see Baucis and Philemon as perfectly before me as if some ancient painter had drawn them; and all the pilgrims in the *Canterbury Tales*, their humours, their features, and the very dress, as distinctly as if I had supped with them at the Tabard in Southwark. Yet even there, too, the figures of Chaucer are much more lively, and set in a better light; which though I have not time to prove, yet I appeal to the reader, and am sure he will clear me from partiality. The thoughts and words remain to be considered, in the comparison of the two poets; and I have saved myself one-half of the labour, by owning that Ovid lived when the Roman tongue was in its meridian; Chaucer, in the dawning of our language: therefore that part of the comparison stands not on an equal foot, any more than the diction of Ennius and Ovid, or of Chaucer and our present English. The words are given up, as a post not to be defended in our poet, because he wanted the modern art of fortifying. The thoughts remain to be considered; and they are to be measured only by their propriety; that is, as they flow more or less naturally from the persons described, on such and such occasions. The vulgar judges, which are nine parts in ten of all nations, who call conceits and jingles wit, who see Ovid full of them, and Chaucer altogether without them, will think me little less than mad for preferring the Englishman to the Roman. Yet, with their leave, I must presume to say, that the things they admire are only glittering trifles, and so far from being witty, that in a serious poem they are nauseous, because they are unnatural. Would any man, who is ready to die for love, describe his passion like Narcissus? Would he think of *inopem me copia fecit*, and a dozen more of such expressions, poured on the neck of one another, and signifying all the same thing? If this were wit, was this a time to be witty, when the poor wretch was in the agony of death? This is just John Littlewit, in *Bartholomew Fair*, who had a conceit (as he tells you) left him in his misery; a miserable conceit. On these occasions the poet should endeavour to raise pity; but, instead of this, Ovid is tickling you to laugh. Virgil never made use of such machines when he was moving you to commiserate the death of Dido: he would not destroy what he was building. Chaucer makes Arcite violent in his love, and unjust in the pursuit of it; yet, when he came to die, he made him think more reasonably: he repents not of his love, for that had altered his character; but acknowledges the injustice of his proceedings, and resigns Emilia to Palamon. What would Ovid have done on this occasion? He would certainly have made Arcite witty on his death-bed; he had complained he was farther off from possession by being so near, and a thousand such boyisms, which Chaucer rejected as below the dignity of the subject. They who think otherwise, would, by the same reason, prefer Lucan and Ovid to Homer and Virgil, and Martial to all four of them. As for the turn of words, in which Ovid particularly excels all poets, they are sometimes a fault, and sometimes a beauty, as they are used properly or improperly; but in strong passions always to be shunned, because passions are serious, and will admit no playing. The French have a high value for them; and, I confess, they are often what they call delicate, when they are introduced with judgement; but Chaucer writ with more simplicity, and followed Nature more closely than to use them. I have thus far, to the best of my knowledge, been an upright judge betwixt the parties in competition, not meddling with the design nor the disposition of it; because the design was not their own; and in the disposing of it they were equal. It remains that I say somewhat of Chaucer in particular.

In the first place, as he is the father of English poetry, so I hold him in the same degree of veneration as the Grecians held Homer, or the Romans Virgil. He is a perpetual fountain of good sense; learned in all sciences; and, therefore, speaks properly on all subjects. As he knew what to say, so he knows also when to leave off; a continence which is practised by few writers, and scarcely by any of the ancients, excepting Virgil and Horace. One of our late great poets is sunk in his reputation, because he could never forgive any conceit which came in his way; but swept like a drag-net, great and small. There was plenty enough, but the dishes were ill sorted; whole pyramids of sweetmeats for boys and women, but little of solid meat for men. All this proceeded not from any want of knowledge, but of judgement. Neither did he want that in discerning the beauties and faults of other poets, but only indulged himself in the luxury of writing; and perhaps knew it was a fault, but hoped the reader would not find it. For this reason, though he must always be thought a great poet, he is no longer esteemed a good writer; and for ten impressions, which his works had in so many successive years, yet at present a hundred books are scarcely purchased once a twelvemonth; for, as my last Lord Rochester said, though somewhat profanely, *Not being of God, he could not stand.*

Chaucer followed Nature everywhere, but was never so bold to go beyond her; and there is a great difference of being *poeta* and *nimis poeta,* if we may believe Catullus, as much as betwixt a modest behaviour and affectation. The verse of Chaucer, I confess, is not harmonious to us; but 'tis like the eloquence of one whom Tacitus commends, it was *auribus istius temporis accommodata:* they who lived with him, and some time after him, thought it musical; and it continues so, even in our judgement, if compared with the numbers of Lydgate and Gower, his contemporaries: there is the rude sweetness of a Scotch tune in it, which is natural and pleasing, though not perfect. 'Tis true, I cannot go so far as he who published the last edition of him; for he would make us believe the fault is in our ears, and that there were really ten syllables in a verse where we find but nine: but this opinion is not worth confuting; 'tis so gross and obvious an error, that common sense (which is a rule in everything but matters of Faith and Revelation) must convince the reader, that equality of numbers in every verse which we call *heroic* was either not known, or not always practised, in Chaucer's age. It were an easy matter to produce some thousands of his verses which are lame for want of half a foot, and sometimes a whole one, and which no pronunciation can make otherwise. We can only say, that he lived in the infancy of our poetry, and that nothing is brought to perfection at the first. We must be children before we grow men. There was an Ennius, and in process of time a Lucilius, and a Lucretius, before Virgil and Horace; even after Chaucer there was a Spenser, a Harington, a Fairfax, before Waller and Denham were in being; and our numbers were in their nonage till these last appeared. I need say little of his parentage, life, and fortunes; they are to be found at large in all the editions of his works. He was employed abroad, and favoured, by Edward the Third, Richard the Second, and Henry the Fourth, and was poet, as I suppose, to all three of them. In Richard's time, I doubt, he was a little dipped in the rebellion of the Commons; and being brother-in-law to John of Gaunt, it was no wonder if he followed the fortunes of that family; and was well with Henry the Fourth when he had deposed his predecessor. Neither is it to be admired, that Henry, who was a wise as well as a valiant prince, who claimed by succession, and was sensible that his title was not sound, but was rightfully in Mortimer who had married the heir of York; it was not to be admired, I say, if that great politician should be pleased to have the greatest wit of those times in his interests, and to be the trumpet of his praises. Augustus had given him the example, by the advice of Maecenas, who recommended Virgil and Horace to him; whose praises helped to make him popular while he was alive, and after his death have made him precious to posterity. As for the religion of our poet, he seems to have some little bias towards the opinions of Wicliffe, after John of Gaunt his patron; somewhat of which appears in the tale of *Piers Plowman*: yet I cannot blame him for inveighing so sharply against the vices of the clergy in his age: their pride, their ambition, their pomp, their avarice, their worldly interest, deserved the lashes which he gave them, both in that, and in most of his *Canterbury Tales*. Neither has his contemporary Boccace spared them: yet both those poets lived in much esteem with good and holy men in orders; for the scandal which is given by particular priests reflects not on the sacred function. Chaucer's Monk, his Canon, and his Friar, took not from the character of his Good Parson. A satirical poet is the check of the laymen on bad priests. We are only to take care, that we involve not the innocent with the guilty in the same condemnation. The good cannot be too much honoured, nor the bad too coarsely used; for the corruption of the best becomes the worst. When a clergyman is whipped, his gown is first taken off, by which the dignity of his order is secured. If he be wrongfully accused, he has his action of slander; and 'tis at the poet's peril if he transgress the law. But they will tell us, that all kind of satire, though never so well deserved by particular priests, yet brings the whole order into contempt. Is then the peerage of England anything dishonoured when a peer suffers for his treason? If he be libelled, or any way defamed, he has his *scandalum magnatum* to punish the offender. They who use this kind of argument seem to be conscious to themselves of somewhat which has deserved the poet's lash, and are less concerned for their public capacity than for their private; at least there is pride at the bottom of their reasoning. If the faults of men in orders are only to be judged among themselves, they are all in some sort parties; for, since they say the honour of their order is concerned in every member of it, how can we be sure that they will be impartial judges? How far I may be allowed to speak my opinion in this case, I know not; but I am sure a dispute of this nature caused mischief in abundance betwixt a King of England and an Archbishop of Canterbury; one standing up for the laws of his land, and the other for the honour (as he called it) of God's Church; which ended in the murder of the prelate, and in the whipping of his Majesty from post to pillar for his penance. The learned and ingenious Dr. Drake has saved me the labour of inquiring into the esteem and reverence which the priests have had of old; and I would rather extend than diminish any part of it: yet I must needs say, that when a priest provokes me without any occasion given him, I have no reason, unless it be the charity of a Christian, to forgive him: *prior laesit* is justification sufficient in the civil law. If I answer him in his own language, self-defence I am sure must be allowed me; and if I carry it farther, even to a sharp recrimination, somewhat may be indulged to human frailty. Yet my resentment has not wrought so far but that I have followed Chaucer, in his character of a holy man, and have enlarged on that subject with some pleasure; reserving to myself the right, if I shall think fit hereafter, to describe another sort of priests, such as are more easily to be found than the Good Parson; such as have given the last blow to Christianity in this age, by a practice so contrary to their doctrine. But this will keep cold till another time. In the meanwhile, I take up Chaucer where I left him.

He must have been a man of a most wonderful comprehensive nature, because, as it has been truly observed of him, he has taken into the compass of his *Canterbury Tales* the various manners and humours (as we now call them) of the whole English nation in his age. Not a single character has escaped him. All his pilgrims are severally distinguished from each other; and not only in their inclinations, but in their very physiognomies and persons. Baptista Porta could not have described their natures better than by the marks which the poet gives them. The matter and manner of their tales, and of their telling, are so suited to their different educations, humours, and callings, that each of them would be improper in any other mouth. Even the grave and serious characters are distinguished by their several sorts of gravity; their discourses are such as belong to their age, their calling, and their breeding; such as are becoming of them, and of them only. Some of his persons are vicious, and some virtuous; some are unlearned, or (as Chaucer calls them) lewd, and some are learned. Even the ribaldry of the low characters is different: the Reeve, the Miller, and the Cook are several men, and distinguished from each other as much as the mincing Lady Prioress and the broad-speaking gap-toothed Wife of Bath. But enough of this; there is such a variety of game springing up before me that I am distracted in my choice, and know not which to follow. 'Tis sufficient to say, according to the proverb, that *here is God's plenty*. We have our forefathers and great-grand-dames all before us, as they were in Chaucer's days: their general characters are still remaining in mankind, and even in England, though they are called by other names than those of monks and friars and canons and lady abbesses and nuns: for mankind is ever the same, and nothing lost out of Nature, though everything is altered. May I have leave to do myself the justice (since my enemies will do me none, and are so far from granting me to be a good poet, that they will not allow me so much as to be a Christian, or a moral man), may I have leave, I say, to inform my reader, that I have confined my choice to such tales of Chaucer as savour nothing of immodesty. If I had desired more to please than to instruct, the Reeve, the Miller, the Shipman, the Merchant, the Sumner, and, above all, the Wife of Bath, in the Prologue to her Tale, would have procured me as many friends and readers, as there are beaux and ladies of pleasure in the town. But I will no more offend against good manners: I am sensible as I ought to be of the scandal I have given by my loose writings; and make what reparation I am able, by this public acknowledgement. If anything of this nature, or of profaneness, be crept into these poems, I am so far from defending it that I disown it. *Totum hoc indictum volo.* Chaucer makes another manner of apology for his broad speaking, and Boccace makes the like; but I will follow neither of them. Our countryman, in the end of his characters before the *Canterbury Tales*, thus excuses the ribaldry, which is very gross in many of his novels:

> *But firste, I pray you, of your courtesy,*
> *That ye ne arrete it not my villany,*
> *Though that I plainly speak in this mattere,*
> *To tellen you her words, and eke her chere:*
> *Ne though I speke her words properly,*
> *For this ye knowen as well as I,*

Who shall tellen a tale after a man,
He mote rehearse as nye as ever he can:
Everich word of it ben in his charge,
All speke he, never so rudely, ne **large:**
Or else he mote tellen his tale untrue,
Or feine things, or find words new:
He may not spare, altho he were his brother
He mote as wel say o word as another.
Crist spake himself ful broad in holy Writ,
And well I wote no villany is it,
Eke Plato saith, who so can him rede,
The words mote been cousin to the dede.

Yet if a man should have inquired of Boccace or
of Chaucer, what need they had of introducing such
characters, where obscene words were proper in their
mouths, but very indecent to be heard; I know not
what answer they could have made; for that reason
such tales shall be left untold by me. You have here
a specimen of Chaucer's language, which is so obsolete
that his sense is scarce to be understood; and you
have likewise more than one example of his unequal
numbers, which were mentioned before. Yet many
of his verses consist of ten syllables, and the words not
much behind our present English: as for example,
these two lines, in the description of the carpenter's
young wife:

Wincing she was, as is a jolly colt,
Long as a mast, and upright as a bolt.

I have almost done with Chaucer, when I have
answered some objections relating to my present work.
I find some people are offended that I have turned
these tales into modern English; because they think
them unworthy of my pains, and look on Chaucer
as a dry, old-fashioned wit, not worth reviving. I
have often heard the late Earl of Leicester say that
Mr. Cowley himself was of that opinion; who, having
read him over at my lord's request, declared he had
no taste of him. I dare not advance my opinion
against the judgement of so great an author; but I

think it fair, however, to leave the decision to the public. Mr. Cowley was too modest to set up for a dictator; and being shocked perhaps with his old style, never examined into the depth of his good sense. Chaucer, I confess, is a rough diamond, and must first be polished ere he shines. I deny not likewise, that, living in our early days of poetry, he writes not always of a piece; but sometimes mingles trivial things with those of greater moment. Sometimes also, though not often, he runs riot like Ovid, and knows not when he has said enough. But there are more great wits besides Chaucer whose fault is their excess of conceits, and those ill sorted. An author is not to write all he can, but only all he ought. Having observed this redundancy in Chaucer (as it is an easy matter for a man of ordinary parts to find a fault in one of greater), I have not tied myself to a literal translation; but have often omitted what I judged unnecessary, or not of dignity enough to appear in the company of better thoughts. I have presumed further, in some places, and added somewhat of my own where I thought my author was deficient, and had not given his thoughts their true lustre, for want of words in the beginning of our language. And to this I was the more emboldened, because (if I may be permitted to say it of myself) I found I had a soul congenial to his, and that I had been conversant in the same studies. Another poet, in another age, may take the same liberty with my writings; if at least they live long enough to deserve correction. It was also necessary sometimes to restore the sense of Chaucer, which was lost or mangled in the errors of the press. Let this example suffice at present: in the story of *Palamon and Arcite*, where the temple of Diana is described, you find these verses, in all the editions of our author:

> *There saw I* Danè *turned into a tree,*
> *I mean not the goddess* Diane,
> *But* Venus *daughter, which that hight* Danè.

Which, after a little consideration, I knew was to be reformed into this sense, that *Daphne*, the daughter of Peneus, was turned into a tree. I durst not make thus bold with Ovid, lest some future Milbourne should arise, and say, I varied from my author because I understood him not.

But there are other judges, who think I ought not to have translated Chaucer into English, out of a quite contrary notion: they suppose there is a certain veneration due to his old language; and that it is little less than profanation and sacrilege to alter it. They are further of opinion, that somewhat of his good sense will suffer in this transfusion, and much of the beauty of his thoughts will infallibly be lost, which appear with more grace in their old habit. Of this opinion was that excellent person whom I mentioned, the late Earl of Leicester, who valued Chaucer as much as Mr. Cowley despised him. My lord dissuaded me from this attempt (for I was thinking of it some years before his death), and his authority prevailed so far with me, as to defer my undertaking while he lived, in deference to him: yet my reason was not convinced with what he urged against it. If the first end of a writer be to be understood, then, as his language grows obsolete, his thoughts must grow obscure:

> *Multa renascentur, quae nunc cecidere; cadentque*
> *Quae nunc sunt in honore vocabula, si volet usus,*
> *Quem penes arbitrium est et ius et norma loquendi.*

When an ancient word, for its sound and significancy, deserves to be revived, I have that reasonable veneration for antiquity to restore it. All beyond this is superstition. Words are not like landmarks, so sacred as never to be removed; customs are changed, and even statutes are silently repealed, when the reason ceases for which they were enacted. As for the other part of the argument, that his thoughts will lose of their original beauty by the innovation of words; in the first place, not only their beauty but their being is lost where they are no longer understood, which is the present case. I grant that something must be lost in all transfusion, that is, in all translations; but the sense will remain, which would otherwise be lost, or at least be maimed, when it is scarce intelligible, and that but to a few. How few are there, who can read Chaucer so as to understand him perfectly? And if imperfectly, then with less profit, and no pleasure. It is not for the use of some old Saxon friends that I have taken these pains with him: let them neglect my version, because they have no need of it. I made it for their sakes who understand sense and poetry as well as they, when that poetry and sense is put into words which they understand. I will go farther, and dare to add, that what beauties I lose in some places, I give to others which had them not originally: but in this I may be partial to myself; let the reader judge, and I submit to his decision. Yet I think I have just occasion to complain of them, who, because they understand Chaucer, would deprive the greater part of their countrymen of the same advantage, and hoard him up, as misers do their grandam gold, only to look on it themselves, and hinder others from making use of it. In sum, I seriously protest that no man ever had, or can have, a greater veneration for Chaucer than myself. I have translated some part of his works, only that I might perpetuate his memory, or at least refresh it, amongst my countrymen. If I have altered him anywhere for the better, I must at the same time acknowledge that I could have done nothing without him. *Facile est inventis addere* is no great commendation; and I am not so vain to think I have deserved a greater. I will conclude what I have to say of him singly, with this one remark: a lady of my acquaintance, who keeps a kind of correspondence with some authors of the fair sex in France, has been informed by them, that Mademoiselle de Scudéry, who is as old as Sibyl, and inspired like her by the same god of poetry, is at this time translating Chaucer into modern French. From which I gather, that he has been formerly translated into the old Provençal; for how she should come to understand old English, I know not. But the matter of fact being true, it makes me think that there is something in it like fatality; that, after certain periods of time, the fame and memory of great wits should be renewed, as Chaucer is both in France and England. If this be wholly chance, 'tis extraordinary; and I dare not call it more, for fear of being taxed with superstition.

Boccace comes last to be considered, who, living in the same age with Chaucer, had the same genius, and followed the same studies. Both writ novels, and each of them cultivated his mother tongue. But the greatest resemblance of our two modern authors being in their familiar style and pleasing way of relating comical adventures, I may pass it over, because I have translated nothing from Boccace of that nature. In the serious part of poetry, the advantage is wholly on Chaucer's side; for though the Englishman has borrowed many tales from the Italian, yet it appears that those of Boccace were not generally of his own making, but taken from authors of former ages, and by him only modelled; so that what there was of invention in either of them may be judged equal. But Chaucer has refined on Boccace, and has mended the stories, which he has borrowed, in his way of telling; though prose allows more liberty of thought, and the expression is more easy when unconfined by numbers. Our countryman carries weight, and yet wins the race at disadvantage. I desire not the reader should take my word; and, therefore, I will set two of their discourses, on the same subject, in the same light, for every man to judge betwixt them. I translated Chaucer first, and, amongst the rest, pitched on *The Wife of Bath's Tale*; not daring, as I have said, to adventure on her Prologue, because 'tis too licentious. There Chaucer introduces an old woman, of mean parentage, whom a youthful knight of noble blood was forced to marry, and consequently loathed her. The crone being in bed with him on the wedding-night, and finding his aversion, endeavours to win his affection by reason, and speaks a good word for herself (as who could blame her?) in hope to mollify the sullen bridegroom. She takes her topics from the benefits of poverty, the advantages of old age and ugliness, the vanity of youth, and the silly pride of ancestry and titles without inherent virtue, which is the true nobility. When I had closed Chaucer, I returned to Ovid, and translated some more of his fables; and, by this time, had so far forgotten *The Wife of Bath's Tale*, that when I took up Boccace, unawares I fell on the same argument, of preferring virtue to nobility of blood and titles, in the story of *Sigismonda*; which I had certainly avoided for the resemblance of the two discourses, if my memory had not failed me. Let the reader weigh them both; and, if he thinks me partial to Chaucer, 'tis in him to right Boccace.

I prefer in our countryman, far above all his other stories, the noble poem of *Palamon and Arcite*, which is of the epic kind, and perhaps not much inferior to the *Ilias* or the *Æneis*. The story is more pleasing than either of them, the manners as perfect, the diction as poetical, the learning as deep and various, and the disposition full as artful: only it includes a greater length of time, as taking up seven years at least; but Aristotle has left undecided the duration of the action; which yet is easily reduced into the compass of a year by a narration of what preceded the return of Palamon to Athens. I had thought, for the honour of our narration, and more particularly for his, whose laurel, though unworthy, I have worn after him, that this story was of English growth, and Chaucer's own: but I was undeceived by Boccace; for, casually looking on the end of his seventh *Giornata*, I found Dioneo (under which name he shadows himself), and Fiametta (who represents his mistress, the natural daughter of Robert, King of Naples), of whom these words are spoken: *Dioneo e Fiametta gran pezza cantarono insieme d'Arcita, e di Palemone*; by which it appears, that this story was written before the time of Boccace; but the name of its author being wholly lost, Chaucer is now become an original; and I question not but the poem has received many beauties by passing through his noble hands. Besides this tale, there is another of his own invention after the manner of the Provençals, called *The Flower and the Leaf*, with which I was so particularly pleased, both for the invention and the moral, that I cannot hinder myself from recommending it to the reader.

As a corollary to this preface, in which I have done justice to others, I owe somewhat to myself; not that I think it worth my time to enter the lists with one Milbourne and one Blackmore, but barely to take notice, that such men there are, who have written scurrilously against me, without any provocation. Milbourne, who is in orders, pretends, amongst the rest, this quarrel to me, that I have fallen foul on priesthood: if I have, I am only to ask pardon of good priests, and am afraid his part of the reparation will come to little. Let him be satisfied, that he shall not be able to force himself upon me for an adversary. I contemn him too much to enter into competition with him. His own translations of Virgil have answered his criticisms on mine. If (as they say he has declared in print) he prefers the version of Ogilby to mine, the world has made him the same compliment; for 'tis agreed on all hands that he writes even below Ogilby. That, you will say, is not easily to be done; but what cannot Milbourne bring about? I am satisfied, however, that while he and I live together, I shall not be thought the worst poet of the age. It looks as if I had desired him underhand to write so ill against me; but upon my honest word I have not

bribed him to do me service, and am wholly guiltless
of his pamphlet. 'Tis true I should be glad if I could
persuade him to continue his good offices, and write
such another critique on anything of mine; for I find,
by experience, he has a great stroke with the reader,
when he condemns any of my poems, to make the
world have a better opinion of them. He has taken
some pains with my poetry; but nobody will be persuaded to take the same with his. If I had taken to
the Church, as he affirms, but which was never in
my thoughts, I should have had more sense, if not
more grace, than to have turned myself out of my
benefice by writing libels on my parishioners. But
his account of my manners and my principles are of
a piece with his cavils and his poetry; and so I have
done with him for ever.

As for the City Bard, or Knight Physician, I hear
his quarrel to me is, that I was the author of *Absalom
and Achitophel*, which, he thinks, is a little hard on his
fanatic patrons in London.

But I will deal the more civilly with his two poems,
because nothing ill is to be spoken of the dead; and
therefore peace be to the *manes* of his *Arthurs*. I will
only say, that it was not for this noble knight that
I drew the plan of an epic poem on King Arthur, in
my preface to the translation of *Juvenal*. The guardian
angels of kingdoms were machines too ponderous for
him to manage; and therefore he rejected them, as
Dares did the whirl-bats of Eryx when they were
thrown before him by Entellus: yet from that preface
he plainly took his hint; for he began immediately
upon the story, though he had the baseness not to
acknowledge his benefactor, but instead of it, to
traduce me in a libel.

I shall say the less of Mr. Collier, because in many
things he has taxed me justly; and I have pleaded
guilty to all thoughts and expressions of mine which
can be truly argued of obscenity, profaneness, or
immorality, and retract them. If he be my enemy,

let him triumph; if he be my friend, as I have given him no personal occasion to be otherwise, he will be glad of my repentance. It becomes me not to draw my pen in the defence of a bad cause, when I have so often drawn it for a good one. Yet it were not difficult to prove that in many places he has perverted my meaning by his glosses, and interpreted my words into blasphemy and bawdry of which they were not guilty. Besides that, he is too much given to horse-play in his raillery, and comes to battle like a dictator from the plough. I will not say, *the zeal of God's house has eaten him up*; but I am sure it has devoured some part of his good manners and civility. It might also be doubted whether it were altogether zeal which prompted him to this rough manner of proceeding; perhaps it became not one of his function to rake into the rubbish of ancient and modern plays: a divine might have employed his pains to better purpose than in the nastiness of Plautus and Aristophanes, whose examples, as they excuse not me, so it might be possibly supposed that he read them not without some pleasure. They who have written commentaries on those poets, or on Horace, Juvenal, and Martial, have explained some vices, which, without their interpretation, had been unknown to modern times. Neither has he judged impartially betwixt the former age and us. There is more bawdry in one play of Fletcher's, called *The Custom of the Country*, than in all ours together. Yet this has been often acted on the stage in my remembrance. Are the times so much more reformed now than they were five-and-twenty years ago? If they are, I congratulate the amendment of our morals. But I am not to prejudice the cause of my fellow poets, though I abandon my own defence: they have some of them answered for themselves; and neither they nor I can think Mr. Collier so formidable an enemy, that we should shun him. He has lost ground, at the latter end of the day, by pursuing his point too far, like the Prince of Condé

at the battle of Senneph: from immoral plays to no
plays, *ab abusu ad usum, non valet consequentia.* But,
being a party, I am not to erect myself into a judge.
As for the rest of those who have written against me,
they are such scoundrels that they deserve not the
least notice to be taken of them. Blackmore and
Milbourne are only distinguished from the crowd
by being remembered to their infamy:

> ... *Demetri, teque, Tigelli,*
> *Discipulorum inter jubeo plorare cathedras.*

JOHN DENNIS

From *THE ADVANCEMENT AND REFORMA-
TION OF MODERN POETRY* (Chapters IV–VI)

[1701]

*That the ancient Poets derived their greatness from the nature
of their subjects.*

IF the ancient poets excelled the moderns in the
greatness of poetry, that is, in epic poetry, in
tragedy, and in the greater ode, they must necessarily
derive their pre-eminence from the subjects of which
they treated, since it has been plainly made to appear
that they could not derive it from any external or
internal advantage. And it follows, that the subjects
which were handled by the ancients must be different
from those which have been treated of by the moderns.
And if the poems which have been written by the
ancients of the forementioned kinds were very much
greater than those which have been produced by the
moderns, why then it follows that the subjects were
very different. But here the favourers of the moderns
assert that the advantage which is to be drawn from
the subject is purely on the side of the moderns. For
who, for example, will compare the achievements of
Achilles and Aeneas, the event of which was only the
reducing two pitiful paltry bourgs with the glorious
actions of some of our modern captains. But then the
partisans of the ancients reply that there is a difference between one subject and another, which their
adversaries seem not to have thought of. For, say
they, human subjects can never differ so much among
themselves as sacred subjects differ from human, for
the difference between the two last is as great as that
between God and Man, which we know is infinite.
Now, say they, sacred subjects are infinitely more

susceptible of the greatness of poetry than profane
ones can be. And the subjects of the ancients in the
forementioned poems were sacred. Now that we may
engage the lovers of the ancients in their turns by
supporting their just pretensions, let us endeavour to
show in the following chapters that sacred poems
must be greater than profane ones can be, supposing
equality of genius and equal art in the writers, and
that the poems of the ancients in the forementioned
kinds were sacred. But in order to the doing that,
we must declare what poetry is and what is its chief
excellence.

*That passion is the chief thing in poetry and that all passion
is either ordinary passion or enthusiasm.*

But, before we proceed, let us define poetry; which
is the first time that a definition has been given of
that noble art; for neither ancient nor modern critics
have defined poetry in general.

Poetry, then, is an imitation of Nature by a pathetic
and numerous speech. Let us explain it.

As poetry is an art, it must be an imitation of
Nature. That the instrument with which it makes
its imitation is speech need not be disputed. That
that speech must be musical no one can doubt: for
numbers distinguish the parts of poetic diction from
the periods of prose. Now numbers are nothing but
articulate sounds, and their pauses measured by their
proper proportions of time. And the periods of prosaic diction are articulate sounds, and their pauses
unmeasured by such proportions. That the speech
by which poetry makes its imitation must be pathetic
is evident, for passion is still more necessary to it than
harmony. For harmony only distinguishes its instrument from that of prose, but passion distinguishes its
very nature and character. For therefore poetry is
poetry, because it is more passionate and sensual than
prose. A discourse that is written in very good

numbers, if it wants passion, can be but measured prose. But a discourse that is everywhere extremely pathetic, and consequently everywhere bold and figurative, is certainly poetry without numbers.

Passion, then, is the characteristical mark of poetry, and consequently must be everywhere. For wherever a discourse is not pathetic, there it is prosaic. As passion in a poem must be everywhere, so harmony is usually diffused throughout it. But passion answers the two ends of poetry better than harmony can do, and upon that account is preferable to it: for first it pleases more, which is evident: for passion can please without harmony, but harmony tires without passion. And in tragedy and in epic poetry a man may instruct without harmony, but never without passion: for the one instructs by admiration, and the other by compassion and terror. And as for the greater ode, if it wants passion, it becomes hateful and intolerable, and its sentences grow contemptible.

Passion is the characteristical mark of poetry, and therefore it must be everywhere; for without passion there can be no poetry, no more than there can be painting. And though the Poet and the Painter describe action, they must describe it with passion. Let any one who beholds a piece of painting, where the figures are shown in action, conclude that if the figures are without passion the painting is contemptible. There must be passion everywhere in poetry and painting, and the more passion there is, the better the poetry and the painting, unless the passion is too much for the subject; and the Painter and the Poet arrive at the height of their art when they describe a great deal of action with a great deal of passion. It is plain, then, from what has been said, that passion in poetry must be everywhere, for where there is no passion there can be no poetry, but that which we commonly call passion cannot be everywhere in any poem. There must be passion, then, that must be distinct from ordinary passion, and that must be enthusiasm. I call that ordinary passion, whose cause is clearly comprehended by him who feels it, whether it be admiration, terror, or joy; and I call the very same passions enthusiasms, when their cause is not clearly comprehended by him who feels them. And those enthusiastic passions are sometimes simple, and sometimes complicated, of all which we shall show examples lower. And thus I have shown that the chief thing in poetry is passion; but here the reader is desired to observe, that by poetry we mean poetry in general, and the body of poetry; for as for the form or soul of particular poems, that is allowed by all to be a fable. But passion is the chief thing in the body of poetry, as spirit is in the human body. For without spirit the body languishes, and the soul is impotent: now everything that they call spirit or genius in poetry, in short, everything that pleases, and consequently moves in the poetic diction, is passion, whether it be ordinary or enthusiastic.

And thus we have shown what the chief excellence in the body of poetry is, which we have proved to be passion. Let us now proceed to the proofs of what we propounded, that sacred subjects are more susceptible of passion than profane ones, and that the subjects of the ancients were sacred in their greater poetry—I mean either sacred in their own natures, or by their manner of handling them.

That passion is more to be derived from a sacred subject than from a profane one.

We have proved that passion is the chief thing in poetry, and that spirit or genius, and in short everything that moves, is passion. Now if the chief thing in poetry be passion, why, then, the chief thing in great poetry must be great passion. We have shown, too, that passion in poetry is of two sorts, ordinary passion or enthusiasm. Let us now proceed to convince the reader that a sacred poem is more susceptible of passion than a profane one can be; which to effect, let us show two things, that a sacred subject is as susceptible of ordinary passions as a profane one can be, and more susceptible of the enthusiastic.

The first is evident from experience: for the poetry among the ancients which shall be hereafter proved to be sacred, had in it greater ordinary passions than their human poetry either had or could possibly have.

'Tis now our business to show that religious subjects are capable of supplying us with more frequent and stronger enthusiasms than the profane. And in order to the clearing this, let us inquire what poetical enthusiasm is. Poetical enthusiasm is a passion guided by judgement, whose cause is not comprehended by us. That it is a passion is plain, because it moves. That the cause is not comprehended is self-evident. That it ought to be guided by judgement is indubitable. For otherwise it would be madness, and not poetical passion. But now let us inquire what the cause of poetical enthusiasm is, that has been hitherto not comprehended by us. That enthusiasm moves, is plain to sense; why, then, it moved the writer: but if it moved the writer, it moved him while he was thinking. Now what can move a man while he is thinking but the thoughts that are in his mind? In short, enthusiasm as well as ordinary passions must proceed from the thoughts, as the passions of all reasonable creatures must certainly do; but the reason why we know not the causes of enthusiastic as well as of ordinary passions, is because we are not so used to them, and because they proceed from thoughts, that latently and unobserved by us carry passion along with them. Here it would be no hard matter to prove that most of our thoughts are naturally attended with some sort and some degree of passion. And 'tis the expression of this passion which gives us so much pleasure, both in conversation and in human authors. For I appeal to any man who is not altogether a philosopher, whether he is not most pleased with conversation and books that are spirited. Now how can this spirit please him, but because it moves him, or what can move him but passion? We never speak for so much as a minute together without different inflexions of voice. Now any one will find upon reflection that these variations and those inflexions mark our different passions. But all this passes unregarded by us, by reason of long use, and the incredible celerity of our thoughts, whose motion is so swift that it is even to ourselves imperceptible; unless we come to reflect, and every one will not be at the trouble of that. Now these passions, when they grow strong, I call enthusiastic motions, and the stronger they are the greater the enthusiasm must be. If any one asks what sort of passions these are, that thus unknown to us flow from these thoughts, to him I answer, that the same sort of passions flow from the thoughts that would do from the things of which those thoughts are ideas. As for example, if the thing that we think of is great, why, then, admiration attends the idea of it; and if it is very great, amazement. If the thing is pleasing and delightful, why then joy and gaiety flow from the idea of it; if it is sad, melancholy; if it is mischievous and powerful, then the imagination of it is attended with terror; and if 'tis both great and likely to do hurt and powerful, why then the thought of it is at once accompanied with wonder, terror, and astonishment. Add to all this that the mind producing these thoughts conceives by reflection a certain pride and joy and admiration, as at the conscious view of its own excellence.

Now he who strictly examines the enthusiasm that is to be met with in the greater poetry will find that it is nothing but the fore-mentioned passions, either simple or complicated, proceeding from the thoughts from which they naturally flow, as being the thoughts or images of things that carry those passions along with them, as we shall show by examples in the following chapter.

But these passions that attend upon our thoughts are seldom so strong as they are in those kind of thoughts which we call images. For they, being the very lively pictures of the things which they represent, set them, as it were, before our very eyes. But images are never so admirably drawn as when they are drawn in motion; especially if the motion is violent. For the mind can never imagine violent motion without being in a violent agitation itself; and the imagination being fired with that agitation sets the very things before our eyes, and consequently makes us have the same passions that we should have from the things themselves. For the warmer the imagination is, the more present the things are to us of which we draw the images; and, therefore, when once the imagination is so inflamed as to get the better of the understanding, there is no difference between the images and the things themselves; as we see, for example, in fears and madmen.

Thus have we shown that enthusiasm flows from the thoughts, and consequently from the subject from which the thoughts proceed. For, as the spirit in poetry is to be proportioned to the thought—for otherwise it does not naturally flow from it, and consequently is not guided by judgement—so the thought is to be proportioned to the subject. Now no subject is so capable of supplying us with thoughts that necessarily produce these great and strong enthusiasms as a religious subject: for all which is great in religion is most exalted and amazing, all that is joyful is transporting, all that is sad is dismal, and all that is terrible is astonishing.

ALEXANDER POPE

AN ESSAY ON CRITICISM

[1711]

I

'TIS hard to say if greater want of skill
  Appear in writing or in judging ill;
But of the two, less dang'rous is th' offence
To tire our patience than mislead our sense.
Some few in that, but numbers err in this,
Ten censure wrong for one who writes amiss;
A fool might once himself alone expose,
Now one in verse makes many more in prose.
  'Tis with our judgements as our watches, none
Go just alike, yet each believes his own.
In poets as true genius is but rare,
True taste as seldom is the critic's share;
Both must alike from heav'n derive their light,
These born to judge, as well as those to write.
Let such teach others who themselves excel,
And censure freely who have written well.
Authors are partial to their wit, 'tis true,
But are not critics to their judgement too?
  Yet if we look more closely, we shall find
Most have the seeds of judgement in their mind;
Nature affords at least a glimm'ring light;
The lines, tho' touch'd but faintly, are drawn right.
But as the slightest sketch, if justly trac'd,
Is by ill colouring but the more disgrac'd,
So by false learning is good sense defac'd:
Some are bewilder'd in the maze of schools,
And some made coxcombs Nature meant but fools.
In search of wit these lose their common sense,
And then turn critics in their own defence.
Each burns alike, who can or cannot write,
Or with a rival's or a eunuch's spite.

All fools have still an itching to deride,
And fain would be upon the laughing side.
If Maevius scribble in Apollo's spite,
There are who judge still worse than he can write.

Some have at first for wits, then poets passed,
Turn'd critics next, and prov'd plain fools at last.
Some neither can for wits nor critics pass,
As heavy mules are neither horse nor ass.
Those half-learn'd witlings, num'rous in our isle,
As half-form'd insects on the banks of Nile;
Unfinish'd things, one knows not what to call,
Their generation's so equivocal:
To tell 'em would a hundred tongues require,
Or one vain wit's, that might a hundred tire.

But you who seek to give and merit fame,
And justly bear a critic's noble name,
Be sure yourself and your own reach to know,
How far your genius, taste, and learning go;
Launch not beyond your depth, but be discreet,
And mark that point where sense and dullness meet.

Nature to all things fix'd the limits fit,
And wisely curb'd proud man's pretending wit.
As on the land while here the ocean gains,
In other parts it leaves wide sandy plains;
Thus in the soul while memory prevails,
The solid power of understanding fails;
Where beams of warm imagination play,
The memory's soft figures melt away.
One science only will one genius fit;
So vast is art, so narrow human wit:
Not only bounded to peculiar arts,
But oft in those confin'd to single parts.
Like kings we lose the conquests gain'd before,
By vain ambition still to make them more:
Each might his sev'ral province well command,
Would all but stoop to what they understand.

First follow NATURE, and your judgement frame
By her just standard, which is still the same:
Unerring Nature, still divinely bright,

One clear, unchang'd, and universal light,
Life, force, and beauty, must to all impart,
At once the source, and end, and test of art.
Art from that fund each just supply provides,
Works without show, and without pomp presides:
In some fair body thus th' informing soul
With spirits feeds, with vigour fills the whole,
Each motion guides, and ev'ry nerve sustains;
Itself unseen, but in th' effects, remains.
Some, to whom heav'n in wit has been profuse,
Want as much more, to turn it to its use;
For wit and judgement often are at strife,
Tho' meant each other's aid, like man and wife.
'Tis more to guide, than spur the Muse's steed;
Restrain his fury, than provoke his speed;
The winged courser, like a gen'rous horse,
Shows most true mettle when you check his course.

Those RULES of old discover'd, not devis'd,
Are Nature still, but Nature methodiz'd;
Nature, like liberty, is but restrain'd
By the same laws which first herself ordain'd.

Hear how learn'd Greece her useful rules indites,
When to repress, and when indulge our flights:
High on Parnassus' top her sons she show'd,
And pointed out those arduous paths they trod;
Held from afar, aloft, th' immortal prize,
And urged the rest by equal steps to rise.
Just precepts thus from great examples giv'n,
She drew from them what they deriv'd from heav'n.
The gen'rous critic fann'd the poet's fire,
And taught the world with reason to admire.
Then criticism the Muse's handmaid prov'd,
To dress her charms, and make her more belov'd:
But following wits from that intention stray'd;
Who could not win the mistress, woo'd the maid;
Against the poets their own arms they turn'd,
Sure to hate most the men from whom they learn'd.
So modern 'pothecaries, taught the art
By doctor's bills to play the doctor's part,

Bold in the practice of mistaken rules,
Prescribe, apply, and call their masters fools.
Some on the leaves of ancient authors prey;
Nor time nor moths e'er spoil'd so much as they:
Some drily plain, without invention's aid,
Write dull receipts how poems may be made.
These leave the sense, their learning to display,
And those explain the meaning quite away.

   You then whose judgement the right course would
      steer,
Know well each ANCIENT's proper character;
His fable, subject, scope in ev'ry page;
Religion, country, genius of his age:
Without all these at once before your eyes,
Cavil you may, but never criticize.
Be Homer's works your study and delight,
Read them by day, and meditate by night;
Thence form your judgement, thence your maxims
      bring,
And trace the Muses upward to their spring;
Still with itself compar'd, his text peruse;
And let your comment be the Mantuan Muse.

   When first young Maro in his boundless mind
A work t' outlast immortal Rome design'd,
Perhaps he seem'd above the critic's law,
And but from Nature's fountains scorn'd to draw:
But when t' examine ev'ry part he came,
Nature and Homer were, he found, the same.
Convinc'd, amaz'd, he checks the bold design;
And rules as strict his labour'd work confine,
As if the Stagirite o'erlook'd each line.
Learn hence for ancient rules a just esteem;
To copy Nature is to copy them.

   Some beauties yet no precepts can declare,
For there's a happiness as well as care.
Music resembles poetry; in each
Are nameless graces which no methods teach,
And which a master-hand alone can reach.
If, where the rules not far enough extend

(Since rules were made but to promote their end),
Some lucky Licence answer to the full
Th' intent propos'd, that licence is a rule.
Thus Pegasus, a nearer way to take,
May boldly deviate from the common track.
Great wits sometimes may gloriously offend
And rise to faults true critics dare not mend;
From vulgar bounds with brave disorder part,
And snatch a grace beyond the reach of art,
Which, without passing thro' the judgement, gains
The heart, and all its end at once attains.
In prospects thus, some objects please our eyes,
Which out of Nature's common order rise,
The shapeless rock, or hanging precipice.
But tho' the ancients thus their rules invade
(As kings dispense with laws themselves have made),
Moderns, beware! Or if you must offend
Against the precept, ne'er transgress its end;
Let it be seldom, and compell'd by need;
And have, at least, their precedent to plead.
The critic else proceeds without remorse,
Seizes your fame, and puts his laws in force.

   I know there are to whose presumptuous thoughts
Those freer beauties, ev'n in them, seem faults.
Some figures monstrous and mis-shap'd appear,
Consider'd singly, or beheld too near,
Which, but proportion'd to their light, or place,
Due distance reconciles to form and grace.
A prudent chief not always must display
His pow'rs in equal ranks, and fair array,
But with th' occasion and the place comply,
Conceal his force, may seem sometimes to fly.
Those oft are stratagems which errors seem,
Nor is it Homer nods, but we that dream.

   Still green with bays each ancient altar stands,
Above the reach of sacrilegious hands;
Secure from flames, from envy's fiercer rage,
Destructive war, and all-involving age.
See, from each clime the learn'd their incense bring!

Hear, in all tongues consenting paeans ring!
In praise so just let ev'ry voice be join'd,
And fill the gen'ral chorus of mankind!
Hail, bards triumphant! born in happier days;
Immortal heirs of universal praise!
Whose honours with increase of ages grow,
As streams roll down, enlarging as they flow;
Nations unborn your mighty names shall sound,
And worlds applaud that must not yet be found!
Oh may some spark of your celestial fire,
The last, the meanest of your sons inspire
(That on weak wings, from far, pursues your flights,
Glows while he reads, but trembles as he writes)
To teach vain wits a science little known,
T' admire superior sense, and doubt their own!

II

Of all the causes which conspire to blind
Man's erring judgement, and misguide the mind,
What the weak head with strongest bias rules,
Is pride, the never-failing vice of fools.
Whatever Nature has in worth denied,
She gives in large recruits of needful pride;
For as in bodies, thus in souls, we find
What wants in blood and spirits, swell'd with wind:
Pride, where wit fails, steps in to our defence,
And fills up all the mighty void of sense.
If once right reason drives that cloud away
Truth breaks upon us with resistless day.
Trust not your self; but your defects to know,
Make use of ev'ry friend—and ev'ry foe.
  A little learning is a dang'rous thing;
Drink deep, or taste not the Pierian spring:
There shallow draughts intoxicate the brain,
And drinking largely sobers us again.
Fir'd at first sight with what the Muse imparts,
In fearless youth we tempt the heights of Arts,
While from the bounded level of our mind

Short views we take, nor see the lengths behind;
But more advanc'd, behold with strange surprise
New distant scenes of endless science rise!
So pleas'd at first the tow'ring Alps we try,
Mount o'er the vales, and seem to tread the sky,
Th' eternal snows appear already past,
And the first clouds and mountains seem the last:
But those attain'd, we tremble to survey
The growing labours of the lengthen'd way,
Th' increasing prospect tires our wand'ring eyes,
Hills peep o'er hills, and Alps on Alps arise!
    A perfect judge will read each work of wit
With the same spirit that its author writ:
Survey the whole, nor seek slight faults to find
Where Nature moves, and rapture warms the mind;
Nor lose, for that malignant dull delight,
The gen'rous pleasure to be charm'd with wit.
But in such lays as neither ebb, nor flow,
Correctly cold, and regularly low,
That shunning faults one quiet tenor keep;
We cannot blame indeed—but we may sleep.
In wit, as nature, what affects our hearts
Is not th' exactness of peculiar parts;
'Tis not a lip, or eye, we beauty call,
But the joint force and full result of all.
Thus when we view some well-proportion'd dome
(The world's just wonder, and ev'n thine, O Rome!),
No single parts unequally surprise,
All comes united to th' admiring eyes;
No monstrous height, or breadth, or length appear;
The whole at once is bold, and regular.
    Whoever thinks a faultless piece to see,
Thinks what ne'er was, nor is, nor e'er shall be.
In ev'ry work regard the writer's end,
Since none can compass more than they intend;
And if the means be just, the conduct true,
Applause, in spite of trivial faults, is due;
As men of breeding, sometimes men of wit,
T' avoid great errors, must the less commit:

Neglect the rules each verbal critic lays,
For not to know some trifles, is a praise.
Most critics, fond of some subservient art,
Still make the whole depend upon a part:
They talk of principles, but notions prize,
And all to one lov'd folly sacrifice.

Once on a time, La Mancha's knight, they say,
A certain bard encount'ring on the way,
Discours'd in terms as just, with looks as sage,
As e'er could Dennis, of the Grecian stage;
Concluding all were desp'rate sots and fools,
Who durst depart from Aristotle's rules.
Our author, happy in a judge so nice,
Produc'd his play, and begg'd the knight's advice;
Made him observe the subject, and the plot,
The manners, passions, unities; what not?
All which, exact to rule, were brought about,
Were but a combat in the lists left out.
'What! leave the combat out?' exclaims the knight.
Yes, or we must renounce the Stagirite.
'Not so, by Heav'n' (he answers in a rage),
'Knights, squires, and steeds, must enter on the stage.'
So vast a throng the stage can ne'er contain.
'Then build a new, or act it in a plain.'

Thus critics, of less judgement than caprice,
Curious, not knowing, not exact but nice,
Form short ideas; and offend in arts
(As most in manners) by a love to parts.

Some to *conceit* alone their taste confine,
And glitt'ring thoughts struck out at ev'ry line;
Pleas'd with a work where nothing's just or fit,
One glaring chaos and wild heap of wit.
Poets, like painters, thus unskill'd to trace
The naked nature and the living grace,
With gold and jewels cover ev'ry part,
And hide with ornaments their want of art.
True wit is Nature to advantage dressed,
What oft was thought, but ne'er so well expressed;
Something, whose truth convinc'd at sight we find,

That gives us back the image of our mind.
As shades more sweetly recommend the light,
So modest plainness sets off sprightly wit.
For works may have more wit than does 'em good,
As bodies perish through excess of blood,

Others for *language* all their care express,
And value books, as women men, for dress:
Their praise is still—the style is excellent;
The sense, they humbly take upon content.
Words are like leaves; and where they most abound,
Much fruit of sense beneath is rarely found.
False eloquence, like the prismatic glass,
Its gaudy colours spreads on ev'ry place;
The face of Nature we no more survey,
All glares alike, without distinction gay:
But true expression, like th' unchanging sun,
Clears and improves whate'er it shines upon,
It gilds all objects but it alters none.
Expression is the dress of thought, and still
Appears more decent, as more suitable;
A vile conceit in pompous words expressed
Is like a clown in regal purple dressed:
For diff'rent styles with diff'rent subjects sort,
As several garbs with country, town, and court.
Some by old words to fame have made pretence,
Ancients in phrase, mere moderns in their sense;
Such labour'd nothings, in so strange a style,
Amaze th' unlearn'd, and make the learned smile.
Unlucky, as Fungoso in the play,
These sparks with awkward vanity display
What the fine gentleman wore yesterday!
And but so mimic ancient wits at best,
As apes our grandsires, in their doublets dressed.
In words, as fashions, the same rule will hold,
Alike fantastic, if too new, or old:
Be not the first by whom the new are tried,
Nor yet the last to lay the old aside.

But most by *numbers* judge a poet's song,
And smooth or rough, with them, is right or wrong:

In the bright Muse tho' thousand charms conspire,
Her voice is all these tuneful fools admire:
Who haunt Parnassus but to please their ear,
Not mend their minds; as some to church repair,
Not for the doctrine, but the music there.
These equal syllables alone require,
Tho' oft the ear the open vowels tire;
While expletives their feeble aid do join,
And ten low words oft creep in one dull line:
While they ring round the same unvaried chimes,
With sure returns of still expected rhymes;
Where'er you find 'the cooling western breeze',
In the next line, it 'whispers thro' the trees':
If 'crystal streams with pleasing murmurs creep',
The reader's threaten'd (not in vain) with 'sleep':
Then, at the last and only couplet fraught
With some unmeaning thing they call a thought,
A needless Alexandrine ends the song,
That, like a wounded snake, drags its slow length
    along.
Leave such to tune their own dull rhymes, and know
What's roundly smooth or languishingly slow;
And praise the eager vigour of a line,
Where Denham's strength, and Waller's sweetness
    join.
True ease in writing comes from art, not chance,
As those move easiest who have learn'd to dance.
'Tis not enough no harshness gives offence.
The sound must seem an echo to the sense:
Soft is the strain when Zephyr gently blows,
And the smooth stream in smoother numbers flows;
But when loud surges lash the sounding shore,
The hoarse, rough verse should like the torrent roar:
When Ajax strives some rock's vast weight to throw,
The line too labours, and the words move slow;
Not so, when swift Camilla scours the plain,
Flies o'er th' unbending corn, and skims along the
    main.
Hear how Timotheus' varied lays surprise,

And bid alternate passions fall and rise!
While, at each change, the son of Libyan Jove
Now burns with glory, and then melts with love;
Now his fierce eyes with sparkling fury glow,
Now sighs steal out, and tears begin to flow:
Persians and Greeks like turns of nature found,
And the world's victor stood subdu'd by Sound!
The pow'r of music all our hearts allow,
And what Timotheus was, is Dryden now.

Avoid extremes; and shun the fault of such
Who still are pleas'd too little or too much.
At ev'ry trifle scorn to take offence,
That always shows great pride, or little sense;
Those heads, as stomachs, are not sure the best,
Which nauseate all, and nothing can digest.
Yet let not each gay turn thy rapture move;
For fools admire, but men of sense approve:
As things seem large which we thro' mists descry,
Dullness is ever apt to magnify.

Some foreign writers, some our own despise;
The ancients only, or the moderns prize.
Thus wit, like faith, by each man is applied
To one small sect, and all are damn'd beside.
Meanly they seek the blessing to confine,
And force that sun but on a part to shine,
Which not alone the southern wit sublimes,
But ripens spirits in cold northern climes;
Which from the first has shone on ages past,
Enlights the present, and shall warm the last;
(Tho' each may feel increases and decays,
And see now clearer and now darker days.)
Regard not then if wit be old or new,
But blame the false, and value still the true.

Some ne'er advance a judgement of their own,
But catch the spreading notion of the town;
They reason and conclude by precedent,
And own stale nonsense which they ne'er invent.
Some judge of authors' names, not works, and then
Nor praise nor blame the writings, but the men.

Of all this servile herd the worst is he
That in proud dulness joins with quality.
A constant critic at the great man's board,
To fetch and carry nonsense for my lord.
What woful stuff this madrigal would be,
In some starv'd hackney sonneteer or me!
But let a lord once own the happy lines,
How the wit brightens! How the style refines
Before his sacred name flies ev'ry fault,
And each exalted stanza teems with thought!

    The vulgar thus through imitation err;
As oft the learn'd by being singular;
So much they scorn the crowd, that if the throng
By chance go right, they purposely go wrong;
So schismatics the plain believers quit,
And are but damn'd for having too much wit.

    Some praise at morning what they blame at night;
But always think the last opinion right.
A Muse by these is like a mistress us'd,
This hour she's idoliz'd, the next abus'd;
While their weak heads like towns unfortified,
'Twixt sense and nonsense daily change their side.
Ask them the cause; they're wiser still, they say;
And still to-morrow's wiser than to-day.
We think our fathers fools, so wise we grow,
Our wiser sons, no doubt, will think us so.
Once school-divines this zealous isle o'erspread;
Who knew most 'sentences' was deepest read;
Faith, gospel, all, seem'd made to be disputed,
And none had sense enough to be confuted:
Scotists and Thomists now in peace remain,
Amidst their kindred cobwebs in Duck-Lane.
If faith itself has diff'rent dresses worn,
What wonder modes in wit should take their turn?
Oft, leaving what is natural and fit,
The current folly proves the ready wit;
And authors think their reputation safe,
Which lives as long as fools are pleas'd to laugh.

    Some valuing those of their own side or mind,

Still make themselves the measure of mankind:
Fondly we think we honour merit then,
When we but praise ourselves in other men.
Parties in wit attend on those of state,
And public faction doubles private hate.
Pride, malice, folly, against Dryden rose,
In various shapes of parsons, critics, beaux;
But sense surviv'd, when merry jests were past;
For rising merit will buoy up at last.
Might he return, and bless once more our eyes,
New Blackmores and new Milbourns must arise:
Nay should great Homer lift his awful head,
Zoilus again would start up from the dead.
Envy will merit, as its shade, pursue;
But like a shadow, proves the substance true;
For envied wit, like Sol eclips'd, makes known
Th' opposing body's grossness, not its own,
When first that sun too pow'rful beams displays,
It draws up vapours which obscure its rays;
But ev'n those clouds at last adorn its way,
Reflect new glories and augment the day.

Be thou the first true merit to befriend;
His praise is lost, who stays till all commend.
Short is the date, alas, of modern rhymes,
And 'tis but just to let 'em live betimes.
No longer now that golden age appears,
When patriarch-wits surviv'd a thousand years:
Now length of fame (our second life) is lost,
And bare threescore is all ev'n that can boast;
Our sons their fathers' failing language see,
And such as Chaucer is, shall Dryden be.
So when the faithful pencil has design'd
Some bright idea of the master's mind,
Where a new world leaps out at his command,
And ready nature waits upon his hand;
When the ripe colours soften and unite,
And sweetly melt into just shade and light;
When mellowing years their full perfection give,
And each bold figure just begins to live,

The treach'rous colours the fair art betray,
And all the bright creation fades away!
　Unhappy wit, like most mistaken things,
Atones not for that envy which it brings.
In youth alone its empty praise we boast,
But soon the short-liv'd vanity is lost:
Like some fair flow'r the early spring supplies,
That gaily blooms, but ev'n in blooming dies.
What is this wit, which must our cares employ?
The owner's wife, that other men enjoy;
Then most our trouble still when most admir'd,
And still the more we give, the more requir'd;
Whose fame with pains we guard, but lose with
　　ease,
Sure some to vex, but never all to please;
'Tis what the vicious fear, the virtuous shun,
By fools 'tis hated, and by knaves undone!
　If wit so much from ign'rance undergo,
Ah let not learning too commence its foe!
Of old, those met rewards who could excel,
And such were prais'd who but endeavour'd well:
Tho' triumphs were to gen'rals only due,
Crowns were reserv'd to grace the soldiers too.
Now, they who reach Parnassus' lofty crown,
Employ their pains to spurn some others down;
And while self-love each jealous writer rules,
Contending wits become the sport of fools:
But still the worst with most regret commend,
For each ill author is as bad a friend.
To what base ends, and by what abject ways,
Are mortals urg'd thro' sacred lust of praise!
Ah ne'er so dire a thirst of glory boast,
Nor in the critic let the man be lost!
Good-nature and good-sense must ever join;
To err is human, to forgive, divine.
　But if in noble minds some dregs remain,
Not yet purg'd off, of spleen and sour disdain;
Discharge that rage on more provoking crimes,
Nor fear a dearth in these flagitious times.

No pardon vile obscenity should find,
Tho' wit and art conspire to move your mind;
But dulness with obscenity must prove
As shameful, sure, as impotence in love.
In the fat age of pleasure, wealth, and ease,
Sprung the rank weed, and thriv'd with large in-
 crease:
When love was all an easy monarch's care,
Seldom at council, never in a war,
Jilts rul'd the state, and statesmen farces writ;
Nay, wits had pensions, and young lords had wit:
The fair sat panting at a courtier's play,
And not a mask went unimprov'd away:
The modest fan was lifted up no more,
And virgins smil'd at what they blush'd before.—
The following licence of a foreign reign
Did all the dregs of bold Socinus drain;
Then unbelieving priests reform'd the nation,
And taught more pleasant methods of salvation;
Where Heav'n's free subjects might their rights
 dispute,
Lest God himself should seem too absolute:
Pulpits their sacred satire learn'd to spare,
And Vice admir'd to find a flatt'rer there!
Encourag'd thus, Wit's Titans brav'd the skies,
And the press groan'd with licenc'd blasphemies.
These monsters, critics! with your darts engage,
Here point your thunder, and exhaust your rage!
Yet shun their fault, who, scandalously nice,
Will needs mistake an author into vice;
All seems infected that th' infected spy,
As all looks yellow to the jaundic'd eye.

III

 Learn then what morals critics ought to show,
For 'tis but half a judge's task, to know.
'Tis not enough, taste, judgement, learning, join;
In all you speak, let truth and candour shine:

That not alone what to your sense is due
All may allow; but seek your friendship too.
Be silent always when you doubt your sense;
And speak, tho' sure, with seeming diffidence:
Some positive, persisting fops we know,
Who, if once wrong, will needs be always so;
But you, with pleasure own your errors past,
And make each day a critique on the last.

　'Tis not enough, your counsel still be true;
Blunt truths more mischief than nice falsehoods **do;**
Men must be taught as if you taught them **not,**
And things unknown propos'd as things forgot.
Without good breeding, truth is disapprov'd:
That only makes superior sense belov'd.

　Be niggards of advice on no pretence;
For the worst avarice is that of sense.
With mean complacence ne'er betray your trust,
Nor be so civil as to prove unjust.
Fear not the anger of the wise to raise:
Those best can bear reproof, who merit praise.

　'Twere well might critics still this freedom **take,**
But Appius reddens at each word you speak,
And stares, tremendous, with a threat'ning **eye,**
Like some fierce tyrant in old tapestry.
Fear most to tax an honourable fool,
Whose right it is, uncensur'd, to be dull;
Such without wit are poets when they please,
As without learning they can take degrees.
Leave dang'rous truths to unsuccessful satires,
And flattery to fulsome dedicators,
Whom, when they praise, the world believes no **more**
Than when they promise to give scribbling o'er.
'Tis best sometimes your censure to restrain,
And charitably let the dull be vain:
Your silence there is better than your spite,
For who can rail so long as they can write?
Still humming on, their drowsy course they keep,
And lash'd so long, like tops, are lash'd asleep.
False steps but help them to renew the race,

As, after stumbling, jades will mend their pace.
What crowds of these, impenitently bold,
In sounds and jingling syllables grown old,
Still run on poets, in a raging vein,
Ev'n to the dregs and squeezings of the brain,
Strain out the last dull droppings of their sense,
And rhyme with all the rage of impotence!
    Such shameless bards we have; and yet 'tis true,
There are as mad, abandon'd critics too.
The bookful blockhead, ignorantly read,
With loads of learned lumber in his head,
With his own tongue still edifies his ears,
And always list'ning to himself appears.
All books he reads, and all he reads assails,
From Dryden's fables down to Durfy's tales.
With him, most authors steal their works, or buy;
Garth did not write his own *Dispensary*.
Name a new play, and he's the poet's friend,
Nay, show'd his faults—but when would poets mend?
No place so sacred from such fops is barr'd,
Nor is Paul's Church more safe than Paul's church-
    yard:
Nay, fly to altars; there they'll talk you dead:
For fools rush in where angels fear to tread.
Distrustful sense with modest caution speaks,
It still looks home, and short excursions makes;
But rattling nonsense in full volleys breaks,
And never shock'd, and never turn'd aside,
Bursts out, resistless, with a thund'ring tide!
    But where's the man who counsel can bestow,
Still pleas'd to teach, and yet not proud to know?
Unbiass'd or by favour, or by spite;
Not dully prepossess'd, nor blindly right;
Tho' learn'd, well-bred; and tho' well-bred, sincere,
Modestly bold, and humanly severe:
Who to a friend his faults can freely show,
And gladly praise the merit of a foe;
Blest with a taste exact, yet unconfin'd;
A knowledge both of books and humankind:

Gen'rous converse; a soul exempt from pride;
And love to praise, with reason on his side?

Such once were critics; such the happy few,
Athens and Rome in better ages knew.
The mighty Stagirite first left the shore,
Spread all his sails, and durst the deeps explore:
He steer'd securely, and discover'd far,
Led by the light of the Maeonian star.
Poets, a race long unconfin'd, and free,
Still fond and proud of savage liberty,
Received his laws; and stood convinc'd 'twas fit,
Who conquer'd Nature, should preside o'er Wit.

Horace still charms with graceful negligence,
And without method talks us into sense;
Will, like a friend, familiarly convey
The truest notions in the easiest way.
He, who supreme in judgement, as in wit,
Might boldly censure, as he boldly writ,
Yet judg'd with coolness, tho' he sung with fire;
His precepts teach but what his works inspire.
Our critics take a contrary extreme,
They judge with fury, but they write with phlegm:
Nor suffers Horace more in wrong translations
By wits, than critics in as wrong quotations.

See Dionysius Homer's thoughts refine,
And call new beauties forth from ev'ry line!

Fancy and art in gay Petronius please,
The scholar's learning, with the courtier's ease.

In grave Quintilian's copious work, we find
The justest rules, and clearest method join'd:
Thus useful arms in magazines we place,
All rang'd in order, and dispos'd with grace;
But less to please the eye, than arm the hand,
Still fit for use, and ready at command.

Thee, bold Longinus! all the Nine inspire,
And bless their critic with a poet's fire.
An ardent judge, who zealous in his trust,
With warmth gives sentence, yet is always just;
Whose own example strengthens all his laws;

And is himself that great sublime he draws.

Thus long succeeding critics justly reign'd,
Licence repress'd, and useful laws ordain'd.
Learning and Rome alike in empire grew;
And arts still follow'd where her eagles flew;
From the same foes, at last, both felt their doom,
And the same age saw learning fall, and Rome.
With tyranny then superstition join'd,
As that the body, this enslav'd the mind;
Much was believ'd, but little understood,
And to be dull was constru'd to be good;
A second deluge learning thus o'er-run,
And the monks finish'd what the Goths begun.

At length Erasmus, that great, injur'd name
(The glory of the priesthood, and the shame!),
Stemm'd the wild torrent of a barb'rous age,
And drove those holy vandals off the stage.

But see! each Muse, in Leo's golden days,
Starts from her trance, and trims her wither'd bays.
Rome's ancient genius, o'er its ruins spread,
Shakes off the dust, and rears his rev'rend head.
Then sculpture and her sister-arts revive;
Stones leap'd to form, and rocks began to live;
With sweeter notes each rising temple rung;
A Raphael painted, and a Vida sung!
Immortal Vida! on whose honour'd brow
The poet's bays and critic's ivy grow:
Cremona now shall ever boast thy name,
As next in place to Mantua, next in fame!

But soon by impious arms from Latium chas'd,
Their ancient bounds the banish'd Muses pass'd;
Thence arts o'er all the northern world advance,
But critic-learning flourish'd most in France.
The rules a nation, born to serve, obeys;
And Boileau still in right of Horace sways.
But we, brave Britons, foreign laws despis'd,
And kept unconquer'd, and uncviliz'd;
Fierce for the liberties of wit, and bold,
We still defied the Romans, as of old.

Yet some there were, among the sounder few
Of those who less presum'd, and better knew,
Who durst assert the juster ancient cause,
And here restor'd Wit's fundamental laws.
Such was the Muse, whose rules and practice tell,
'Nature's chief masterpiece is writing well.'
Such was Roscommon—not more learn'd than good,
With manners gen'rous as his noble blood;
To him the wit of Greece and Rome was known,
And ev'ry author's merit, but his own.
Such late was Walsh—the Muse's judge and friend,
Who justly knew to blame or to commend;
To failings mild, but zealous for desert;
The clearest head, and the sincerest heart.
This humble praise, lamented shade! receive,
This praise at least a grateful Muse may give:
The Muse, whose early voice you taught to sing,
Prescrib'd her heights, and prun'd her tender wing,
(Her guide now lost) no more attempts to rise,
But in low numbers short excursions tries:
Content, if hence th' unlearn'd their wants may view,
The learn'd reflect on what before they knew:
Careless of censure, nor too fond of fame;
Still pleas'd to praise, yet not afraid to blame,
Averse alike to flatter, or offend;
Not free from faults, nor yet too vain to mend.

JOSEPH ADDISON

CHEVY CHASE

[*The Spectator*, Nos. 70, 74: 1711]

I

Interdum vulgus rectum videt.

HOR. *Epist.* ii. 1. 63.

WHEN I travelled, I took a particular delight in
hearing the songs and fables that are come from
father to son, and are most in vogue among the
common people of the countries through which I
passed; for it is impossible that anything should be
universally tasted and approved by a multitude,
though they are only the rabble of a nation, which
hath not in it some peculiar aptness to please and
gratify the mind of man. Human nature is the same
in all reasonable creatures; and whatever falls in
with it will meet with admirers amongst readers of all
qualities and conditions. Molière, as we are told by
Monsieur Boileau, used to read all his comedies to
an old woman who was his housekeeper, as she sat
with him at her work by the chimney-corner; and
could foretell the success of his play in the theatre,
from the reception it met at his fire-side: for he tells
us that the audience always followed the old woman,
and never failed to laugh in the same place.

I know nothing which more shows the essential and
inherent perfection of simplicity of thought, above
that which I call the Gothic manner in writing, than
this, that the first pleases all kinds of palates, and the
latter only such as have formed to themselves a wrong
artificial taste upon little fanciful authors and writers
of epigram. Homer, Virgil, or Milton, so far as the
language of their poems is understood, will please
a reader of plain common sense, who could neither

relish nor comprehend an epigram of Martial, or a poem of Cowley: so, on the contrary, an ordinary song or ballad that is the delight of the common people cannot fail to please all such readers as are not unqualified for the entertainment by their affectation or ignorance; and the reason is plain, because the same paintings of nature which recommend it to the most ordinary reader will appear beautiful to the most refined.

The old song of Chevy-Chase is the favourite ballad of the common people of England, and Ben Jonson used to say he had rather have been the author of it than of all his works. Sir Philip Sidney in his Discourse of Poetry speaks of it in the following words: 'I never heard the old song of Piercy and Douglas, that I found not my heart more moved than with a trumpet; and yet it is sung but by some blind crowder with no rougher voice than rude style; which being so evil apparelled in the dust and cobwebs of that uncivil age, what would it work trimmed in the gorgeous eloquence of Pindar?' For my own part, I am so professed an admirer of this antiquated song, that I shall give my reader a critique upon it without any further apology for so doing.

The greatest modern critics have laid it down as a rule, that an heroic poem should be founded upon some important precept of morality, and adapted to the constitution of the country in which the poet writes. Homer and Virgil have formed their plans in this view. As Greece was a collection of many governments, who suffered very much among themselves, and gave the Persian emperor, who was their common enemy, many advantages over them by their mutual jealousies and animosities, Homer, in order to establish among them a union which was so necessary for their safety, grounds his poem upon the discords of the several Grecian princes who were engaged in a confederacy against an Asiatic prince, and the several advantages which the enemy gained

by such their discords. At the time the poem we are
now treating of was written, the dissensions of the
barons, who were then so many petty princes, ran
very high, whether they quarrelled among them
selves or with their neighbours, and produced un
speakable calamities to the country: the poet, to deter
men from such unnatural contentions, describes a
bloody battle and dreadful scene of death, occasioned
by the mutual feuds which reigned in the families of
an English and Scotch nobleman: that he designed
this for the instruction of his poem, we may learn
from his four last lines, in which, after the example
of the modern tragedians, he draws from it a precept
for the benefit of his readers:

> God save the King, and bless the land
> In plenty, joy, and peace;
> And grant henceforth that foul debate
> 'Twixt noblemen may cease.

The next point observed by the greatest heroic
poets hath been, to celebrate persons and actions
which do honour to their country: thus Virgil's hero
was the founder of Rome, Homer's a prince of Greece;
and for this reason Valerius Flaccus and Statius, who
were both Romans, might be justly derided for having
chosen the expedition of the Golden Fleece, and the
Wars of Thebes, for the subject of their epic writings.

The poet before us has not only found out an hero
in his own country, but raises the reputation of it by
several beautiful incidents. The English are the first
who take the field, and the last who quit it. The
English bring only fifteen hundred to the battle, the
Scotch two thousand. The English keep the field
with fifty-three; the Scotch retire with fifty-five; all
the rest on each side being slain in the battle. But the
most remarkable circumstance of this kind is, the
different manner in which the Scotch and English
kings receive the news of this fight, and of the great
men's deaths who commanded in it.

This news was brought to Edinburgh,
  Where Scotland's king did reign,
That brave Earl Douglas suddenly
  Was with an arrow slain.

O heavy news! King James did say,
  Scotland can witness be,
I have not any captain more
  Of such account as he.

Like tidings to King Henry came
  Within as short a space,
That Piercy of Northumberland
  Was slain in Chevy-Chase.

Now God be with him, said our King,
  Sith 'twill no better be,
I trust I have within my realm
  Five hundred as good as he.

Yet shall not Scot nor Scotland say
  But I will vengeance take,
And be revenged on them all
  For brave Lord Piercy's sake.

This vow full well the King perform'd
  After on Humble-down,
In one day fifty knights were slain,
  With lords of great renown.

And of the rest of small account
  Did many thousands die, &c.

At the same time that the poet shows a laudable
partiality to his countrymen, he represents the Scots
after a manner not unbecoming so bold and brave a
people.

Earl Douglas on a milk-white steed,
  Most like a baron bold,
Rode foremost of the company,
  Whose armour shone like gold.

His sentiments and actions are every way suitable
to an hero. One of us two, says he, must die: I am

an earl as well as yourself, so that you can have no pretence for refusing the combat: however, says he, it is pity, and indeed would be a sin, that so many innocent men should perish for our sakes; rather let you and I end our quarrel in single fight.

> Ere thus I will outbraved be,
>   One of us two shall die;
> I know thee well, an earl thou art,
>   Lord Piercy, so am I.

> But trust me, Piercy, pity it were,
>   And great offence, to kill
> Any of these our harmless men,
>   For they have done no ill.

> Let thou and I the battle try,
>   And set our men aside;
> Accurs'd be he, Lord Piercy said,
>   By whom this is denied.

When these brave men had distinguished themselves in the battle and in single combat with each other, in the midst of a generous parley, full of heroic sentiments, the Scotch earl falls; and with his dying words encourages his men to revenge his death, representing to them, as the most bitter circumstance of it, that his rival saw him fall.

> With that there came an arrow keen
>   Out of an English bow,
> Which struck Earl Douglas to the heart
>   A deep and deadly blow.

> Who never spake more words than these,
>   Fight on, my merry men all,
> For why, my life is at an end,
>   Lord Piercy sees my fall.

Merry men, in the language of those times, is no more than a cheerful word for companions and fellow-soldiers. A passage in the eleventh book of Virgil's *Aeneid* is very much to be admired, where Camilla in her last agonies, instead of weeping over the wound she had received, as one might have expected from a warrior of her sex, considers only (like the hero of whom we are now speaking) how the battle should be continued after her death.

> *Tum sic expirans, etc.*

> A gathering mist o'erclouds her cheerful eyes;
> And from her cheeks the rosy colour flies.
> Then turns to her, whom of her female train
> She trusted most, and thus she speaks with pain.
> Acca, 'tis past! he swims before my sight,
> Inexorable death; and claims his right.
> Bear my last words to Turnus, fly with speed,
> And bid him timely to my charge succeed:
> Repel the Trojans, and the town relieve:
> Farewell.——

> DRYDEN.

Turnus did not die in so heroic a manner: though our poet seems to have had his eye upon Turnus's speech in the last verse.

> Lord Piercy sees my fall.

> *Vicisti, et victum tendere palmas*
> *Ausonii videre.*

> AEN. xii. 936.

Earl Piercy's lamentation over his enemy is generous, beautiful, and passionate: I must only caution the reader not to let the simplicity of the style, which one may well pardon in so old a poet, prejudice him against the greatness of the thought.

> Then leaving life, Earl Piercy took
>   The dead man by the hand,
> And said, Earl Douglas, for thy life
>   Would I had lost my land.

> O Christ! my very heart doth bleed
>   With sorrow for thy sake;
> For sure a more renowned knight
>   Mischance did never take.

That beautiful line, *Taking the dead man by the hand,*

will put the reader in mind of Aeneas's behaviour towards Lausus, whom he himself had slain as he came to the rescue of his aged father.

> *At vero ut vultum vidit morientis, et ora,*
> *Ora modis Anchisiades pallentia miris,*
> *Ingemuit, miserans graviter, dextramque tetendit, etc.*
>
> AEN. x. 822.

> The pious prince beheld young Lausus dead;
> He griev'd, he wept; then grasp'd his hand, and said,
> Poor hapless youth! what praises can be paid
> To worth so great!
>
> DRYDEN.

I shall take another opportunity to consider the other parts of this old song.

II

Pendent opera interrupta.—VIRG. Aen. iv. 88.

In my last Monday's paper I gave some general instances of those beautiful strokes which please the reader in the old song of Chevy-Chase: I shall here, according to my promise, be more particular, and show that the sentiments in that ballad are extremely natural and poetical, and full of the majestic simplicity we admire in the greatest of the ancient poets; for which reason I shall quote several passages of it, in which the thought is altogether the same with what we meet in several passages of the *Aeneid*; not that I would infer from thence, that the poet (whoever he was) proposed to himself any imitation of those passages, but that he was directed to them in general by the same kind of poetical genius, and by the same copyings after nature.

Had this old song been filled with epigrammatical turns and points of wit, it might perhaps have pleased the wrong taste of some readers; but it would never have become the delight of the common people, nor

have warmed the heart of Sir Philip Sidney like the
sound of a trumpet; it is only nature that can have
this effect, and please those tastes which are the most
unprejudiced or the most refined. I must, however,
beg leave to dissent from so great an authority as
that of Sir Philip Sidney, in the judgement which
he has passed as to the rude style and evil apparel
of this antiquated song; for there are several parts
in it where not only the thought but the language
is majestic, and the numbers sonorous; at least, the
apparel is much more *gorgeous* than many of the poets
made use of in Queen Elizabeth's time, as the reader
will see in several of the following quotations.

What can be greater than either the thought or
the expression in that stanza:

> To drive the deer with hound and horn
>   Earl Piercy took his way;
> The child may rue that is unborn
>   The hunting of that day.

This way of considering the misfortunes which this
battle would bring upon posterity, not only on those
who were born immediately after the battle, and
lost their fathers in it, but on those also who perished
in future battles, which took their rise from this
quarrel of the two earls, is wonderfully beautiful, and
conformable to the way of thinking among the ancient poets.

> *Audiet pugnas vitio parentum*
>   *Rara juventus.*
>   HOR. *Od.* i. 2, 23.

What can be more sounding and poetical, or resemble
more the majestic simplicity of the ancients, than the
following stanzas:

> The stout Earl of Northumberland
>   A vow to God did make,
> His pleasure in the Scottish woods
>   Three summer's days to take.

With fifteen hundred bowmen bold,
    All chosen men of might,
Who knew full well, in time of need,
    To aim their shafts aright.

The hounds ran swiftly through the woods,
    The nimble deer to take;
And with their cries the hills and dales
    An echo shrill did make.

Vocat ingenti clamore Cithaeron
Taygetique canes, domitrixque Epidaurus equorum:
Et vox assensu nemorum ingeminata remugit.

GEORG. iii. 43.

Lo, yonder doth Earl Douglas come,
    His men in armour bright;
Full twenty hundred Scottish spears,
    All marching in our sight.

All men of pleasant Tividale,
    Fast by the river Tweed, &c.

The country of the Scotch warriors, described in
these two last verses, has a fine romantic situation,
and affords a couple of smooth words for verse. If
the reader compares the foregoing six lines of the
song with the following Latin verses, he will see how
much they are written in the spirit of Virgil:

Adversi campo apparent hastasque reductis
Protendunt longe dextris, et spicula vibrant;

Quique altum Praeneste viri, quique arva Gabinae
Junonis, gelidumque Anienem, et roscida rivis
Hernica saxa colunt:

—qui rosea rura Velini,
Qui Tetricae horrentis rupes, montemque Severum,
Casperiamque colunt, Forulosque et flumen Himellae:
Qui Tiberim Fabarimque bibunt.

AEN. xi. 605; vii. 682, 712.

But to proceed:

Earl Douglas on a milk-white steed,
    Most like a baron bold,
Rode foremost of the company,
    Whose armour shone like gold.

Turnus ut antevolans tardum praecesserat agmen, etc.
Vidisti, quo Turnus equo, quibus ibat in armis
Aureus.

> Our English archers bent their bows,
>   Their hearts were good and true;
> At the first flight of arrows sent,
>   Full threescore Scots they slew.

> They closed full fast on ev'ry side,
>   No slackness there was found;
> And many a gallant gentleman
>   Lay gasping on the ground.

> With that there came an arrow keen
>   Out of an English bow,
> Which struck Earl Douglas to the heart
>   A deep and deadly blow.

Aeneas was wounded after the same manner by an
unknown hand in the midst of a parley:

> *Has inter voces, media inter talia verba,*
> *Ecce viro stridens alis allapsa sagitta est,*
> *Incertum qua pulsa manu.*
>
> AEN. xii. 318.

But of all the descriptive parts of this song, there
are none more beautiful than the four following
stanzas, which have a great force and spirit in them,
and are filled with very natural circumstances. The
thought in the third stanza was never touched by
any other poet, and is such a one as would have
shined in Homer or Virgil.

> So thus did both these nobles die,
>   Whose courage none could stain:
> An English archer then perceived
>   The noble Earl was slain.

> He had a bow bent in his hand,
>   Made of a trusty tree,
> An arrow of a cloth-yard long
>   Unto the head drew he.

> Against Sir Hugh Montgomery
>   So right his shaft he set,
> The gray goose wing that was thereon
>   In his heart-blood was wet.

> This sight did last from break of day
>   Till setting of the sun;
> For when they rung the ev'ning-bell,
>   The battle scarce was done.

One may observe likewise, that in the catalogue of the slain the author has followed the example of the greatest ancient poets, not only in giving a long list of the dead, but by diversifying it with little characters of particular persons:

> And with Earl Douglas there was slain
>   Sir Hugh Montgomery,
> Sir Charles Carrel, that from the field
>   One foot would never fly:

> Sir Charles Murrel of Ratcliff too,
>   His sister's son was he:
> Sir David Lamb, so well esteem'd,
>   Yet saved could not be.

The familiar sound in these names destroys the majesty of the description; for this reason I do not mention this part of the poem but to show the natural cast of thought which appears in it, as the two last verses look almost like a translation of Virgil:

> *Cadit et Ripheus, justissimus unus*
> *Qui fuit in Teucris et servantissimus aequi,*
> *Diis aliter visum est.*

> AEN. ii. 426.

In the catalogue of the English who fell, Witherington's behaviour is in the same manner particularized very artfully, as the reader is prepared for it by that account which is given of him in the beginning of the battle; though I am satisfied that your little buffoon readers (who have seen that passage ridiculed in *Hudibras*) will not be able to take the beauty of it: for which reason I dare not so much as quote it.

> Then stept a gallant squire forth,
>   Witherington was his name,
> Who said, I would not have it told
>   To Henry our King for shame,
> That e'er my captain fought on foot,
>   And I stood looking on.

We meet with the same heroic sentiments in Virgil:

> *Non pudet, O Rutuli, cunctis pro talibus unam*
> *Objectare animam? numerone an viribus aequi*
> *Non sumus?*
>
> AEN. xii. 229.

What can be more natural or more moving, than the circumstances in which he describes the behaviour of those women who had lost their husbands on this fatal day:

> Next day did many widows come,
>   Their husbands to bewail;
> They wash'd their wounds in brinish tears,
>   But all would not prevail.
>
> Their bodies bathed in purple blood,
>   They bore with them away:
> They kiss'd them dead a thousand times,
>   When they were clad in clay.

Thus we see how the thoughts of this poem, which naturally arise from the subject, are always simple, and sometimes exquisitely noble; that the language is often very sounding; and that the whole is written with a true poetical spirit.

If this song had been written in the Gothic manner, which is the delight of all our little wits, whether writers or readers, it would not have hit the taste of so many ages, and have pleased the readers of all ranks and conditions. I shall only beg pardon for such a profusion of Latin quotations; which I should not have made use of, but that I feared my own judgement would have looked too singular on such a subject, had not I supported it by the practice and authority of Virgil.

CRITICISMS ON *PARADISE LOST*

[*The Spectator*, Nos. 267, 273, 279, 285: 1712]

i. *The Fable.*

Cedite Romani scriptores, cedite Graii.—PROPERT.

THERE is nothing in Nature so irksome as general discourses, especially when they turn chiefly upon words. For this reason I shall waive the discussion of that point which was started some years since, whether Milton's *Paradise Lost* may be called an heroic poem. Those who will not give it that title may call it (if they please) a divine poem. It will be sufficient to its perfection, if it has in it all the beauties of the highest kind of poetry; and as for those who allege it is not an heroic poem, they advance no more to the diminution of it than if they should say Adam is not Aeneas, nor Eve Helen.

I shall therefore examine it by the rules of epic poetry, and see whether it falls short of the *Iliad* or *Aeneid*, in the beauties which are essential to that kind of writing. The first thing to be considered in an epic poem is the fable, which is perfect or imperfect, according as the action which it relates is more or less so. This action should have three qualifications in it. First, it should be but one action. Secondly, it should be an entire action; and thirdly, it should be a great action. To consider the action of the *Iliad*, *Aeneid*, and *Paradise Lost*, in these three several lights. Homer to preserve the unity of his action hastens into the midst of things, as Horace has observed. Had he gone up to Leda's Egg, or begun much later, even at the rape of Helen, or the investing of Troy, it is manifest that the story of the poem would have been a series of several actions. He therefore opens his poem with the discord of his princes, and with great art interweaves in the several succeeding parts of it an account of everything material which relates to them, and had passed before that fatal dissension. After the same manner Aeneas makes his first appearance in the Tyrrhene Seas, and within sight of Italy, because the action proposed to be celebrated was that of his settling himself in Latium. But because it was necessary for the reader to know what had happened to him in the taking of Troy, and in the preceding parts of his voyage, Virgil makes his hero relate it by way of episode in the second and third books of the *Aeneid*. The contents of both which books come before those of the first book in the thread of the story, though for preserving of this unity of action they follow them in the disposition of the poem. Milton, in imitation of these two great poets, opens his *Paradise Lost* with an infernal council plotting the fall of man, which is the action he proposed to celebrate; and as for those great actions which preceded, in point of time, the battle of the angels and the creation of the world (which would have entirely destroyed the unity of his principal action, had he related them in the same order that they happened), he cast them into the fifth, sixth, and seventh books, by way of episode to this noble poem.

Aristotle himself allows that Homer has nothing to boast of as to the unity of his fable, though at the same time that great critic and philosopher endeavours to palliate this imperfection in the Greek poet, by imputing it in some measure to the very nature of an epic poem. Some have been of opinion that the *Aeneid* labours also in this particular, and has episodes which may be looked upon as excrescences rather than as parts of the action. On the contrary, the poem which we have now under our consideration, hath no other episodes than such as naturally arise from the subject, and yet is filled with such a multitude of astonishing incidents that it gives us at the same time a pleasure of the greatest variety, and of the greatest simplicity.

I must observe also, that as Virgil in the poem which was designed to celebrate the original of the Roman Empire, has described the birth of its great rival, the Carthaginian Commonwealth: Milton, with the like art in his poem on the fall of man, has related the fall of those angels who are his professed enemies. Besides the many other beauties in such an episode, its running parallel with the great action of the poem hinders it from breaking the unity so much as another episode would have done, that had not so great an affinity with the principal subject. In short, this is the same kind of beauty which the critics admire in the *Spanish Friar*, or the *Double Discovery*, where the two different plots look like counterparts and copies of one another.

The second qualification required in the action of an epic poem is that it should be an *entire* action. An action is entire when it is complete in all its parts; or, as Aristotle describes it, when it consists of a beginning, a middle, and an end. Nothing should go before it, be intermixed with it, or follow after it, that is not related to it. As on the contrary, no single step should be omitted in that just and regular process which it must be supposed to take from its original to its consummation. Thus we see the anger of Achilles in its birth, its continuance and effects; and Aeneas's settlement in Italy, carried on through all the oppositions in his way to it both by sea and land. The action in Milton excels (I think) both the former in this particular; we see it contrived in Hell, executed upon Earth, and punished by Heaven. The parts of it are told in the most distinct manner, and grow out of one another in the most natural method.

The third qualification of an epic poem is its greatness. The anger of Achilles was of such consequence that it embroiled the kings of Greece, de-

stroyed the heroes of Troy, and engaged all the gods
in factions. Aeneas's settlement in Italy produced the
Caesars, and gave birth to the Roman Empire.
Milton's subject was still greater than either of the
former; it does not determine the fate of single persons or nations, but of a whole species. The united
powers of hell are joined together for the destruction
of mankind, which they effected in part, and would
have completed had not Omnipotence itself interposed. The principal actors are Man in his greatest
perfection and Woman in her highest beauty. Their
enemies are the fallen angels; the Messiah their
friend, and the Almighty their protector. In short,
everything that is great in the whole circle of being,
whether within the verge of Nature or out of it, has
a proper part assigned it in this noble poem.

In poetry, as in architecture, not only the whole,
but the principal members, and every part of them,
should be great. I will not presume to say that the
book of games in the *Aeneid*, or that in the *Iliad*, are
not of this nature, nor to reprehend Virgil's 'simile
of the top', and many other of the same nature in
the *Iliad*, as liable to any censure in this particular;
but I think we may say, without derogating from those
wonderful performances, that there is an unquestionable magnificence in every part of *Paradise Lost*, and
indeed a much greater than could have been formed
upon any pagan system.

But Aristotle, by the greatness of the action, does
not only mean that it should be great in its nature,
but also in its duration, or, in other words, that it
should have a due length in it, as well as what we
properly call greatness. The just measure of the kind
of magnitude he explains by the following similitude.
An animal, no bigger than a mite, cannot appear
perfect to the eye, because the sight takes it in at
once, and has only a confused idea of the whole, and
not a distinct idea of all its parts. If, on the contrary,
you should suppose an animal of ten thousand

furlongs in length, the eye would be so filled with a
single part of it that it could not give the mind an
idea of the whole. What these animals are to the
eye, a very short or a very long action would be to
the memory. The first would be, as it were, lost and
swallowed up by it, and the other difficult to be
contained in it. Homer and Virgil have shown their
principal art in this particular; the action of the *Iliad*,
and that of the *Aeneid*, were in themselves exceeding
short, but are so beautifully extended and diversified
by the invention of episodes and the machinery of
gods with the like poetical ornaments, that they make
up an agreeable story sufficient to employ the memory
without overcharging it. Milton's action is enriched
with such a variety of circumstances that I have taken
as much pleasure in reading the Contents of his
Books as in the best invented story I ever met with.
It is possible that the traditions on which the *Iliad*
and *Aeneid* were built had more circumstances in them
than the history of the fall of man, as it is related
in Scripture. Besides, it was easier for Homer and
Virgil to dash the truth with fiction, as they were
in no danger of offending the religion of their country
by it. But as for Milton, he had not only a very few
circumstances upon which to raise his poem, but was
also obliged to proceed with the greatest caution in
everything that he added out of his own invention.
And, indeed, notwithstanding all the restraints he
was under, he has filled his story with so many
surprising incidents, which bear so close an analogy
with what is delivered in Holy Writ, that it is capable
of pleasing the most delicate reader without giving
offence to the most scrupulous.

The modern critics have collected from several
hints in the *Iliad* and *Aeneid* the space of time which
is taken up by the action of each of those poems;
but as a great part of Milton's story was transacted
in regions that lie out of the reach of the sun and the
sphere of day, it is impossible to gratify the reader

with such a calculation, which indeed would be more curious than instructive; none of the critics, either ancient or modern, having laid down rules to circumscribe the action of an epic poem with any determined number of years, days, or hours.

ii. *The Characters.*

—— *Notandi sunt tibi mores.*—HOR.

Having examined the action of *Paradise Lost*, let us in the next place consider the actors. This is Aristotle's method of considering: first the fable, and secondly the manners, or as we generally call them in English, the fable and the characters.

Homer has excelled all the heroic poets that ever wrote, in the multitude and variety of his characters. Every god that is admitted into his poem, acts a part which would have been suitable to no other deity. His princes are as much distinguished by their manners as by their dominions; and even those among them whose characters seem wholly made up of courage, differ from one another as to the particular kinds of courage in which they excel. In short, there is scarce a speech or action in the *Iliad* which the reader may not ascribe to the person that speaks or acts, without seeing his name at the head of it.

Homer does not only outshine all other poets in the variety, but also in the novelty of his characters. He has introduced among his Grecian princes a person who had lived thrice the age of man, and conversed with Theseus, Hercules, Polyphemus, and the first race of heroes. His principal actor is the son of a goddess, not to mention the offspring of other deities, who have likewise a place in his poem, and the venerable Trojan prince who was the father of so many kings and heroes. There is in these several characters of Homer a certain dignity as well as novelty, which adapts them in a more peculiar manner to the nature of an heroic poem. Though, at the same time, to give them the greater variety, he has described a Vulcan, that is a buffoon among his gods, and a Thersites among his mortals.

Virgil falls infinitely short of Homer in the characters of his poem, both as to their variety and novelty. Aeneas is indeed a perfect character, but as for Achates, though he is styled the hero's friend, he does nothing in the whole poem which may deserve that title. Gyas, Mnesteus, Sergestus, and Cloanthus, are all of them men of the same stamp and character:

Fortemque Gyan, fortemque Cloanthum.—Virg.

There are indeed several very natural incidents in the part of Ascanius; as that of Dido cannot be sufficiently admired. I do not see anything new or particular in Turnus. Pallas and Evander are copies of Hector and Priam, as Lausus and Mezentius are almost parallels to Pallas and Evander. The characters of Nisus and Euryalus are beautiful, but common. We must not forget the parts of Sinon, Camilla, and some few others, which are beautiful improvements on the Greek poet. In short, there is neither that variety nor novelty in the persons of the *Aeneid*, which we meet with in those of the *Iliad*.

If we look into the characters of Milton we shall find that he has introduced all the variety his poem was capable of receiving. The whole species of mankind was in two persons at the time to which the subject of his poem is confined. We have, however, four distinct characters in these two persons. We see Man and Woman in the highest innocence and perfection, and in the most abject state of guilt and infirmity. The two last characters are, indeed, very common and obvious, but the two first are not only more magnificent, but more new than any characters either in Virgil or Homer, or indeed in the whole circle of nature.

Milton was so sensible of this defect in the subject

of his poem, and of the few characters it would afford him, that he has brought into it two actors of a shadowy and fictitious nature, in the persons of Sin and Death, by which means he has interwoven in the body of his fable a very beautiful and well-invented allegory. But notwithstanding the fineness of this allegory may atone for it in some measure, I cannot think that persons of such a chimerical existence are proper actors in an epic poem; because there is not that measure of probability annexed to them, which is requisite in writings of this kind, as I shall show more at large hereafter.

Virgil has, indeed, admitted Fame as an actress in the *Aeneid*, but the part she acts is very short, and none of the most admired circumstances in that divine work. We find in mock-heroic poems, particularly in the *Dispensary* and the *Lutrin*, several allegorical persons of this nature, which are very beautiful in those compositions, and may, perhaps, be used as an argument, that the authors of them were of opinion such characters might have a place in an epic work. For my own part I should be glad the reader would think so, for the sake of the poem I am now examining, and must further add, that if such empty unsubstantial beings may be ever made use of on this occasion, there were never any more nicely imagined and employed in more proper actions, than those of which I am now speaking.

Another principal actor in this poem is the great enemy of mankind. The part of Ulysses in Homer's *Odyssey* is very much admired by Aristotle, as perplexing that fable with very agreeable plots and intricacies, not only by the many adventures in his voyage, and the subtilty of his behaviour, but by the various concealments and discoveries of his person in several parts of that poem. But the crafty being I have now mentioned makes a much longer voyage than Ulysses, puts in practice many more wiles and stratagems, and hides himself under a greater variety

of shapes and appearances, all of which are severally
detected, to the great delight and surprise of the
reader.

We may likewise observe with how much art the
poet has varied several characters of the persons that
speak in his infernal assembly. On the contrary, how
has he represented the whole Godhead exerting itself
towards man in its full benevolence under the three-
fold distinction of a Creator, a Redeemer, and a
Comforter!

Nor must we omit the person of Raphael, who
amidst his tenderness and friendship for man, shows
such a dignity and condescension in all his speech and
behaviour as are suitable to a superior nature. The
angels are indeed as much diversified in Milton, and
distinguished by their proper parts, as the gods are
in Homer or Virgil. The reader will find nothing
ascribed to Uriel, Gabriel, Michael, or Raphael, which
is not in a particular manner suitable to their respective characters.

There is another circumstance in the principal
actors of the *Iliad* and *Aeneid*, which gives a peculiar
beauty to those two poems, and was therefore contrived with very great judgement. I mean the authors
having chosen for their heroes persons who were so
nearly related to the people for whom they wrote.
Achilles was a Greek, and Aeneas the remote founder
of Rome. By this means their countrymen (whom
they principally proposed to themselves for their
readers) were particularly attentive to all the parts of
their story, and sympathized with their heroes in all
their adventures. A Roman could not but rejoice in
the escapes, successes, and victories of Aeneas, and be
grieved at any defeats, misfortunes, or disappointments
that befell him; as a Greek must have had the same
regard for Achilles. And it is plain that each of those
poems have lost this great advantage, among those
readers to whom their heroes are as strangers, or
indifferent persons.

Milton's poem is admirable in this respect, since it is impossible for any of its readers, whatever nation, country, or people he may belong to, not to be related to the persons who are the principal actors in it; but what is still infinitely more to its advantage, the principal actors in this poem are not only our progenitors but our representatives. We have an actual interest in everything they do, and no less than our utmost happiness is concerned, and lies at stake in all their behaviour.

I shall subjoin as a corollary to the foregoing remark, an admirable observation out of Aristotle, which hath been very much misrepresented in the quotations of some modern critics: 'If a man of perfect and consummate virtue falls into a misfortune, it raises our pity, but not our terror, because we do not fear that it may be our own case, who do not resemble the suffering person.' But, as that great philosopher adds, 'If we see a man of virtues mixed with infirmities fall into any misfortune, it does not only raise our pity but our terror; because we are afraid that the like misfortunes may happen to ourselves, who resemble the character of the suffering person.'

I shall take another opportunity to observe that a person of an absolute and consummate virtue should never be introduced in tragedy, and shall only remark in this place that the foregoing observation of Aristotle, though it may be true in other occasions, does not hold in this; because in the present case, though the persons who fall into misfortune are of the most perfect and consummate virtue, it is not to be considered as what may possibly be, but what actually is our own case; since we are embarked with them on the same bottom, and must be partakers of their happiness or misery.

In this, and some other very few instances, Aristotle's rules for epic poetry (which he had drawn from his reflections upon Homer) cannot be supposed to quadrate exactly with the heroic poems which have been made since his time; as it is plain his rules would have been still more perfect, could he have perused the *Aeneid* which was made some hundred years after his death.

In my next I shall go through other parts of Milton's poem; and hope that what I shall there advance, as well as what I have already written, will not only serve as a comment upon Milton, but upon Aristotle.

iii. *The Sentiment.*

Reddere personae scit convenientia cuique.—Hor.

We have already taken a general survey of the fable and characters in Milton's *Paradise Lost.* The parts which remain to be considered, according to Aristotle's method, are the sentiments and the language. Before I enter upon the first of these, I must advertise my reader, that it is my design as soon as I have finished my general reflections on these four several heads, to give particular instances out of the poem which is now before us of beauties and imperfections which may be observed under each of them, as also of such other particulars as may not properly fall under any of them. This I thought fit to premise, that the reader may not judge too hastily of this piece of criticism, or look upon it as imperfect, before he has seen the whole extent of it.

The sentiments in all epic poems are the thoughts and behaviour which the author ascribes to the persons whom he introduces, and are *just* when they are conformable to the characters of the several persons. The sentiments have likewise a relation to things as well as persons, and are then perfect when they are such as are adapted to the subject. If in either of these cases the poet argues, or explains, magnifies or diminishes, raises love or hatred, pity or terror, or any other passion, we ought to consider whether the sentiments he makes use of are proper for their ends. Homer is censured by the critics for his defect as to this particular in several parts of the *Iliad* and *Odyssey*, though at the same time those who have treated this great poet with candour, have attributed this defect to the times in which he lived. It was the fault of the age, and not of Homer, if there wants that delicacy in some of his sentiments, which appears in the works of men of a much inferior genius. Besides, if there are blemishes in any particular thoughts, there is an infinite beauty in the greatest part of them. In short, if there are many poets who would not have fallen into the meanness of some of his sentiments, there are none who could have risen up to the greatness of others. Virgil has excelled all others in the propriety of his sentiments. Milton shines likewise very much in this particular: nor must we omit one consideration which adds to his honour and reputation. Homer and Virgil introduced persons whose characters are commonly known among men, and such as are to be met with either in history or in ordinary conversation. Milton's characters, most of them, lie out of Nature, and were to be formed purely by his own invention. It shows a greater genius in Shakespeare to have drawn his Caliban than his Hotspur or Julius Caesar: the one was to be supplied out of his own imagination, whereas the other might have been formed upon tradition, history, and observation. It was much easier therefore for Homer to find proper sentiments for an assembly of Grecian generals, than for Milton to diversify his infernal council with proper characters, and inspire them with a variety of sentiments. The loves of Dido and Aeneas are only copies of what has passed between other persons. Adam and Eve, before the fall, are a different species from that of mankind, who are descended from them; and none but a poet of the most unbounded invention, and the most exquisite judgement, could have filled their conversation and behaviour with such beautiful circumstances during their state of innocence.

Nor is it sufficient for an epic poem to be filled with such thoughts as are natural, unless it abound also with such as are sublime. Virgil in this particular falls short of Homer. He has not indeed so many thoughts that are low and vulgar, but at the same time has not so many thoughts that are sublime and noble. The truth of it is, Virgil seldom rises into very astonishing sentiments, where he is not fired by the *Iliad*. He everywhere charms and pleases us by the force of his own genius, but seldom elevates and transports us where he does not fetch his hints from Homer.

Milton's chief talent, and indeed his distinguishing excellence, lies in the sublimity of his thoughts. There are others of the moderns who rival him in every other part of poetry; but in the greatness of his sentiments he triumphs over all the poets both modern and ancient, Homer only excepted. It is impossible for the imagination of man to distend itself with greater ideas than those which he has laid together in his first, second, and tenth books. The seventh, which describes the creation of the world, is likewise wonderfully sublime, though not so apt to stir up emotion in the mind of the reader, nor consequently so perfect in the epic way of writing, because it is filled with less action. Let the reader compare what Longinus has observed on several passages in Homer, and he will find parallels for most of them in the *Paradise Lost*.

From what has been said we may infer that as there are two kinds of sentiments, the natural and the sublime, which are always to be pursued in an heroic poem, there are also two kinds of thoughts which are carefully to be avoided. The first are such as are affected and unnatural; the second such as are mean and vulgar. As for the first kind of thoughts we meet with little or nothing that is like them in Virgil. He has none of those little points and puerilities that are so often to be met with in Ovid, none of the epigrammatic turns of Lucan, none of those swelling sentiments which are so frequently in Statius and Claudian, none of those mixed embellishments of Tasso. Everything is just and natural. His sentiments show that he had a perfect insight into human nature, and that he knew everything which was the most proper to affect it.

Mr. Dryden has in some places, which I may hereafter take notice of, misrepresented Virgil's way of thinking as to this particular, in the translation he has given us of the *Aeneid*. I do not remember that Homer anywhere falls into the faults above-mentioned, which were indeed the false refinements of later ages. Milton, it must be confessed, has sometimes erred in this respect, as I shall show more at large in another paper; though considering all the poets of the age in which he wrote were infected with this wrong way of thinking, he is rather to be admired that he did not give more into it, than that he did sometimes comply with the vicious taste which prevails so much among modern writers.

But since several thoughts may be natural which are low and grovelling, an epic poet should not only avoid such sentiments as are unnatural or affected, but also such as are low and vulgar. Homer has opened a great field of raillery to men of more delicacy than greatness of genius by the homeliness of some of his sentiments. But, as I have before said, these are rather to be imputed to the simplicity of the age in which he lived, to which I may also add of that which he described, than to any imperfection in that divine poet. Zoilus, among the Ancients, and Monsieur Perrault among the Moderns, pushed their ridicule very far upon him, on account of some such sentiments. There is no blemish to be observed in Virgil, under this head, and but very few in Milton.

I shall give but one instance of this impropriety of sentiments in Homer, and at the same time compare it with an instance of the same nature, both in Virgil and Milton. Sentiments which raise laughter can very

seldom be admitted with any decency into an heroic
poem, whose business it is to excite passions of a much
nobler nature. Homer, however, in his characters of
Vulcan and Thersites, in his story of Mars and Venus,
in his behaviour of Irus, and in other passages, has
been observed to have lapsed into the burlesque
character, and to have departed from that serious air
which seems essential to the magnificence of an epic
poem. I remember but one laugh in the whole *Aeneid*,
which rises in the fifth book upon Monoetes, where
he is represented as thrown overboard, and drying
himself upon a rock. But this piece of mirth is so
well timed that the severest critic can have nothing
to say against it, for it is in the book of games and
diversions where the reader's mind may be supposed
to be sufficiently relaxed for such an entertainment.
The only piece of pleasantry in *Paradise Lost* is where
the evil spirits are described as rallying the angels
upon the success of their new invented artillery. This
passage I look upon to be the most exceptionable in
the whole poem, as being nothing else but a string
of puns, and those, too, very indifferent ones:

> —— Satan beheld their plight,
> And to his mates thus in derision call'd.
> O friends, why come not on these victors proud?
> Ere while they fierce were coming, and when we,
> To entertain them fair with *open front*,
> And breast (what could we more?), propounded terms
> Of composition; straight they chang'd their minds,
> *Flew off*, and into strange vagaries fell,
> As they would dance: yet for a dance they seem'd
> Somewhat extravagant and wild, perhaps
> For joy of offer'd peace: but I suppose
> If our proposals once again were *heard*,
> We should compel them to a quick *result*.
> To whom thus Belial in like gamesome mood.
> Leader, the terms we sent were terms of *weight*,
> Of *hard contents*, and full of force urg'd home,
> Such as we might perceive amus'd them all,
> And *stumbled* many; who receives them right,

Had need, from head to foot, well *understand*;
Not *understood*, this gift they have besides,
They shew us when our foes *walk not upright*.
   Thus they among themselves in pleasant vein
Stood scoffing ——

iv. *The Language*

Ne, quicunque Deus, quicunque adhibebitur heros,
Regali conspectus in auro nuper et ostro,
Migret in obscuras humili sermone tabernas:
Aut, dum vitat humum, nubes et inania captet.—Hor.

Having already treated of the fable, the characters,
and sentiments in the *Paradise Lost*, we are in the last
place to consider the language; and as the learned
world is very much divided upon Milton as to this
point, I hope they will excuse me if I appear particular
in any of my opinions and incline to those who judge
the most advantageously of the author.

It is requisite that the language of an heroic poem
should be both perspicuous and sublime. In proportion as either of these two qualities are wanting, the
language is imperfect. Perspicuity is the first and
most necessary qualification; insomuch, that a good-
natured reader sometimes overlooks a little slip even
in the grammar or syntax, where it is impossible for
him to mistake the poet's sense. Of this kind is that
passage in Milton, wherein he speaks of Satan:

   —— God and his Son except,
Created thing nought valu'd he nor shunn'd.

And that in which he describes Adam and Eve:

Adam the goodliest man of men since born
His sons, the fairest of her daughters *Eve*.

It is plain that in the former of these passages,
according to the natural syntax, the divine persons
mentioned in the first line are represented as created
beings; and that in the other, Adam and Eve are
confounded with their sons and daughters. Such little

blemishes as these, when the thought is great and natural, we should, with Horace, impute to a pardonable inadvertency, or to the weakness of human nature, which cannot attend to each minute particular, and give the last finishing to every circumstance in so long a work. The ancient critics, therefore, who were acted by a spirit of candour, rather than that of cavilling, invented certain figures of speech on purpose to palliate little errors of this nature in the writings of those authors who had so many greater beauties to atone for them.

If clearness and perspicuity were only to be consulted the poet would have nothing else to do but to clothe his thoughts in the most plain and natural expressions. But, since it often happens that the most obvious phrases, and those which are used in ordinary conversation, become too familiar to the ear, and contract a kind of meanness by passing through the mouths of the vulgar, a poet should take particular care to guard himself against idiomatic ways of speaking. Ovid and Lucan have many poornesses of expression upon this account, as taking up with the first phrases that offered, without putting themselves to the trouble of looking after such as would not only have been natural, but also elevated and sublime. Milton has but few failings in this kind, of which, however, you may meet with some instances, as in the following passages:

> Embryos and idiots, eremites and friars
> *White, black, and grey, with all their trumpery,*
> Here pilgrims roam—
> . . . A while discourse they hold,
> *No fear lest dinner cool*; when thus began
> Our author . . .
> Who of all ages to succeed, but feeling
> The evil on him brought by me, will curse
> My head, Ill fare our ancestor impure,
> *For this we may thank* Adam . . .

The great masters in composition know very well that many an elegant phrase becomes improper for a poet or an orator, when it has been debased by common use. For this reason the works of ancient authors, which are written in dead languages, have a great advantage over those which are written in languages that are now spoken. Were there any mean phrases or idioms in Virgil and Homer, they would not shock the ear of the most delicate modern reader so much as they would have done that of an old Greek or Roman, because we never hear them pronounced in our streets, or in ordinary conversation.

It is not therefore sufficient that the language of an epic poem be perspicuous, unless it be also sublime. To this end it ought to deviate from the common forms and ordinary phrases of speech. The judgement of a poet very much discovers itself in shunning the common roads of expression without falling into such ways of speech as may seem stiff and unnatural; he must not swell into a false sublime by endeavouring to avoid the other extreme. Among the Greeks, Aeschylus, and sometimes Sophocles, were guilty of this fault; among the Latins, Claudian and Statius; and among our own countrymen, Shakespeare and Lee. In these authors the affectation of greatness often hurts the perspicuity of the style, as in many others the endeavour after perspicuity prejudices its greatness.

Aristotle has observed that the idiomatic style may be avoided, and the sublime formed, by the following methods. First, by the use of metaphors, like those in Milton:

> *Imparadised* in one another's arms.
> . . . And in his hand a reed
> Stood waving *tipt* with fire; . . .
> The grassy clods now *calv'd*. . . .

In these and innumerable other instances the metaphors are very bold but beautiful. I must, however, observe that the metaphors are not thick sown in Milton, which always savours too much of wit; that they never clash with one another, which, as Aristotle observes, turns a sentence into a kind of an enigma or riddle; and that he seldom makes use of them where the proper and natural words will do as well.

Another way of raising the language, and giving it a poetical turn, is to make use of the idioms of other tongues. Virgil is full of the Greek forms of speech, which the critics call *Hellenisms*, as Horace in his Odes abounds with them much more than Virgil. I need not mention the several dialects which Homer has made use of for this end. Milton, in conformity with the practice of the ancient poets, and with Aristotle's rule, has infused a great many Latinisms, as well as Graecisms, into the language of his poem, as towards the beginning of it:

> *Nor* did they *not* perceive the evil plight
> In which they were, *or* the fierce pains *not* feel.
> Yet *to* their gen'ral's voice they soon obey'd.
> . . . Who shall tempt with wand'ring feet
> The dark unbottom'd infinite abyss,
> And through the *palpable obscure* find out his way,
> His uncouth way, or spread his airy flight
> Upborn with indefatigable wings
> Over the *vast abrupt!* . . .
> . . . So both ascend
> In the visions of God. . . .

Under this head may be reckoned the placing the adjective after the substantive, the transposition of words, the turning the adjective into a substantive, with several other foreign modes of speech, which this poet has naturalized to give his verse the greater sound and throw it out of prose.

The third method mentioned by Aristotle is what agrees with the genius of the Greek language more than with that of any other tongue, and is therefore more used by Homer than by any other poet. I mean the lengthening of a phrase by the addition of words, which may either be inserted or omitted, as also by the extending or contracting of particular words by the insertion or omission of certain syllables. Milton has put in practice this method of raising his language, as far as the nature of our tongue will permit, as in the passage above-mentioned, Eremite, for what is hermit in common discourse. If you observe the measure of his verse, he has with great judgement suppressed a syllable in several words, and shortened those of two syllables into one, by which method, besides the above-mentioned advantage, he has given a greater variety to his numbers. But this practice is more particularly remarkable in the names of persons and of countries, as Beelzebub, Hessebon, and in many other particulars, wherein he has either changed the name, or made use of that which is not the most commonly known, that he might the better deviate from the language of the vulgar.

The same reason recommended to him several old words, which also makes his poem appear the more venerable, and gives it a greater air of antiquity.

I must likewise take notice that there are in Milton several words of his own coining, as Cerberean, miscreated, hell-doomed, embryon atoms, and many others. If the reader is offended at this liberty in our English poet I would recommend him to a discourse in Plutarch, which shows us how frequently Homer has made use of the same liberty.

Milton, by the above-mentioned helps, and by the choice of the noblest words and phrases which our tongue would afford him, has carried our language to a greater height than any of the English poets have ever done before or after him, and made the sublimity of his style equal to that of his sentiments.

I have been the more particular in these observations of Milton's style, because it is that part of him in which he appears the most singular. The remarks I have here made upon the practice of other poets, with my observations out of Aristotle, will perhaps alleviate the prejudice which some have taken to his poem upon this account; though, after all, I must confess that I think his style, though admirable in general, is in some places too much stiffened and obscured by the frequent use of those methods which Aristotle has prescribed for the raising of it.

This redundancy of those several ways of speech which Aristotle calls *foreign language*, and with which Milton has so very much enriched, and in some places darkened the language of his poem, was the more proper for his use, because his poem is written in blank verse; rhyme, without any other assistance, throws the language off from prose, and very often makes an indifferent phrase pass unregarded; but where the verse is not built upon rhymes, there pomp of sound and energy of expression are indispensably necessary to support the style, and keep it from falling into the flatness of prose.

Those who have not a taste for this elevation of style and are apt to ridicule a poet when he departs from the common forms of expression, would do well to see how Aristotle has treated an ancient author, called Euclid, for his insipid mirth upon this occasion. Mr. Dryden used to call this sort of men his prose-critics.

I should, under this head of the language, consider Milton's numbers, in which he has made use of several elisions that are not customary among other English poets, as may be particularly observed in his cutting off the letter *y* when it precedes a vowel. This, and some other innovations in the measure of his verse, has varied his numbers in such a manner as makes them incapable of satiating the ear and cloying the reader, which the same uniform measure would certainly have done, and which the perpetual returns of rhyme never fail to do in long narrative poems. I shall close these reflections upon the language of *Paradise Lost*, with observing that Milton has copied after Homer, rather than Virgil, in the length of his periods, the copiousness of his phrases, and the running of his verses into one another.

THE FAIRY WAY OF WRITING

[*The Spectator*, No. 419: 1712.]

——*Mentis gratissimus error.*—HOR.

THERE is a kind of writing wherein the poet quite loses sight of Nature, and entertains his reader's imagination with the characters and actions of such persons as have many of them no existence, but what he bestows on them. Such are fairies, witches, magicians, demons, and departed spirits. This Mr. Dryden calls *the Fairy Way of Writing*, which is, indeed, more difficult than any other that depends on the poet's fancy, because he has no pattern to follow in it, and must work altogether out of his own invention.

There is a very odd turn of thought required for this sort of writing, and it is impossible for a poet to succeed in it, who has not a particular cast of fancy, and an imagination naturally fruitful and superstitious. Besides this, he ought to be very well versed in legends and fables, antiquated romances, and the traditions of nurses and old women, that he may fall in with our natural prejudices, and humour those notions which we have imbibed in our infancy. For, otherwise, he will be apt to make his fairies talk like people of his own species, and not like other sets of beings, who converse with different objects, and think in a different manner from that of mankind:

Sylvis deducti caveant, me iudice, fauni
Ne velut innati triviis, ac pene forenses,
Aut nimium teneris iuvenentur versibus——.—HOR.

I do not say with Mr. Bayes in the *Rehearsal* that spirits must not be confined to speak sense, but it is certain their sense ought to be a little discoloured, that it may seem particular and proper to the person and condition of the speaker.

These descriptions raise a pleasing kind of horror in the mind of the reader, and amuse his imagination with the strangeness and novelty of the persons who are represented in them. They bring up into our memory the stories we have heard in our childhood, and favour those secret terrors and apprehensions to which the mind of man is naturally subject. We are pleased with surveying the different habits and behaviours of foreign countries; how much more must we be delighted and surprised when we are led, as it were, into a new creation, and see the persons and manners of another species? Men of cold fancies and philosophical dispositions object to this kind of poetry, that it has not probability enough to affect the imagination. But to this it may be answered, that we are sure, in general, there are many intellectual beings in the world besides ourselves, and several species of spirits, who are subject to different laws and economies from those of mankind; when we see, therefore, any of these represented naturally, we cannot look upon the representation as altogether impossible; nay, many are prepossessed with such false opinions as dispose them to believe these particular delusions; at least, we have all heard so many pleasing relations in favour of them, that we do not care for seeing through the falsehood, and willingly give ourselves up to so agreeable an imposture.

The ancients have not much of this poetry among them, for, indeed, almost the whole substance of it owes its original to the darkness and superstition of later ages, when pious frauds were made use of to amuse mankind and frighten them into a sense of their duty. Our forefathers looked upon Nature with more reverence and horror, before the world was enlightened by learning and philosophy, and loved to astonish themselves with the apprehensions of witchcraft, prodigies, charms, and enchantments. There was not a village in England that had not a ghost in it, the churchyards were all haunted, every large common had a circle of fairies belonging to it, and there was scarce a shepherd to be met with who had not seen a spirit.

Among all the poets of this kind our English are much the best, by what I have yet seen, whether it be that we abound with more stories of this nature or that the genius of our country is fitter for this sort of poetry. For the English are naturally fanciful, and very often disposed by that gloominess and melancholy of temper, which is so frequent in our nation, to many wild notions and visions, to which others are not so liable.

Among the English, Shakespeare has incomparably excelled all others. That noble extravagance of fancy, which he had in so great perfection, thoroughly qualified him to touch this weak superstitious part of his reader's imagination, and made him capable of succeeding where he had nothing to support him besides the strength of his own genius. There is something so wild and yet so solemn in the speeches of his ghosts, fairies, witches, and the like imaginary persons, that we cannot forbear thinking them natural, though we have no rule by which to judge of them, and must confess, if there are such beings in the world, it looks highly probable they should talk and act as he has represented them.

There is another sort of imaginary beings, that we sometimes meet with among the poets, when the author represents any passion, appetite, virtue, or vice, under a visible shape, and makes it a person or an actor in his poem. Of this nature are the descriptions of Hunger and Envy in Ovid, of Fame in Virgil, and of Sin and Death in Milton. We find a whole creation of the like shadowy persons in Spenser, who had an admirable talent in representations of this kind. I have discoursed of these emblematical persons in former papers, and shall therefore only mention them in this place. Thus we see how many ways Poetry addresses itself to the imagination, as it has not only the whole circle of nature for its province, but makes new worlds of its own, shows us persons who are not to be found in being, and represents even the faculties of the soul, with her several virtues and vices, in a sensible shape and character.

THOMAS GRAY

POETIC DICTION

[From a letter to Richard West, 1742]

. . . .

I HAVE myself, upon your recommendation, been reading *Joseph Andrews*. The incidents are ill-laid and without invention; but the characters have a great deal of nature, which always pleases even in her lowest shapes. Parson Adams is perfectly well; so is Mrs. Slipslop, and the story of Wilson; and throughout he shows himself well read in stage-coaches, country squires, inns, and Inns of Court. His reflections upon high people and low people, and misses and masters, are very good. However the exaltedness of some minds (or rather as I shrewdly suspect their insipidity and want of feeling or observation) may make them insensible to these light things (I mean such as characterize and paint nature), yet surely they are as weighty and much more useful than your grave discourses upon the mind, the passions, and what not. Now as the paradisaical pleasures of the Mohammedans consist in playing upon the flute and lying with Houris, be mine to read eternal new romances of Marivaux and Crébillon.

You are very good in giving yourself the trouble to read and find fault with my long harangues. Your freedom (as you call it) has so little need of apologies, that I should scarce excuse your treating me any otherwise; which, whatever compliment it might be to my vanity, would be making a very ill one to my understanding. As to matter of style, I have this to say: the language of the age is never the language of poetry; except among the French, whose verse, where the thought or image does not support it, differs in nothing from prose. Our poetry, on the contrary, has a language peculiar to itself; to which almost every one, that has written, has added something by enriching it with foreign idioms and derivatives: nay sometimes words of their own composition or invention. Shakespeare and Milton have been great creators this way; and no one more licentious than Pope or Dryden, who perpetually borrow expressions from the former. Let me give you some instances from Dryden, whom everybody reckons a great master of our poetical tongue. Full of *museful mopings*—unlike the *trim* of love—a pleasant *beverage*—a *roundelay* of love—stood silent in his *mood*—with knots and *knares* deformed—his *ireful mood*—in proud *array*—his *boon* was granted—and *disarray* and shameful rout—*wayward* but wise—*furbished* for the field—the *foiled doddered* oaks—*disherited*—*smouldering* flames—*retchless* of laws—*crones* old and ugly—the *beldam* at his side—the *grandam-hag*—*villanise* his Father's fame. But they are infinite; and our language not being a settled thing (like the French) has an undoubted right to words of an hundred years old, provided antiquity have not rendered them unintelligible. In truth, Shakespeare's language is one of his principal beauties; and he has no less advantage over your Addisons and Rowes in this, than in those other great excellencies you mention. Every word in him is a picture. Pray put me the following lines into the tongue of our modern dramatics:

> But I, that am not shaped for sportive tricks,
> Nor made to court an amorous looking-glass:
> I, that am rudely stampt, and want love's majesty
> To strut before a wanton ambling nymph:
> I, that am curtail'd of this fair proportion,
> Cheated of feature by dissembling nature,
> Deform'd, unfinish'd, sent before my time
> Into this breathing world, scarce half made up—

And what follows. To me they appear untranslatable; and if this be the case, our language is greatly degenerated. However, the affectation of imitating

Shakespeare may doubtless be carried too far; and is no sort of excuse for sentiments ill-suited, or speeches ill-timed, which I believe is a little the case with me. I guess the most faulty expressions may be these— *silken* son of *dalliance*—*drowsier* pretensions—*wrinkled beldams*—*arched* the hearer's brow and *riveted* his eyes in *fearful ecstasy*. These are easily altered or omitted; and indeed if the thoughts be wrong or superfluous, there is nothing easier than to leave out the whole. The first ten or twelve lines are, I believe, the best; and as for the rest, I was betrayed into a good deal of it by Tacitus; only what he has said in five words, I imagine I have said in fifty lines. Such is the misfortune of imitating the inimitable. Now, if you are of my opinion, *una litura* may do the business better than a dozen; and you need not fear unravelling my web. I am a sort of spider; and have little else to do but spin it over again, or creep to some other place and spin there. Alas! for one who has nothing to do but amuse himself, I believe my amusements are as little amusing as most folks. . . .

DODSLEY'S MISCELLANY

[From a letter to Horace Walpole, 1748]

I AM obliged to you for Mr. Dodsley's book, and having pretty well looked it over, will (as you desire) tell you my opinion of it. He might, methinks, have shared the Graces in his frontispiece, if he chose to be economical, and dressed his authors in a little more decent raiment—not in whited-brown paper, and distorted characters, like an old ballad. I am ashamed to see myself; but the company keeps me in countenance: so to begin with Mr. Tickell. This is not only a state-poem (my ancient aversion) but a state-poem on the peace of Utrecht. If Mr. Pope had wrote a panegyric on it, one could hardly have read him with patience: but this is only a poor short-winded

imitator of Addison, who had himself not above three
or four notes in poetry, sweet enough indeed, like
those of a German flute, but such as soon tire and
satiate the ear with their frequent return. Tickell has
added to this a great poverty of sense, and a string
of transitions that hardly become a school-boy. However, I forgive him for the sake of his ballad, which
I always thought the prettiest in the world.

All there is of Mr. Green here, has been printed
before; there is a profusion of wit everywhere; reading
would have formed his judgement, and harmonized
his verse, for even his wood-notes often break out into
strains of real poetry and music. The *School-Mistress*
is excellent in its kind and masterly; and (I am sorry
to differ from you, but) *London* is to me one of those
few imitations that have all the ease and all the spirit
of an original. The same man's verses at the opening
of Garrick's theatre are far from bad. Mr. Dyer (here
you will despise me highly) has more of poetry in his
imagination than almost any of our number; but
rough and injudicious. I should range Mr. Bramston
only a step or two above Dr. King, who is as low in
my estimation as in yours. Dr. Evans is a furious
madman; and *Pre-existence* is nonsense in all her
altitudes. Mr. Lyttelton is a gentle elegiac person.
Mr. Nugent sure did not write his own Ode. I like
Mr. Whitehead's little poems, I mean the Ode on a
Tent, the Verses to Garrick, and particularly those
to Charles Townsend, better than anything I had
seen before of him. I gladly pass over H. Browne and
the rest, to come at you. You know I was of the
publishing side, and thought your reasons against it
none; for though, as Mr. Chute said extremely well,
the *still small voice* of poetry was not made to be heard
in a crowd; yet satire will be heard, for all the
audience are by nature her friends; especially when
she appears in the spirit of Dryden, with his strength,
and often with his versification, such as you have
caught in those lines on the royal unction, on the

papal dominion, and convents of both sexes; on Henry VIII and Charles II, for these are to me the shining parts of your Epistle. There are many lines I could wish corrected, and some blotted out, but beauties enough to atone for a thousand worse faults than these. The opinion of such as can at all judge, who saw it before in Dr. Middleton's hands, concurs nearly with mine. As to what any one says, since it came out; our people (you must know) are slow of judgement; they wait till some bold body saves them the trouble, and then follow his opinion; or stay till they hear what is said in town, that is at some Bishop's table, or some coffee-house about the Temple. When they are determined I will tell you faithfully their verdict.

. . . . .

I like Mr. Aston Hervey's Fable; and an Ode (the last of all) by Mr. Mason, a new acquaintance of mine, whose *Musaeus* too seems to carry with it the promise at least of something good to come. I was glad to see you distinguished who poor West was, before his charming Ode, and called it anything rather than a Pindaric. The town is an owl if it don't like Lady Mary, and I am surprised at it: we here are owls enough to think her eclogues very bad; but that I did not wonder at. Our present taste is Sir T. Fitz-Osborne's Letters. . . .

EDWARD YOUNG

CONJECTURES ON ORIGINAL COMPOSITION

IN A LETTER TO THE AUTHOR OF SIR CHARLES GRANDISON

[1759]

DEAR SIR,—We confess the follies of youth without a blush; not so those of age. However, keep me a little in countenance, by considering, that age wants amusements more, though it can justify them less, than the preceding periods of life. How you may relish the pastime here sent you, I know not. It is miscellaneous in its nature, somewhat licentious in its conduct; and, perhaps, not over important in its end. However, I have endeavoured to make some amends, by digressing into subjects more important, and more suitable to my season of life. A serious thought, standing single among many of a lighter nature, will sometimes strike the careless wanderer after amusement only, with useful awe: as monumental marbles scattered in a wide pleasure garden (and such there are) will call to recollection those who would never have sought it in a churchyard walk of mournful yews.

To one such monument I may conduct you, in which is a hidden lustre, like the sepulchral lamps of old; but not like those will this be extinguished, but shine the brighter for being produced, after so long concealment, into open day.

You remember that your worthy patron, and our common friend, put some questions on the serious drama, at the same time when he desired our sentiments on original and on moral composition. Though I despair of breaking through the frozen obstructions of age, and care's incumbent cloud, into that flow of thought, and brightness of expression, which subjects so polite require; yet will I hazard some conjectures on them.

I begin with original composition; and the more willingly, as it seems an original subject to me, who have seen nothing hitherto written on it: But first, a few thoughts on composition in general. Some are of opinion that its growth, at present, is too luxuriant; and that the press is overcharged. Overcharged, I think, it could never be, if none were admitted, but such as brought their imprimatur from sound understanding, and the public good. Wit indeed, however brilliant, should not be permitted to gaze self-enamoured on its useless charms, in that fountain of fame (if so I may call the press), if beauty is all that it has to boast; but, like the first Brutus, it should sacrifice its most darling offspring to the sacred interests of virtue, and real service of mankind.

This restriction allowed, the more composition the better. To men of letters, and leisure, it is not only a noble amusement, but a sweet refuge; it improves their parts, and promotes their peace: it opens a back-door out of the bustle of this busy and idle world into a delicious garden of moral and intellectual fruits and flowers; the key of which is denied to the rest of mankind. When stung with idle anxieties, or teased with fruitless impertinence, or yawning over insipid diversions, then we perceive the blessing of a lettered recess. With what a gust do we retire to our disinterested and immortal friends in our closet, and find our minds, when applied to some favourite theme, as naturally, and as easily quieted and refreshed, as a peevish child (and peevish children are we all till we fall asleep) when laid to the breast? Our happiness no longer lives on charity; nor bids fair for a fall, by leaning on that most precarious and thorny pillow, another's pleasure, for our repose. How independent of the world is he who can daily find new acquaintance, that at once entertain, and improve him, in the little world, the minute but fruitful creation, of his own mind?

These advantages composition affords us, whether we write ourselves, or in more humble amusement peruse the works of others. While we bustle through the thronged walks of public life, it gives us a respite, at least, from care; a pleasing pause of refreshing recollection. If the country is our choice, or fate, there it rescues us from sloth and sensuality, which, like obscene vermin, are apt gradually to creep unperceived into the delightful bowers of our retirement, and to poison all its sweets. Conscious guilt robs the rose of its scent, the lily of its lustre; and makes an Eden a deflowered and dismal scene.

Moreover, if we consider life's endless evils, what can be more prudent than to provide for consolation under them? A consolation under them the wisest of men have found in the pleasures of the pen. Witness, among many more, Thucydides, Xenophon, Tully, Ovid, Seneca, Pliny the Younger, who says, *In uxoris infirmitate, et amicorum periculo, aut morte turbatus, ad studia, unicum doloris levamentum, confugio.* And why not add to these their modern equals, Chaucer, Raleigh, Bacon, Milton, Clarendon, under the same shield, unwounded by misfortune, and nobly smiling in distress?

Composition was a cordial to these under the frowns of fortune; but evils there are which her smiles cannot prevent or cure. Among these are the languors of old age. If those are held honourable, who in a hand benumbed by time have grasped the just sword in defence of their country; shall they be less esteemed, whose unsteady pen vibrates to the last in the cause of religion, of virtue, of learning? Both these are happy in this, that by fixing their attention on objects most important, they escape numberless little anxieties, and that *taedium vitae* which often hangs so heavy on its evening hours. May not this insinuate some apology for my spilling ink, and spoiling paper, so late in life?

But there are who write with vigour, and success, to the world's delight, and their own renown. These are the glorious fruits where genius prevails. The mind of a man of genius is a fertile and pleasant field, pleasant as Elysium, and fertile as Tempe; it enjoys a perpetual spring. Of that spring, originals are the fairest flowers: imitations are of quicker growth, but fainter bloom. Imitations are of two kinds: one of nature, one of authors. The first we call originals, and confine the term imitation to the second. I shall not enter into the curious inquiry of what is, or is not, strictly speaking, original, content with what all must allow, that some compositions are more so than others; and the more they are so, I say, the better. Originals are, and ought to be, great favourites, for they are great benefactors; they extend the republic of letters, and add a new province to its dominion. Imitators only give us a sort of duplicates of what we had, possibly much better, before; increasing the mere drug of books, while all that makes them valuable, knowledge and genius, are at a stand. The pen of an original writer, like Armida's wand, out of a barren waste calls a blooming spring. Out of that blooming spring an imitator is a transplanter of laurels, which sometimes die on removal, always languish in a foreign soil.

But suppose an imitator to be most excellent (and such there are), yet still he but nobly builds on another's foundation; his debt is, at least, equal to his glory; which, therefore, on the balance, cannot be very great. On the contrary, an original, though but indifferent (its originality being set aside), yet has something to boast; it is something to say with him in *Horace*,

Meo sum Pauper in aere;

and to share ambition with no less than Caesar, who declared he had rather be the first in a village than the second at Rome.

Still farther: an imitator shares his crown, if he has one, with the chosen object of his imitation; an original enjoys an undivided applause. An original may be said to be of a vegetable nature; it rises spontaneously from the vital root of genius; it grows, it is not made. Imitations are often a sort of manufacture wrought up by those mechanics, art and labour, out of pre-existent materials not their own.

Again: we read imitation with somewhat of his languor, who listens to a twice-told tale. Our spirits rouse at an original; that is a perfect stranger, and all throng to learn what news from a foreign land: and though it comes, like an Indian prince, adorned with feathers only, having little of weight; yet of our attention it will rob the more solid, if not equally new. Thus every telescope is lifted at a new-discovered star; it makes a hundred astronomers in a moment, and denies equal notice to the sun. But if an original, by being as excellent as new, adds admiration to surprise, then are we at the writer's mercy; on the strong wing of his imagination, we are snatched from Britain to Italy, from climate to climate, from pleasure to pleasure; we have no home, no thought, of our own; till the magician drops his pen. And then falling down into ourselves, we awake to flat realities, lamenting the change, like the beggar who dreamt himself a prince.

It is with thoughts as it is with words; and with both as with men; they may grow old and die. Words tarnished, by passing through the mouths of the vulgar, are laid aside as inelegant and obsolete. So thoughts, when become too common, should lose their currency; and we should send new metal to the mint, that is, new meaning to the press. The division of tongues at Babel did not more effectually debar men from making themselves a name (as the Scripture speaks), than the too great concurrence, or union of tongues will do for ever. We may as well grow good by another's virtue, or fat by another's food, as famous by another's thought. The world will pay its debt of praise but once; and instead of applauding, explode a second demand, as a cheat.

If it is said, that most of the Latin classics, and all the Greek, except, perhaps, Homer, Pindar, and Anacreon, are in the number of imitators, yet receive our highest applause; our answer is, That they, though not real, are accidental originals; the works they imitated, few excepted, are lost; they, on their father's decease, enter as lawful heirs, on their estates in fame. The fathers of our copyists are still in possession; and secured in it, in spite of Goths, and flames, by the perpetuating power of the Press. Very late must a modern imitator's fame arrive, if it waits for their decease.

An original enters early on reputation: Fame, fond of new glories, sounds her trumpet in triumph at its birth; and yet how few are awakened by it into the noble ambition of like attempts! Ambition is sometimes no vice in life; it is always a virtue in composition. High in the towering Alps is the fountain of the Po; high in fame and in antiquity is the fountain of an imitator's undertaking; but the river, and the imitation, humbly creep along the vale. So few are our originals, that, if all other books were to be burnt, the lettered world would resemble some metropolis in flames, where a few incombustible buildings, a fortress, temple, or tower, lift their heads, in melancholy grandeur, amid the mighty ruin. Compared with this conflagration, old Omar lighted up but a small bonfire, when he heated the baths of the barbarians, for eight months together, with the famed Alexandrian library's inestimable spoils, that no profane book might obstruct the triumphant progress of his holy Alcoran round the globe.

But why are originals so few? not because the writer's harvest is over, the great reapers of antiquity having left nothing to be gleaned after them; nor because the human mind's teeming time is past, or because it is incapable of putting forth unprecedented births; but because illustrious examples engross, prejudice, and intimidate. They engross our attention, and so prevent a due inspection of ourselves; they prejudice our judgement in favour of their abilities, and so lessen the sense of our own; and they intimidate us with the splendour of their renown, and thus under diffidence bury our strength. Nature's impossibilities, and those of diffidence lie wide asunder.

Let it not be suspected, that I would weakly insinuate anything in favour of the moderns, as compared with ancient authors; no, I am lamenting their great inferiority. But I think it is no necessary inferiority; that it is not from divine destination, but from some cause far beneath the moon: I think that human souls, through all periods, are equal; that due care and exertion would set us nearer our immortal predecessors than we are at present; and he who questions and confutes this, will show abilities not a little tending toward a proof of that equality which he denies.

After all, the first ancients had no merit in being originals: they could not be imitators. Modern writers have a choice to make; and therefore have a merit in their power. They may soar in the regions of liberty, or move in the soft fetters of easy imitation; and imitation has as many plausible reasons to urge, as pleasure had to offer to Hercules. Hercules made the choice of an hero, and so became immortal.

Yet let not assertors of classic excellence imagine, that I deny the tribute it so well deserves. He that admires not ancient authors, betrays a secret he would conceal, and tells the world that he does not understand them. Let us be as far from neglecting, as from copying, their admirable compositions: sacred be their rights, and inviolable their fame. Let our understanding feed on theirs; they afford the noblest nourishment; but let them nourish, not annihilate, our own. When we read, let our imagination kindle at their charms; when we write, let our judgement shut them out of our thoughts; treat even Homer himself as his royal admirer was treated by the cynic; bid him stand aside, nor shade our composition from the beams of our own genius; for nothing original can rise, nothing immortal can ripen, in any other sun.

Must we then, you say, not imitate ancient authors? Imitate them by all means; but imitate aright. He that imitates the divine *Iliad* does not imitate Homer; but he who takes the same method, which Homer took, for arriving at a capacity of accomplishing a work so great. Tread in his steps to the sole fountain of immortality; drink where he drank, at the true Helicon, that is, at the breast of Nature: imitate; but imitate not the composition, but the man. For may not this paradox pass into a maxim? viz. 'The less we copy the renowned ancients, we shall resemble them the more.'

But possibly you may reply, that you must either imitate Homer, or depart from Nature. Not so: for suppose you was to change place, in time, with Homer; then, if you write naturally, you might as well charge Homer with an imitation of you. Can you be said to imitate Homer for writing so, as you would have written, if Homer had never been? As far as a regard to Nature, and sound sense, will permit a departure from your great predecessors; so far, ambitiously, depart from them; the farther from them in similitude, the nearer are you to them in excellence; you rise by it into an original; become a noble collateral, not an humble descendant from them. Let us build our compositions with the spirit, and in the taste, of the ancients; but not with their materials: thus will they resemble the structures of Pericles at Athens, which Plutarch commends for having had an air of antiquity as soon as they were built. All eminence, and distinction, lies out of the beaten road; excursion and deviation are necessary to find it; and the more remote your path from the highway, the more reputable; if, like poor Gulliver (of whom anon), you fall not into a ditch, in your way to glory.

What glory to come near, what glory to reach, what glory (presumptuous thought!) to surpass our predecessors! And is that then in Nature absolutely impossible? Or is it not, rather, contrary to Nature to fail in it? Nature herself sets the ladder, all wanting is our ambition to climb. For by the bounty of Nature we are as strong as our predecessors; and by the favour of time (which is but another round in Nature's scale) we stand on higher ground. As to the first, were they more than men? Or are we less? Are not our minds cast in the same mould with those before the flood? The flood affected matter; mind escaped. As to the second; though we are moderns, the world is an ancient; more ancient far, than when they, whom we most admire, filled it with their fame. Have we not their beauties, as stars, to guide; their defects, as rocks, to be shunned; the judgement of ages on both, as a chart to conduct, and a sure helm to steer us in our passage to greater perfection than theirs? And shall we be stopped in our rival pretensions to fame by this just reproof?

Stat contra, dicitque tibi tua pagina, fur es.
MART.

It is by a sort of noble contagion, from a general familiarity with their writings, and not by any particular sordid theft, that we can be the better for those who went before us. Hope we, from plagiarism, any dominion in literature; as that of Rome arose from a nest of thieves?

Rome was a powerful ally to many states; ancient authors are our powerful allies; but we must take heed, that they do not succour till they enslave, after the manner of Rome. Too formidable an idea of their superiority, like a spectre, would fright us out of a proper use of our wits; and dwarf our understanding, by making a giant of theirs. Too great awe for them lays genius under restraint, and denies it that free scope, that full elbow-room, which is requisite for striking its most masterly strokes. Genius is a master-workman, learning is but an instrument; and an instrument, though most valuable, yet not always indispensable. Heaven will not admit of a partner in the accomplishment of some favourite spirits; but rejecting all human means, assumes the whole glory to itself. Have not some, though not famed for erudition, so written, as almost to persuade us, that they shone brighter, and soared higher, for escaping the boasted aid of that proud ally?

Nor is it strange; for what, for the most part, mean we by genius, but the power of accomplishing great things without the means generally reputed necessary to that end? A genius differs from a good understanding, as a magician from a good architect: that raises his structure by means invisible; this by the skilful use of common tools. Hence genius has ever been supposed to partake of something divine. *Nemo unquam vir magnus fuit, sine aliquo afflatu divino.*

Learning, destitute of this superior aid, is fond and proud of what has cost it much pains; is a great lover of rules, and boaster of famed examples: as beauties less perfect, who owe half their charms to cautious art, learning inveighs against natural un-studied graces, and small harmless inaccuracies, and sets rigid bounds to that liberty, to which genius often owes its supreme glory; but the no-genius its frequent ruin. For unprescribed beauties, and unexampled excellence, which are characteristics of genius, lie without the pale of learning's authorities, and laws; which pale, genius must leap to come at them: but by that leap, if genius is wanting, we break our necks; we lose that little credit which possibly we might have enjoyed before. For rules, like crutches, are a needful aid to the lame, though an impediment to the strong. A Homer casts them away; and, like his Achilles,

Jura negat sibi nata, nihil non arrogat,

by native force of mind. There is something in poetry beyond prose-reason; there are mysteries in it not to be explained, but admired; which render mere prose-men infidels to their divinity. And here pardon a second paradox; viz. 'Genius often then deserves most to be praised, when it is most sure to be condemned; that is, when its excellence, from mounting high, to weak eyes is quite out of sight.'

If I might speak further of learning, and genius, I would compare genius to virtue, and learning to riches. As riches are most wanted where there is least virtue; so learning where there is least genius. As virtue without much riches can give happiness, so genius without much learning can give renown. As it is said in Terence, *Pecuniam negligere interdum maximum est lucrum*; so to neglect of learning, genius sometimes owes its greater glory. Genius, therefore, leaves but the second place, among men of letters, to the learned. It is their merit, and ambition, to fling light on the works of genius, and point out its charms. We most justly reverence their informing radius for that favour; but we must much more admire the radiant stars pointed out by them.

A star of the first magnitude among the moderns was Shakespeare; among the ancients, Pindar, who (as Vossius tells us) boasted of his no-learning, calling himself the eagle, for his flight above it. And such genii as these may, indeed, have much reliance on their own native powers. For genius may be compared to the natural strength of the body; learning to the super-induced accoutrements of arms: if the first is equal to the proposed exploit, the latter rather encumbers than assists; rather retards than promotes the victory. *Sacer nobis inest Deus*, says Seneca. With regard to the moral world, conscience, with regard to the intellectual, genius, is that god within. Genius can set us right in composition, without the rules of the learned; as conscience sets us right in life, without the laws of the land: this, singly, can make us good, as men: that, singly, as writers, can sometimes make us great.

I say, sometimes, because there is a genius, which stands in need of learning to make it shine. Of genius there are two species, an earlier and a later; or call them infantine and adult. An adult genius comes out of Nature's hand, as Pallas out of Jove's head, at full growth and mature: Shakespeare's genius was of this kind; on the contrary, Swift stumbled at the threshold, and set out for distinction on feeble knees: his was an infantine genius; a genius, which, like other infants, must be nursed, and educated, or it will come to naught: learning is its nurse and tutor; but this nurse may overlay with an indigested load, which smothers common sense; and this tutor may mislead, with pedantic prejudice, which vitiates the best understanding: as too great admirers of the fathers of the Church have sometimes set up their authority against the true sense of Scripture; so too great admirers of the classical fathers have sometimes set up their authority, or example, against reason.

> *Neve minor, neu sit quinto productior actu*
> *Fabula.*

So says Horace, so says ancient example. But reason has not subscribed. I know but one book that can justify our implicit acquiescence in it: and (by the way) on that book a noble disdain of undue deference to prior opinion has lately cast, and is still casting, a new and inestimable light.

But, superstition for our predecessors set aside, the classics are for ever our rightful and revered masters in composition; and our understandings bow before them: but when? When a master is wanted; which, sometimes, as I have shown, is not the case. Some are pupils of nature only, nor go farther to school: from such we reap often a double advantage; they not only rival the reputation of the great ancient authors, but also reduce the number of mean ones among the moderns. For when they enter on subjects which have been in former hands, such is their superiority, that, like a tenth wave, they overwhelm and bury in oblivion all that went before: and thus not only enrich and adorn, but remove a load, and lessen the labour, of the lettered world.

'But, you say, since originals can arise from genius only, and since genius is so very rare, it is scarce worth while to labour a point so much, from which we can reasonably expect so little.' To show that genius is not so very rare as you imagine, I shall point out strong instances of it, in a far distant quarter from that mentioned above. The minds of the schoolmen were almost as much cloistered as their bodies; they had but little learning, and few books; yet may the most learned be struck with some astonishment at their so singular natural sagacity, and most exquisite edge of thought. Who would expect to find Pindar and Scotus, Shakespeare and Aquinas, of the same party? Both equally show an original, unindebted energy; the *vigor igneus*, and *caelestis origo*, burns in both; and leaves us in doubt whether genius is more evident in the sublime flights and beauteous flowers of poetry, or in the profound penetrations, and marvellously keen and minute distinctions, called the thorns of the schools. There might have been more able consuls called from the plough than ever arrived at that honour: many a genius probably there has been which could neither write nor read. So that genius, that supreme lustre of literature, is less rare than you conceive.

By the praise of genius we detract not from learning; we detract not from the value of gold, by saying that diamond has greater still. He who disregards learning shows that he wants its aid; and he that overvalues it shows that its aid has done him harm. Overvalued indeed it cannot be, if genius, as to composition, is valued more. Learning we thank, genius we revere; that gives us pleasure, this gives us rapture;

that informs, this inspires; and is itself inspired; for genius is from heaven, learning from man: this sets us above the low and illiterate; that, above the learned and polite. Learning is borrowed knowledge; genius is knowledge innate, and quite our own. Therefore, as Bacon observes, it may take a nobler name, and be called wisdom; in which sense of wisdom some are born wise.

But here a caution is necessary against the most fatal of errors in those automaths, those self-taught philosophers of our age, who set up genius, and often mere fancied genius, not only above human learning, but divine truth. I have called genius wisdom; but let it be remembered, that in the most renowned ages of the most refined heathen wisdom (and theirs is not Christian) 'the world by wisdom knew not God, and it pleased God by the foolishness of preaching to save those that believed.' In the fairyland of fancy, genius may wander wild; there it has a creative power, and may reign arbitrarily over its own empire of chimeras. The wide field of Nature also lies open before it, where it may range unconfined, make what discoveries it can, and sport with its infinite objects uncontrolled, as far as visible Nature extends, painting them as wantonly as it will. But what painter of the most unbounded and exalted genius can give us the true portrait of a seraph? He can give us only what, by his own or others' eyes, has been seen; though that indeed infinitely compounded, raised, burlesqued, dishonoured, or adorned: in like manner, who can give us divine truth unrevealed? Much less should any presume to set aside divine truth when revealed, as incongruous to their own sagacities—Is this too serious for my subject? I shall be more so before I close.

Having put in a caveat against the most fatal of errors, from the too great indulgence of genius, return we now to that too great suppression of it, which is detrimental to composition; and endeavour to rescue the writer, as well as the man. I have said that some

are born wise; but they, like those that are born rich,
by neglecting the cultivation and produce of their
own possessions, and by running in debt, may be
beggared at last; and lose their reputations, as younger
brothers estates, not by being born with less abilities
than the rich heir, but at too late an hour.

Many a great man has been lost to himself, and
the public, purely because great ones were born before
him. Hermias, in his collections on Homer's blindness, says, that Homer, requesting the gods to grant
him a sight of Achilles, that hero rose, but in armour
so bright, that it struck Homer blind with the blaze.
Let not the blaze of even Homer's muse darken us
to the discernment of our own powers; which may
possibly set us above the rank of imitators; who,
though most excellent and even immortal (as some
of them are) yet are still but *Dii minorum gentium*, nor
can expect the largest share of incense, the greatest
profusion of praise, on their secondary altars.

But further still: a spirit of imitation hath many
ill effects; I shall confine myself to three. First, it
deprives the liberal and politer arts of an advantage
which the mechanic enjoy: in these, men are ever
endeavouring to go beyond their predecessors; in the
former, to follow them. And since copies surpass not
their originals, as streams rise not higher than their
spring, rarely so high; hence, while arts mechanic
are in perpetual progress and increase, the liberal are
in retrogradation and decay. *These* resemble pyramids, are broad at bottom, but lessen exceedingly as
they rise; *those* resemble rivers which, from a small
fountain-head, are spreading ever wider and wider
as they run. Hence it is evident that different portions
of understanding are not (as some imagine) allotted
to different periods of time; for we see, in the same
period, understanding rising in one set of artists and
declining in another. Therefore Nature stands ab-
solved and our inferiority in composition must be
charged on ourselves.

Nay, so far are we from complying with a necessity, which Nature lays us under, that, secondly, by a spirit of imitation we counteract Nature, and thwart her design. She brings us into the world all originals: no two faces, no two minds, are just alike; but all bear Nature's evident mark of separation on them. Born originals, how comes it to pass that we die copies? That meddling ape Imitation, as soon as we come to years of indiscretion (so let me speak), snatches the pen and blots out Nature's mark of separation, cancels her kind intention, destroys all mental individuality; the lettered world no longer consists of singulars, it is a medley, a mass; and a hundred books, at bottom, are but one. Why are monkeys such masters of mimicry? Why receive they such a talent at imitation? Is it not as the Spartan slaves received a licence for ebriety; that their betters might be ashamed of it?

The third fault to be found with a spirit of imitation is, that with great incongruity it makes us poor and proud: makes us think little, and write much; gives us huge folios, which are little better than more reputable cushions to promote our repose. Have not some sevenfold volumes put us in mind of Ovid's sevenfold channels of the Nile at the conflagration?

> *Ostia septem*
> *Pulverulenta vacant septem sine flumine valles.*

Such leaden labours are like Lycurgus's iron money, which was so much less in value than in bulk, that it required barns for strong-boxes, and a yoke of oxen to draw five hundred pounds.

But notwithstanding these disadvantages of imitation, imitation must be the lot (and often an honourable lot it is) of most writers. If there is a famine of invention in the land, like Joseph's brethren we must travel far for food; we must visit the remote and rich ancients; but an inventive genius may safely stay at home; that, like the widow's cruse, is divinely replenished from within; and affords us a miraculous delight. Whether our own genius be such or not, we diligently should inquire; that we may not go a-begging with gold in our purse. For there is a mine in man, which must be deeply dug ere we can conjecture its contents. Another often sees that in us, which we see not ourselves; and may there not be that in us which is unseen by both? That there may, chance often discovers, either by a luckily chosen theme, or a mighty premium, or an absolute necessity of exertion, or a noble stroke of emulation from another's glory; as that on Thucydides from hearing Herodotus repeat part of his history at the Olympic games: had there been no Herodotus, there might have been no Thucydides, and the world's admiration might have begun at Livy for excellence in that province of the pen. Demosthenes had the same stimulation on hearing Callistratus; or Tully might have been the first of consummate renown at the bar.

Quite clear of the dispute concerning ancient and modern learning, we speak not of performance, but powers. The modern powers are equal to those before them; modern performance in general is deplorably short. How great are the names just mentioned! Yet who will dare affirm, that as great may not rise up in some future, or even in the present age? Reasons there are why talents may not appear, none why they may not exist as much in one period as another. An evocation of vegetable fruits depends on rain, air, and sun; an evocation of the fruits of genius no less depends on externals. What a marvellous crop bore it in Greece and Rome! And what a marvellous sunshine did it there enjoy! What encouragement from the nature of their governments, and the spirit of their people! Virgil and Horace owed their divine talents to Heaven; their immortal works to men; thank Maecenas and Augustus for them. Had it not been for these, the genius of those poets had lain buried in their ashes. Athens expended on her theatre, painting, sculpture, and architecture, a tax levied for the

support of a war. Caesar dropped his papers when
Tully spoke; and Philip trembled at the voice of
Demosthenes: and has there arisen but one Tully,
one Demosthenes, in so long a course of years? The
powerful eloquence of them both in one stream,
should never bear me down into the melancholy persuasion, that several have not been born, though they
have not emerged. The sun as much exists in a cloudy
day, as in a clear; it is outward, accidental circumstances that with regard to genius either in nation
or age

> *Collectas fugat nubes, solemque reducit.*
> VIRG.

As great, perhaps greater than those mentioned
(presumptuous as it may sound) may possibly arise;
for who hath fathomed the mind of man? Its bounds
are as unknown as those of the creation; since the
birth of which, perhaps, not one has so far exerted,
as not to leave his possibilities beyond his attainments,
his powers beyond his exploits. Forming our judgements altogether by what *has* been done, without
knowing, or at all inquiring, what possibly *might* have
been done, we naturally enough fall into too mean an
opinion of the human mind. If a sketch of the divine
Iliad before Homer wrote, had been given to mankind,
by some superior being, or otherwise, its execution
would, probably, have appeared beyond the power of
man. Now, to surpass it, we think impossible. As the
first of these opinions would evidently have been a
mistake, why may not the second be so too? Both are
founded on the same bottom; on our ignorance of the
possible dimensions of the mind of man.

Nor are we only ignorant of the dimensions of the
human mind in general, but even of our own. That
a man may be scarce less ignorant of his own powers,
than an oyster of its pearl, or a rock of its diamond;
that he may possess dormant, unsuspected abilities,
till awakened by loud calls, or stung up by striking
emergencies, is evident from the sudden eruption of

some men, out of perfect obscurity, into public admiration, on the strong impulse of some animating
occasion; not more to the world's great surprise than
their own. Few authors of distinction but have ex-
perienced something of this nature, at the first beam-
ings of their yet unsuspected genius on their hitherto
dark composition: the writer starts at it, as at a lucid
meteor in the night; is much surprised; can scarce
believe it true. During his happy confusion it may
be said to him, as to Eve at the lake,

> What there thou seest, fair creature, is thyself.
>
> MILT.

Genius, in this view, is like a dear friend in our company under disguise; who, while we are lamenting
his absence, drops his mask, striking us, at once, with
equal surprise and joy. This sensation, which I speak of
in a writer, might favour, and so promote, the fable
of poetic inspiration: a poet of a strong imagination,
and stronger vanity, on feeling it, might naturally
enough realize the world's mere compliment, and
think himself truly inspired. Which is not improbable;
for enthusiasts of all kinds do no less.

Since it is plain that men may be strangers to their
own abilities; and by thinking meanly of them without just cause, may possibly lose a name, perhaps
a name immortal; I would find some means to prevent these evils. Whatever promotes virtue, promotes
something more, and carries its good influence beyond
the moral man: to prevent these evils, I borrow two
golden rules from ethics, which are no less golden in
composition than in life. 1st. *Know thyself;* 2ndly,
Reverence thyself: I design to repay ethics in a future
letter, by two rules from rhetoric for its service.

1st. Know thyself. Of ourselves it may be said, as
Martial says of a bad neighbour,

> *Nil tam prope, proculque nobis.*

Therefore dive deep into thy bosom; learn the depth,

extent, bias, and full fort of thy mind; contract full intimacy with the stranger within thee; excite and cherish every spark of intellectual light and heat, however smothered under former negligence, or scattered through the dull, dark mass of common thoughts; and collecting them into a body, let thy genius rise (if a genius thou hast) as the sun from chaos; and if I should then say, like an Indian, *Worship it*, (though too bold) yet should I say little more than my second rule enjoins, (viz.) Reverence thyself.

That is, let not great examples, or authorities, browbeat thy reason into too great a diffidence of thyself: thyself so reverence, as to prefer the native growth of thy own mind to the richest import from abroad; such borrowed riches make us poor. The man who thus reverences himself, will soon find the world's reverence to follow his own. His works will stand distinguished; his the sole property of them; which property alone can confer the noble title of an author; that is, of one who (to speak accurately) thinks and composes; while other invaders of the press, how voluminous and learned soever, (with due respect be it spoken) only read and write.

This is the difference between those two luminaries in literature, the well-accomplished scholar, and the divinely-inspired enthusiast; the first is, as the bright morning star; the second, as the rising sun. The writer who neglects those two rules above will never stand alone; he makes one of a group, and thinks in wretched unanimity with the throng: incumbered with the notions of others, and impoverished by their abundance, he conceives not the least embryo of new thought; opens not the least vista through the gloom of ordinary writers, into the bright walks of rare imagination, and singular design; while the true genius is crossing all public roads into fresh un-trodden ground; he, up to the knees in antiquity, is treading the sacred footsteps of great examples, with

the blind veneration of a bigot saluting the papal toe;
comfortably hoping full absolution for the sins of his
own understanding, from the powerful charm of touching his idol's infallibility.

Such meanness of mind, such prostration of our
own powers, proceeds from too great admiration of
others. Admiration has, generally, a degree of two
very bad ingredients in it; of ignorance, and of fear;
and does mischief in composition, and in life. Proud
as the world is, there is more superiority in it *given*
than *assumed;* and its grandees of all kinds owe more
of their elevation to the littleness of others' minds,
than to the greatness of their own. Were not pros-
trate spirits their voluntary pedestals, the figure
they make among mankind would not stand so
high. Imitators and translators are somewhat of
the pedestal-kind, and sometimes rather raise their
original's reputation, by showing him to be by them
inimitable, than their own. Homer has been translated into most languages; Aelian tells us that the
Indians (hopeful tutors!) have taught him to speak
their tongue. What expect we from them? Not
Homer's Achilles, but something which, like Patroclus,
assumes his name, and at its peril appears in his
stead; nor expect we Homer's Ulysses, gloriously
bursting out of his cloud into royal grandeur, but an
Ulysses under disguise, and a beggar to the last. Such
is that inimitable father of poetry, and oracle of all
the wise, whom Lycurgus transcribed; and for an
annual public recital of whose works Solon enacted a
law; that it is much to be feared, that his so numerous
translations are but as the published testimonials of
so many nations and ages, that this author so divine
is untranslated still.

But here,

Cynthius aurem

Vellit,—

VIRG.

and demands justice for his favourite, and ours. Great

things he has done; but he might have done greater. What a fall is it from Homer's numbers, free as air, lofty and harmonious as the spheres, into childish shackles, and tinkling sounds! But, in his fall, he is still great:

> Nor appears
> Less than archangel ruin'd, and the excess
> Of glory obscur'd.—
>
> MILT.

Had Milton never wrote, Pope had been less to blame: but when in Milton's genius, Homer, as it were, personally rose to forbid Britons doing him that ignoble wrong, it is less pardonable, by that effeminate decoration, to put Achilles in petticoats a second time. How much nobler had it been, if his numbers had rolled on in full flow, through the various modulations of masculine melody, into those grandeurs of solemn sound, which are indispensably demanded by the native dignity of heroic song! How much nobler, if he had resisted the temptation of that Gothic demon, which, modern poesy tasting, became mortal! Oh, how unlike the deathless, divine harmony of three great names (how justly joined!), of Milton, Greece, and Rome! His verse, but for this little speck of mortality in its extreme parts, as his hero had in his heel, like him, had been invulnerable and immortal. But, unfortunately, that was undipped in Helicon; as this, in Styx. Harmony as well as eloquence is essential to poesy; and a murder of his music is putting half Homer to death. Blank is a term of diminution; what we mean by blank verse, is, verse unfallen, uncurst; verse reclaimed, reinthroned in the true language of the gods; who never thundered nor suffered their Homer to thunder, in rhyme; and therefore, I beg you, my friend, to crown it with some nobler term; nor let the greatness of the thing lie under the defamation of such a name.

But supposing Pope's *Iliad* to have been perfect in its kind; yet it is a translation still; which differs as much from an original, as the moon from the sun:

—*Phoeben alieno jusserat igne*
Impleri, solemque suo.

CLAUD.

But as nothing is more easy than to write originally wrong, originals are not here recommended, but under the strong guard of my first rule—Know thyself. Lucian, who was an original, neglected not this rule, if we may judge by his reply to one who took some freedom with him. He was, at first, an apprentice to a statuary; and when he was reflected on as such, by being called Prometheus, he replied, 'I am indeed the inventor of new work, the model of which I owe to none; and, if I do not execute it well, I deserve to be torn by twelve vultures, instead of one.'

If so, O Gulliver! dost thou not shudder at thy brother Lucian's vultures hovering o'er thee? Shudder on! they cannot shock thee more than decency has been shocked by thee. How have thy Houyhnhnms thrown thy judgement from its seat, and laid thy imagination in the mire! In what ordure hast thou dipped thy pencil! What a Monster hast thou made of the

Human face divine!

MILTON.

This writer has so satirized human nature, as to give a demonstration in himself, that it deserves to be satirized. But, say his wholesale admirers, few could so have written; true, and fewer would. If it required great abilities to commit the fault, greater still would have saved him from it. But whence arise such warm advocates for such a performance? From hence, viz. before a character is established, merit makes fame; afterwards fame makes merit. Swift is not commended for this piece, but this piece for Swift. He has given us some beauties which deserve all our praise; and our comfort is, that his faults will not become common; for none can be guilty of them, but who have wit as well as reputation to spare. His wit had been less wild, if his temper had not jostled his judgement. If his favourite houyhnhnms could write, and Swift had been one of them, every horse with him would have been an ass, and he would have written a panegyric on mankind, saddling with much reproach the present heroes of his pen. On the contrary, being born amongst men, and, of consequence, piqued by many, and peevish at more, he has blasphemed a nature little lower than that of angels, and assumed by far higher than they: but surely the contempt of the world is not a greater virtue than the contempt of mankind is a vice. Therefore I wonder that, though forborne by others, the laughter-loving Swift was not reproved by the venerable Dean, who could sometimes be very grave.

For I remember, as I and others were taking with him an evening's walk, about a mile out of Dublin, he stopped short; we passed on; but perceiving that he did not follow us, I went back; and found him fixed as a statue, and earnestly gazing upward at a noble elm, which in its uppermost branches was much withered, and decayed. Pointing at it, he said, 'I shall be like that tree, I shall die at top.' As in this he seemed to prophesy like the Sibyls; if, like one of them, he had burnt part of his works, especially *this* blasted branch of a noble genius, like her too, he might have risen in his demand for the rest.

Would not his friend Pope have succeeded better in an original attempt? Talents untried are talents unknown. All that I know is, that, contrary to these sentiments, he was not only an avowed professor of imitation, but a zealous recommender of it also. Nor could he recommend any thing better, except emulation, to those who write. One of these all writers must call to their aid; but aids they are of unequal repute. Imitation is inferiority confessed; emulation is superiority contested, or denied; imitation is servile, emulation generous; that fetters, this fires; that may give a name; this, a name immortal: this made Athens to succeeding ages the rule of taste, and the standard of perfection. Her men of genius struck fire against each other; and kindled, by conflict, into glories, which no time shall extinguish. We thank Aeschylus for Sophocles; and Parrhasius for Zeuxis; emulation, for both. That bids us fly the general fault of imitators; bids us not be struck with the loud report of former fame, as with a knell, which damps the spirits; but as with a trumpet, which inspires ardour to rival the renowned. Emulation exhorts us, instead of learning our discipline for ever, like raw troops, under ancient leaders in composition, to put those laurelled veterans in some hazard of losing their superior posts in glory.

Such is emulation's high-spirited advice, such her immortalizing call. Pope would not hear, preengaged with Imitation, which blessed him with all her charms. He chose rather, with his namesake of Greece, to triumph in the old world, than to look out for a new. His taste partook the error of his religion; it denied not worship to saints and angels; that is, to writers, who, canonized for ages, have received their apotheosis from established and universal fame. True poesy, like true religion, abhors idolatry; and though it honours the memory of the exemplary, and takes them willingly (yet cautiously) as guides in the way to glory; real, though unexampled, excellence is its only aim; nor looks it for any inspiration less than divine.

Though Pope's noble Muse may boast her illustrious descent from Homer, Virgil, Horace, yet is an original author more nobly born. As Tacitus says of Curtius Rufus, an original author is born of himself, is his own progenitor, and will probably propagate a numerous offspring of imitators, to eternize his glory; while mule-like imitators die without issue. Therefore, though we stand much obliged for his giving us an Homer, yet had he doubled our obligation by giving us—a Pope. Had he a strong imagination,

and the true sublime? That granted, we might have
had two Homers instead of one, if longer had been
his life; for I heard the dying swan talk over an epic
plan a few weeks before his decease.

Bacon, under the shadow of whose great name I
would shelter my present attempt in favour of originals, says, 'Men seek not to know their own stock, and
abilities; but fancy their possessions to be greater, and
their abilities less, than they really are.' Which is, in
effect, saying, 'That we ought to exert more than we
do; and that, on exertion, our probability of success
is greater than we conceive.'

Nor have I Bacon's opinion only, but his assistance
too, on my side. His mighty mind travelled round the
intellectual world; and, with a more than eagle's eye,
saw, and has pointed out, blank spaces, or dark spots
in it, on which the human mind never shone: some
of these have been enlightened since; some are be-
nighted still.

Moreover, so boundless are the bold excursions of
the human mind, that, in the vast void beyond real
existence, it can call forth shadowy beings, and unknown worlds, as numerous, as bright, and, perhaps,
as lasting, as the stars; such quite-original beauties
we may call paradisaical.

> *Natos sine semine flores.*
> Ovid.

When such an ample area for renowned adventure
in original attempts lies before us, shall we be as mere
leaden pipes, conveying to the present age small
streams of excellence from its grand reservoir in
antiquity; and those too, perhaps, muddled in the
pass? Originals shine, like comets; have no peer in
their path; are rivalled by none, and the gaze of all.
All other compositions (if they shine at all) shine in
clusters; like the stars in the galaxy; where, like bad
neighbours, all suffer from all; each particular being
diminished, and almost lost in the throng.

If thoughts of this nature prevailed; if ancients and moderns were no longer considered as masters and pupils, but as hard-matched rivals for renown; then moderns, by the longevity of their labours, might, one day, become ancients themselves: and old Time, that best weigher of merits, to keep his balance even, might have the golden weight of an Augustan age in both his scales: or rather our scale might descend; and that of antiquity (as a modern match for it strongly speaks) might *kick the beam*.

And why not? For consider, since an impartial Providence scatters talents indifferently, as through all orders of persons, so through all periods of time; since, a marvellous light, unenjoyed of old, is poured on us by revelation, with larger prospects extending our understanding, with brighter objects enriching our imagination, with an inestimable prize setting our passions on fire, thus strengthening every power that enables composition to shine; since there has been no fall in man on this side Adam, who left no works, and the works of all other ancients are our auxiliars against themselves, as being perpetual spurs to our ambition, and shining lamps in our path to fame; since this world is a school, as well for intellectual, as moral, advance; and the longer human nature is at school, the better scholar it should be; since, as the moral world expects its glorious millennium, the world intellectual may hope, by the rules of analogy, for some superior degrees of excellence to crown her later scenes; nor may it only hope, but must enjoy them too; for Tully, Quintilian, and all true critics allow, that virtue assists genius, and that the writer will be more able, when better is the man—all these particulars, I say, considered, why should it seem altogether impossible, that heaven's latest editions of the human mind may be the most correct, and fair? that the day may come, when the moderns may proudly look back on the comparative darkness of former ages, on the children of antiquity; reputing

Homer and Demosthenes as the dawn of divine genius, and Athens as the cradle of infant fame? What a glorious revolution would this make in the rolls of renown!

What a rant, say you, is here?—I partly grant it. Yet, consider, my friend! knowledge physical, mathematical, moral, and divine, increases; all arts and sciences are making considerable advance; with them, all the accommodations, ornaments, delights, and glories of human life; and these are new food to the genius of a polite writer; these are as the root, and composition as the flower; and as the root spreads and thrives, shall the flower fail? As well may a flower flourish, when the root is dead. It is prudence to read, genius to relish, glory to surpass, ancient authors; and wisdom to try our strength, in an attempt in which it would be no great dishonour to fail.

Why condemned Maro his admirable epic to the flames? Was it not because his discerning eye saw some length of perfection beyond it? And what he saw, may not others reach? And who bid fairer than our countrymen for that glory? Something new may be expected from Britons particularly; who seem not to be more severed from the rest of mankind by the surrounding sea, than by the current in their veins; and of whom little more appears to be required, in order to give us originals, than a consistency of character, and making their compositions of a piece with their lives. May our genius shine; and proclaim us in that nobler view!

> . . . *minimâ contentos nocte Britannos.*
> VIRG.

And so it does; for in polite composition, in natural and mathematical knowledge, we have great originals already—Bacon, Boyle, Newton Shakespeare, Milton, have showed us, that all the winds cannot blow the British flag farther, than an original spirit can convey the British fame; their names go round the world;

and what foreign genius strikes not as they pass?
Why should not their posterity embark in the same
bold bottom of new enterprise, and hope the same
success? Hope it they may; or you must assert,
either that those originals which we already enjoy,
were written by angels, or deny that we are men. As
Simonides said to Pausanias, reason should say to the
writer, 'Remember thou art a man.' And for man
not to grasp at all which is laudable within his reach,
is a dishonour to human nature, and a disobedience
to the divine; for as heaven does nothing in vain, its
gift of talents implies an injunction of their use.

A friend of mine has obeyed that injunction; he
has relied on himself, and with a genius, as well moral
as original (to speak in bold terms), has cast out evil
spirits; has made a convert to virtue of a species of
composition, once most its foe. As the first Christian
emperors expelled demons, and dedicated their tem-
ples to the living God.

But you, I know, are sparing in your praise of this
author; therefore I will speak of one, which is sure
of your applause. Shakespeare mingled no water with
his wine, lowered his genius by no vapid imitation.
Shakespeare gave us a Shakespeare, nor could the
first in ancient fame have given us more! Shakespeare is not their son, but brother; their equal; and
that, in spite of all his faults. Think you this too
bold? Consider, in those ancients what it is the world
admires! Not the fewness of their faults, but the
number and brightness of their beauties; and if
Shakespeare is their equal (as he doubtless is) in that
which in them is admired, then is Shakespeare as
great as they; and not impotence, but some other
cause, must be charged with his defects. When we
are setting these great men in competition, what but
the comparative size of their genius is the subject of
our inquiry? And a giant loses nothing of his size,
though he should chance to trip in his race. But it is
a compliment to those heroes of antiquity to suppose

Shakespeare their equal only in dramatic powers; therefore, though his faults had been greater, the scale would still turn in his favour. There is at least as much genius on the British as on the Grecian stage, though the former is not swept so clean—so clean from violations not only of the dramatic, but moral rule; for an honest heathen, on reading some of our celebrated scenes, might be seriously concerned to see, that our obligations to the religion of Nature were cancelled by Christianity.

Jonson, in the serious drama, is as much an imitator as Shakespeare is an original. He was very learned, as Samson was very strong, to his own hurt: blind to the nature of tragedy, he pulled down all antiquity on his head, and buried himself under it; we see nothing of Jonson, nor indeed of his admired (but also murdered) ancients; for what shone in the historian is a cloud on the poet; and *Catiline* might have been a good play, if Sallust had never written.

Who knows whether Shakespeare might not have thought less, if he had read more? Who knows, if he might not have laboured under the load of Jonson's learning, as Enceladus under Etna? His mighty genius, indeed, through the most mountainous oppression would have breathed out some of his inextinguishable fire; yet, possibly, he might not have risen up into that giant, that much more than common man, at which we now gaze with amazement, and delight. Perhaps he was as learned as his dramatic province required; for whatever other learning he wanted, he was master of two books, unknown to many of the profoundly read, though books which the last conflagration alone can destroy; the book of Nature, and that of man. These he had by heart, and has transcribed many admirable pages of them, into his immortal works. These are the fountainhead, whence the Castalian streams of original composition flow; and these are often muddied by other waters, though waters in their distinct channel, most wholesome and pure: as two chemical liquors, separately clear as crystal, grow foul by mixture, and offend the sight. So that he had not only as much learning as his dramatic province required, but, perhaps, as it could safely bear. If Milton had spared some of his learning, his muse would have gained more glory, than he would have lost by it.

Dryden, destitute of Shakespeare's genius, had almost as much learning as Jonson, and, for the buskin, quite as little taste. He was a stranger to the pathos, and, by numbers, expression, sentiment, and every other dramatic cheat, strove to make amends for it; as if a saint could make amends for the want of conscience; a soldier, for the want of valour; or a vestal, of modesty. The noble nature of tragedy disclaims an equivalent; like virtue, it demands the heart; and Dryden had none to give. Let epic poets think, the tragedian's point is rather to feel; such distant things are a tragedian and a poet, that the latter indulged destroys the former. Look on Barnwell, and Essex, and see how as to these distant characters Dryden excels, and is excelled. But the strongest demonstration of his no-taste for the buskin are his tragedies fringed with rhyme; which, in epic poetry, is a sore disease, in the tragic, absolute death. To Dryden's enormity, Pope's was a light offence. As lacemen are foes to mourning, these two authors, rich in rhyme, were no great friends to those solemn ornaments, which the noble nature of their works required.

Must rhyme then, say you, be banished? I wish the nature of our language could bear its entire expulsion; but our lesser poetry stands in need of a toleration for it; it raises that, but sinks the great; as spangles adorn children, but expose men. Prince Henry bespangled all over in his eyelet-hole suit, with glittering pins; and an Achilles, or an Almanzor, in his Gothic array; are very much on a level, as to the majesty of the poet, and the prince. Dryden had a great, but a general capacity; and as for a general genius, there is no such thing in Nature. A genius implies the rays of the mind concentred, and determined to some particular point; when they are scattered widely, they act feebly, and strike not with sufficient force, to fire, or dissolve, the heart. As what comes from the writer's heart reaches ours; so what comes from his head sets our brains at work, and our hearts at ease. It makes a circle of thoughtful critics, not of distressed patients; and a passive audience is what tragedy requires. Applause is not to be given, but extorted; and the silent lapse of a single tear does the writer more honour than the rattling thunder of a thousand hands. Applauding hands and dry eyes (which during Dryden's theatrical reign often met) are a satire on the writer's talent, and the spectator's taste. When by such judges the laurel is blindly given, and by such a poet proudly received, they resemble an intoxicated host, and his tasteless guests, over some sparkling adulteration, commending their champagne.

But Dryden has his glory, though not on the stage. What an inimitable original is his ode! A small one, indeed, but of the first lustre, and without a flaw; and, amid the brightest boasts of antiquity, it may find a foil.

Among the brightest of the moderns, Mr. Addison must take his place. Who does not approach his character with great respect? They who refuse to close with the public in his praise, refuse at their peril. But, if men will be fond of their own opinions, some hazard must be run. He had, what Dryden and Jonson wanted, a warm and feeling heart; but, being of a grave and bashful nature, through a philosophic reserve and a sort of moral prudery, he concealed it, where he should have let loose all his fire, and have showed the most tender sensibilities of heart. At his celebrated *Cato*, few tears are shed, but Cato's own; which, indeed, are truly great, but unaffecting, except to the noble few, who love their country better than themselves. The bulk of mankind want virtue enough to be touched by them. His strength of genius has reared up one glorious image, more lofty and truly golden than that in the plains of Dura, for cool admiration to gaze at, and warm patriotism (how rare!) to worship; while those two throbbing pulses of the drama, by which alone it is shown to live, terror and pity, neglected through the whole, leave our unmolested hearts at perfect peace. Thus the poet, like his hero, through mistaken excellence, and virtue overstrained, becomes a sort of suicide; and that which is most dramatic in the drama, dies. All his charms of poetry are but as funeral flowers, which adorn; all his noble sentiments but as rich spices, which embalm, the tragedy deceased.

Of tragedy, pathos is not only the life and soul, but the soul inextinguishable; it charms us through a thousand faults. Decorations, which in this author abound, though they might immortalize other poesy, are the *splendida peccata* which damn the drama; while, on the contrary, the murder of all other beauties is a venial sin, nor plucks the laurel from the tragedian's brow. Was it otherwise, Shakespeare himself would run some hazard of losing his crown.

Socrates frequented the plays of Euripides; and what living Socrates would decline the theatre, at the representation of *Cato*? Tully's assassins found him in the litter, reading the *Medea* of the Grecian poet, to prepare himself for death. Part of *Cato* might be read to the same end. In the weight and dignity of moral reflection, Addison resembles that poet, who was called the dramatic philosopher; and is himself, as he says of Cato, 'ambitiously sententious'. But as to the singular talent so remarkable in Euripides, at melting down hearts into the tender streams of grief and pity, there the resemblance fails. His beauties sparkle, but do not warm; they sparkle as stars in a frosty night. There is, indeed, a constellation in his play; there is the philosopher, patriot, orator, and poet; but where is the tragedian? And, if that is wanting,

Cur in theatrum Cato severe venisti?
                                        MART.

And, when I recollect what passed between him and Dryden in relation to this drama, I must add the next line,

An ideo tantum veneras, ut exires?

For, when Addison was a student at Oxford, he sent up this play to his friend Dryden, as a proper person to recommend it to the theatre, if it deserved it; who returned it, with very great commendation; but with his opinion, that, on the stage, it could not meet with its deserved success. But though the performance was denied the theatre, it brought its author on the public stage of life. For persons in power inquiring soon after of the head of his college for a youth of parts, Addison was recommended, and readily received, by means of the great reputation which Dryden had just then spread of him above.

There is this similitude between the poet and the play; as this is more fit for the closet than the stage; so, that shone brighter in private conversation than on the public scene. They both had a sort of local excellency, as the heathen gods a local divinity; beyond such a bound they, unadmired; and these, unadored. This puts me in mind of Plato, who denied Homer to the public; that Homer, which, when in his closet, was rarely out of his hand. Thus, though Cato is not calculated to signalize himself in the warm emotions of the theatre, yet we find him a most amiable companion in our calmer delights of recess.

Notwithstanding what has been offered, this, in many views, is an exquisite piece. But there is so much more of art than nature in it, that I can scarce forbear calling it an exquisite piece of statuary,

Where the smooth chisel all its skill has shown,
To soften into flesh the rugged stone.

                                        ADDISON.

That is, where art has taken great pains to labour undramatic matter into dramatic life; which is impossible. However, as it is, like Pygmalion, we cannot but fall in love with it, and wish it was alive. How would a Shakespeare, or an Otway, have answered our wishes? They would have outdone Prometheus, and, with their heavenly fire, have given him not only life, but immortality. At their dramas (such is the force of nature) the poet is out of sight, quite hid behind his Venus, never thought of, till the curtain falls. Art brings our author forward, he stands before his piece; splendidly indeed, but unfortunately; for the writer must be forgotten by his audience during the representation, if for ages he would be remembered by posterity. In the theatre, as in life, delusion is the charm; and we are undelighted the first moment we are undeceived. Such demonstration have we, that the theatre is not yet opened in which solid happiness can be found by man; because none are more than comparatively good; and folly has a corner in the heart of the wise.

A genius fond of ornament should not be wedded to the tragic muse, which is in mourning: we want not to be diverted at an entertainment, where our greatest pleasure arises from the depth of our concern. But whence (by the way) this odd generation of pleasure from pain? The movement of our melancholy passions is pleasant, when we ourselves are safe: we love to be at once miserable and unhurt. So are we made; and so made, perhaps, to show us the divine goodness; to show that none of our passions were designed to give us pain, except when being pained is for our advantage on the whole; which is evident from this instance, in which we see that passions the most painful administer greatly, sometimes, to our delight. Since great names have accounted otherwise for this particular, I wish this solution, though to me probable, may not prove a mistake.

To close our thoughts on *Cato*: he who sees not much beauty in it, has no taste for poetry; he who sees nothing else, has no taste for the stage. Whilst it justifies censure, it extorts applause. It is much to be admired, but little to be felt. Had it not been a tragedy, it had been immortal; as it is a tragedy, its uncommon fate somewhat resembles his, who, for conquering gloriously, was condemned to die. Both shone, but shone fatally—because in breach of their respective laws, the laws of the drama, and the laws of arms. But how rich in reputation must that author be, who can spare a *Cato*, without feeling the loss!

That loss by our author would scarce be felt; it would be but dropping a single feather from a wing that mounts him above his contemporaries. He has a more refined, decent, judicious, and extensive genius, than Pope or Swift. To distinguish this triumvirate from each other, and, like Newton, to discover the different colours in these genuine and meridian rays of literary light, Swift is a singular wit, Pope a correct poet, Addison a great author. Swift looked on wit as the *jus divinum* to dominion and sway in the world, and considered as usurpation all power that was lodged in persons of less sparkling understandings. This inclined him to tyranny in wit; Pope was somewhat of his opinion, but was for softening tyranny into lawful monarchy; yet were there some acts of severity in his reign. Addison's crown was elective, he reigned by the public voice:

> ... *Volentes*
> *Per populos dat iura, viamque affectat Olympo.*
> VIRG.

But as good books are the medicine of the mind, if we should dethrone these authors, and consider them, not in their royal, but their medicinal capacity, might it not then be said, that Addison prescribed a wholesome and pleasant regimen, which was universally relished, and did much good; that Pope

preferred a purgative of satire, which, though wholesome, was too painful in its operation; and that
Swift insisted on a large dose of ipecacuanha, which,
though readily swallowed from the fame of the physician, yet, if the patient had any delicacy of taste,
he threw up the remedy, instead of the disease?

Addison wrote little in verse, much in sweet, elegant,
Virgilian prose; so let me call it, since Longinus calls
Herodotus most Homeric, and Thucydides is said to
have formed his style on Pindar. Addison's compositions are built with the finest materials, in the taste
of the ancients, and (to speak his own language)
on truly classic ground: and though they are the
delight of the present age, yet am I persuaded that
they will receive more justice from posterity. I never
read him, but I am struck with such a disheartening
idea of perfection that I drop my pen. And, indeed,
far superior writers should forget his compositions, if
they would be greatly pleased with their own.

And yet (perhaps you have not observed it) what
is the common language of the world, and even of
his admirers, concerning him? They call him an
elegant writer: that elegance which shines on the surface of his compositions, seems to dazzle their understanding, and render it a little blind to the depth of
sentiment which lies beneath: thus (hard fate!) he
loses reputation with them, by doubling his title to it.
On subjects the most interesting and important, no
author of his age has written with greater, I had
almost said with equal, weight: and they who commend him for his elegance, pay him such a sort of
compliment, by their abstemious praise, as they
would pay to Lucretia, if they should commend her
only for her beauty.

But you say that you know his value already.
You know, indeed, the value of his writings, and
close with the world in thinking them immortal; but,
I believe, you know not that his name would have
deserved immortality, though he had never written;

and that, by a better title than the pen can give: you know too, that his life was amiable; but, perhaps, you are still to learn that his death was triumphant: that is a glory granted to very few. And the paternal hand of Providence, which, sometimes, snatches home its beloved children in a moment, must convince us, that it is a glory of no great consequence to the dying individual; that, when it is granted, it is granted chiefly for the sake of the surviving world, which may profit by his pious example, to whom is indulged the strength and opportunity to make his virtue shine out brightest at the point of death. And here, permit me to take notice, that the world will, probably, profit more by a pious example of lay-extraction, than by one born of the church; the latter being, usually, taxed with an abatement of influence by the bulk of mankind: therefore, to smother a bright example of this superior good influence, may be reputed a sort of murder injurious to the living, and unjust to the dead.

Such an example have we in Addison; which, though hitherto suppressed, yet, when once known, is insuppressible, of a nature too rare, too striking to be forgotten. For, after a long and manly, but vain struggle with his distemper, he dismissed his physicians, and with them all hopes of life: but with his hopes of life he dismissed not his concern for the living, but sent for a youth nearly related, and finely accomplished, yet not above being the better for good impressions from a dying friend. He came; but life now glimmering in the socket, the dying friend was silent: after a decent and proper pause, the youth said, 'Dear Sir! you sent for me: I believe, and I hope, that you have some commands; I shall hold them most sacred.' May distant ages not only hear, but feel, the reply! Forcibly grasping the youth's hand, he softly said, 'See in what peace a Christian can die.' He spoke with difficulty, and soon expired. Through grace divine, how great is man! Through

divine mercy, how stingless is death! Who would not
thus expire?

What an inestimable legacy were those few dying
words to the youth beloved! What a glorious supple-
ment to his own valuable fragment on the truth of
Christianity! What a full demonstration, that his
fancy could not feign beyond what his virtue could
reach! For when he would strike us most strongly
with the grandeur of Roman magnanimity, his dying
hero is ennobled with this sublime sentiment,

> While yet I live, let me not live in vain.
> CATO.

But how much more sublime is that sentiment when
realized in life; when dispelling the languors, and
appeasing the pains of a last hour, and brightening
with illustrious action the dark avenue, and all-awful
confines of an eternity! When his soul scarce animated
his body, strong faith and ardent charity animated
his soul into divine ambition of saving more than his
own. It is for our honour, and our advantage, to hold
him high in our esteem: for the better men are, the
more they will admire him; and the more they admire
him, the better will they be.

By undrawing the long closed curtain of his death-
bed, have I not showed you a stranger in him whom
you knew so well? Is not this of your favourite
author,

> —Notâ maior imago?
> VIRG.

His compositions are but a noble preface; the grand
work is his death: that is a work which is read in
heaven: how has it joined the final approbation of
angels to the previous applause of men! How gloriously has he opened a splendid path, through fame
immortal, into eternal peace! How has he given
religion to triumph amidst the ruins of his nature!
And, stronger than death, risen higher in virtue when
breathing his last!

If all our men of genius had so breathed their last; if all our men of genius, like him, had been men of genius for eternals; *then* had we never been pained by the report of a latter end—oh! how unlike to this! But a little to balance our pain, let us consider that such reports as make us, at once, adore and tremble, are of use, when too many there are who must tremble before they will adore; and who convince us, to our shame, that the surest refuge of our endangered virtue is in the fears and terrors of the disingenuous human heart.

'But reports, you say, may be false; and you farther ask me, If all reports were true, how came an anecdote of so much honour to human nature, as mine, to lie so long unknown? What inauspicious planet interposed to lay its lustre under so lasting and so surprising an eclipse?'

The fact is indisputably true; nor are you to rely on me for the truth of it: my report is but a second edition: it was published before, though obscurely, and with a cloud before it. As clouds before the sun are often beautiful, so this of which I speak. How finely pathetic are those two lines, which this so solemn and affecting scene inspired!

> He taught us how to live; and, oh! too high
> A price for knowledge, taught us how to die.
> TICKELL.

With truth wrapped in darkness, so sung our oracle to the public, but explained himself to me: he was present at his patron's death, and that account of it here given, he gave to me before his eyes were dry. By what means Addison taught us how to die, the poet left to be made known by a late, and less able hand; but one more zealous for his patron's glory—zealous, and impotent, as the poor Egyptian, who gathered a few splinters of a broken boat, as a funeral pile for the great Pompey, studious of doing honour to so renowned a name: yet had not this poor plank (permit me, here, so to call this imperfect page) been thrown out, the chief article of his patron's glory would probably have been sunk for ever, and late ages have received but a fragment of his fame: a fragment glorious indeed, for his genius how bright! But to commend him for composition, though immortal, is detraction now, if there our encomium ends: let us look farther to that concluding scene, which spoke human nature not unrelated to the divine. To that let us pay the long and large arrear of our greatly posthumous applause.

This you will think a long digression, and justly, if that may be called a digression, which was my chief inducement for writing at all. I had long wished to deliver up to the public this sacred deposit, which by Providence was lodged in my hands; and I entered on the present undertaking partly as an introduction to that, which is more worthy to see the light; of which I gave an intimation in the beginning of my letter: for this is the monumental marble there mentioned, to which I promised to conduct you; this is the sepulchral lamp, the long-hidden lustre of our accomplished countryman, who now rises as from his tomb, to receive the regard so greatly due to the dignity of his death; a death to be distinguished by tears of joy; a death which angels beheld with delight.

And shall that, which would have shone conspicuous amid the resplendent lights of Christianity's glorious morn, by these dark days be dropped into oblivion? Dropped it is; and dropped by our sacred, august, and ample register of renown, which has entered in its marble memoirs the dim splendour of far inferior worth: though so lavish of praise, and so talkative of the dead, yet is it silent on a subject, which (if any) might have taught its unlettered stones to speak. If powers were not wanting, a monument more durable than those of marble should proudly rise in this ambitious page, to the new and far nobler Addison, than that which you, and the public, have so long and so much admired: nor this nation only; for it is Europe's Addison, as well as ours; though Europe knows not half his title to her esteem; being as yet unconscious that the dying Addison far outshines her Addison immortal. Would we resemble him? Let us not limit our ambition to the least illustrious part of his character; heads, indeed, are crowned on earth; but hearts only are crowned in heaven: a truth, which, in such an age of authors, should not be forgotten.

It is piously to be hoped, that this narrative may have some effect, since all listen, when a death-bed speaks; and regard the person departing as an actor of a part, which the great master of the drama has appointed us to perform to-morrow. This was a Roscius on the stage of life; his exit how great! Ye lovers of virtue, *plaudite*! and let us, my friend! ever 'remember his end, as well as our own, that we may never do amiss.'—I am,

Dear Sir,
Your most obliged,
humble servant.

P.S.—How far Addison is an original, you will see in my next; where I descend from this consecrated ground into his sublunary praise; and great is the descent, though into noble heights of intellectual power.

RICHARD HURD

From *LETTERS ON CHIVALRY*, 1762

HEROIC AND GOTHIC MANNERS

(*Letter VI*)

LET it be no surprise to you that, in the close of my last letter, I presumed to bring the *Gierusalemme liberata* into competition with the *Iliad*.

So far as the heroic and Gothic manners are the same, the pictures of each, if well taken, must be equally entertaining. But I go farther, and maintain that the circumstances, in which they differ, are clearly to the advantage of the Gothic designers.

You see my purpose is to lead you from this forgotten chivalry to a more amusing subject, I mean the poetry we still read, and which was founded upon it.

Much has been said, and with great truth, of the felicity of Homer's age, for poetical manners. But as Homer was a citizen of the world, when he had seen in Greece, on the one hand, the manners he has described, could he, on the other hand, have seen in the west the manners of the feudal ages, I make no doubt but he would certainly have preferred the latter. And the grounds of this preference would, I suppose, have been 'the improved gallantry of the feudal times; and the superior solemnity of their superstitions'.

If any great poet, like Homer, had lived amongst, and sung of, the Gothic knights (for after all Spenser and Tasso came too late, and it was impossible for them to paint truly and perfectly what was no longer seen or believed) this preference, I persuade myself, had been very sensible. But their fortune was not so happy.

—omnes illacrymabiles
Urgentur, ignotique longâ
Nocte, carent quia vate sacro.

As it is, we may take a guess of what the subject was capable of affording to real genius from the rude sketches we have of it, in the old romancers. And it is but looking into any of them to be convinced that the gallantry, which inspirited the feudal times, was of a nature to furnish the poet with finer scenes and subjects of description in every view, than the simple and uncontrolled barbarity of the Grecian.

The principal entertainment arising from the delineation of these consists in the exercise of the boisterous passions, which are provoked and kept alive from one end of the *Iliad* to the other, by every imaginable scene of rage, revenge, and slaughter. In the other, together with these, the gentler and more humane affections are awakened in us by the most interesting displays of love and friendship; of love, elevated to its noblest heights; and of friendship, operating on the purest motives. The mere variety of these paintings is a relief to the reader as well as writer. But their beauty, novelty, and pathos give them a vast advantage on the comparison.

Consider, withal, the surprises, accidents, adventures which probably and naturally attend on the life of wandering knights; the occasion there must be for describing the wonders of different countries, and of presenting to view the manners and policies of distant states: all which make so conspicuous a part of the materials of the greater poetry.

So that, on the whole, though the spirit, passions, rapine, and violence of the two sets of manners were equal, yet there was a dignity, a magnificence, a variety in the feudal, which the other wanted.

As to religious machinery, perhaps the popular system of each was equally remote from reason, yet the latter had something in it more amusing, as well as more awakening to the imagination.

The current popular tales of elves and fairies were even fitter to take the credulous mind, and charm it into a willing admiration of the specious miracles which wayward fancy delights in, than those of the old traditionary rabble of pagan divinities. And then, for the more solemn fancies of witchcraft and incantation, the horrors of the Gothic were above measure striking and terrible. The mummeries of the pagan priests were childish, but the Gothic enchanters shook and alarmed all nature.

We feel this difference very sensibly in reading the ancient and modern poets. You would not compare the Canidia of Horace with the witches in *Macbeth*. And what are Virgil's myrtles dropping blood, to Tasso's enchanted forest?

Ovid indeed, who had a fancy turned to romance, makes Medea, in a rant, talk wildly. But was this the common language of their other writers? The enchantress in Virgil says coolly of the very chiefest prodigies of her charms and poisons,

> *His ego saepè lupum fieri, et se condere sylvis*
> *Moerin; saepè animas imis excire sepulchris,*
> *Atque satas alio vidi traducere messes.*

The admirable poet has given an air of the marvellous to his subject, by the magic of his expression. Else, what do we find here, but the ordinary effects of melancholy, the vulgar superstition of evoking spirits, and the supposed influence of fascination on the hopes of rural industry?

> *Non isthic obliquo oculo mihi commoda quisquam*
> *Limat . . .*

says the poet of his country-seat, as if this security from a fascinating eye were a singular privilege, and the mark of a more than common good fortune.

Shakespeare, on the other hand, with a terrible sublime (which not so much the energy of his genius, as the nature of his subject drew from him) gives us

another idea of the rough magic, as he calls it, of
fairy enchantment:

> . . . I have bedimm'd
> The noon-tide sun, call'd forth the mutinous winds,
> And 'twixt the green sea and the azure vault
> Set roaring war; to the dread rattling thunder
> Have I giv'n fire, and rifted Jove's stout oak
> With his own bolt: The strong-bas'd promontory
> Have I made shake, and by the spurs pluck'd up
> The pine and cedar: Graves, at my command,
> Have open'd, and let forth their sleepers . . .

The last circumstance, you will say, is but the
animas imis excire sepulchris of the Latin poet. But a
very significant word marks the difference. The
pagan necromancers had a hundred little tricks by
which they pretended to call up the ghosts, or shadows
of the dead: but these, in the ideas of paganism, were
quite another thing from Shakespeare's sleepers.

This may serve for a cast of Shakespeare's magic:
and I can't but think that when Milton wanted to
paint the horrors of that night (one of the noblest
parts in his *Paradise Regained*), which the devil himself
is feigned to conjure up in the wilderness, the Gothic
language and ideas helped him to work up his
tempest with such terror. You will judge from these
lines:

> . . . nor staid the terror there;
> Infernal ghosts and hellish furies round
> Environ'd thee; some howl'd, some yell'd, some shriek'd,
> Some bent at thee their fiery darts . . .

But above all from the following:

> Thus pass'd the night so foul, till morning fair
> Came forth with pilgrim steps in amice gray,
> Who with her *radiant finger* still'd the roar
> Of thunder, chas'd the clouds, and laid the winds
> And *griesly specters* . . .

Where the radiant finger points at the potent wand
of the Gothic magicians, which could reduce the

calm of nature, upon occasion, as well as disturb it; and the grisly spectres laid by the approach of morn, were apparently of their raising, as a sagacious critic perceived when he took notice 'how very injudicious it was to retail the popular superstition in this place'.

After all, the conclusion is not to be drawn so much from particular passages, as from the general impression left on our minds in reading the ancient and modern poets. And this is so much in favour of the latter that Mr. Addison scruples not to say, 'The ancients have not much of this poetry among them; for, indeed (continues he) almost the whole substance of it owes its original to the darkness and superstition of later ages. Our forefathers looked upon nature with more reverence and horror, before the world was enlightened by learning and philosophy, and loved to astonish themselves with the apprehensions of witchcraft, prodigies, charms, and enchantments. There was not a village in England, that had not a ghost in it, the churchyards were all haunted, every large common had a circle of fairies belonging to it, and there was scarce a shepherd to be met with who had not seen a spirit.'

We are upon enchanted ground, my friend; and you are to think yourself well used that I detain you no longer in this fearful circle. The glimpse, you have had of it, will help your imagination to conceive the rest. And without more words you will readily apprehend that the fancies of our modern bards are not only more gallant, but, on a change of the scene, more sublime, more terrible, more alarming, than those of the classic fablers. In a word, you will find that the manners they paint, and the superstitions they adopt, are the more poetical for being Gothic.

SPENSER AND MILTON

(*Letter VII*)

BUT nothing shows the difference of the two systems under consideration more plainly, than the effect they really had on the two greatest of our poets; at least the two which an English reader is most fond to compare with Homer, I mean Spenser and Milton.

It is not to be doubted but that each of these bards had kindled his poetic fire from classic fables. So that, of course, their prejudices would lie that way. Yet they both appear, when most inflamed, to have been more particularly wrapt with the Gothic fables of chivalry.

Spenser, though he had been long nourished with the spirit and substance of Homer and Virgil, chose the times of chivalry for his theme, and fairy land for the scene of his fictions. He could have planned, no doubt, an heroic design on the exact classic model: or, he might have trimmed between the Gothic and classic, as his contemporary Tasso did. But the charms of fairy prevailed. And if any think he was seduced by Ariosto into this choice, they should consider that it could be only for the sake of his subject; for the genius and character of these poets was widely different.

Under this idea then of a Gothic, not classical poem, the *Faerie Queene* is to be read and criticized. And on these principles, it would not be difficult to unfold its merit in another way than has been hitherto attempted.

Milton, it is true, preferred the classic model to the Gothic. But it was after long hesitation; and his favourite subject was Arthur and his knights of the round table. On this he had fixed for the greater part of his life. What led him to change his mind was, partly, as I suppose, his growing fanaticism; partly, his ambition to take a different route from Spenser;

but chiefly perhaps, the discredit into which the stories of chivalry had now fallen by the immortal satire of Cervantes. Yet we see through all his poetry, where his enthusiasm flames out most, a certain predilection for the legends of chivalry before the fables of Greece.

This circumstance, you know, has given offence to the austerer and more mechanical critics. They are ready to censure his judgement, as juvenile and unformed, when they see him so delighted, on all occasions, with the Gothic romances. But do these censors imagine that Milton did not perceive the defects of these works, as well as they? No: it was not the composition of books of chivalry, but the manners described in them, that took his fancy; as appears from his *Allegro*:

> Towred cities please us then
> And the busy hum of men,
> Where throngs of knights and barons bold
> In weeds of peace high triumphs hold,
> With store of ladies, whose bright eyes
> Rain influence, and judge the prize
> Of wit, or arms, while both contend
> To win her grace, whom all commend.

And when in the *Penseroso* he draws, by a fine contrivance, the same kind of image to soothe melancholy which he had before given to excite mirth, he indeed extols an author of one of these romances, as he had before, in general, extolled the subject of them; but it is an author worthy of his praise; not the writer of *Amadis* or *Sir Launcelot of the Lake*, but Chaucer himself, who has left an unfinished story on the Gothic or feudal model:

> Or call up him that left half-told
> The story of Cambuscan bold,
> Of Camball and of Algarsife,
> And who had Canace to wife
> That own'd the virtuous ring and glass
> And of the wondrous horse of brass,

> On which the Tartar king did ride;
> And if aught else great bards beside
> In sage and solemn tunes have sung
> Of tourneys and of trophies hung,
> Of forests and enchantments drear,
> Where more is meant than meets the ear.

The conduct then of these two poets may incline us to think with more respect than is commonly done of the Gothic manners, I mean as adapted to the uses of the greater poetry.

I say nothing of Shakespeare because the sublimity (the divinity, let it be, if nothing else will serve) of his genius kept no certain route, but rambled at hazard into all the regions of human life and manners. So that we can hardly say what he preferred or what he rejected on full deliberation. Yet one thing is clear, that even he is greater when he uses Gothic manners and machinery than when he employs classical: which brings us again to the same point, that the former have, by their nature and genius, the advantage of the latter in producing the sublime.

THE FAERIE QUEENE

(Letter VIII)

I spoke 'of criticizing Spenser's poem, under the idea not of a classical but Gothic composition'.

It is certain much light might be thrown on that singular work, were an able critic to consider it in this view. For instance, he might go some way towards explaining, perhaps justifying, the general plan and conduct of the *Faerie Queene*, which to classical readers has appeared indefensible.

I have taken the fancy, with your leave, to try my hand on this curious subject.

When an architect examines a Gothic structure by Grecian rules, he finds nothing but deformity.

But the Gothic architecture has its own rules, by which when it comes to be examined, it is seen to have its merit, as well as the Grecian. The question is not, which of the two is conducted in the simplest or truest taste: but whether there be not sense and design in both, when scrutinized by the laws on which each is projected.

The same observation holds of the two sorts of poetry. Judge of the *Faerie Queene* by the classic models, and you are shocked with its disorder: consider it with an eye to its Gothic original, and you find it regular. The unity and simplicity of the former are more complete: but the latter has that sort of unity and simplicity which results from its nature.

The *Faerie Queene* then, as a Gothic poem, derives its method, as well as the other characters of its composition, from the established modes and ideas of chivalry.

It was usual, in the days of knight-errantry, at the holding of any great feast, for knights to appear before the prince who presided at it, and claim the privilege of being sent on any adventure, to which the solemnity might give occasion. For it was supposed that, when such a throng of knights and barons bold as Milton speaks of, were got together, the distressed would flock in from all quarters, as to a place where they knew they might find and claim redress for all their grievances.

This was the real practice, in the days of pure and ancient chivalry. And an image of this practice was afterwards kept up in the castles of the great, on any extraordinary festival or solemnity: of which, if you want an instance, I refer you to the description of a feast made at Lisle in 1453, in the court of Philip the Good, Duke of Burgundy, for a crusade against the Turks: as you may find it given at large in the memoirs of Matthieu de Conci, Olivier de la Marche, and Monstrelet.

That feast was held for twelve days: and each day

was distinguished by the claim and allowance of some adventure.

Now laying down this practice, as a foundation for the poet's design, you will see how properly the *Faerie Queene* is conducted.

'I devise,' says the poet himself in his Letter to Sir W. Raleigh, 'that the Faery Queen kept her annual feaste xii days: upon which xii several days, the occasions of the xii several adventures hapened; which being undertaken by xii several knights, are in these xii books severally handled.'

Here you have the poet delivering his own method, and the reason of it. It arose out of the order of his subject. And would you desire a better reason for his choice?

Yes, you will say; a poet's method is not that of his subject. I grant you, as to the order of time, in which the recital is made; for here, as Spenser observes (and his own practice agrees to the rule), lies the main difference between the poet historical and the historiographer. The reason of which is drawn from the nature of epic composition itself, and holds equally, let the subject be what it will, and whatever the system of manners be on which it is conducted. Gothic or classic makes no difference in this respect.

But the case is not the same with regard to the general plan of a work, or what may be called the order of distribution, which is and must be governed by the subject-matter itself. It was as requisite for the *Faerie Queene* to consist of the adventures of twelve knights as for the *Odyssey* to be confined to the adventures of one hero: justice had otherwise not been done to his subject.

So that if you will say anything against the poet's method, you must say that he should not have chosen this subject. But this objection arises from your classic ideas of unity, which have no place here; and are in every view foreign to the purpose, if the poet has found means to give his work, though consisting of many parts, the advantage of unity. For in some reasonable sense or other it is agreed every work of art must be one, the very idea of a work requiring it.

If you ask then what is this unity of Spenser's poem? I say it consists in the relation of its several adventures to one common original, the appointment of the Faerie Queen; and to one common end, the completion of the Faerie Queen's injunctions. The knights issued forth on their adventures on the breaking up of this annual feast; and the next annual feast, we are to suppose, is to bring them together again from the achievement of their several charges.

This, it is true, is not the classic unity, which consists in the representation of one entire action: but it is a unity of another sort, a unity resulting from the respect which a number of related actions have to one common purpose. In other words, it is a unity of design and not of action.

This Gothic method of design in poetry may be, in some sort, illustrated by what is called the Gothic method of design in gardening. A wood or grove cut out into many separate avenues or glades was amongst the most favourite of the works of art, which our fathers attempted in this species of cultivation. These walks were distinct from each other, had each their several destination, and terminated on their own proper objects. Yet the whole was brought together and considered under one view by the relation which these various openings had, not to each other, but to their common and concurrent centre. You and I are, perhaps, agreed that this sort of gardening is not of so true a taste as that which Kent and Nature have brought us acquainted with; where the supreme art of the designer consists in disposing his ground and objects into an entire landscape; and grouping them, if I may use the term, in so easy a manner, that the careless observer, though he be taken with the symmetry of the whole, discovers no art in the combination:

In lieto aspetto il bel giardin s'aperse,
  Acque stagnanti, mobili cristalli,
Fior vari, e varie piante, herbe diverse,
  Apriche collinette, ombrose valli,
Selve, e spelunche in UNA VISTA offerse:
  E quel, che'l bello, e'l caro accresce à l'opre,
  L'Arte, che tutto fà, nulla si scopre.
                            TASSO. C. xvi. S. ix.

This, I say, may be the truest taste in gardening,
because the simplest. Yet there is a manifest regard
to unity in the other method; which has had its
admirers, as it may have again, and is certainly not
without its design and beauty.

But to return to our poet. Thus far he drew from
Gothic ideas, and these ideas, I think, would lead
him no farther. But, as Spenser knew what belonged
to classic composition, he was tempted to tie his
subject still closer together by one expedient of his
own, and by another taken from his classic models.

His own was to interrupt the proper story of each
book, by dispersing it into several; involving by this
means, and as it were intertwisting the several
actions together, in order to give something like the
appearance of one action to his twelve adventures.
And for this conduct, as absurd as it seems, he had
some great examples in the Italian poets, though I
believe they were led into it by different motives.

The other expedient which he borrowed from the
classics, was by adopting one superior character which
should be seen throughout. Prince Arthur, who had a
separate adventure of his own, was to have his part in
each of the others; and thus several actions were to be
embodied by the interest which one principal hero had
in them all. It is even observable that Spenser gives this
adventure of Prince Arthur, in quest of Gloriana, as the
proper subject of his poem. And upon this idea the late
learned editor of the *Faerie Queene* has attempted, but I
think without success, to defend the unity and simplicity of its fable. The truth was, the violence of

classic prejudices forced the poet to affect this appearance of unity, though in contradiction to his Gothic system. And as far as we can judge of the tenor of the whole work from the finished half of it, the adventure of Prince Arthur, whatever the author pretended, and his critic too easily believed, was but an afterthought; and at least with regard to the historical fable, which we are now considering, was only one of the expedients by which he would conceal the disorder of his Gothic plan.

And if this was his design, I will venture to say that both his expedients were injudicious. Their purpose was to ally two things in nature incompatible, the Gothic, and the classic unity; the effect of which mis-alliance was to discover and expose the nakedness of the Gothic.

I am of opinion then, considering the *Faerie Queene* as an epic or narrative poem constructed on Gothic ideas, that the poet had done well to effect no other unity than that of design, by which his subject was connected. But his poem is not simply narrative; it is throughout allegorical: he calls it 'a perpetual allegory or dark conceit': and this character, for reasons I may have occasion to observe hereafter, was even predominant in the *Faerie Queene*. His narration is subservient to his moral, and but serves to colour it. This he tells us himself at setting out:

Fierce wars and faithful loves shall *moralize* my song,

that is, shall serve for a vehicle, or instrument to convey the moral.

Now under this idea the unity of the *Faerie Queene* is more apparent. His twelve knights are to exemplify as many virtues, out of which one illustrious character is to be composed. And in this view the part of Prince Arthur in each book becomes essential, and yet not principal; exactly as the poet has contrived it. They who rest in the literal story, that is, who criticize it on the footing of a narrative poem, have constantly objected to this management. They say it necessarily breaks the unity of design. Prince Arthur, they affirm, should either have had no part in the other adventures or he should have had the chief part. He should either have done nothing or more. And the objection is unanswerable; at least I know of nothing that can be said to remove it but what I have supposed above might be the purpose of the poet, and which I myself have rejected as insufficient.

But how faulty soever this conduct be in the literal story, it is perfectly right in the moral: and that for an obvious reason, though his critics seem not to have been aware of it. His chief hero was not to have the twelve virtues in the *degree* in which the knights had, each of them, their own; (such a character would be a monster) but he was to have so much of each as was requisite to form his superior character. Each virtue in its perfection is exemplified in its own knight: they are all, in a due degree, concentred in Prince Arthur.

This was the poet's moral: and what way of expressing this moral in the history but by making Prince Arthur appear in each adventure, and in a manner subordinate to its proper hero? Thus, though inferior to each in his own specific virtue, he is superior to all by uniting the whole circle of their virtues in himself. And thus he arrives, at length, at the possession of that bright form of Glory, whose ravishing beauty, as seen in a dream or vision, had led him out into these miraculous adventures in the land of Faerie.

The conclusion is that, as an allegorical poem, the method of the *Faerie Queene* is governed by the justness of the moral: as a narrative poem it is conducted on the ideas and usages of chivalry. In either view, if taken by itself, the plan is defensible. But from the union of the two designs there arises a perplexity and confusion, which is the proper, and only considerable, defect of this extraordinary poem.

SAMUEL JOHNSON

DRYDEN AS CRITIC AND POET

[From *Lives of the English Poets*, 1779]

DRYDEN may be properly considered as the father of English criticism, as the writer who first taught us to determine upon principles the merit of composition. Of our former poets the greatest dramatist wrote without rules, conducted through life and nature by a genius that rarely misled and rarely deserted him. Of the rest, those who knew the laws of propriety had neglected to teach them.

Two *Arts of English Poetry* were written in the days of Elizabeth by Webb and Puttenham, from which something might be learned, and a few hints had been given by Jonson and Cowley; but Dryden's *Essay on Dramatic Poetry* was the first regular and valuable treatise on the art of writing.

He who, having formed his opinions in the present age of English literature, turns back to peruse this dialogue, will not perhaps find much increase of knowledge or much novelty of instruction; but he is to remember that critical principles were then in the hands of a few, who had gathered them partly from the ancients and partly from the Italians and French. The structure of dramatic poems was then not generally understood. Audiences applauded by instinct, and poets perhaps often pleased by chance.

A writer who obtains his full purpose loses himself in his own lustre. Of an opinion which is no longer doubted, the evidence ceases to be examined. Of an art universally practised, the first teacher is forgotten. Learning once made popular is no longer learning; it has the appearance of something which we have bestowed upon ourselves, as the dew appears to rise from the field which it refreshes.

To judge rightly of an author, we must transport

ourselves to his time, and examine what were the wants of his contemporaries, and what were his means of supplying them. That which is easy at one time was difficult at another. Dryden at least imported his science, and gave his country what it wanted before; or rather, he imported only the materials, and manufactured them by his own skill.

The dialogue on the Drama was one of his first essays of criticism, written when he was yet a timorous candidate for reputation, and therefore laboured with that diligence which he might allow himself somewhat to remit, when his name gave sanction to his positions, and his awe of the public was abated, partly by custom, and partly by success. It will not be easy to find, in all the opulence of our language, a treatise so artfully variegated with successive representations of opposite probabilities, so enlivened with imagery, so brightened with illustrations. His portraits of the English dramatists are wrought with great spirit and diligence. The account of Shakespeare may stand as a perpetual model of encomiastic criticism; exact without minuteness, and lofty without exaggeration. The praise lavished by Longinus, on the attestation of the heroes of Marathon, by Demosthenes, fades away before it. In a few lines is exhibited a character, so extensive in its comprehension, and so curious in its limitations, that nothing can be added, diminished, or reformed; nor can the editors and admirers of Shakespeare, in all their emulation of reverence, boast of much more than of having diffused and paraphrased this epitome of excellence, of having changed Dryden's gold for baser metal, of lower value though of greater bulk.

In this, and in all his other essays on the same subject, the criticism of Dryden is the criticism of a poet; not a dull collection of theorems, nor a rude detection of faults, which perhaps the censor was not able to have committed; but a gay and vigorous dissertation, where delight is mingled with instruction, and where the author proves his right of judgement by his power of performance.

The different manner and effect with which critical knowledge may be conveyed, was perhaps never more clearly exemplified than in the performances of Rymer and Dryden. It was said of a dispute between two mathematicians, 'malim cum Scaligero errare, quam cum Clavio recte sapere'; that 'it was more eligible to go wrong with one than right with the other'. A tendency of the same kind every mind must feel at the perusal of Dryden's prefaces and Rymer's discourses. With Dryden we are wandering in quest of Truth; whom we find, if we find her at all, dressed in the graces of elegance, and if we miss her, the labour of the pursuit rewards itself; we are led only through fragrance and flowers: Rymer, without taking a nearer, takes a rougher way; every step is to be made through thorns and brambles; and Truth, if we meet her, appears repulsive by her mien, and ungraceful by her habit. Dryden's criticism has the majesty of a queen; Rymer's has the ferocity of a tyrant.

As he had studied with great diligence the art of poetry, and enlarged or rectified his notions, by experience perpetually increasing, he had his mind stored with principles and observations; he poured out his knowledge with little labour; for of labour, notwithstanding the multiplicity of his productions, there is sufficient reason to suspect that he was not a lover. To write *con amore*, with fondness for the employment, with perpetual touches and retouches, with unwillingness to take leave of his own idea, and an unwearied pursuit of unattainable perfection was, I think, no part of his character.

His criticism may be considered as general or occasional. In his general precepts, which depend upon the nature of things, and the structure of the human mind, he may doubtless be safely recommended to the confidence of the reader; but his occasional and particular positions were sometimes interested sometimes negligent, and sometimes capricious. It is not without reason that Trapp, speaking of the praises which he bestows on *Palamon and Arcite*, says, 'Novimus iudicium Drydeni de poemate quodam Chauceri, pulchro sane illo, et plurimum laudando; nimirum quod non modo vere epicum sit, sed Iliada etiam atque Aeneada aequet, imo superet. Sed novimus eodem tempore viri illius maximi non semper accuratissimas esse censuras, nec ad severissimam critices normam exactas: illo iudice, optimum est plerumque, quod ille prae manibus habet, et in quo nunc occupatur'.

He is therefore by no means constant to himself. His defence and desertion of dramatic rhyme is generally known. Spence, in his remarks on Pope's *Odyssey*, produces what he thinks an unconquerable quotation from Dryden's preface to the *Aeneid*, in favour of translating an epic poem into blank verse; but he forgets that when his author attempted the *Iliad*, some years afterwards, he departed from his own decision, and translated into rhyme.

When he has any objection to obviate, or any licence to defend, he is not very scrupulous about what he asserts, nor very cautious, if the present purpose be served, not to entangle himself in his own sophistries. But when all arts are exhausted, like other hunted animals, he sometimes stands at bay; when he cannot disown the grossness of one of his plays, he declares that he knows not any law that prescribes morality to a comic poet.

His remarks on ancient or modern writers are not always to be trusted. His parallel of the versification of Ovid with that of Claudian has been very justly censured by Sewel. His comparison of the first line of Virgil with the first of Statius is not happier. Virgil, he says, is soft and gentle, and would have thought Statius mad if he had heard him thundering out

Quae superimposito moles geminata colosso.

Statius perhaps heats himself, as he proceeds, to exaggerations somewhat hyperbolical; but undoubtedly Virgil would have been too hasty, if he had condemned him to straw for one sounding line. Dryden wanted an instance, and the first that occurred was impressed into the service.

What he wishes to say, he says at hazard; he cited *Gorboduc*, which he had never seen; gives a false account of Chapman's versification; and discovers, in the preface to his *Fables*, that he translated the first book of the *Iliad*, without knowing what was in the second.

It will be difficult to prove that Dryden ever made any great advances in literature. As, having distinguished himself at Westminster under the tuition of Busby, who advanced his scholars to a height of knowledge very rarely attained in grammar-schools, he resided afterwards at Cambridge, it is not to be supposed, that his skill in the ancient languages was deficient, compared with that of common students; but his scholastic acquisitions seem not proportionate to his opportunities and abilities. He could not, like Milton or Cowley, have made his name illustrious merely by his learning. He mentions but few books, and those such as lie in the beaten track of regular study; from which if ever he departs, he is in danger of losing himself in unknown regions.

In his dialogue on the Drama, he pronounces with great confidence that the Latin tragedy of *Medea* is not Ovid's, because it is not sufficiently interesting and pathetic. He might have determined the question upon surer evidence; for it is quoted by Quintilian as the work of Seneca; and the only line which remains of Ovid's play, for one line is left us, is not there to be found. There was therefore no need of the gravity of conjecture, or the discussion of plot or sentiment, to find what was already known upon higher authority than such discussions can ever reach.

His literature, though not always free from ostentation, will be commonly found either obvious, and made his own by the art of dressing it; or superficial, which, by what he gives, shows what he wanted; or erroneous, hastily collected, and negligently scattered.

Yet it cannot be said that his genius is ever unprovided of matter, or that his fancy languishes in penury of ideas. His works abound with knowledge, and sparkle with illustrations. There is scarcely any science or faculty that does not supply him with occasional images and lucky similitudes; every page discovers a mind very widely acquainted both with art and nature, and in full possession of great stores of intellectual wealth. Of him that knows much, it is natural to suppose that he has read with diligence; yet I rather believe that the knowledge of Dryden was gleaned from accidental intelligence and various conversation, by a quick apprehension, a judicious selection and a happy memory, a keen appetite of knowledge and a powerful digestion; by vigilance that permitted nothing to pass without notice, and a habit of reflection that suffered nothing useful to be lost. A mind like Dryden's, always curious, always active, to which every understanding was proud to be associated, and of which every one solicited the regard, by an ambitious display of himself, had a more pleasant, perhaps a nearer way, to knowledge than by the silent progress of solitary reading. I do not suppose that he despised books, or intentionally neglected them; but that he was carried out, by the impetuosity of his genius, to more vivid and speedy instructors; and that his studies were rather desultory and fortuitous than constant and systematical.

It must be confessed that he scarcely ever appears to want book-learning but when he mentions books: and to him may be transferred the praise which he gives his master Charles.

> His conversation, wit, and parts,
> His knowledge in the noblest useful arts,
>   Were such, dead authors could not give,
>   But habitudes of those that live;

Who, lighting him, did greater lights receive:
    He drain'd from all, and all they knew,
His apprehension quick, his judgement true:
    That the most learn'd with shame confess
His knowledge more, his reading only less.

Of all this, however, if the proof be demanded,
I will not undertake to give it; the atoms of probability, of which my opinion has been formed, lie
scattered over all his works; and by him who thinks
the question worth his notice, his works must be perused with very close attention.

Criticism, either didactic or defensive, occupies
almost all his prose, except those pages which he has
devoted to his patrons; but none of his prefaces were
ever thought tedious. They have not the formality
of a settled style, in which the first half of the sentence
betrays the other. The clauses are never balanced,
nor the periods modelled; every word seems to drop
by chance, though it falls into its proper place.
Nothing is cold or languid; the whole is airy, animated, and vigorous; what is little, is gay; what is
great, is splendid. He may be thought to mention
himself too frequently; but while he forces himself
upon our esteem, we cannot refuse him to stand high
in his own. Everything is excused by the play of
images and the spriteliness of expression. Though all is
easy, nothing is feeble; though all seems careless,
there is nothing harsh; and though, since his earlier
works, more than a century has passed, they have
nothing yet uncouth or obsolete.

He who writes much will not easily escape a
manner, such a recurrence of particular modes as may
be easily noted. Dryden is always another and the
same, he does not exhibit a second time the same
elegances in the same form, nor appears to have any
art other than that of expressing with clearness what
he thinks with vigour. His style could not easily be
imitated, either seriously or ludicrously; for, being
always equable and always varied, it has no promi-

nent or discriminative characters. The beauty who is totally free from disproportion of parts and features, cannot be ridiculed by an overcharged resemblance.

From his prose, however, Dryden derives only his accidental and secondary praise; the veneration with which his name is pronounced by every cultivator of English literature, is paid to him as he refined the language, improved the sentiments, and tuned the numbers of English poetry.

After about half a century of forced thoughts, and rugged metre, some advances towards nature and harmony had been already made by Waller and Denham; they had shown that long discourses in rhyme grew more pleasing when they were broken into couplets, and that verse consisted not only in the number but the arrangement of syllables.

But though they did much, who can deny that they left much to do? Their works were not many, nor were their minds of very ample comprehension. More examples of more modes of composition were necessary for the establishment of regularity, and the introduction of propriety in word and thought.

Every language of a learned nation necessarily divides itself into diction scholastic and popular, grave and familiar, elegant and gross; and from a nice distinction of these different parts arises a great part of the beauty of style. But if we except a few minds, the favourites of nature, to whom their own original rectitude was in the place of rules, this delicacy of selection was little known to our authors; our speech lay before them in a heap of confusion, and every man took for every purpose what chance might offer him.

There was therefore before the time of Dryden no poetical diction, no system of words at once refined from the grossness of domestic use, and free from the harshness of terms appropriated to particular arts. Words too familiar, or too remote, defeat the purpose of a poet. From those sounds which we hear on small or on coarse occasions, we do not easily receive strong impressions or delightful images; and words to which we are nearly strangers, whenever they occur, draw that attention on themselves which they should transmit to things.

Those happy combinations of words which distinguish poetry from prose, had been rarely attempted; we had few elegances or flowers of speech, the roses had not yet been plucked from the bramble, or different colours had not been joined to enliven one another.

It may be doubted whether Waller and Denham could have overborne the prejudices which had long prevailed, and which even then were sheltered by the protection of Cowley. The new versification, as it was called, may be considered as owing its establishment to Dryden; from whose time it is apparent that English poetry has had no tendency to relapse to its former savageness.

The affluence and comprehension of our language is very illustriously displayed in our poetical translations of ancient writers; a work which the French seem to relinquish in despair, and which we were long unable to perform with dexterity. Ben Jonson thought it necessary to copy Horace almost word by word; Feltham, his contemporary and adversary, considers it as indispensably requisite in a translation to give line for line. It is said that Sandys, whom Dryden calls the best versifier of the last age, has struggled hard to comprise every book of his English *Metamorphoses* in the same number of verses with the original. Holyday had nothing in view but to show that he understood his author, with so little regard to the grandeur of his diction, or the volubility of his numbers, that his metres can hardly be called verses; they cannot be read without reluctance, nor will the labour always be rewarded by understanding them. Cowley saw that such copyers were a servile race; he asserted his liberty and spread his wings so boldly that he left his authors. It was reserved for Dryden to fix the limits of poetical liberty, and give us just rules and examples of translation.

When languages are formed upon different principles, it is impossible that the same modes of expression should always be elegant in both. While they run on together, the closest translation may be considered as the best; but when they divaricate, each must take its natural course. Where correspondence cannot be obtained, it is necessary to be content with something equivalent. 'Translation therefore,' says Dryden, 'is not so loose as paraphrase, nor so close as metaphrase.'

All polished languages have different styles; the concise, the diffuse, the lofty, and the humble. In the proper choice of style consists the resemblance which Dryden principally exacts from the translator. He is to exhibit his author's thoughts in such a dress of diction as the author would have given them, had his language been English: rugged magnificence is not to be softened: hyperbolical ostentation is not to be repressed, nor sententious affectation to have its points blunted. A translator is to be like his author: it is not his business to excel him.

The reasonableness of these rules seems sufficient for their vindication; and the effects produced by observing them were so happy, that I know not whether they were ever opposed but by Sir Edward Sherburne, a man whose learning was greater than his powers of poetry; and who, being better qualified to give the meaning than the spirit of Seneca, has introduced his version of three tragedies by a defence of close translation. The authority of Horace, which the new translators cited in defence of their practice, he has, by a judicious explanation, taken fairly from them; but reason wants not Horace to support it.

It seldom happens that all the necessary causes concur to any great effect: will is wanting to power, or power to will, or both are impeded by external obstructions. The exigences in which Dryden was condemned to pass his life, are reasonably supposed to have blasted his genius, to have driven out his works in a state of immaturity, and to have intercepted the full-blown elegance which longer growth would have supplied.

Poverty, like other rigid powers, is sometimes too hastily accused. If the excellence of Dryden's works was lessened by his indigence, their number was increased; and I know not how it will be proved, that if he had written less he would have written better; or that indeed he would have undergone the toil of an author, if he had not been solicited by something more pressing than the love of praise.

But as is said by his Sebastian,

What had been, is unknown; what is, appears.

We know that Dryden's several productions were so many successive expedients for his support; his plays were therefore often borrowed, and his poems were almost all occasional.

In an occasional performance no height of excellence can be expected from any mind, however fertile in itself, and however stored with acquisitions. He whose work is general and arbitrary, has the choice of his matter, and takes that which his inclination and his studies have best qualified him to display and decorate. He is at liberty to delay his publication, till he has satisfied his friends and himself; till he has reformed his first thoughts by subsequent examination; and polished away those faults which the precipitance of ardent composition is likely to leave behind it. Virgil is related to have poured out a great number of lines in the morning, and to have passed the day in reducing them to fewer.

The occasional poet is circumscribed by the narrowness of his subject. Whatever can happen to man has happened so often, that little remains for fancy or invention. We have been all born; we have most of us been married; and so many have died before us, that our deaths can supply but few materials for a poet. In the fate of princes the public has an interest; and what happens to them of good or evil, the poets have always considered as business for the Muse. But after so many inauguratory gratulations, nuptial hymns, and funeral dirges, he must be highly favoured by nature, or by fortune, who says anything not said before. Even war and conquest, however splendid, suggest no new images; the triumphal chariot of a victorious monarch can be decked only with those ornaments that have graced his predecessors.

Not only matter but time is wanting. The poem must not be delayed till the occasion is forgotten. The lucky moments of animated imagination cannot be attended; elegances and illustrations cannot be multiplied by gradual accumulation; the composition must be dispatched while conversation is yet busy, and admiration fresh; and haste is to be made, lest some other event should lay hold upon mankind.

Occasional compositions may however secure to a writer the praise both of learning and facility; for they cannot be the effect of long study, and must be furnished immediately from the treasures of the mind.

The death of Cromwell was the first public event which called forth Dryden's poetical powers. His heroic stanzas have beauties and defects; the thoughts are vigorous, and though not always proper, show a mind replete with ideas; the numbers are smooth, and the diction, if not altogether correct, is elegant and easy.

Davenant was perhaps at this time his favourite author, though *Gondibert* never appears to have been popular: and from Davenant he learned to please his ear with the stanza of four lines alternately rhymed.

Dryden very early formed his versification: there are in this early production no traces of Donne's or

Jonson's ruggedness; but he did not so soon free his mind from the ambition of forced conceits. In his verses on the Restoration, he says of the king's exile:

> He, toss'd by Fate,
> Could taste no sweets of youth's desired age,
> But found his life too true a pilgrimage.

And afterwards, to show how virtue and wisdom are increased by adversity, he makes this remark:

> Well might the ancient poets then confer
> On Night the honour'd name of *counsellor*,
> Since, struck with rays of prosperous fortune blind,
> We light alone in dark afflictions find.

His praise of Monk's dexterity comprises such a cluster of thoughts unallied to one another, as will not elsewhere be easily found:

> 'Twas Monk, whom Providence design'd to loose
> Those real bonds false freedom did impose.
> The blessed saints that watch'd this turning scene,
> Did from their stars with joyful wonder lean,
> To see small clues draw vastest weights along,
> Not in their bulk, but in their order strong.
> Thus pencils can by one slight touch restore
> Smiles to that changed face that wept before.
> With ease such fond chimaeras we pursue,
> As fancy frames for fancy to subdue:
> But, when ourselves to action we betake
> It shuns the mint like gold that chemists make:
> How hard was then his task, at once to be
> What in the body natural we see!
> Man's Architect distinctly did ordain
> The charge of muscles, nerves, and of the brain,
> Through viewless conduits spirits to dispense
> The springs of motion from the seat of sense.
> 'Twas not the hasty product of a day,
> But the well-ripen'd fruit of wise delay.
> He, like a patient angler, ere he strook,
> Would let them play a-while upon the hook.
> Our healthful food the stomach labours thus,
> At first embracing what it straight doth crush.

> Wise leeches will not vain receipts obtrude,
> While growing pains pronounce the humours crude;
> Deaf to complaints, they wait upon the ill,
> Till some safe crisis authorize their skill.

He had not yet learned, indeed he never learned
well, to forbear the improper use of mythology.
After having rewarded the heathen deities for their
care,

> With Alga who the sacred altar strows?
> To all the sea-gods Charles an offering owes;
> A bull to thee, Portunus, shall be slain;
> A ram to you, ye Tempests of the Main:

he tells us, in the language of religion,

> Prayer storm'd the skies, and ravish'd Charles from thence,
> As heaven itself is took by violence.

And afterwards mentions one of the most awful
passages of sacred history.

Other conceits there are, too curious to be quite
omitted; as,

> For by example most we sinn'd before,
> And, glass-like, clearness mix'd with frailty bore.

How far he was yet from thinking it necessary to
found his sentiments on Nature, appears from the
extravagance of his fictions and hyperboles:

> The winds, that never moderation knew,
> Afraid to blow too much, too faintly blew;
> Or, out of breath with joy, could not enlarge
> Their straiten'd lungs.—

> It is no longer motion cheats your view;
> As you meet it, the land approacheth you;
> The land returns, and in the white it wears
> The marks of penitence and sorrow bears.

I know not whether this fancy, however little be its
value, was not borrowed. A French poet read to
Malherbe some verses, in which he represents France

as moving out of its place to receive the king. 'Though this,' said Malherbe, 'was in my time, I do not remember it.'

His poem on the Coronation has a more even tenor of thought. Some lines deserve to be quoted:

> You have already quench'd sedition's brand,
> And zeal, that burnt it, only warms the land;
> The jealous sects that durst not trust their cause
> So far from their own will as to the laws,
> Him for their umpire and their synod take,
> And their appeal alone to Caesar make.

Here may be found one particle of that old versification, of which, I believe, in all his works, there is not another:

> Nor is it duty, or our hope alone,
> Creates that joy, but full *fruition*.

In the verses to the Lord Chancellor Clarendon, two years afterwards, is a conceit so hopeless at the first view, that few would have attempted it, and so successfully laboured, that though at last it gives the reader more perplexity than pleasure, and seems hardly worth the study that it costs, yet it must be valued as a proof of a mind at once subtle and comprehensive:

> In open prospect nothing bounds our eye,
> Until the earth seems join'd unto the sky:
> So in this hemisphere our utmost view
> Is only bounded by our king and you:
> Our sight is limited where you are join'd,
> And beyond that no farther heaven can find.
> So well your virtues do with his agree,
> That, though your orbs of different greatness be,
> Yet both are for each other's use dispos'd,
> His to enclose, and yours to be enclos'd.
> Nor could another in your room have been,
> Except an emptiness had come between.

The comparison of the Chancellor to the Indies leaves all resemblance too far behind it:

> And as the Indies were not found before
> Those rich perfumes which from the happy shore
> The winds upon their balmy wings convey'd,
> Whose guilty sweetness first their world betray'd
> So by your counsels we are brought to view
> A new and undiscover'd world in you.

There is another comparison, for there is little else in the poem, of which, though perhaps it cannot be explained into plain prosaic meaning, the mind perceives enough to be delighted, and readily forgives its obscurity for its magnificence:

> How strangely active are the arts of peace,
> Whose restless motions less than wars do cease;
> Peace is not freed from labour, but from noise;
> And war more force, but not more pains employs:
> Such is the mighty swiftness of your mind,
> That, like the earth's, it leaves our sense behind,
> While you so smoothly turn and roll our sphere,
> That rapid motion does but rest appear.
> For as in nature's swiftness, with the throng
> Of flying orbs while ours is borne along,
> All seems at rest to the deluded eye,
> Mov'd by the soul of the same harmony:
> So carried on by your unwearied care,
> We rest in peace, and yet in motion share.

To this succeed four lines, which perhaps afford Dryden's first attempt at those penetrating remarks on human nature, for which he seems to have been peculiarly formed:

> Let envy then those crimes within you see,
> From which the happy never must be free;
> Envy that does with misery reside,
> The joy and the revenge of ruin'd pride.

Into this poem he seems to have collected all his powers; and after this he did not often bring upon his anvil such stubborn and unmalleable thoughts; but, as a specimen of his abilities to unite the most unsociable matter, he has concluded with lines of which I think not myself obliged to tell the meaning:

> Yet unimpaired with labours, or with time,
> Your age but seems to a new youth to climb.
> Thus heavenly bodies do our time beget,
> And measure change, but share no part of it:
> And still it shall without a weight increase,
> Like this new year, whose motions never cease.
> For since the glorious course you have begun
> Is led by Charles, as that is by the sun,
> It must both weightless and immortal prove,
> Because the centre of it is above.

In the *Annus Mirabilis* he returned to the quatrain, which from that time he totally quitted, perhaps from this experience of its inconvenience, for he complains of its difficulty. This is one of his greatest attempts. He had subjects equal to his abilities, a great naval war, and the Fire of London. Battles have always been described in heroic poetry, but a sea-fight and artillery had yet something of novelty. New arts are long in the world before poets describe them, for they borrow everything from their predecessors, and commonly derive very little from nature or from life. Boileau was the first French writer that had ever hazarded in verse the mention of modern war, or the effects of gunpowder. We, who are less afraid of novelty, had already possession of those dreadful images: Waller had described a sea-fight. Milton had not yet transferred the invention of fire-arms to the rebellious angels.

This poem is written with great diligence, yet does not fully answer the expectation raised by such subjects and such a writer. With the stanza of Davenant he has sometimes his vein of parenthesis, and incidental disquisition, and stops his narrative for a wise remark.

The general fault is, that he affords more sentiment than description, and does not so much impress scenes upon the fancy, as deduce consequences and make comparisons.

The initial stanzas have rather too much resemblance to the first lines of Waller's poem on the war with Spain; perhaps such a beginning is natural, and could not be avoided without affectation. Both Waller and Dryden might take their hint from the poem on the civil war of Rome, *Orbem iam totum, etc.*

Of the king collecting his navy, he says:

> It seems as every ship their sovereign knows,
>   His awful summons they so soon obey;
> So hear the scaly herds when Proteus blows,
>   And so to pasture follow through the sea.

It would not be hard to believe that Dryden had written the first two lines seriously, and that some wag had added the two latter in burlesque. Who would expect the lines that immediately follow, which are indeed perhaps indecently hyperbolical, but certainly in a mode totally different?

> To see this fleet upon the ocean move,
>   Angels drew wide the curtains of the skies;
> And heaven, as if there wanted lights above,
>   For tapers made two glaring comets rise.

The description of the attempt at Bergen will afford a very complete specimen of the descriptions in this poem:

> And now approach'd their fleet from India, fraught
>   With all the riches of the rising sun:
> And precious sand from southern climates brought,
>   The fatal regions where the war begun.

> Like hunted castors, conscious of their store,
>   Their way-laid wealth to Norway's coast they bring:
> Then first the North's cold bosom spices bore,
>   And winter brooded on the eastern spring.

> By the rich scent we found our perfum'd prey,
>   Which, flank'd with rocks, did close in covert lie:
> And round about their murdering cannon lay,
>   At once to threaten and invite the eye.

Fiercer than cannon, and than rocks more hard,
  The English undertake th' unequal war:
Seven ships alone, by which the port is barr'd,
  Besiege the Indies, and all Denmark dare.

These fight like husbands, but like lovers those:
  These fain would keep, and those more fain enjoy;
And to such height their frantic passion grows,
  That what both love, both hazard to destroy:

Amidst whole heaps of spices lights a ball,
  And now their odours arm'd against them fly:
Some preciously by shatter'd porcelain fall,
  And some by aromatic splinters die.

And though by tempests of the prize bereft,
  In heaven's inclemency some ease we find:
Our foes we vanquish'd by our valour left,
  And only yielded to the seas and wind.

In this manner is the sublime too often mingled
with the ridiculous. The Dutch seek a shelter for a
wealthy fleet: this surely needed no illustration; yet
they must fly, not like all the rest of mankind on the
same occasion, but like hunted castors; and they
might with strict propriety be hunted; for we winded
them by our noses—their perfumes betrayed them.
The husband and the lover, though of more dignity
than the castor, are images too domestic to mingle
properly with the horrors of war. The two quatrains
that follow are worthy of the author.

The account of the different sensations with which
the two fleets retired, when the night parted them, is
one of the fairest flowers of English poetry:

The night comes on, we eager to pursue
  The combat still, and they asham'd to leave:
'Till the last streaks of dying day withdrew,
  And doubtful moon-light did our rage deceive.

In th' English fleet each ship resounds with joy,
  And loud applause of their great leader's fame:
In fiery dreams the Dutch they still destroy,
  And, slumbering, smile at the imagin'd flame.

Not so the Holland fleet, who, tir'd and done,
  Stretch'd on their decks like weary oxen lie;
Faint sweats all down their mighty members run
  (Vast bulks, which little souls but ill supply).

In dreams they fearful precipices tread,
  Or, shipwreck'd, labour to some distant shore:
Or, in dark churches, walk among the dead;
  They wake with horror, and dare sleep no more.

It is a general rule in poetry, that all appropriated
terms of art should be sunk in general expressions,
because poetry is to speak a universal language.
This rule is still stronger with regard to arts not
liberal, or confined to few, and therefore far removed
from common knowledge; and of this kind, certainly,
is technical navigation. Yet Dryden was of opinion
that a sea-fight ought to be described in the nautical
language; 'and certainly,' says he, 'as those who in
a logical disputation keep to general terms would hide
a fallacy, so those who do it in any poetical description would veil their ignorance.'

Let us then appeal to experience; for by experience
at last we learn as well what will please as what will
profit. In the battle, his terms seem to have been
blown away; but he deals them liberally in the dock:

So here, some pick out bullets from the side,
  Some drive old *okum* thro' each *seam* and *rift*:
Their left-hand does the *calking-iron* guide,
  The rattling *mallet* with the right they lift.

With boiling pitch another near at hand
  (From friendly Sweden brought) the *seams instops*:
Which, well laid o'er, the salt-sea waves withstand,
  And shake them from the rising beak in drops.

Some the *gall'd* ropes with dauby *marling* bind,
  Or sear-cloth masts with strong *tarpaulin* coats:
To try new *shrouds* one mounts into the wind,
  And one below, their ease or stiffness notes.

I suppose here is not one term which every reader
does not wish away.

His digression to the original and progress of navigation, with his prospect of the advancement which it shall receive from the Royal Society, then newly instituted, may be considered as an example seldom equalled of seasonable excursion and artful return.

One line, however, leaves me discontented; he says, that by the help of the philosophers,

> Instructed ships shall sail to quick commerce,
> By which remotest regions are allied.—

which he is constrained to explain in a note, 'By a more exact measure of longitude'. It had better become Dryden's learning and genius to have laboured science into poetry, and have shown, by explaining longitude, that verse did not refuse the ideas of philosophy.

His description of the Fire is painted by resolute meditation, out of a mind better formed to reason than to feel. The conflagration of a city, with all its tumults of concomitant distress, is one of the most dreadful spectacles which this world can offer to human eyes; yet it seems to raise little emotion in the breast of the poet; he watches the flame coolly from street to street, with now a reflection, and now a simile, till at last he meets the king, for whom he makes a speech, rather tedious in a time so busy, and then follows again the progress of the fire.

There are, however, in this part some passages that deserve attention; as in the beginning:

> The diligence of trades and noiseful gain,
>   And luxury, more late, asleep were laid;
> All was the night's, and in her silent reign
>   No sound the rest of Nature did invade
> In this deep quiet——

The expression 'All was the night's' is taken from Seneca, who remarks on Virgil's line,

> *Omnia noctis erant placida composta quiete,*

that he might have concluded better,

> *Omnia noctis erant.*

The following quatrain is vigorous and animated:

> The ghosts of traitors from the bridge descend
> With bold fanatic spectres to rejoice;
> About the fire into a dance they bend,
> And sing their hellish Sabbath notes with feeble voice.

His prediction of the improvements which shall be made in the new city is elegant and poetical, and, with an event which poets cannot always boast, has been happily verified. The poem concludes with a simile that might have better been omitted.

Dryden, when he wrote this poem, seems not yet fully to have formed his versification, or settled his system of propriety.

From this time, he addicted himself almost wholly to the stage, 'to which', says he, 'my genius never much inclined me', merely as the most profitable market for poetry. By writing tragedies in rhyme, he continued to improve his diction and his numbers. According to the opinion of Harte, who had studied his works with great attention, he settled his principles of versification in 1676, when he produced the play of *Aureng Zebe*; and according to his own account of the short time in which he wrote *Tyrannic Love* and the *State of Innocence*, he soon obtained the full effect of diligence, and added facility to exactness.

Rhyme has been so long banished from the theatre, that we know not its effect upon the passions of an audience; but it has this convenience, that sentences stand more independent on each other, and striking passages are therefore easily selected and retained. Thus the description of night in the *Indian Emperor*, and the rise and fall of empire in the *Conquest of Granada*, are more frequently repeated than any lines in *All for Love*, or *Don Sebastian*.

To search his plays for vigorous sallies, and sententious elegances, or to fix the dates of any little pieces which he wrote by chance, or by solicitation, were labour too tedious and minute.

His dramatic labours did not so wholly absorb his thoughts, but that he promulgated the laws of translation in a preface to the English Epistles of Ovid; one of which he translated himself, and another in conjunction with the Earl of Mulgrave.

Absalom and Achitophel is a work so well known, that particular criticism is superfluous. If it be considered as a poem political and controversial, it will be found to comprise all the excellences of which the subject is susceptible; acrimony of censure, elegance of praise, artful delineation of characters, variety and vigour of sentiment, happy turns of language, and pleasing harmony of numbers; and all these raised to such a height as can scarcely be found in any other English composition.

It is not, however, without faults; some lines are inelegant or improper, and too many are irreligiously licentious. The original structure of the poem was defective; allegories drawn to great length will always break; Charles could not run continually parallel with David.

The subject had likewise another inconvenience: it admitted little imagery or description, and a long poem of mere sentiments easily becomes tedious; though all the parts are forcible, and every line kindles new rapture, the reader, if not relieved by the interposition of something that soothes the fancy, grows weary of admiration, and defers the rest.

As an approach to historical truth was necessary, the action and catastrophe were not in the poet's power; there is therefore an unpleasing disproportion between the beginning and the end. We are alarmed by a faction formed out of many sects various in their principles, but agreeing in their purpose of mischief, formidable for their numbers, and strong by their supports, while the king's friends are few and weak. The chiefs on either part are set forth to view; but when expectation is at the height, the king makes a speech, and

Henceforth a series of new times began.

Who can forbear to think of an enchanted castle, with a wide moat and lofty battlements, walls of marble and gates of brass, which vanishes at once into air, when the destined knight blows his horn before it?

In the second part, written by Tate, there is a long insertion, which, for poignancy of satire, exceeds any part of the former. Personal resentment, though no laudable motive to satire, can add great force to general principles. Self-love is a busy prompter.

The *Medal*, written upon the same principles with *Absalom and Achitophel*, but upon a narrower plan, gives less pleasure, though it discovers equal abilities in the writer. The superstructure cannot extend beyond the foundation; a single character or incident cannot furnish as many ideas as a series of events or multiplicity of agents. This poem, therefore, since time has left it to itself, is not much read, nor perhaps generally understood, yet it abounds with touches both of humorous and serious satire. The picture of a man whose propensions to mischief are such, that his best actions are but inability of wickedness, is very skilfully delineated and strongly coloured:

Power was his aim: but, thrown from that pretence,
The wretch turn'd loyal in his own defence,
And malice reconcil'd him to his Prince.
Him, in the anguish of his soul, he serv'd;
Rewarded faster still than he deserv'd:
Behold him now exalted into trust;
His counsels oft convenient, seldom just.
Ev'n in the most sincere advice he gave,
He had a grudging still to be a knave.
The frauds he learnt in his fanatic years,
Made him uneasy in his lawful gears:
At least as little honest as he could:
And, like white witches, mischievously good.
To this first bias, longingly, he leans;
And rather would be great by wicked means.

The *Threnodia*, which, by a term I am afraid neither
authorized nor analogical, he calls *Augustalis*, is not
among his happiest productions. Its first and obvious
defect is the irregularity of its metre, to which the
ears of that age, however, were accustomed. What
is worse, it has neither tenderness nor dignity, it is
neither magnificent nor pathetic. He seems to look
round him for images which he cannot find, and what
he has he distorts by endeavouring to enlarge them.
He is, he says, petrified with grief; but the marble
sometimes relents, and trickles in a joke:

> The sons of art all med'cines try'd,
> And every noble remedy apply'd;
>   With emulation each essay'd
>   His utmost skill; *nay, more, they pray'd*:
> Never was losing game with better conduct play'd.

He had been a little inclined to merriment before
upon the prayers of a nation for their dying sovereign,
nor was he serious enough to keep heathen fables out
of his religion.

> With him th' innumerable crowd of armed prayers
> Knock'd at the gates of heaven, and knock'd aloud;
> *The first well-meaning rude petitioners*
> All for his life assail'd the throne,
> All would have brib'd the skies by offering up their own.
> So great a throng not heaven itself could bar;
> 'Twas almost borne by force *as in the giants' war.*
>   The prayers, at least, for his reprieve were heard;
> His death, like Hezekiah's, was deferr'd.

There is throughout the composition a desire of
splendour without wealth. In the conclusion he
seems too much pleased with the prospect of the new
reign to have lamented his old master with much
sincerity.

He did not miscarry in this attempt for want of
skill either in lyric or elegiac poetry. His poem *On the
Death of Mrs. Killigrew* is undoubtedly the noblest
ode that our language has ever produced. The first

part flows with a torrent of enthusiasm. *Fervet immensusque ruit.* All the stanzas indeed are not equal. An imperial crown cannot be one continued diamond; the gems must be held together by some less valuable matter.

In his first ode for Cecilia's day, which is lost in the splendour of the second, there are passages which would have dignified any other poet. The first stanza is vigorous and elegant, though the word *diapason* is too technical, and the rhymes are too remote from one another.

> From harmony, from heavenly harmony,
>   This universal frame began:
> When nature underneath a heap of jarring atoms lay,
>   And could not heave her head.
> The tuneful voice was heard from high,
>   Arise, ye more than dead.
> Then cold and hot, and moist and dry,
> In order to their stations leap,
>   And music's power obey.
> From harmony, from heavenly harmony,
>   This universal frame began:
>   From harmony to harmony
> Through all the compass of the notes it ran,
>   The diapason closing full in man.

The conclusion is likewise striking, but it includes an image so awful in itself, that it can owe little to poetry; and I could wish the antithesis of music untuning had found some other place.

> As from the power òf sacred lays
>   The spheres began to move,
> And sung the great Creator's praise
>   To all the bless'd above.
> So, when the last and dreadful hour
> This crumbling pageant shall devour,
> The trumpet shall be heard on high,
> The dead shall live, the living die,
> And music shall untune the sky.

Of his skill in elegy he has given a specimen in his

Eleonora, of which the following lines discover their author:

> Though all these rare endowments of the mind
> Were in a narrow space of life confin'd,
> The figure was with full perfection crown'd;
> Though not so large an orb, as truly round:
> As when in glory, through the public place,
> The spoils of conquer'd nations were to pass,
> And but one day for triumph was allow'd,
> The consul was constrain'd his pomp to crowd;
> And so the swift procession hurried on,
> That all, though not distinctly, might be shown:
> So in the straiten'd bounds of life confin'd,
> She gave but glimpses of her glorious mind:
> And multitudes of virtues pass'd along;
> Each pressing foremost in the mighty throng,
> Ambitious to be seen, and then make room
> For greater multitudes that were to come.
> Yet unemploy'd no minute slipp'd away;
> Moments were precious in so short a stay.
> The haste of heaven to have her was so great,
> That some were single acts, though each complete;
> And every act stood ready to repeat.

This piece, however, is not without its faults; there is so much likeness in the initial comparison, that there is no illustration. As a king would be lamented, Eleonora was lamented.

> As when some great and gracious monarch dies,
> Soft whispers, first, and mournful murmurs rise
> Among the sad attendants; then the sound
> Soon gathers voice, and spreads the news around,
> Through town and country, till the dreadful blast
> Is blown to distant colonies at last;
> Who, then, perhaps, were offering vows in vain,
> For his long life, and for his happy reign:
> So slowly by degrees, unwilling fame
> Did matchless Eleonora's fate proclaim,
> Till public as the loss the news became.

This is little better than to say in praise of a shrub, that it is as green as a tree, or of a brook, that it waters a garden, as a river waters a country.

Dryden confesses that he did not know the lady whom he celebrates; the praise being therefore inevitably general, fixes no impression upon the reader, nor excites any tendency to love, nor much desire of imitation. Knowledge of the subject is to the poet what durable materials are to the architect.

The *Religio Laici*, which borrows its title from the *Religio Medici* of Browne, is almost the only work of Dryden which can be considered as a voluntary effusion; in this, therefore, it might be hoped, that the full effulgence of his genius would be found. But unhappily the subject is rather argumentative than poetical: he intended only a specimen of metrical disputation:

> And this unpolish'd rugged verse I chose,
> As fittest for discourse, and nearest prose.

This, however, is a composition of great excellence in its kind, in which the familiar is very properly diversified with the solemn, and the grave with the humorous; in which metre has neither weakened the force, nor clouded the perspicuity of argument; nor will it be easy to find another example equally happy of this middle kind of writing, which, though prosaic in some parts, rises to high poetry in others, and neither towers to the skies, nor creeps along the ground.

Of the same kind, or not far distant from it, is the *Hind and Panther*, the longest of all Dryden's original poems; an allegory intended to comprise and to decide the controversy between the Romanists and Protestants. The scheme of the work is injudicious and incommodious; for what can be more absurd than that one beast should counsel another to rest her faith upon a pope and council? He seems well enough skilled in the usual topics of argument, endeavours to show the necessity of an infallible judge, and reproaches the Reformers with want of unity; but is weak enough to ask, why, since we see without knowing how, we may not have an infallible judge without knowing where.

The Hind at one time is afraid to drink at the common brook, because she may be worried; but walking home with the Panther, talks by the way of the Nicene Fathers, and at last declares herself to be the Catholic Church.

This absurdity was very properly ridiculed in the *City Mouse and Country Mouse* of Montague and Prior; and in the detection and censure of the incongruity of the fiction chiefly consists the value of their performance, which, whatever reputation it might obtain by the help of temporary passions, seems to readers almost a century distant, not very forcible or animated.

Pope, whose judgement was perhaps a little bribed by the subject, used to mention this poem as the most correct specimen of Dryden's versification. It was, indeed, written when he had completely formed his manner, and may be supposed to exhibit, negligence excepted, his deliberate and ultimate scheme of metre.

We may therefore reasonably infer that he did not approve the perpetual uniformity which confines the sense to couplets; since he has broken his lines in the initial paragraph:

A milk-white Hind, immortal and unchang'd,
Fed on the lawns, and in the forest rang'd;
Without unspotted, innocent within,
She fear'd no danger, for she knew no sin.
Yet had she oft been chas'd with horns and hounds
And Scythian shafts, and many winged wounds
Aim'd at her heart; was often forc'd to fly,
And doom'd to death, though fated not to die.

These lines are lofty, elegant, and musical, notwithstanding the interruption of the pause, of which the effect is rather increase of pleasure by variety, than offence by ruggedness.

To the first part it was his intention, he says, 'to give the majestic turn of heroic poesy'; and perhaps he might have executed his design not unsuccessfully, had not an opportunity of satire, which he cannot forbear, fallen sometimes in his way. The character of a Presbyterian, whose emblem is the wolf, is not very heroically majestic:

> More haughty than the rest, the wolfish race
> Appear with belly gaunt and famish'd face:
> Never was so deform'd a beast of grace.
> His ragged tail betwixt his legs he wears,
> Close clapp'd for shame; but his rough crest he rears,
> And pricks up his predestinating ears.

His general character of the other sorts of beasts that never go to church, though spritely and keen, has, however, not much of heroic poesy:

> These are the chief; to number o'er the rest,
> And stand like Adam naming every beast,
> Were weary work; nor will the Muse describe
> A slimy-born and sun-begotten tribe;
> Who, far from steeples and their sacred sound,
> In fields their sullen conventicles found.
> These gross, half-animated, lumps I leave;
> Nor can I think what thoughts they can conceive;
> But if they think at all, 'tis sure no higher
> Than matter, put in motion, may aspire;
> Souls that can scarce ferment their mass of clay;
> So drossy, so divisible are they,
> As would but serve pure bodies for allay:
> Such souls as shards produce, such beetle things
> As only buzz to heaven with evening wings;
> Strike in the dark, offending but by chance;
> Such are the blindfold blows of ignorance.
> They know not beings, and but hate a name;
> To them the Hind and Panther are the same.

One more instance, and that taken from the narrative part, where style was more in his choice, will show how steadily he kept his resolution of heroic dignity:

> For when the herd, suffic'd, did late repair
> To ferny heaths, and to their forest lair,
> She made a mannerly excuse to stay,
> Proffering the Hind to wait her half the way:

That, since the sky was clear, an hour of talk
Might help her to beguile the tedious walk.
With much good-will the motion was embrac'd,
To chat awhile on their adventures past:
Nor had the grateful Hind so soon forgot
Her friend and fellow-sufferer in the plot.
Yet wondering how of late she grew estrang'd,
Her forehead cloudy and her count'nance chang'd,
She thought this hour th' occasion would present
To learn her secret cause of discontent,
Which well she hop'd, might be with ease redress'd,
Considering her a well-bred civil beast,
And more a gentlewoman than the rest.
After some common talk what rumours ran,
The lady of the spotted muff began.

The second and third parts he professes to have
reduced to diction more familiar and more suitable
to dispute and conversation; the difference is not,
however, very easily perceived; the first has familiar,
and the two others have sonorous, lines. The original
incongruity runs through the whole; the king is now
Caesar, and now the Lion; and the name Pan is given
to the Supreme Being.

But when this constitutional absurdity is forgiven,
the poem must be confessed to be written with great
smoothness of metre, a wide extent of knowledge, and
an abundant multiplicity of images; the controversy
is embellished with pointed sentences, diversified by
illustrations, and enlivened by sallies of invective.
Some of the facts to which allusions are made, are
now become obscure, and perhaps there may be
many satirical passages little understood.

As it was by its nature a work of defiance, a composition which would naturally be examined with
the utmost acrimony of criticism, it was probably
laboured with uncommon attention; and there are,
indeed, few negligences in the subordinate parts.
The original impropriety, and the subsequent un-
popularity of the subject, added to the ridiculousness
of its first elements, has sunk it into neglect; but it

may be usefully studied, as an example of poetical ratiocination, in which the argument suffers little from the metre.

In the poem *On the Birth of the Prince of Wales*, nothing is very remarkable but the exorbitant adulation, and that insensibility of the precipice on which the king was then standing, which the Laureate apparently shared with the rest of the courtiers. A few months cured him of controversy, dismissed him from court, and made him again a playwright and translator.

Of Juvenal there had been a translation by Stapylton, and another by Holyday; neither of them is very poetical. Stapylton is more smooth, and Holyday's is more esteemed for the learning of his notes. A new version was proposed to the poets of that time, and undertaken by them in conjunction. The main design was conducted by Dryden, whose reputation was such that no man was unwilling to serve the Muses under him.

The general character of this translation will be given, when it is said to preserve the wit, but to want the dignity of the original. The peculiarity of Juvenal is a mixture of gaiety and stateliness, of pointed sentences and declamatory grandeur. His points have not been neglected; but his grandeur none of the band seemed to consider as necessary to be imitated, except Creech, who undertook the thirteenth satire. It is therefore perhaps possible to give a better representation of that great satirist, even in those parts which Dryden himself has translated, some passages excepted, which will never be excelled.

With Juvenal was published Persius, translated wholly by Dryden. This work, though like all the other productions of Dryden it may have shining parts, seems to have been written merely for wages, in a uniform mediocrity, without any eager endeavour after excellence, or laborious effort of the mind.

There wanders an opinion among the readers of

poetry, that one of these satires is an exercise of the school. Dryden says that he once translated it at school; but not that he preserved or published the juvenile performance.

Not long afterwards he undertook perhaps the most arduous work of its kind, a translation of Virgil, for which he had shown how well he was qualified by his version of the Pollio, and two episodes, one of Nisus and Euryalus, the other of Mezentius and Lausus.

In the comparison of Homer and Virgil, the discriminative excellence of Homer is elevation and comprehension of thought, and that of Virgil is grace and splendour of diction. The beauties of Homer are therefore difficult to be lost, and those of Virgil difficult to be retained. The massy trunk of sentiment is safe by its solidity, but the blossoms of elocution easily drop away. The author, having the choice of his own images, selects those which he can best adorn: the translator must, at all hazards, follow his original, and express thoughts which perhaps he would not have chosen. When to this primary difficulty is added the inconvenience of a language so much inferior in harmony to the Latin, it cannot be expected that they who read the *Georgics* and the *Aeneid* should be much delighted with any version.

All these obstacles Dryden saw, and all these he determined to encounter. The expectation of his work was undoubtedly great; the nation considered its honour as interested in the event. One gave him the different editions of his author, and another helped him in the subordinate parts. The arguments of the several books were given him by Addison.

The hopes of the public were not disappointed. He produced, says Pope, 'the most noble and spirited translation that I know in any language'. It certainly excelled whatever had appeared in English, and appears to have satisfied his friends, and, for the most part, to have silenced his enemies. Milbourne, indeed, a clergyman, attacked it; but his outrages seem to be the ebullitions of a mind agitated by stronger resentment than bad poetry can excite, and previously resolved not to be pleased.

His criticism extends only to the preface, pastorals, and *Georgics;* and, as he professes, to give his antagonist an opportunity of reprisal, he has added his own version of the first and fourth pastorals, and the first *Georgic.* The world has forgotten his book; but since his attempt has given him a place in literary history, I will preserve a specimen of his criticism, by inserting his remarks on the invocation before the first *Georgic,* and of his poetry, by annexing his own version.

'Ver. 1.

> What makes a plenteous harvest, when to turn
> The fruitful soil, and when to sow the corn—

It's unlucky, they say, to stumble at the threshold, but what has a plenteous harvest to do here? Virgil would not pretend to prescribe rules for that which depends not on the husbandman's care, but the disposition of Heaven altogether. Indeed, the plenteous crop depends somewhat on the good method of tillage, and where the land's ill matured, the corn, without a miracle, can be but indifferent; but the harvest may be good, which is its properest epithet, though the husbandman's skill were never so indifferent. The next sentence is too literal, and when to plough had been Virgil's meaning, and intelligible to everybody; and when to sow the corn, is a needless addition.

'Ver. 3.

> The care of sheep, of oxen, and of kine,
> And when to geld the lambs, and sheer the swine,

would as well have fallen under the *cura boum, qui cultus habendo sit pecori,* as Mr. D.'s deduction of particulars.

'Ver. 5.

> The birth and genius of the frugal bee,
> I sing, Maecenas, and I sing to thee.

But where did *experientia* ever signify birth and genius? or what ground was there for such a figure in this place? How much more manly is Mr. Ogilby's version!

> What makes rich grounds, in what celestial signs,
> 'Tis good to plough, and marry elms with vines.
> What best fits cattle, what with sheep agrees,
> And several arts improving frugal bees,
> I sing, Maecenas.

'Which four lines, though faulty enough, are yet much more to the purpose than Mr. D.'s six.

'Ver. 22.

> From fields and mountains to my song repair.

For *patrium linquens nemus, saltusque Lycaei*—Very well explained!

'Ver. 23, 24.

> Inventor, Pallas, of the fattening oil,
> Thou founder of the plough, and ploughman's toil!

Written as if these had been both Pallas's invention. The ploughman's toil's impertinent.

'Ver. 25.

> ——The shroud-like cypress——

Why shroud-like? Is a cypress pulled up by the roots, which the sculpture in the last eclogue fills Silvanus's hand with, so very like a shroud? Or did not Mr. D. think of that kind of cypress used often for scarves and hatbands at funerals formerly, or for widows' veils, &c.? If so, 'twas a deep good thought.

'Ver. 26.

> —That wear
> The rural honours, and increase the year—

What's meant by increasing the year? Did the gods or goddesses add more months, or days, or hours to it? Or how can *arva tueri* signify to wear rural honours? Is this to translate, or abuse an author? The next couplets are borrowed from Ogilby, I suppose, because less to the purpose than ordinary.

'Ver. 33.

> The patron of the world, and Rome's peculiar guard.

Idle, and none of Virgil's, no more than the sense of
the precedent couplet; so again, he interpolates Virgil
with that and "the round circle of the year to guide
powerful of blessings, which thou strew'st around".
A ridiculous Latinism, and an impertinent addition;
indeed the whole period is but one piece of absurdity
and nonsense, as those who lay it with the original
must find.

'Ver. 42, 43.

> And Neptune shall resign the fasces of the sea.

Was he consul or dictator there?

> And watry virgins for thy bed shall strive.

Both absurd interpolations.

'Ver. 47, 48.

> Where in the void of heaven a place is free,
> Ah happy, D——n, were that place for thee!

But where is that void? Or what does our translator
mean by it? He knows what Ovid says God did, to
prevent such a void in heaven; perhaps, this was then
forgotten: but Virgil talks more sensibly.

'Ver. 49.

> The scorpion ready to receive thy laws.

No, he would not then have gotten out of his way
so fast.

'Ver. 56.

> Though Proserpine affects her silent seat—

What made her then so angry with Ascalaphus, for
preventing her return? She was now mused to patience
under the determinations of fate, rather than fond of
her residence.

'Ver. 61, 62, 63.

> Pity the poet's, and the ploughman's cares,
> Interest thy greatness in our mean affairs.
> And use thyself betimes to hear our prayers.

Which is such a wretched perversion of Virgil's noble thought as Vicars would have blushed at; but Mr. Ogilby makes us some amends, by his better lines:

> O wheresoe'er thou art, from thence incline,
> And grant assistance to my bold design!
> Pity with me, poor husbandmen's affairs,
> And now, as if translated, hear our prayers.

This is sense, and to the purpose: the other, poor mistaken stuff.'

Such were the strictures of Milbourne, who found few abettors; and of whom it may be reasonably imagined, that many who favoured his design were ashamed of his insolence.

When admiration had subsided, the translation was more coolly examined, and found, like all others, to be sometimes erroneous, and sometimes licentious. Those who could find faults, thought they could avoid them; and Dr. Brady attempted in blank verse a translation of the *Aeneid*, which, when dragged into the world, did not live long enough to cry. I have never seen it; but that such a version there is, or has been, perhaps some old catalogue informed me.

With not much better success, Trapp, when his tragedy and his prelections had given him reputation, attempted another blank version of the *Aeneid*; to which, notwithstanding the slight regard with which it was treated, he had afterwards perseverance enough to add the *Eclogues* and *Georgics*. His book may continue its existence as long as it is the clandestine refuge of schoolboys.

Since the English ear has been accustomed to the mellifluence of Pope's numbers, and the diction of poetry has become more splendid, new attempts have been made to translate Virgil; and all his works have been attempted by men better qualified to contend with Dryden. I will not engage myself in an invidious comparison by opposing one passage to another; a work of which there would be no end, and which might be often offensive without use.

It is not by comparing line with line that the merit of great works is to be estimated, but by their general effects and ultimate result. It is easy to note a weak line, and to write one more vigorous in its place; to find a happiness of expression in the original, and transplant it by force into the version: but what is given to the parts, may be subducted from the whole, and the reader may be weary, though the critic may commend. Works of imagination excel by their allurement and delight; by their power of attracting and detaining the attention. That book is good in vain, which the reader throws away. He only is the master, who keeps the mind in pleasing captivity; whose pages are perused with eagerness, and in hope of new pleasure are perused again; and whose conclusion is perceived with an eye of sorrow, such as the traveller casts upon departing day.

By his proportion of this predomination I will consent that Dryden should be tried; of this, which, in opposition to reason, makes Ariosto the darling and the pride of Italy; of this, which, in defiance of criticism, continues Shakespeare the sovereign of the drama.

His last work was his *Fables*, in which he gave us the first example of a mode of writing which the Italians call *rifaccimento*, a renovation of ancient writers, by modernizing their language. Thus the old poem of Boiardo has been new-dressed by Domenichi and Berni. The works of Chaucer, upon which this kind of rejuvenescence has been bestowed by Dryden, require little criticism. The tale of the *Cock* seems hardly worth revival; and the story of *Palamon and Arcite*, containing an action unsuitable to the times in which it is placed, can hardly be suffered to pass without censure of the hyperbolical commendation which Dryden has given it in the general preface, and in a poetical dedication, a piece where his original fondness of remote conceits seems to have revived.

Of the three pieces borrowed from Boccace, *Sigismunda* may be defended by the celebrity of the story. *Theodore and Honoria*, though it contains not much moral, yet afforded opportunities of striking description. And *Cymon* was formerly a tale of such reputation, that, at the revival of letters, it was translated into Latin by one of the Beroalds.

Whatever subjects employed his pen, he was still improving our measures and embellishing our language.

In this volume are interspersed some short original poems, which with his prologues, epilogues, and songs, may be comprised in Congreve's remark, that even those, if he had written nothing else, would have entitled him to the praise of excellence in his kind.

One composition must, however, be distinguished. The *Ode for St. Cecilia's Day*, perhaps the last effort of his poetry, has always been considered as exhibiting the highest flight of fancy, and the exactest nicety of art. This is allowed to stand without a rival. If indeed there is any excellence beyond it, in some other of Dryden's works that excellence must be found. Compared with the *Ode on Killigrew*, it may be pronounced perhaps superior in the whole; but without any single part equal to the first stanza of the other.

It is said to have cost Dryden a fortnight's labour; but it does not want its negligences: some of the lines are without correspondent rhymes; a defect, which I never detected but after an acquaintance of many years, and which the enthusiasm of the writer might hinder him from perceiving.

His last stanza has less emotion than the former; but is not less elegant in the diction. The conclusion is vicious; the music of Timotheus, which 'raised a mortal to the skies', had only a metaphorical power; that of Cecilia, which 'drew an angel down', had a real effect; the crown therefore could not reasonably be divided

In a general survey of Dryden's labours, he appears to have a mind very comprehensive by nature, and much enriched with acquired knowledge. His compositions are the effects of a vigorous genius operating upon large materials.

The power that predominated in his intellectual operations was rather strong reason than quick sensibility. Upon all occasions that were presented, he studied rather than felt, and produced sentiments not such as nature enforces, but meditation supplies. With the simple and elemental passions, as they spring separate in the mind, he seems not much acquainted; and seldom describes them but as they are complicated by the various relations of society, and confused in the tumults and agitations of life.

What he says of love may contribute to the explanation of his character:

> Love various minds does variously inspire;
> It stirs in gentle bosoms gentle fire,
> Like that of incense on the altar laid;
> But raging flames tempestuous souls invade;
> A fire which every windy passion blows,
> With pride it mounts, or with revenge it glows.

Dryden's was not one of the 'gentle bosoms'. Love as it subsists in itself, with no tendency but to the person loved, and wishing only for correspondent kindness; such love as shuts out all other interest; the love of the golden age, was too soft and subtle to put his faculties in motion. He hardly conceived it but in its turbulent effervescence with some other desires; when it was inflamed by rivalry, or obstructed by difficulties: when it invigorated ambition, or exasperated revenge.

He is therefore, with all his variety of excellence, not often pathetic; and had so little sensibility of the power of effusions purely natural, that he did not esteem them in others. Simplicity gave him no pleasure; and for the first part of his life he looked on Otway with contempt, though at last, indeed very late, he confessed that in his play 'there was nature, which is the chief beauty'.

We do not always know our own motives. I am not certain whether it was not rather the difficulty which he found in exhibiting the genuine operations of the heart, than a servile submission to an injudicious audience, that filled his plays with false magnificence. It was necessary to fix attention; and the mind can be captivated only by recollection, or by curiosity; by reviving natural sentiments, or impressing new appearances of things; sentences were readier at his call than images; he could more easily fill the ear with some splendid novelty, than awaken those ideas that slumber in the heart.

The favourite exercise of his mind was ratiocination; and, that argument might not be too soon at an end, he delighted to talk of liberty and necessity, destiny and contingence; these he discusses in the language of the school with so much profundity, that the terms which he uses are not always understood. It is indeed learning, but learning out of place.

When once he had engaged himself in disputation, thoughts flowed in on either side: he was now no longer at a loss; he had always objections and solutions at command: *verbaque provisam rem*—give him matter for his verse, and he finds without difficulty verse for his matter.

In comedy, for which he professes himself not naturally qualified, the mirth which he excites will perhaps not be found so much to arise from any original humour, or peculiarity of character nicely distinguished and diligently pursued, as from incidents and circumstances, artifices and surprises; from jests of action rather than of sentiment. What he had of humorous or passionate, he seems to have had not from nature, but from other poets; if not always as a plagiary, at least as an imitator.

Next to argument, his delight was in wild and daring sallies of sentiment, in the irregular and eccentric violence of wit. He delighted to tread upon the brink of meaning, where light and darkness begin to mingle; to approach the precipice of absurdity, and hover over the abyss of unideal vacancy. This inclination sometimes produced nonsense, which he knew; as,

> Move swiftly, sun, and fly a lover's pace,
> Leave weeks and months behind thee in thy race.

> Amariel flies
> To guard thee from the demons of the air;
> My flaming sword above them to display,
> All keen, and ground upon the edge of day.

And sometimes it issued in absurdities, of which perhaps he was not conscious:

> Then we upon our orb's last verge shall go,
>   And see the ocean leaning on the sky;
> From thence our rolling neighbours we shall know,
>   And on the lunar world securely pry.

These lines have no meaning: but may we not say, in imitation of Cowley on another book,

> 'Tis so like *sense* 'twill serve the turn as well?

This endeavour after the grand and the new produced many sentiments either great or bulky, and many images either just or splendid:

> I am as free as Nature first made man,
> Ere the base laws of servitude began,
> When wild in woods the noble savage ran.

> —'Tis but because the Living death ne'er knew,
> They fear to prove it as a thing that's new:
> Let me th' experiment before you try,
> I'll show you first how easy 'tis to die.

> —There with a forest of their darts he strove,
> And stood like Capaneus defying Jove;
> With his broad sword the boldest beating down,
> While Fate grew pale lest he should win the town,
> And turn'd the iron leaves of his dark book
> To make new dooms, or mend what it mistook.

> —I beg no pity for this mouldering clay;
> For if you give it burial, there it takes
> Possession of your earth;
> If burnt, and scatter'd in the air, the winds
> That strew my dust diffuse my royalty,
> And spread me o'er your clime; for where one atom
> Of mine shall light, know there Sebastian reigns.

Of these quotations the two first may be allowed to be great, the two latter only timid.

Of such selection there is no end. I will add only a few more passages; of which the first, though it may perhaps not be quite clear in prose, is not too obscure for poetry, as the meaning that it has is noble:

> No, there is a necessity in Fate,
> Why still the brave bold man is fortunate;
> He keeps his object ever full in sight,
> And that assurance holds him firm and right;
> True, 'tis a narrow way that leads to bliss,
> But right before there is no precipice;
> Fear makes men look aside, and so their footing miss.

Of the images which the two following citations afford, the first is elegant, the second magnificent; whether either be just let the reader judge:

> What precious drops are these,
> Which silently each other's track pursue,
> Bright as young diamonds in their infant dew?

> ——Resign your castle——
> —Enter, brave Sir; for when you speak the word,
> The gates shall open of their own accord;
> The genius of the place its Lord shall meet,
> And bow its towery forehead at your feet.

These bursts of extravagance Dryden calls the Delilahs of the theatre: and owns that many noisy lines of Maximin and Almanzor call out for vengeance upon him; 'but I knew', says he, 'that they were bad enough to please, even when I wrote them'. There is surely reason to suspect that he pleased himself as well as his audience; and that these, like the harlots of other men, had his love, though not his approbation.

He had sometimes faults of a less generous and splendid kind. He makes, like almost all other poets, very frequent use of mythology, and sometimes connects religion and fable too closely without distinction.

He descends to display his knowledge with pedantic ostentation; as when, in translating Virgil, he says 'tack to the larboard'—and 'veer starboard'; and talks in another work of 'virtue spooming before the wind'. His vanity now and then betrays his ignorance:

> They Nature's king through Nature's optics view'd;
> Revers'd they view'd him lessen'd to their eyes.

He had heard of reversing a telescope, and unluckily reverses the object.

He is sometimes unexpectedly mean. When he describes the Supreme Being as moved by prayer to stop the Fire of London, what is his expression?

> A hollow crystal pyramid he takes,
> In firmamental waters dipp'd above,
> Of this a broad *extinguisher* he makes,
> And *hoods* the flames that to their quarry strove.

When he describes the Last Day, and the decisive tribunal, he intermingles this image:

> When rattling bones together fly,
> From the four quarters of the sky.

It was indeed never in his power to resist the temptation of a jest. In his elegy on Cromwell:

> No sooner was the Frenchman's cause embrac'd,
> Than the *light Monsieur* the *grave Don* outweigh'd;
> His fortune turn'd the scale——

He had a vanity, unworthy of his abilities, to show, as may be suspected, the rank of the company with whom he lived, by the use of French words, which had then crept into conversation; such as *fraîcheur* for

coolness, *fougue* for turbulence, and a few more, none
of which the language has incorporated or retained.
They continue only where they stood first, perpetual
warnings to future innovators.

These are his faults of affectation; his faults of negligence are beyond recital. Such is the unevenness of
his compositions, that ten lines are seldom found
together without something of which the reader is
ashamed. Dryden was no rigid judge of his own pages;
he seldom struggled after supreme excellence, but
snatched in haste what was within his reach; and
when he could content others, was himself contented.
He did not keep present to his mind an idea of pure
perfection; nor compare his works, such as they were,
with what they might be made. He knew to whom he
should be opposed. He had more music than Waller,
more vigour than Denham, and more nature than
Cowley; and from his contemporaries he was in no
danger. Standing therefore in the highest place, he
had no care to rise by contending with himself; but
while there was no name above his own, was willing to
enjoy fame on the easiest terms.

He was no lover of labour. What he thought
sufficient, he did not stop to make better; and allowed
himself to leave many parts unfinished, in confidence
that the good lines would overbalance the bad. What
he had once written, he dismissed from his thoughts;
and, I believe, there is no example to be found of any
correction or improvement made by him after publication. The hastiness of his productions might be the
effect of necessity; but his subsequent neglect could
hardly have any other cause than impatience of study.

What can be said of his versification will be little
more than a dilatation of the praise given it by Pope:

> Waller was smooth; but Dryden taught to join
> The varying verse, the full-resounding line,
> The long majestic march, and energy divine.

Some improvements had been already made in

English numbers; but the full force of our language was not yet felt; the verse that was smooth was commonly feeble. If Cowley had sometimes a finished line, he had it by chance. Dryden knew how to choose the flowing and the sonorous words; to vary the pauses, and adjust the accents; to diversify the cadence, and yet preserve the smoothness of his metre.

Of triplets and Alexandrines, though he did not introduce the use, he established it. The triplet has long subsisted among us. Dryden seems not to have traced it higher than to Chapman's *Homer*; but it is to be found in Phaer's *Virgil*, written in the reign of Mary, and in Hall's *Satires*, published five years before the death of Elizabeth.

The Alexandrine was, I believe, first used by Spenser, for the sake of closing his stanza with a fuller sound. We had a longer measure of fourteen syllables, into which the *Aeneid* was translated by Phaer, and other works of the ancients, by other writers; of which Chapman's *Iliad* was, I believe, the last.

The two first lines of Phaer's third *Aeneid* will exemplify this measure:

When Asia's state was overthrown, and Priam's kingdom
        stout,
All guiltless, by the power of gods above was rooted out.

As these lines had their break, or *caesura*, always at the eighth syllable, it was thought, in time, commodious to divide them; and quatrains of lines alternately consisting of eight and six syllables, make the most soft and pleasing of our lyric measures; as,

> Relentless Time, destroying power,
>   Which stone and brass obey,
> Who giv'st to every flying hour
>   To work some new decay.

In the Alexandrine, when its power was once felt, some poems, as Drayton's *Polyolbion*, were wholly written; and sometimes the measures of twelve and fourteen syllables were interchanged with one another.

Cowley was the first that inserted the Alexandrine at pleasure among the heroic lines of ten syllables, and from him Dryden professes to have adopted it.

The triplet and Alexandrine are not universally approved. Swift always censured them, and wrote some lines to ridicule them. In examining their propriety, it is to be considered that the essence of verse is regularity, and its ornament is variety. To write verse is to dispose syllables and sounds harmonically by some known and settled rule; a rule, however, lax enough to substitute similitude for identity, to admit change without breach of order, and to relieve the ear without disappointing it. Thus a Latin hexameter is formed from dactyls and spondees differently combined; the English heroic admits of acute or grave syllables variously disposed. The Latin never deviates into seven feet, or exceeds the number of seventeen syllables; but the English Alexandrine breaks the lawful bounds, and surprises the reader with two syllables more than he expected.

The effect of the triplet is the same: the ear has been accustomed to expect a new rhyme in every couplet; but is on a sudden surprised with three rhymes together, to which the reader could not accommodate his voice, did he not obtain notice of the change from the braces in the margins. Surely there is something unskilful in the necessity of such mechanical direction.

Considering the metrical art simply as a science, and consequently excluding all casualty, we must allow that triplets and Alexandrines, inserted by caprice, are interruptions of that constancy to which science aspires. And though the variety which they produce may very justly be desired, yet to make our poetry exact, there ought to be some stated mode of admitting them.

But till some such regulation can be formed, I wish them still to be retained in their present state. They are sometimes grateful to the reader, and sometimes convenient to the poet. Fenton was of opinion that Dryden was too liberal and Pope too sparing in their use.

The rhymes of Dryden are commonly just, and he valued himself for his readiness in finding them; but he is sometimes open to objection.

It is the common practice of our poets to end the second line with a weak or grave syllable:

> Together o'er the Alps methinks we fly,
> Fill'd with ideas of fair *Italy*.

Dryden sometimes puts the weak rhyme in the first:

> Laugh all the powers that favour *tyranny*,
> And all the standing army of the sky.

Sometimes he concludes a period or paragraph with the first line of a couplet, which, though the French seem to do it without irregularity, always displeases in English poetry.

The Alexandrine, though much his favourite, is not always very diligently fabricated by him. It invariably requires a break at the sixth syllable; a rule which the modern French poets never violate, but which Dryden sometimes neglected:

> And with paternal thunder vindicates his throne.

Of Dryden's works it was said by Pope, that he 'could select from them better specimens of every mode of poetry than any other English writer could supply'. Perhaps no nation ever produced a writer that enriched his language with such variety of models. To him we owe the improvement, perhaps the completion of our metre, the refinement of our language, and much of the correctness of our sentiments. By him we were taught *sapere et fari*, to think naturally and express forcibly. Though Davies has reasoned in rhyme before him, it may be perhaps maintained that he was the first who joined argument with poetry, He showed us the true bounds of a translator's liberty.

What was said of Rome, adorned by Augustus, may
be applied by an easy metaphor to English poetry
embellished by Dryden, *lateritiam invenit, marmoream
reliquit*, 'He found it brick, and he left it marble.'

GRAY

(1781)

THOMAS GRAY, the son of Mr. Philip Gray, a scrivener
of London, was born in Cornhill, November 26, 1716.
His grammatical education he received at Eton under
the care of Mr. Antrobus, his mother's brother, then
assistant to Dr. George; and when he left school, in
1734, entered a pensioner at Peterhouse in Cambridge.

The transition from the school to the college is,
to most young scholars, the time from which they date
their years of manhood, liberty, and happiness; but
Gray seems to have been very little delighted with
academical gratifications; he liked at Cambridge
neither the mode of life nor the fashion of study, and
lived sullenly on to the time when his attendance on
lectures was no longer required. As he intended to
profess the Common Law he took no degree.

When he had been at Cambridge about five years,
Mr. Horace Walpole, whose friendship he had gained
at Eton, invited him to travel with him as his companion. They wandered through France into Italy;
and Gray's letters contain a very pleasing account of
many parts of their journey. But unequal friendships
are easily dissolved: at Florence they quarrelled and
parted, and Mr. Walpole is now content to have it
told that it was by his fault. If we look, however,
without prejudice on the world, we shall find that
men, whose consciousness of their own merit sets
them above the compliances of servility, are apt enough
in their association with superiors to watch their own
dignity with troublesome and punctilious jealousy,
and in the fervour of independence to exact that atten-

tion which they refuse to pay. Part they did, whatever was the quarrel, and the rest of their travels was doubtless more unpleasant to them both. Gray continued his journey in a manner suitable to his own little fortune, with only an occasional servant.

He returned to England in September 1741, and in about two months afterwards buried his father, who had, by an injudicious waste of money upon a new house, so much lessened his fortune, that Gray thought himself too poor to study the law. He therefore retired to Cambridge, where he soon after became Bachelor of Civil Law; and where, without liking the place or its inhabitants, or professing to like them, he passed, except a short residence at London, the rest of his life.

About this time he was deprived of Mr. West, the son of a chancellor of Ireland, a friend on whom he appears to have set a high value, and who deserved his esteem by the powers which he shows in his letters, and in the *Ode to May*, which Mr. Mason has preserved, as well as by the sincerity with which, when Gray sent him part of *Agrippina*, a tragedy that he had just begun, he gave an opinion which probably intercepted the progress of the work, and which the judgement of every reader will confirm. It was certainly no loss to the English stage that *Agrippina* was never finished.

In this year (1742) Gray seems first to have applied himself seriously to poetry; for in this year were produced the *Ode to Spring*, his *Prospect of Eton*, and his *Ode to Adversity*. He began likewise a Latin poem, *De Principiis Cogitandi*.

It may be collected from the narrative of Mr. Mason, that his first ambition was to have excelled in Latin poetry: perhaps it were reasonable to wish that he had prosecuted his design; for though there is at present some embarrassment in his phrase, and some harshness in his lyric numbers, his copiousness of language is such as very few possess, and his lines, even when imperfect, discover a writer whom practice would quickly have made skilful.

He now lived on at Peterhouse, very little solicitous what others did or thought, and cultivated his mind and enlarged his views without any other purpose than of improving and amusing himself; when Mr. Mason, being elected fellow of Pembroke Hall, brought him a companion who was afterwards to be his editor, and whose fondness and fidelity has kindled in him a zeal of admiration, which cannot be reasonably expected from the neutrality of a stranger and the coldness of a critic.

In this retirement he wrote (1747) an *Ode on the Death of Mr. Walpole's Cat*; and the year afterwards attempted a poem of more importance, on *Government and Education*, of which the fragments which remain have many excellent lines.

His next production (1750) was his far-famed *Elegy in the Churchyard*, which, finding its way into a magazine first, I believe, made him known to the public.

An invitation from Lady Cobham about this time gave occasion to an odd composition called *A Long Story*, which adds little to Gray's character.

Several of his pieces were published (1753), with designs by Mr. Bentley; and, that they might in some form or other make a book, only one side of each leaf was printed. I believe the poems and the plates recommended each other so well, that the whole impression was soon bought. This year he lost his mother.

Some time afterwards (1756) some young men of the college, whose chambers were near his, diverted themselves with disturbing him by frequent and troublesome noises, and, as is said, by pranks yet more offensive and contemptuous. This insolence, having endured it awhile, he represented to the governors of the society, among whom perhaps he had no friends; and, finding his complaint little regarded, removed himself to Pembroke Hall.

In 1757 he published *The Progress of Poetry* and *The Bard*, two compositions at which the readers of poetry were at first content to gaze in mute amazement. Some that tried them confessed their inability to understand them, though Warburton said that they were understood as well as the works of Milton and Shakespeare, which it is the fashion to admire. Garrick wrote a few lines in their praise. Some hardy champions undertook to rescue them from neglect, and in a short time many were content to be shown beauties which they could not see.

Gray's reputation was now so high that, after the death of Cibber, he had the honour of refusing the laurel, which was then bestowed on Mr. Whitehead.

His curiosity, not long after, drew him away from Cambridge to a lodging near the Museum, where he resided near three years, reading and transcribing; and, so far as can be discovered, very little affected by two odes on *Oblivion* and *Obscurity*, in which his lyric performances were ridiculed with much contempt and much ingenuity.

When the Professor of Modern History at Cambridge died, he was, as he says, *cockered and spirited up*, till he asked it of Lord Bute, who sent him a civil refusal; and the place was given to Mr. Brocket, the tutor of Sir James Lowther.

His constitution was weak, and believing that his health was promoted by exercise and change of place, he undertook (1765) a journey into Scotland, of which his account, so far as it extends, is very curious and elegant; for as his comprehension was ample, his curiosity extended to all the works of art, all the appearances of nature, and all the monuments of past events. He naturally contracted a friendship with Dr. Beattie, whom he found a poet, a philosopher, and a good man. The Mareschal College at Aberdeen offered him the degree of Doctor of Laws, which, having omitted to take it at Cambridge, he thought it decent to refuse.

What he had formerly solicited in vain, was at last given him without solicitation. The Professorship of

History became again vacant, and he received (1768) an offer of it from the Duke of Grafton. He accepted, and retained it to his death; always designing lectures, but never reading them; uneasy at his neglect of duty, and appeasing his uneasiness with designs of reformation, and with a resolution which he believed himself to have made of resigning the office, if he found himself unable to discharge it.

Ill health made another journey necessary, and he visited (1769) Westmorland and Cumberland. He that reads his epistolary narration wishes that to travel and to tell his travels had been more of his employment; but it is by studying at home that we must obtain the ability of travelling with intelligence and improvement.

His travels and his studies were now near their end. The gout, of which he had sustained many weak attacks, fell upon his stomach, and, yielding to no medicines, produced strong convulsions, which (July 30, 1771) terminated in death.

His character I am willing to adopt, as Mr. Mason has done, from a letter written to my friend Mr. Boswell, by the Rev. Mr. Temple, rector of St. Gluvias in Cornwall; and am as willing as his warmest well-wisher to believe it true.

'Perhaps he was the most learned man in Europe. He was equally acquainted with the elegant and profound parts of science, and that not superficially but thoroughly. He knew every branch of history, both natural and civil; had read all the original historians of England, France, and Italy; and was a great antiquarian. Criticism, metaphysics, morals, politics, made a principal part of his study; voyages and travels of all sorts were his favourite amusements; and he had a fine taste in painting, prints, architecture, and gardening. With such a fund of knowledge, his conversation must have been equally instructing and entertaining; but he was also a good man, a man of virtue and humanity. There is no character without some speck, some imperfection; and I think the greatest defect in his was an affectation in delicacy, or rather effeminacy, and a visible fastidiousness, or contempt and disdain of his inferiors in science. He also had, in some degree, that weakness which disgusted Voltaire so much in Mr. Congreve: though he seemed to value others chiefly according to the progress they had made in knowledge, yet he could not bear to be considered himself merely as a man of letters; and though without birth, or fortune, or station, his desire was to be looked upon as a private independent gentleman, who read for his amusement. Perhaps it may be said, What signifies so much knowledge, when it produced so little? Is it worth taking so much pains to leave no memorial but a few poems? But let it be considered that Mr. Gray was, to others, at least innocently employed; to himself, certainly beneficially. His time passed agreeably; he was every day making some new acquisition in science; his mind was enlarged, his heart softened, his virtue strengthened; the world and mankind were shown to him without a mask; and he was taught to consider every thing as trifling, and unworthy of the attention of a wise man, except the pursuit of knowledge and practice of virtue, in that state wherein God hath placed us.'

To this character Mr. Mason has added a more particular account of Gray's skill in zoology. He has remarked that Gray's effeminacy was affected most before those whom he did not wish to please; and that he is unjustly charged with making knowledge his sole reason of preference, as he paid his esteem to none whom he did not likewise believe to be good.

What has occurred to me, from the slight inspection of his letters in which my undertaking has engaged me, is, that his mind had a large grasp; that his curiosity was unlimited, and his judgement cultivated; that he was a man likely to love much where he loved at all, but that he was fastidious and hard to please.

His contempt, however, is often employed, where I hope it will be approved, upon scepticism and infidelity. His short account of Shaftesbury I will insert.

'You say you cannot conceive how Lord Shaftesbury came to be a philosopher in vogue; I will tell you: first, he was a lord; secondly, he was as vain as any of his readers; thirdly, men are very prone to believe what they do not understand; fourthly, they will believe any thing at all, provided they are under no obligation to believe it; fifthly, they love to take a new road, even when that road leads nowhere; sixthly, he was reckoned a fine writer, and seems always to mean more than he said. Would you have any more reasons? An interval of above forty years has pretty well destroyed the charm. A dead lord ranks with commoners: vanity is no longer interested in the matter; for a new road is become an old one.'

Mr. Mason has added, from his own knowledge, that though Gray was poor, he was not eager of money; and that, out of the little that he had, he was very willing to help the necessitous.

As a writer he had this peculiarity, that he did not write his pieces first rudely, and then correct them, but laboured every line as it arose in the train of composition; and he had a notion not very peculiar, that he could not write but at certain times, or at happy moments; a fantastic foppery, to which my kindness for a man of learning and of virtue wishes him to have been superior.

Gray's poetry is now to be considered; and I hope not to be looked on as an enemy to his name, if I confess that I contemplate it with less pleasure than his life.

His *Ode on Spring* has something poetical, both in the language and the thought; but the language is too luxuriant, and the thoughts have nothing new. There has of late arisen a practice of giving to adjectives, derived from substantives, the termination of participles; such as the cultured plain, the daisied bank; but I was sorry to see, in the lines of a scholar like Gray, the honied spring. The morality is natural, but too stale; the conclusion is pretty.

The poem on the *Cat* was doubtless by its author considered as a trifle, but it is not a happy trifle. In the first stanza the azure flowers that blow, show resolutely a rhyme is sometimes made when it cannot easily be found. Selima, the cat, is called a nymph, with some violence both to language and sense; but there is good use made of it when it is done; for of the two lines,

> What female heart can gold despise?
> What cat's averse to fish?

the first relates merely to the nymph, and the second only to the cat. The sixth stanza contains a melancholy truth, that a favourite has no friend; but the last ends in a pointed sentence of no relation to the purpose; if what glistered had been gold, the cat would not have gone into the water; and, if she had, would not less have been drowned.

The *Prospect of Eton College* suggests nothing to Gray, which every beholder does not equally think and feel. His supplication to Father Thames, to tell him who drives the hoop or tosses the ball, is useless and puerile. Father Thames has no better means of knowing than himself. His epithet 'buxom health' is not elegant; he seems not to understand the word. Gray thought his language more poetical as it was more remote from common use: finding in Dryden honey redolent of spring, an expression that reaches the utmost limits of our language, Gray drove it a little more beyond apprehension, by making gales to be redolent of joy and youth.

Of the *Ode on Adversity*, the hint was at first taken from *O Diva, gratum quae regis Antium*; but Gray has excelled his original by the variety of his sentiments, and by their moral application. Of this piece, at once poetical and rational, I will not by slight objections violate the dignity.

My process has now brought me to the *wonderful Wonder of Wonders*, the two sister odes, by which, though either vulgar ignorance or common sense at first universally rejected them, many have been since persuaded to think themselves delighted. I am one of those that are willing to be pleased, and therefore would gladly find the meaning of the first stanza of *The Progress of Poetry*.

Gray seems in his rapture to confound the images of spreading sound and running water. A stream of music may be allowed; but where does music, however smooth and strong, after having visited the verdant vales, roll down the steep amain, so as that rocks and nodding groves rebellow to the roar? If this be said of music, it is nonsense; if it be said of water, it is nothing to the purpose.

The second stanza, exhibiting Mars's car and Jove's eagle, is unworthy of further notice. Criticism disdains to chase a schoolboy to his commonplaces.

To the third it may likewise be objected, that it is drawn from Mythology, though such as may be more easily assimilated to real life. Idalia's velvet-green has something of cant. An epithet or metaphor drawn from Nature ennobles Art; an epithet or metaphor drawn from Art degrades Nature. Gray is too fond of words arbitrarily compounded. Many-twinkling was formerly censured as not analogical; we may say many-spotted, but scarcely many-spotting. This stanza, however, has something pleasing.

Of the second ternary of stanzas, the first endeavours to tell something, and would have told it, had it not been crossed by Hyperion: the second describes well enough the universal prevalence of poetry; but I am afraid that the conclusion will not rise from the premises. The caverns of the north and the plains of Chili are not the residences of glory and generous shame. But that poetry and virtue go always together is an opinion so pleasing, that I can forgive him who resolves to think it true.

The third stanza sounds big with Delphi, and Egean, and Ilissus, and Meander, and hallowed fountain and solemn sound; but in all Gray's odes there is a kind of cumbrous splendour which we wish away. His position is at last false: in the time of Dante and Petrarch, from whom he derives our first school of poetry, Italy was overrun by tyrant power and coward vice; nor was our state much better when we first borrowed the Italian arts.

Of the third ternary, the first gives a mythological birth of Shakespeare. What is said of that mighty genius is true; but it is not said happily: the real effects of this poetical power are put out of sight by the pomp of machinery. Where truth is sufficient to fill the mind, fiction is worse than useless; the counterfeit debases the genuine.

His account of Milton's blindness, if we suppose it caused by study in the formation of his poem, a supposition surely allowable, is poetically true, and happily imagined. But the car of Dryden, with his two coursers, has nothing in it peculiar; it is a car in which any other rider may be placed.

The Bard appears, at the first view, to be, as Algarotti and others have remarked, an imitation of the prophecy of Nereus. Algarotti thinks it superior to its original; and, if preference depends only on the imagery and animation of the two poems, his judgement is right. There is in *The Bard* more force, more thought, and more variety. But to copy is less than to invent, and the copy has been unhappily produced at a wrong time. The fiction of Horace was to the Romans credible; but its revival disgusts us with apparent and unconquerable falsehood. *Incredulus odi.*

To select a singular event, and swell it to a giant's bulk by fabulous appendages of spectres and predictions, has little difficulty, for he that forsakes the probable may always find the marvellous. And it has little use; we are affected only as we believe; we are improved only as we find something to be imitated or declined. I do not see that *The Bard* promotes any truth, moral or political.

His stanzas are too long, especially his epodes; the ode is finished before the ear has learned its measures, and consequently before it can receive pleasure from their consonance and recurrence.

Of the first stanza the abrupt beginning has been celebrated; but technical beauties can give praise only to the inventor. It is in the power of any man to rush abruptly upon his subject, that has read the ballad of *Johnny Armstrong*,

Is there ever a man in all Scotland—

The initial resemblances, or alliterations, ruin, ruthless, helm or hauberk, are below the grandeur of a poem that endeavours at sublimity.

In the second stanza the Bard is well described; but in the third we have the puerilities of obsolete mythology. When we are told that Cadwallo hushed the stormy main, and that Modred made huge Plinlimmon bow his cloud-topped head, attention recoils from the repetition of a tale that, even when it was first heard, was heard with scorn.

The weaving of the winding sheet he borrowed, as he owns, from the northern bards; but their texture, however, was very properly the work of female powers, as the art of spinning the thread of life in another mythology. Theft is always dangerous; Gray has made weavers of his slaughtered bards by a fiction outrageous and incongruous. They are then called upon to weave the warp, and weave the woof, perhaps with no great propriety; for it is by crossing the woof with the warp that men weave the web or piece; and the first line was dearly bought by the admission of its wretched correspondent, 'Give ample room and verge enough'. He has, however, no other line as bad.

The third stanza of the second ternary is commended, I think, beyond its merit. The personification is indistinct. Thirst and hunger are not alike; and their features, to make the imagery perfect, should have been discriminated. We are told, in the same stanza, how towers are fed. But I will no longer look for particular faults; yet let it be observed that the ode might have been concluded with an action of better example; but suicide is always to be had, without expense of thought.

These odes are marked by glittering accumulations of ungraceful ornaments; they strike, rather than please; the images are magnified by affectation; the language is laboured into harshness. The mind of the writer seems to work with unnatural violence. 'Double, double, toil and trouble.' He has a kind of strutting dignity, and is tall by walking on tiptoe. His art and his struggle are too visible, and there is too little appearance of ease and nature.

To say that he has no beauties would be unjust: a man like him, of great learning and great industry, could not but produce something valuable. When he pleases least, it can only be said that a good design was ill directed.

His translations of Northern and Welsh poetry deserve praise; the imagery is preserved, perhaps often improved; but the language is unlike the language of other poets.

In the character of his *Elegy* I rejoice to concur with the common reader; for by the common sense of readers uncorrupted with literary prejudices, after all the refinements of subtilty and the dogmatism of learning, must be finally decided all claim to poetical honours. The *Churchyard* abounds with images which find a mirror in every mind, and with sentiments to which every bosom returns an echo. The four stanzas beginning 'Yet even these bones', are to me original: I have never seen the notions in any other place; yet he that reads them here, persuades himself that he has always felt them. Had Gray written often thus, it had been vain to blame, and useless to praise him.

THOMAS WARTON

PREFACE TO MILTON'S MINOR POEMS

(1790)

THE poems which compose the present volume were published almost thirty years before the appearance of the *Paradise Lost*. During that interval, they were so totally disregarded, at least by the general reader, as scarcely to have conferred on their author the reputation of a writer of verses; much less the distinction and character of a true poet. After the publication of the *Paradise Lost*, whose acknowledged merit and increasing celebrity might have naturally contributed to call other pieces of the same author, and of a kindred excellence, into a more conspicuous point of view, they long continued to remain in their original state of neglect and obscurity. At the infancy of their circulation, and for some years afterwards, they were overwhelmed in the commotions of faction, the conflict of religious disputation, and the professional ignorance of fanaticism. In succeeding years, when tumults and usurpations were at an end, and leisure and literature returned, the times were still unpropitious, and the public taste was unprepared for their reception. It was late in the present century before they attained their just measure of esteem and popularity. Wit and rhyme, sentiment and satire, polished numbers, sparkling couplets, and pointed periods, having so long kept undisturbed possession in our poetry, would not easily give way to fiction and fancy, to picturesque description, and romantic imagery.

When Sir Henry Wotton, 1637, had received from Milton the compliment of a present of *Comus*, at first separately printed by the care of Henry Lawes, he returned a panegyric on the performance in which real approbation undoubtedly concurred with the partiality of private friendship, and a grateful sense of this kind testimony of Milton's regard. But Wotton, a scholar and a poet, did not perceive the genuine graces of this exquisite masque, which yet he professes to have 'viewed with singular delight'. His conceptions did not reach to the higher poetry of *Comus*. He was rather struck with the pastoral mellifluence of its lyric measures, which he styles 'a certain Doric delicacy in the songs and odes', than with its grave and more majestic tones, with the solemnity and variety of its peculiar vein of original invention. This drama was not to be generally characterized by its songs and odes: nor do I know that softness and sweetness, although they want neither, are particularly characteristical of those passages, which are most commonly rough with strong and crowded images, and rich in personification. However, the Song to Echo, and the initial strains of Comus's invocation, are much in the style which Wotton describes.

The first edition of these poems, comprehending *Comus* already printed, and *Lycidas*, of which there was also a previous impression, is dated in 1645. But I do not recollect, that for seventy years afterwards, they are once mentioned in the whole succession of English literature. Perhaps almost the only instance on record in that period of time of their having received any, even a slight, mark of attention or notice, is to be found in Archbishop Sancroft's papers at Oxford. In these papers is contained a very considerable collection of poetry, but chiefly religious, exactly and elegantly transcribed with his own hand, while he was a fellow of Emmanuel College, and about the year 1648, from Crashaw, Cowley, Herbert, Alabaster, Wotton, and other poets then in fashion. And among these extracts is Milton's *Ode on the Nativity*, said by Sancroft to be selected from 'the first page of John Milton's poems'. Also our author's version of the fifty-third Psalm, noted by the transcriber, I suppose as an example of uncommon exertion of genius, to have been done in the fifteenth year of the translator's age. Sancroft, even to his maturer years, retained his strong early predilection to polite literature, which he still continued to cultivate; and from these and other remains of his studies in that pursuit, now preserved in the Bodleian Library, it appears that he was a diligent reader of the poetry of his times, both in English and Latin. In an old Miscellany, quaintly called *Naps on Parnassus*, and printed in 1658, there is a recital of the most excellent English poets; who, according to this author's enumeration are Chaucer, Hardyng, Lydgate, Spenser, Drayton, Shakespeare, Jonson, Donne, Beaumont and Fletcher, Sandys, Cowley, and Cleveland, with some others then living and perhaps in fashion, but now forgotten. But there is not a syllable of the writer of *L'Allegro, Il Penseroso*, and *Comus*. Langbaine, who wrote his dramatic biography in 1691, a scholar and a student in English poetry, having enumerated Milton's greater English poems, coldly adds, 'He published some *other* poems in Latin and English, printed at London, 1645.' Nor is there the quantity of an hemistich quoted from any of these poems, in the collections of those who have digested the beauties or phrases of the English poets from 1655 to 1738, inclusively. The first of these, is the *English Treasury of Wit and Language*, by John Cotgrave, 1655. The second, the *English Parnassus, or an Help to English Poesy*, by Joshua Poole of Clare Hall, 1657. And not to omit the intermediate labours of Bysshe and Gildon, the latter of whom promises 'to give the reader the *great* images that are to be found in our poets who are *truly great*, as well as their topics and moral reflections', the last, and by far the most copious and judicious compilation of the kind extant, is the *British Muse* in three volumes, by Thomas Hayward, with a good Preface by Oldys, published in 1738. Yet this author professes chiefly to consider, '*neglected* and *expiring* merit, and to *revive* and preserve the excellencies which time and *oblivion* were upon the point of cancelling, rather than to *repeat* what others had extracted before'.

Patrick Hume, a Scotchman, in 1695, published a large and very learned commentary on the *Paradise Lost*, to which some of his successors in the same province, apprehending no danger of detection from a work rarely inspected, and too pedantic and cumbersome to attract many readers, have been often amply indebted, without even the most distant hint of acknowledgement. But Hume, in comparing Milton with himself, perhaps conscious of his importance as a commentator on the sublimities of the epic muse, not once condescends to draw a single illustration from this volume of his author. In 1732, Bentley, mistaking his object, and to the disgrace of his critical abilities, gave a new and splendid edition of the *Paradise Lost*. The principal design of the Notes is to prove, that the poet's native text was vitiated by an infinite variety of licentious interpolations and factitious readings, which as he pretends, proceeded from the artifice, the ignorance, or the misapprehension, of an amanuensis, to whom Milton, being blind, had been compelled to dictate his verses. To ascertain his criticisms in detecting or reforming these imaginary forgeries, he often appeals to words and phrases in the same poem. But he never attempts to confirm his conjectures from the smaller poems, written before the poet was blind: and from which, in the prosecution of the same arbitrary mode of emendation, his analogies in many instances might have consequently derived a much stronger degree of authority and credibility. The truth is, Bentley was here a stranger. I must, however, except that he once quotes a line from the beginning of *Comus*.

One of the earliest encomiums which this volume of Milton seems to have received, was from the pen of Addison. In a *Spectator*, written 1711, he mentions Milton's laughter in the opening of *L'Allegro* as a very poetical figure: and adds, citing the lines at large, that Euphrosyne's group of Mirth is finely described. But this specimen and recommendation, although from so favourite a writer, and so elegant a critic, was probably premature, and I suspect contributed but little to make the poem much better known. In the meantime I will venture to pronounce that although the citation immediately resulted from the subject of Addison's paper, he thought it the finest group or description either in this piece or its companion the *Penseroso*. Had Addison ever entered into the spirit and genius of both poems, he certainly did not want opportunities of bringing them forward, by exhibiting passages of a more poetical character. It has been observed in the *Essay on the Genius of Pope*, that Milton's nephew, E. Philips, in his 'Tractatus de carmine dramatico poetarum veterum cui subjungitur Enumeratio Poetarum, Lond. 1670', mentioning his uncle's *Paradise Lost*, adds, 'praeter alia quae scripsit *elegantissime* tum *Anglicè* tum Latine' (p. 270). And Toland, from the same quarter, says of *Comus*, 'like which piece, in the peculiar disposition of the story, the sweetness of the numbers, the justness of the expression, and the moral it teaches, there is nothing extant in any language' (*Life*, prefixed to Milton's Prose Works, Amst. 1698). And of *Lycidas*, 'the Monody is one o the finest [poems] he ever wrote' (Ibid. p. 44). These indeed are early testimonies; but as coming from his relations are not properly admissible.

My father used to relate, that when he once, at Magdalen College, Oxford, mentioned in high terms this volume to Mr. Digby, the intimate friend of Pope, Mr. Digby expressed much surprise that he had never heard Pope speak of them, went home and immediately gave them an attentive reading, and asked Pope if he knew anything of this hidden treasure. Pope availed himself of the question: and accordingly, we find him soon afterwards sprinkling his *Eloisa to Abelard* with epithets and phrases of a new form and sound, pilfered from *Comus* and the *Penseroso*. It is a phenomenon in the history of English poetry, that Pope, a poet not of Milton's pedigree, should be their first copyer. He was, however, conscious that he might borrow from a book then scarcely remembered, without the hazard of a discovery, or the imputation of plagiarism. Yet the theft was so slight, as hardly to deserve the name: and it must be allowed, that the experiment was happily and judiciously applied, in delineating the sombrous scenes of the pensive Eloisa's convent, the solitary Paraclete.

At length, we perceive these poems emerging in the criticism of the times. In 1733, Doctor Pearce published his *Review of the Text of Paradise Lost*, where they frequently furnish collateral evidences in favour of the established state of that text; and in refutation of Bentley's chimerical corrections. In the following year, the joint labour of the two Richardsons produced *Explanatory Notes on the Paradise Lost*, where they repeatedly lend their assistance, and are treated in such a style of criticism as shows that their beauties were truly felt. Soon afterwards, such respectable names as Jortin, Warburton, and Hurd conspired in examining their excellencies, in adjusting their claims to praise, and extending their reputation. They were yet further recommended to the public regard. In 1738, *Comus* was presented on the stage at Drury Lane, with musical accompaniments by Dr. Arne, and the application of additional songs, selected and adapted from *L'Allegro*, and other pieces of this volume: and although not calculated to shine in theatric exhibition for those very reasons which constitute its essential and specific merit, from this introduction to notice *Comus* grew popular as a poem. *L'Allegro* and *Il Penseroso* were set to music by Handel in 1741; and his expressive harmonies here received the honour which they have so seldom found, but which they so justly deserve, of being *married to immortal verse*. Not long afterwards, *Lycidas* was imitated by Mr. Mason: as

L'Allegro and *Il Penseroso* had been before, in his *Il Bellicoso ed Il Pacifico*. In the meantime the *Paradise Lost* was acquiring more numerous readers: the manly melodies of blank verse, which after its revival by Philips had been long neglected, caught the public ear: and the whole of Milton's poetical works, associating their respective powers as in one common interest, jointly and reciprocally co-operated in diffusing and forming just ideas of a more perfect species of poetry. A visible revolution succeeded in the general cast and character of the national composition. Our versification contracted a new colouring, a new phraseology; and the school of Milton rose in emulation of the school of Pope.

An editor of Milton's juvenile poems cannot but express his concern, in which, however, he may have been anticipated by his reader, that their number is so inconsiderable. With Milton's *mellow hangings*, delicious as they are, we reasonably rest contented: but we are justified in regretting that he has left so few of his early blossoms, not only because they are so exquisitely sweet, but because so many more might have naturally been expected. And this regret is yet aggravated, when we consider the cause which prevented the production of more, and intercepted the progress of so promising a spring: when we recollect that the vigorous portion of his life, that those years in which imagination is on the wing, were unworthily and unprofitably wasted on temporary topics, on elaborate but perishable dissertations in defence of innovation and anarchy. To this employment he sacrificed his eyes, his health, his repose, his native propensities, his elegant studies. Smit with the deplorable polemics of puritanism, he suddenly ceased to gaze on *such sights as youthful poets dream.*

The numerous and noble plans of tragedy which he had deliberately formed with the discernment and selection of a great poetical mind, were at once interrupted and abandoned; and have now left to a disappointed posterity only a few naked outlines, and confused sketches. Instead of embellishing original tales of chivalry, of clothing the fabulous achievements of the early British kings and champions in the gorgeous trappings of epic attire, he wrote *Smectymnuus* and *Tetrachordon*, apologies for fanatical preachers and the doctrine of divorce. In his travels he had intended to visit Sicily and Athens, countries connected with his finer feelings, interwoven with his poetical ideas, and impressed upon his imagination by his habits of reading, and by long and intimate converse with the Grecian literature. But so prevalent were his patriotic attachments, that hearing in Italy of the commencement of the national quarrel, instead of proceeding forward to feast his fancy with the contemplation of scenes familiar to Theocritus and Homer, the pines of Etna and the pastures of Peneus, he abruptly changed his course, and hastily returned home to plead the cause of ideal liberty. Yet in this chaos of controversy, amidst endless disputes concerning religious and political reformation, independency, prelacy, tithes, toleration, and tyranny, he sometimes seems to have heaved a sigh for the peaceable enjoyments of lettered solitude, for his congenial pursuits, and the more mild and ingenuous exercises of the Muse. In a letter to Henry Oldenburgh, written in 1654, he says, 'Hoc cum libertatis adversariis inopinatum certamen, diversis longe, et amoenioribus omnino me studiis intentum, ad se rapuit invitum.' And in one of his prose-tracts, 'I may one day hope to have ye again in a still time, when there shall be no chiding. Not in these noises.' And in another, having mentioned some of his schemes for epic poetry and tragedy, 'of highest hope and hardest attempting', he adds, 'With what small willingness I endure to interrupt the pursuit of no less hopes than these, and leave a calm and pleasing solitariness, fed with cheerful and confident thoughts, to embark in a troubled sea of noises and hoarse disputes, from beholding the bright countenance of

truth in the quiet and still air of delightful studies,
&c.' He still, however, obstinately persisted in what
he thought his duty. But surely these speculations
should have been consigned to the enthusiasts of the
age, to such restless and wayward spirits as Prynne,
Hugh Peters, Goodwyn, and Baxter. Minds less
refined and faculties less elegantly cultivated, would
have been better employed in this task.

>   —Coarse complexions,
> And cheeks of sorry grain, will serve to ply
> The sampler, and to tease the housewife's wool:
> What need a vermeil-tinctur'd lip for that,
> Love-darting eyes, and tresses like the morn?

PRINTED IN GREAT BRITAIN
AT THE UNIVERSITY PRESS, OXFORD
BY VIVIAN RIDLER
PRINTER TO THE UNIVERSITY